BSL
KJG
MEZ

BUSINESS ETHICS IN ACTION

BUSINESS ETHICS IN ACTION

Seeking Human Excellence in Organizations

Domènec Melé

palgrave
macmillan

First published 2009 by
PALGRAVE MACMILLAN

Palgrave Macmillan in the UK is an imprint of Macmillan Publishers Limited,
registered in England, company number 785998, of 4 Crinan Street,
London N1 9XW.

Palgrave® and Macmillan® are registered trademarks in the United States,
the United Kingdom, Europe and other countries.

ISBN 978–0–230–57310–9

This book is printed on paper suitable for recycling and made from fully
managed and sustained forest sources. Logging, pulping and manufacturing
processes are expected to conform to the environmental regulations of the
country of origin.

A catalogue record for this book is available from the British Library.

A catalog record for this book is available from the Library of Congress.

Contents

Part III   Managerial Ethics

List of Tables and Figures

Tables

Figures

Foreword

Financial and corporate crises trigger increasing interest in, and public demand for, business ethics. This happened in the 1980s with insider trading on Wall Street, in the 1990s with massive corporate downsizing in the United States, and in the early 2000s with the scandals concerning Enron, WorldCom, Tyco, Parmalat and others. These crises pressured the business world to emphasize the importance of business ethics. The current massive disruption in financial markets brought on by the collapse of the sub-prime mortgage market in the United States is generating the same reaction.

Many universities and business schools currently offer business ethics and corporate social responsibility courses as a required subject in their programmes. Several research centres and chairs on these matters have also been endowed. Courses in business ethics are essential in order to provide students with an appropriate conceptual background, and help them discover and frame ethical issues in business, gain an understanding of the role of ethical values and moral character in leadership, reason about ethical dilemmas, and reflect on how to improve business and organizational conditions from an ethical perspective. However, courses in business ethics are not sufficient to accomplish all this. Their impact would be very minor if other core courses in the business curriculum suffered from a gaping hole where ethics ought to be. Thus, the real challenge in business education is to introduce business ethics into every area of the curriculum.

With this book, Professor Domènec Melé seeks to contribute to both goals: to offer knowledge of business ethics to be used both in classes devoted to that subject, and to integrate its concepts and frameworks into the entire curriculum. Although designed for use in a business ethics course, it is not removed from other business topics, and those who teach in different business disciplines will find that this book provides very useful ideas that could be integrated in their respective subjects.

This book is also very unique. It adopts a person-centred approach that fits very nicely with the nature of the firm, and the identity and role of business leaders. Companies are made up of people, their success depends on the quality of their people, and managing organizations is mainly about managing people. Furthermore, many crucial points regarding leadership and ethics in organizations are central to this book, such as respect for each individual, the proper use of power, the role of values and mission statements in successful firms, and organizational designs that are not only effective, but also contribute to the personal and professional growth of those involved in the organization. This book not only aims at describing business ethics dilemmas, but also at how to understand that ethics is a foundation of human excellence, and business ethics an indispensable pillar in business excellence.

Professor Domènec Melé is a pioneer in business ethics in Europe, and his work is familiar to many scholars and business people throughout the world. He has been working in the fields of business ethics and business in society for more than 20 years, mainly at IESE Business School, where he holds the Chair of Business Ethics. His vast and rich work in research, teaching and consulting in this field provides him with an excellent background and the expertise with which to write an elegant and practical book on a very complex subject.

This book is simultaneously rigorous, clear and accessible to business people, and includes many cases that help understand the nature and intricacy of business ethics. At the same time, its well-defined frameworks, sound principles, wide use of cases and useful criteria are extremely helpful in dealing with that complexity in a practical way. In all, it is a very significant contribution to business education and will be a great pedagogical tool for leadership development.

JORDI CANALS
Dean of IESE Business School

Preface

I would like to begin with a personal anecdote, if I may. Once, long ago, while travelling to a conference, I was reading a book on business ethics. Beside me was a man who was surreptitiously looking at my book. My travelling companion, who was a businessman, finally spoke:

'You seem interested in business ethics. Are you?'

'Yes, I am,' I answered. 'Actually, I teach business ethics in a business school.'

His response was quick and very frank:

'Oh! This is really important; there is so much corruption nowadays. Look: in my father's times a contract was a page and a handshake. Now, a contract is a tome, and each new contract contains more and more clauses. Good for lawyers, who charge high fees.'

I replied:

> 'Your last point is very true. Most of my colleagues and many people involved in business would agree that ethics and trust are closely related. Cases of deception or fraud, attempts at manipulation or abuse of good faith, lead people to lose trust, and increasingly complex mechanisms of control are introduced. So, the higher the level of ethical behaviour is, the less the cost of control.'

I continued:

> 'However, let me disagree a little with your first point. Business ethics is not only about corruption. Certainly, corruption and misbehaviour are a part of ethics, and we can learn proper conduct through considering misconduct. But I think that ethics is much more than a set of rules to avoid corruption or a set of minimum standards to reinforce the law, or even to go beyond the law in some respects. Many think that ethics, although it includes principles and norms, is basically about moral character and living a good life. Its main reference is how we should act if we would want to become better as human beings.'

My companion seemed a little surprised, and we continued our conversation until the plane landed.

This anecdote reflects two key points of this book. First, it provides a compass for seeking human excellence in corporate life. Second, business ethics is related to good practices in organizations, management and corporate governance: practices that favour trust and quality performance in business relationships. Our aim here is not only to evaluate what is or is not ethically acceptable, but also to provide positive guidelines for improving ethical conduct in corporate life.

During the long elaboration of this book, a colleague asked me:

> 'Are you adopting a deontological or a utilitarian approach? Or maybe you're focusing on "virtue ethics"? That's very much in fashion.'

He was referring to three well-known ethics theories commonly applied to business ethics:

> 'Well, none of these approaches exactly. The book will present information about mainstream theories of business ethics, and even religious approaches. It also provides a brief philosophical discussion, although not too long, to avoid boring the readers. However, the book has its own approach. It considers duties, as the deontological approach does, but also virtues. I have no doubt about the importance of principles and virtues in ethics, but I also take into account consequences – although not in a utilitarian sense – in making moral judgements.'

This book is centred on the human being and the human capacity to acquire good character traits through action. It is in line with ethical traditions dating back to ancient Greece, which stress that every human action has an effect on the person and, first, on the agent: the person who performs it; but also on the human quality of relationships and on the culture, which is continually taking shape.

We adopt a specific view that we call the person-centred approach, which is outlined in Chapter 4. In this view, human virtues are central because they shape character and bring about human excellence, but this approach also considers principles and norms for good behaviour and for achieving harmonious and just human relations.

In writing this book, the author has had in mind as his presumed audience people involved in business, including those who are preparing themselves to become managers, business executives and consultants. It provides numerous cases to be discussed, along with illustrative examples. This practical orientation is reflected in the title: *Business Ethics in Action*. However, conceptual foundations have not been neglected. For every topic, the book provides a short but rigorous philosophical discussion easily accessible to those unfamiliar with moral philosophy. It also provides the theoretical framework, which can be of decisive assistance in reflecting on particular situations and in finding responses to specific problems in order to render business ethics practical. Whenever necessary, an historical view has been introduced for a better understanding of specific issues, although always briefly, and always avoiding erudite but superfluous elaboration. The book generally focuses on managerial work, including aspects relevant for managerial decision-making, for organizational design, and for managing the relationships between business and society. However, it is our belief that this book provides useful perspectives not only for managers, but also for anybody involved in business organizations, from those in corporate governance to supervisors and employees.

The study of ethical issues has increased dramatically in the last three decades, both as an academic discipline and in business activity. Thus, it is not possible to discuss in any depth all the specific issues that might arise in operations, marketing, finance, accounting, information technology and other business areas. However, most of the current topics, ethical issues and dilemmas generally discussed in the business ethics field have a place in this textbook, and are addressed in a clear and succinct manner. Furthermore, some key bibliographical references are included for those who desire to delve deeper into a given topic.

Another characteristic of the book is the international perspective of its contents and cases. It has not been written for use in any particular country or culture. Many issues considered have relevance in most countries and, in fact, the cases originate from a great variety of countries worldwide. The above-mentioned person-centred approach is not limited to any particular geographical area. It includes basic and commonly accepted human principles, such as the Golden Rule (putting oneself in the place of the other) and human values. Particular importance is granted to human dignity and human rights. Its international perspective is also reinforced through a consistent consideration of standards for business ethics and corporate social responsibility proposed by recognized international organizations, such as the United Nations, the International Labour Organization, the Organization for Economic Cooperation and Development and so on. In light of the potential audience, the book uses an uncomplicated writing style, with a limited vocabulary. In addition, tables and figures are introduced when necessary to clarify and aid in the discussion.

Every chapter begins with an introductory case, usually related to cases considered as 'classics' in the business ethics field. These cases generally include scandals and questionable behaviours, and permit us to introduce the topic of each chapter. Through these cases, the reader will be able to discover certain ethical points that can then be studied at any depth desired. These cases can also foster learning through discussing behaviours that have gained notoriety: they teach what to avoid. By contrast, at the end of each chapter there is another case that is generally much more positive. These cases (Business ethics in practice) present companies or managers who seek to put business ethics into action in some respect addressed in the chapter. In order to discuss specific ethical dilemmas, a short case (Dilemma) is provided in every chapter.

At the beginning of each chapter there is a checklist of 'chapter aims'. At the end is a summary that identifies the main points of the chapter. Every chapter has an Insight inserted to give supplementary information or to introduce a controversial point.

The book is structured in five parts, with three chapters in each. Part I is introductory. This begins with a chapter that explores the role of ethics in business by discussing frequently asked questions on business ethics, about such topics as the relationship between ethics and profitability, and the use of ethics as a tool for public relations. It also includes some conceptual clarifications on ethics and related matters.

The second chapter introduces the role of ethics in the economic and social context of business. It analyses prompts and problems of the free market and the role of laws, along with social demands directed at business. Specifically, it discusses why business ethics is necessary if market, laws and social claims already provide economic and social controls for business. The last chapter of this introductory part deals with cultural diversity and standards of international ethical and corporate responsibility. Particular attention is paid to the controversy on cultural relativism, as well as universal ethical principles and common human values.

Part II, 'The Individual within the Organization', starts with a chapter that considers human action and how ethics is at its core. It also presents the person-centred approach used in the book, along with an overview of the mainstream theories of business ethics. The next chapter deals with individual responsibility and how to make sound moral judgements in decision-making. Some principles and criteria are proposed to overcome dilemmas in business and management. Finally, Chapter 6 presents and discusses frequently arising ethical issues in business, such as frauds, bribes, extortion, questionable payments, insider trading, conflicts of interest, tax evasion and whistle-blowing.

Part III focuses on managerial ethics, with some insights for corporate governance ethics. Chapter 7 poses a crucial question: For the sake of whom should a company be managed? The answer, which has enormous ethical consequences, passes through discussions of different views of the firm and conceptions of its purpose within society. The next chapter discusses how power can be used with justice in corporations, reviewing misuses of managerial power and good practices in both corporate governance and management. Chapter 9 considers leadership and some human virtues especially relevant to being a moral leader.

Part IV deals with organizational ethics. The key idea in this part is that organizational structure, culture and activities should respect people's dignity and rights. Far from impeding the ethical behaviours and personal growth of those involved in the organization, structure and culture should foster them. The first chapter of this part discusses this point. It also includes the role of corporate values, codes of conduct and ethical programmes in favouring an ethical culture. Chapter 11 deals with ethics in the organization of work and workers' rights. Chapter 12 concludes this part with ethics in the organizing of marketing.

Part V, 'Societal Business Ethics', considers managing the relationships between business and society from a business ethics perspective. Chapter 13 deals with corporate social responsibility and corporate accountability, presenting an historical view, the mainstream theories and practical proposals. The following chapter focuses on corporate citizenship as a comprehensive concept for the social responsibility of business, proposing ethical bases for an appropriate implementation of this concept. Finally, Chapter 15 presents some key issues in environmental business ethics and possible business strategies for being an environmentally responsible corporation.

Finally, the author would like to thank Prof. Jordi Canals, Dean of IESE, for suggesting that I write the present book, and Palgrave Macmillan for accepting this project. Ursula Gavin, as Palgrave's representative, gave me support and sound advice during the preparation of the manuscript. I offer my special thanks to Kinga Dygulska for her collaboration in the task of preparing documentation for the cases, and to John Fennar, Devra Torres, and Keith Povey for their help in the editing process. Gratitude is also due to several colleagues and reviewers for their constructive and thoughtful comments and suggestions on the manuscript drafts. They have no doubt contributed to the improvement of this book in many respects. Interacting with MBA and doctoral students of IESE Business School and undergraduate students of the International University of Catalonia has been a continuous challenge to enhancing the study cases and teaching materials. My thanks to them all.

Barcelona   Domènec Melé

Part I
Introduction to
Business Ethics

I don't believe ethical behaviour should depend on its paying. To suggest that doing right needs to be justified by its economic reward is amoral, a self-inflicted wound hugely damaging to corporate reputation... Doing right because it is right, not because it pays, needs to be the foundation of business.[1]

Sir Geoffrey Chandler (1922–)
Former Director, Shell International

Chapter Aims

This chapter will allow you to:
- distinguish between 'spontaneous morality' and 'rational ethics'
- gain an understanding of how the current interest in business ethics emerged
- introduce yourself to the idea of business ethics, its constitutive parts, and the place of ethics in business
- provide arguments to think about the possible link between ethics and economic performance
- understand why companies introduce ethical practices into their organizations
- distinguish between ethics as a real commitment and ethics as 'window-dressing'
- understand rational ethics more deeply, including how it differs from moral judgements, personal and social values, religious ethics and moral theology.

Key terms:

Behavioural ethics	Ethics	Rational ethics
Business ethics	Management ethics	Religious ethics
Corporate citizenship	Moral development	Social values
Corporate reputation	Moral experience	Societal business ethics
Corporate social responsibility	Moral judgements	Spontaneous ethics
Ethical dilemmas	Moral theology	Stakeholder management
Ethical improvements	Organizational ethics	Subjectivism
Ethical issues	Personal values	Sustainability

The Role of Ethics in Business

INTRODUCTORY CASE 1:

THE RISE AND FALL OF ARTHUR ANDERSEN

Arthur Andersen was a respected firm. Once, it was known for its high standards in accounting, but it lost its way and later met its demise. In the 1990s, it was one of the 'Big Five' accounting firms worldwide, operating in 84 countries.

Arthur Andersen co-founded the firm in 1913 and headed it until his death in 1947. Leonard Spacek, who succeeded him, continued the legacy of his predecessor and conducted the firm's auditing services in the same way. Thus, both Andersen and Spacek ensured that the firm would follow a solid path by creating a strong culture of integrity.

In a speech delivered in 1932, Arthur Andersen revealed his ideals:

> If the confidence of the public in the integrity of accountants' reports is shaken, their value is gone. To preserve the integrity of his reports, the accountant must insist upon absolute independence of judgement and action. The necessity of preserving this position of independence indicates certain standards of conduct.[2]

A story, often repeated in the early years of Arthur Andersen, tells of an executive from a local company. The executive asked Andersen to sign off on accounts that contained flawed accounting. Even knowing that if he did not do so he would lose a major client, Andersen replied that he would not sign the accounts 'for all the money in America'. He is also quoted as having said that the accountant's responsibility was to investors, not to their clients. For many years, the motto of Andersen was 'Think straight, talk straight.'

Arthur Andersen led the way in many accounting standards and, for ethical reasons, he severed his firm's links with several clients in the 1970s. For years, the cornerstones of Arthur Andersen were people management, quality, thought leadership, and financial performance. In addition, values such as integrity, stewardship, and public responsibility were of paramount importance.

Arthur Andersen and other accounting firms in the 1980s tried to expand their activity with the growing and profitable business of consulting. They sought out opportunities for consultancy fees from existing audit clients. Arthur Andersen increased its consultancy practices to the point that this activity made up the bulk of its revenues. However, this compromised their auditing independence.

In 1989, due to the growth rate of the consulting business in comparison with accounting, auditing and tax practice, the firm split into Arthur Andersen and Andersen Consulting, two separate units of Andersen Worldwide. By the late 1990s, Andersen Consulting showed triple the per-share revenues of Arthur Andersen. However, the disparity in growth in the accounting and consulting arms led to many disputes between these two business units. This continued until August 2000, when the International Chamber of Commerce granted Andersen Consulting its independence from Arthur Andersen, but awarded US$1.2 billion in past payments to Arthur Andersen, also declaring that Andersen Consulting would no longer be able to use the Andersen name. As a result, Andersen Consulting changed its name to Accenture at the beginning of 2001.

In June 2001, the Securities and Exchange Commission (SEC), the US government agency responsible for enforcing the federal securities laws and regulating the security industry/stock market, issued a cease-and-desist order against Andersen regarding securities violations for its participation in a 1.7 billion dollars accounting fraud at Waste Management.

A year later, on 15 June 2002, the Federal Court of Houston convicted Arthur Andersen of obstruction of justice and shredding documents related to its audit of Enron, the infamous energy corporation responsible for one of corporate America's greatest frauds. The case referred to David Duncan, the audit partner assigned to Enron by Arthur Andersen. In October 2001, he ordered his audit team in Houston and several other regional offices to destroy a large quantity of work documents within a span of three days.

The CEO, Joseph Berardino, notified the SEC about the procedure and fired Duncan, even though the latter set a goal of 20 per cent increase in sales, and Andersen's Houston office was billing such companies as Enron one million dollars per week.

A few weeks after the trial, Arthur Andersen surrendered its licences to practice as a Certified Public Accountant in the USA, pending the result of prosecution by the Department of Justice over the firm's handling of the auditing of Enron. The firm lost almost all of its clients when it was indicted, with over 100 civil suits pending against the firm related to its audits of Enron and other companies. After the indictment, it began winding down its American operations. The firm shrank quickly: 28,000 employees in the USA and 85,000 worldwide lost their jobs. Three other major corporations for which Andersen issued unqualified or clean audit opinions – Global Crossing, Qwest and WorldCom – were being investigated by the SEC and reinstated the previous financial statements or declared bankruptcy. In 2005, the United States Supreme Court overturned the obstruction of justice verdict based on faulty jury instructions. However, it came too late, as there was nothing left of the company.

For Barbara L. Toffler, a former partner-in-charge of Andersen's Ethics and Responsible Business Practices consulting services, who joined Arthur Andersen in 1995, the symptoms of Andersen's 'fatal disease' were evident long before Enron. She thought that an organization once proudly dedicated to professional integrity became corrupted by greed. She added that, in the latter stages of the existence of Andersen, money was seen as the great healer, and so the leaders who emerged were those whose clear focus was only on raising the revenues. This was far from the early business philosophy of the first two leaders. When Leonard Spacek was running the firm, he was somehow able to convince his partners, time and time again, to sacrifice earnings for integrity.

From the beginning of 1959 and throughout 1960, the firm put a cap on partner compensations and allowed them to be reviewed only every three to five years, so that the rest of the money could flow down to the new partners and to the cost of developing the firm. Partners did not expect to enrich themselves in those days. They hoped for a good career at a business with a good name.[3]

In the last years, 'the four cornerstones of success at Arthur Andersen – people management, quality, thought leadership, and financial performance' – were referred to colloquially as 'three pebbles and a boulder. The boulder was financial performance. The rest, it seemed, was a joke.'[4]

Toffler reveals that:

> at Andersen, Tradition dictates that we serve the clients well but also that we stand up to the client when it does something wrong. Yet in the new leadership, clients had become too valuable to defy. The distortion of the tradition meant that you could best serve the client – and therefore keep the client – by keeping it happy. This created a natural tension and mistrust between auditors and consultants, particularly when working with powerful, high-paying clients, referred to as the Crown Jewels.[5]

Despite the new creed of keeping clients happy, Toffler also noted the strong culture within Andersen persisted, but it had now lost its focus on integrity. 'At Arthur Andersen, Tradition also dictated obedience to the partner. If upsetting the client was a bad thing, so was questioning your superior.'[6]

Questions:

1. What led Arthur Andersen to its demise?
2. Do you think that ethics plays a role in auditing? What about other types of businesses?
3. In this particular case, is there any link between ethics, or lack of ethics, and economic results? Might a similar link exist in other businesses?

Sources: D. Collins, 'Arthur Andersen' in R. W. Kolb, *Encyclopedia of Business Ethics and Society* (Los Angeles: Sage, 2008): 115–17; F. D. Hawkins and J. Cohen, case study, *Arthur Andersen LLP* (Cambridge, MA: Harvard Business School Publishing, 2003); A. Nanda and S. Landry, case study, *Family Feud: Andersen vs Andersen (A) and (B)* (Cambridge, MA: Harvard Business School Publishing, 1999 and 2000); B. L. Toffler, *Final Accounting: Ambition, Greed, and the Fall of Arthur Andersen* (New York: Broadway Books, 2003); M. Torres, case study, *The Demise of Arthur Andersen* (Barcelona, Spain: IESE Publishing, 2007); Wikipedia (Arthur Andersen); D. Windsor, 'Enron Corporation', in R. W. Kolb, *Encyclopedia of Business Ethics and Society* (Los Angeles: Sage, 2008): 716–19.

SPONTANEOUS ETHICS AND RATIONAL ETHICS

When a business scandal appears on page 1 of the *Financial Times*, people usually blame those who have taken advantage of their position for personal enrichment, or for their negligence, or for abusing others in some way. This makes clear that human beings have the capacity to make value judgements: a certain moral sense by which we discern good and bad, right and wrong.

One can evaluate the sale of a product with regard to financial gain or to the satisfaction of both customer and salesperson, but these are not the sole criteria. The sale might be fraudulent, if it has been carried out deceptively and occasioned damage to the buyer; or, to the contrary, it might be a fair sale, and even a real act of service to the buyer. These latter judgements – as to fraudulence or fairness – are moral ones.

Language also bears witness to a certain spontaneous moral sense that permits us to make moral evaluations. Every language is full of words with moral connotations. We approve or criticize human behaviours, employing terms such as good and bad, right and wrong, fair and unfair, praiseworthy and blameworthy, responsible and irresponsible, rights and duties, licit and illicit, and so on. The list can be lengthened by the inclusion of value-laden words such as integrity, honesty, truthfulness, benevolence, friendship, kindness, and gratitude.

The fact that we make moral judgements, and the way language expresses them, both denote a common moral experience: a state of consciousness in which an individual passes judgement about good and bad. Morality is integral to the human condition. However, some people have a more cultivated moral sense than others, just as an ear for music or other human capabilities might be more or less cultivated.

Family, school, religion, cultural environment and study exert a significant influence on individual moral development.[7] Other relevant factors are one's own behaviour and personal reflection, as ancient thinkers – particularly Aristotle – have pointed out. When an individual tries to act well, doing what he or she believes is right, that person's moral sensibility regarding that action increases. By contrast, if one persistently avoids evaluating what is right, his or her moral sensitivity will decrease. Learning from past actions and their consequences, as well as discovering mistakes in moral judgements, can improve our capacity for such evaluation. Asking for advice from the wise and learning from their accumulated moral wisdom are additional means of developing wisdom and improving moral judgements.

Moral experience is a starting point for ethics, but ethics differs from the spontaneous sense of morality. Ethics is a rational or philosophical approach to morality. While each individual can have a particular sense of morality, ethics presents objective references and universal principles for moral reasoning, which provide a rational tool for contrasting personal views and a coherent system for the moral evaluation of human actions and behaviour.

Ethics is about the 'moral quality' of human action. This is different from the 'technical' aspects of efficacy or effectiveness in obtaining a given objective or goal. In considering an action in a business context, both technical and moral aspects can be qualified by the adjective 'good' – but in different senses. A business can be 'good' (profitable) in economic terms and 'good' in ethical terms. A profitable business can also be a good (fair) one or a bad (unfair) one. Ethics is a guide for acting well. As we will see, ethics comes first, but the managerial challenge is to harmonize doing good and doing well.

Ancient Greece was the cradle of ethics and the home of Socrates (fifth century BC), generally considered the founding father of ethics, understood as 'moral philosophy'. Although there were excellent instances of ethics in several earlier cultures, which included precepts for business activities,[8] it was Socrates – and then Plato and Aristotle – who introduced a systematic, rational approach to morality: 'rational ethics', or simply 'ethics'.

In his early discussions of the subject, Socrates confronted the Sophists, who employed rhetoric to convince others to collaborate in their own purposes, whatever those might be, including unjust lawsuits. It seems that Sophists taught their skills for a fee, often an exorbitant one, to enable others to succeed in the litigious social life of Athens. Socrates opposed this approach, proposing instead a rational search for moral truth, using arguments to identify what is really right and not merely profitable or beneficial in a particular sense.

Employing reason as an approach to morality is by now a long tradition. Throughout the entire history of humanity, many thinkers and ordinary people have professed great esteem for reason and its capacity to discover the morality of human acts.

Ethics aids in moral reasoning, but it is much more than a guide for making moral evaluations. Its own etymology throws some light on its meaning. The word 'ethics' comes from the Greek *ethos*, meaning 'custom' or 'habit', something belonging to character and, more specifically, *virtues*: good, stable attitudes or dispositions of an individual for a 'good life'. Such virtues denote human excellence. Ethics is also related to the social conditions that can foster human excellence.

In the eighteenth century, and even earlier, the meaning of ethics changed. The main concern of moral philosophers was to establish principles, and the subsequent norms, for determining which actions are ethically acceptable. Although this vision of ethics remains, there is also an increasing tendency to recover the classical notion of virtue-based ethics.

There are a number of concepts related to, but distinct from, ethics. Among these are moral judgements, personal and social values, behavioural ethics, religious ethics and moral theology (see the Appendix to this chapter for a conceptual clarification).

CONTEMPORARY DEVELOPMENT OF BUSINESS ETHICS AND RELATED MATTERS

Ethics in business is not new. In many religious traditions, one finds abundant references to the moral aspects of business. Nevertheless, in the past two hundred years, influential streams of thought have viewed business as belonging exclusively to the economic domain, and thus as an amoral activity. Consequently, ethics, generally reduced to subjective values, was regarded as wholly separate from business administration. The well-known expression 'business is business' expresses its presumed amorality.

Nonetheless, a sense of morality has always persisted in many business people and executives. Some corporations are built up within a strong ethical framework – HP, IBM or Medtronic, for example. Johnson & Johnson launched its now famous 'Credo' in 1942. Other companies developed codes of conduct.[9] Moreover, since at least the 1950s, many scholars and practitioners have taken an interest in social issues and corporate social responsibility. Still, it was not until the 1970s that 'business ethics' became a strong movement, with an evident influence on both academics and business practitioners.[10] Since then, numerous companies have introduced activities and practices of business ethics into their organizations, and few remain that still contend that ethics has nothing to do with business.

◀ Insight 1: ▶

How the business ethics movement started

Before the 1970s, some considered the impact of business on society and spoke of social issues and corporate social responsibilities, but they rarely mentioned ethical principles or standards, or other ethical concepts, such as moral virtues, justice or human values. They preferred to use such terms as 'social values', 'social demands' and, somewhat later, 'corporate reputation'. Moral obligations and ethical principles were viewed as pertaining more to individuals than to business. Nevertheless, certain events contributed to a shift in perspective. These included the anti-capitalism protests of the late 1960s, increasing demands for consumer rights and respect for the environment; the impact of Martin Luther King's assassination in 1968, which led to some corporations reviewing their civil rights policies (equality, discrimination, affirmative action); the Watergate scandal, which revealed the existence of a White House 'dirty tricks' squad and brought about the resignation of President Nixon in 1974; and, finally, large-scale corporate bribes to foreign politicians, including the $12 million Lockheed bribery case related to an aircraft sale which caused the fall of the Japanese prime minister at the time.[11] Public opinion demanded more ethical behaviour from both the administration and business corporations.

Neither have other countries been lacking in events leading to greater insistence on ethics in business: financial scandals, negligence-fuelled accidents, unsafe products, environmental damage, inhumane work conditions, and numerous varieties of fraud. These realities demand objective ethical standards, laws and a sense of responsibility in business.

The business ethics movement has been characterized by both theory and practice. The former includes conceptual developments regarding the integration of ethics and business. Early on, academics suggested applying ethical principles to business and using methods of moral reasoning in decision-making.[12] Later, from a broader perspective, business ethics also began addressing virtues and values.[13]

The corporate answer was to introduce codes of conduct, corporate values and ethical programmes to avoid misbehaviours. Before long, business ethics was presented as an increasing body of knowledge and a new academic discipline, and courses were offered at numerous business schools. Later, conferences, books and specialized journals throughout the world analysed countless ethical issues in business.

The business ethics movement soon met *stakeholder management,* a concept introduced in the 1980s that has gained increasing acceptance.[14] Although stakeholders have to be defined with reference to particular situations, the typical ones are the main constituencies of the firm: shareholders, employees, suppliers, customers and the local community. Stakeholder management focuses on satisfying the needs and interests of all who have a stake in the firm's actions, not only shareholders. Initially, stakeholder management was regarded as an alternative way to formulate strategies, divorced from any ethical or social considerations, but normative bases and an ethical foundation were subsequently integrated.

In the early 1990s, an increasing interest emerged in good practices of *corporate governance* – that is, how a corporation is directed, administered or controlled. This deals with the role of the board of directors and includes the internal means by which corporations are operated and controlled. There was particular concern with avoiding abuses (especially of minority shareholders and investors) and underlining fiduciary duties, due diligence, accountability, transparency and social responsibility. The relationships among the main players of corporate governance – including the board of directors, the Chief Executive Officer, management, shareholders and other stakeholders – were frequently complex and involved specific ethical issues that deserved attention.

At the beginning of the twenty-first century, a new demand for business ethics emerged due to a series of well-known business scandals, such as Arthur Andersen, Enron, WorldCom, Tyco, Parmalat, and many others. At the same time, ethical behaviour was increasingly appreciated by many business people as fostering trust, which is essential for organizations and commerce. Moreover, since the turn of the current century, a renewed interest in *corporate social responsibility* has emerged, and two new concepts related to business ethics are becoming increasingly popular. One is the concept of *sustainability,* which, simply put, refers to concern for future generations. The other is considering corporations as a 'citizen' of the society. This leads to talk of *corporate citizenship,* a concept that introduces the idea that business is not merely an economic entity, but also a part of the society, and should contribute to a good society beyond what is required by law. In this way, business corporations do not appear as isolated groups whose only concern is money making, but as institutions trying to work hand in hand with citizens, governments and social organizations in order to build a good society, even in a global context.[15]

BUSINESS ETHICS AND ITS CONSTITUTIVE ASPECTS

Having completed these introductory remarks, let us discuss the nature of business ethics – a specific field of ethics focused on business activity. Business activity is accomplished by people working within business organizations or on behalf of their respective organizations. Thus, the specific scope of business ethics embraces everything related to business organizations, and everything undertaken on their behalf.

Business ethics, then, does not pertain to individual actions carried out in contexts outside business but, rather, to actions of individuals while involved in business and to actions performed cooperatively within an organization – just as 'political ethics' deals with actions of individuals in their political activity, not in their private life. However, business ethics, as political ethics, is first of all 'ethics', based on common fundamental standards for any human activity. As Nash has pointed out, business ethics 'is not a separate moral standard, but the study of how the business context poses its own unique problems for the moral person who acts as agent of the system'.[16]

Given the existence of this unique ethics, defined as a guide for human excellence, 'business ethics' can be defined as a guide for human excellence in business organizations or, more colloquially, as a guideline for human quality in business.

A crucial point is that, within organizations, some people are managing other people through corporate statements, strategies and objectives, policies, organizational structures, systems and specific practices. Thus, to some extent, they condition the activity of other people (managers, employees). At the same time, workers, unions, managers, clients and consumers, the market and other groups or factors all condition business decisions.

Four main constitutive aspects can be distinguished in business ethics:

- *Individual business ethics* includes all action related to individual behaviour within the organization, or on behalf of the organization, including individual decision-making and personal responsibility.
- *Managerial ethics* deals with managerial activities within the firm and in the leadership of organizations. Managers direct, coordinate, motivate and supervise people in order to perform actions for a common purpose. Managerial responsibility and decision-making have special connotations for influence upon others and for the organization as a whole. This is why management ethics is a specific area of study. Ethics in entrepreneurship, corporate governance and leadership can also be included in this constitutive aspect of business ethics.
- *Organizational ethics* refers to organizations or business firms as a whole. Organizations are managed by strategies, objectives, structure, systems, procedures, rules and so on. As a result of several factors, cultures are developed within organizations. All of these can be inspired and evaluated by ethics. Organizational ethics considers organizations from an ethical perspective and

addresses the question of how to enhance the fostering of human excellence within organizations.

- *Societal business ethics* covers the vast field of business–society relationships and environmental responsibility, including business, government and civil society relationships; the responsibilities of business in society, in both local and global contexts; the contribution of business to sustainable development; corporate community involvement, the responsibilities of business to the environment, and so on.

ETHICAL ISSUES, DILEMMAS AND IMPROVEMENTS

Some authors contend that the role of business ethics is simply to evaluate which actions are ethically acceptable and which are not. While the ethical evaluation of some cases generally does not present any particular difficulties, others situations can be more problematic.[17] In this respect, they distinguish between 'ethical issues' and 'ethical dilemmas'.

Ethical issues are well defined and the right course of action clearly prescribed; for example, stealing company products, commercial fraud, or dumping toxic waste into a local river; whereas ethical dilemmas are situations in which the decision-maker (generally, the manager) faces a difficult choice with no clear-cut right answer. An ethical dilemma might be, for instance, how to address competing claims of two or more individuals to whom one has an obligation. Another might be how to decide whether to accept a job that would provide greater income to support one's family but would be very demanding in terms of travel abroad, leaving less time for the children.

The distinction between ethical issues and ethical dilemmas is based on the idea that ethics is only a tool to evaluate whether an action is ethically acceptable or not. However, if we accept ethics as a guide for human excellence, it is much more than a tool for evaluation. It is an intrinsic dimension of human action, which has different degrees of goodness. This goodness entails asking not only what is acceptable, but also what is the best one can do under the given circumstances. A similar state of affairs is found in medicine: health is not only about diseases and what behaviour causes or cures them, but also about improving health and creating the conditions for longevity and fitness.

According to this second, broader position, ethical issues and dilemmas should be enlarged to consider possible courses of action for the improvement of a given situation. Thus, business ethics through its constitutive aspects (individual, managerial, organizational and societal), faces three types of problems (see Figure 1.1) each demanding a suitable course of action:

- *Ethical issues*: Ethics defines a few unacceptable actions. Frequently, these actions receive specific names (fraud, bribery, embezzlement and so on) and are formalized in laws, and perhaps in written corporate policies (codes of conduct).

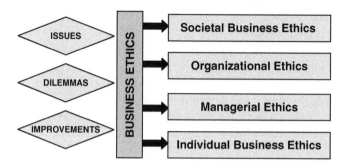

Figure 1.1   Constitutive aspects of Business Ethics and types of problems considered

- *Ethical dilemmas*: These emerge when it is not easy to identify and character-ize ethical issues, within specific contexts, or to demand accurate judgements that consider all relevant circumstances to determine the appropriate action.
- *Ethical improvements*: In some situations, one seeks to improve ethical excel-lence. For instance, in selling a product, behaviours that treat customers with fairness is acceptable as a minimum standard, but a higher standard is possible; for instance, willingness and kindness in attending to clients, and putting oneself in their shoes to understand their needs and provide the best possible service.

ARE PROFITS AND ETHICS TRULY RELATED?

A frequently asked question is whether ethics leads to profits or whether the two are irreconcilable enemies. First, we must make clear that ethics focuses on what is good or bad from a moral perspective. Consequently, the value of ethics is not as an instrument for profits but lies in its intrinsic worth. However, business enterprises exist within a competitive system, and it is reasonable to inquire into the financial impact of good conduct.

People have long debated whether ethics and corporate social responsibilities contribute to profits. Some enthusiastically proclaim, 'Good ethics is good busi-ness', or promote the slogan: 'From values to value'. Others, however, are more sceptical about the profitability of business ethics. Finally, a third group holds that the 'ethics pays' argument might be valid if one takes a broader view and looks to long-term effects.[18]

In the short term, unethical behaviours – such as abusive labour contracts, fraud, bribes and embezzlement – can lead to profits more readily than fairness can. However, such conduct runs the risk of losing the confidence of those affected, or of others who have observed the conduct. In some cases, such prac-tices can even lead to costly legal penalties. If a public scandal ensues, the loss of reputation can be dramatic; drastic action, as well as the investment of much time and money, might be necessary to recover credibility and trust.

Trust, with its underlying assumption of an implicit moral duty, is closely related to ethics.[19] Trust is created through conversation and dialogue, and through various motions, gestures, and simple forms of behaviour by which individuals exercise negative and positive duties towards each other.[20] For instance, research shows that a salesperson's ethical behaviour leads to greater customer satisfaction, trust and loyalty to the firm that the salesperson represents.[21] Within organizations, perceptions of a leader's integrity and fairness are key determinants of trust.[22] The conclusion is that ethical behaviours tend to generate trust, and trust is crucial to good business performance.[23]

Similar results show the findings of a global research survey among 9,500 senior executives from 365 companies representing a broad range of industries in 30 countries around the world.[24] Surveyed executives believe that corporate values – defined as 'a corporation's institutional standards of behaviour' – influence corporate reputation, employee recruitment, customer loyalty, brand equity, product quality/innovation, supplier relationships and risk management. In addition, in accordance with this survey, companies that report superior financial results emphasize such values as commitment to employees, drive to succeed and adaptability.

Professor Lynn Sharp Paine of Harvard Business School has noted that in the past few years many corporate initiatives have shown concern for strengthening corporate reputation or becoming more responsive to the needs and interests of their various constituencies.[25] She suggested that companies must merge social and financial imperatives to achieve superior performance.

One can argue that acting ethically might mean some additional cost or the loss of a contract. Investing in worker safety could lead to a loss in competitiveness if one's rivals fail to do likewise. Laws and their reinforcement can help to avoid such situations but, if this is not the case, managers should do their best. Competent managers will seek to run businesses that are both ethical and profitable. With imagination, they can find alternative means of solving difficult problems.

In extreme cases, managers need the courage to say 'no', since, for a manager with integrity, profits cannot come at any cost. Even when ethical behaviour does not pay off in economic terms,[26] it pays off in personal terms, because, in acting wrongly, an individual harms his or her own integrity, becoming worse as a human being.[27] Religious convictions add motivations for right behaviour regardless of whether ethics would be profitable.

WHY DO CORPORATIONS ENGAGE IN BUSINESS ETHICS?

Some people wonder if business ethics is a real commitment or just a catchphrase. The answer: it depends on the company. Many corporations or business firms[28] have, indeed, institutionalized business ethics practices, and are seeking to manage ethical and social issues in organizations, or are in some way incorporating ethics into their organizations and management. But what are the real motives that impel a company to introduce ethics? Is ethics just 'window dressing' or a substantial commitment? Is business ethics a transitory fashion or a permanent necessity? What is the real role of ethics in business?

In reviewing the reasons why companies are trying to integrate ethics more effectively into management or introducing ethics programmes into their organizations, several types of motives can be outlined:

To recover a company's image after a notorious business scandal

Triggered by public scandals that destroyed corporate credibility and public trust, many companies have introduced strong ethical programmes, focused on compliance. These include codes of ethics, employee training, ethics committees, direct lines for consultations, sanctions and so on. This has been the case in companies such as Lockheed-Martin, Nike, Tyco, Boeing and many others.

To avoid the loss of a good corporate image or being sued for misconduct

This aim has been especially apparent since at least the 1960s. It has been noted that companies who do not take responsibility for their power will ultimately lose it.[29] More recently, risks have increased due to tightening regulatory pressures, demands of transparency from investors and public opinion, and greater pressures – particularly on large corporations – from non-governmental organizations and the mass media.

Apropos avoiding risks, in the United States the Federal Sentencing Guidelines (a set of rules that federal judges almost invariably employ, at least as a starting point) favour corporate ethics programmes in such a way that if a company is condemned for employee misbehaviours, the fine is reduced if the company has implemented such a programme. Business ethics compliance and corporate values statements can contribute to business risk avoidance.

To build corporate reputation

Corporate reputation attracts customers to products, investors to securities and employees to jobs, and therefore constitutes a competitive advantage. Reputation is now an important strategic area for many companies and, as we have seen, ethics is deemed key to reputation. Ethical behaviour and good corporate governance build credibility, and thereby corporate reputation and a competitive advantage. Corporate concern for reputation has increased as a consequence of legal regulations in certain countries, which require information on social activities, social and environmental reports, and reputation indexes (especially for listed companies). The 'Dow Jones Sustainability World Indexes' are used by investors and lenders around the world to screen the social and environmental performance of corporations. Similarly, the FTSE4Good Index is also used to screen good corporate citizenship.

To enhance stakeholder relationships

If ethical behaviour is linked to trust in relationships, business ethics will be particularly important in another strategic area: stakeholder relationships. The behaviours of the firm towards, the stakeholder affect their commitment and trust, creative cooperation, stakeholder loyalty, compliance and future trust-related behaviours of the stakeholders.[30] Corporate values concerned with legitimate stakeholder needs will foster strong and cooperative relationships and better performance.

To act with real commitment

This derives from the understanding that businesses need to do the right thing and contribute to the society to which they belong. While the previous aims respond exclusively to the profit motive, commitment responds to moral duty. The first contribution of businesses to society is avoidance of behaviours that erode the common good. However, the business contribution to society is much more than avoiding the negative. With reason, some founders of well-known companies have expressed a real commitment to contribute to the well-being of society as do some companies in their mission statement. A sense of commitment is not incompatible with other motives, such as maintaining fair relations with stakeholders, enhancing reputation or avoiding risks. But the acid test is maintaining commitment, even in the absence of other motives.

To return to the initial question, one can indeed find companies that take business ethics as a catch phrase or a public relations stratagem – 'window dressing' – but many others have a real commitment to business ethics. Some research[31] shows that there are companies that show apparent commitment, presumably due to external pressures, but do little to foster ethical behaviour within their organizations. Other companies, however, are active both in showing external commitment and in promoting ethical practices. The findings indicate that social and environmental factors pushing for programmes of corporate ethics had some influence, but that management commitment was a stronger determinant of what companies were really doing.

In practice, there could be different motivations for companies to adopt policies of business ethics.

APPENDIX:

SOME CONCEPTUAL CLARIFICATIONS OF ETHICS AND RELATED CONCEPTS

To conclude this chapter, let us present a few conceptual clarifications regarding the difference between rational ethics and other related concepts with which ethics is often confused.

Moral judgements

When someone claims: 'This business is unfair', he or she is making a moral judgement. Moral judgements are about particular situations or events occurring under specific circumstances, while ethics presents rational foundations for making sound moral judgements. Consider, for instance, the case of selling a toy with toxic paint to little children. A moral judgement would be: 'It is unfair to sell this product.' This is the result of the following implicit ethical reasoning: 'It is unfair to sell this product because it is unsafe, and people have the right to buy safe products.' Deliberation could follow regarding the idea that everyone has the right to avoid danger to health and that life is a universal human value deserving of respect. Ethics provides these kinds of grounds for making moral judgements.

Moral judgements sometimes arise from feelings of approval or rejection. However, feelings do not guarantee sound judgement. For instance, if you are a manager, your decision to fire somebody who has committed a crime against the company might provoke bitter feelings in you if you are sympathetic towards this individual. None-theless, from an ethical perspective, it might be the right thing to do.

Personal values

Ethics – and, more specifically, ethical values – differ conceptually from personal values. 'Personal' values express what is appreciated by someone because of its moral, religious or aesthetic quality, or its utility. 'Ethical' values are based on moral qualities that contribute to human excellence: for example, integrity, justice, truthfulness, gratitude, friendship and generosity. Although ethical values are objective, they have a subjective dimension as well, since they can be discovered by individuals.

Personal values, therefore, depend on each individual. An honest person would hold quite different values than those of a criminal. In spite of this, some people adopt the position that only personal values or 'moral opinions', and not any objective ethics, are relevant. This position, called 'subjectivism', makes any dialogue on morality problematic because of a lack of any objective ethical reference. In practice, subjectivism is difficult to hold, especially when one is a victim of a clear abuse of power or other unfair treatment, or is living under a tyranny. In such situations, the victim generally claims a right to fair treatment. However, a subjectivist cannot coherently claim any objective right, only the right to a personal opinion.

Cultural values

Social or cultural values are those that are widely shared by members of groups and communities within a common cultural environment. Some personal values might be similar, or even identical to, the social values of groups or communities to which the individual belongs.

Social values that indicate appreciation of specific issues can be a spur to reflection. However, ethics is distinct from cultural values. The latter concerns descriptions (what *is*) of a social group's beliefs and values, but not prescriptions (what *ought to be*). Some cultural values are fully compatible with ethical principles. Others are not: think of a social environment whose 'values' lead it to be tolerant with inhumane working conditions, corruption, lack of respect for minority rights, or to show scant concern for environmental issues.

Behavioural ethics

There are countless empirical studies about the real behaviour of people in organizations.[32] They focus on psychological or situational factors – such as age, sex or organizational context – which can influence behaviour or decision-making. These studies are behavioural descriptions of what occurs at a certain place and time, but they do not reveal anything about whether such behaviour is right or wrong. The aim of ethics, by contrast, is not *describing* what people are doing but *prescribing* what they ought to do.

Religious ethics and moral theology

Religions and moral theology contain commendable ethical values and requirements, and provide moral guidelines to believers, as do some non-religious
wisdom traditions. Rational ethics coincides with many religious precepts but
derives from rational inquiry rather than from any religion.

The question of the relationship between rational ethics and religious ethics
is not new. In Socrates' time, it was commonly held that moral obligation came
from the gods, or God. Socrates, although he was a pious man, defended the
position that reason can understand what is morally good, and that gods only
command what is good.[33] In other words, Socrates held that there are standards
of goodness that can be known by human reason.

There are respected ethical systems built on religious faith and deep treatises
on moral theology developed from both faith and reason. Both religious ethics
and moral theology deserve consideration and, in a global world, where religion
is salient for many people, familiarity with the basic aspects of religious ethics
applied to business seems a necessity for those who manage businesses and organizations in an international context. (Chapter 3 devotes its appendix to some
significant religious insights for business ethics.)

However, religious ethics has limitations, especially in the field of business
ethics, if it is limited to statements of faith. Religious ethics requires rational
development if it is to be applied to a great variety of business problems.[34]
Furthermore, in a pluralistic society it seems necessary to propound rational
arguments, not merely religious approaches. Thus, without neglecting personal
beliefs, we need rational ethics to be able to present rational arguments beyond
religion, and also as a tool for fruitful dialogue. In this sense, the aim of ethics is
to provide a rational basis as common ground for people from different religions
and cultures.

Business ethics in practice 1:

Johnson & Johnson and the Tylenol Affair

Johnson & Johnson (J&J), founded in 1886 by General Robert Johnson, man-
ufactures and sells pharmaceuticals, biotechnology products and personal
hygiene products, among many others. It is listed among the *Fortune 500* and
its common stock is a component of the Dow Jones Industrial Average. Currently, J&J appears at the top of some rankings of corporate reputation in the
USA.[35]

In 1943, Robert Wood Johnson, chairman from 1932 to 1963 and a member of the company's founding family, crafted what in J&J is known as 'Our
Credo', following principles set down by the founder of J&J. It was shortly
before the company became a publicly traded company. This is the text of the
J&J Credo, now translated into 36 languages and disseminated wherever this
multinational company operates in the world:

Business ethics in practice 1: (cont'd)

Our Credo

We believe our first responsibility is to the doctors, nurses and patients,
to mothers and fathers and all others who use our products and services.
In meeting their needs everything we do must be of high quality.
We must constantly strive to reduce our costs
in order to maintain reasonable prices.
Customers' orders must be serviced promptly and accurately.
Our suppliers and distributors must have an opportunity
to make a fair profit.

We are responsible to our employees,
the men and women who work with us throughout the world.
Everyone must be considered as an individual.
We must respect their dignity and recognize their merit.
They must have a sense of security in their jobs.
Compensation must be fair and adequate,
and working conditions clean, orderly and safe.
We must be mindful of ways to help our employees fulfill
their family responsibilities.
Employees must feel free to make suggestions and complaints.
There must be equal opportunity for employment, development
and advancement for those qualified.
We must provide competent management,
and their actions must be just and ethical.

We are responsible to the communities in which we live and work
and to the world community as well.
We must be good citizens – support good works and charities
and bear our fair share of taxes.
We must encourage civic improvements and better health and education.
We must maintain in good order
the property we are privileged to use,
protecting the environment and natural resources.

Our final responsibility is to our stockholders.
Business must make a sound profit.
We must experiment with new ideas.
Research must be carried on, innovative programs developed
and mistakes paid for.
New equipment must be purchased, new facilities provided
and new products launched.
Reserves must be created to provide for adverse times.
When we operate according to these principles,
the stockholders should realize a fair return.

Business ethics in practice 1: (cont'd)

'Our Credo' defines a hierarchy of people to whom J&J have a responsibility, rather than a specific set of values. People working in J&J are encouraged to make decisions inspired by the philosophy embodied in the Credo, which challenges them to put first the needs and well-being of the people J&J serve. According to J&J's corporate website, 'Our Credo is more than just a moral compass. We believe it's a recipe for business success. The fact that Johnson & Johnson is one of only a handful of companies that have flourished through more than a century of change is proof of that.'[36]

The 'Tylenol case' was a paradigmatic example of how the J&J Credo works. Tylenol was a popular analgesic in the USA and in other countries, until the sudden death of seven people in Chicago after having taken Extra-Strength Tylenol brand capsules. This caused great alarm among the executives of McNeil Consumer Products, a division of J&J. The case was heard in autumn 1982, and it was also proved that Tylenol capsules contained cyanide. The company's reaction was determined and quick. Within a few days of the incident, the recall of all Extra-Strength Tylenol was made. In addition, the company offered to exchange Tylenol capsules for Tylenol tablets. The nationwide recall involved 31 million bottles of Tylenol, which cost the company $100 million. Moreover, the company itself prevented consumers from using any Tylenol product until the cause of the tampering had been established. As a result, the production and advertising of Tylenol also ceased. The senior executives were accessible to the media and a toll-free crisis phone line was set up for consumers.

Such a huge operation was mounted despite the company having no real knowledge of the extent of the contamination and, consequently, being unable to ensure that no one else would be poisoned. As the investigation proceeded, they discovered that the contamination was caused externally, probably during some part of the distribution process. But it was sure that the contamination was not the effect of the production process or of any other internal operation.

J&J received recognition from the media for having acted quickly, openly and honestly, both during the crisis and in bringing it to an end. Consequently, the company was able to preserve its good name and reputation. No one was convicted of the tampering incidents and deaths: the company was able to reintroduce Tylenol – acetaminophen capsules – with new triple-seal tamper-resistant packaging. Despite its market share drop from 33 per cent to 18 per cent, it recovered its position in less than one year.

Many believe that the Tylenol affair was guided by the J&J culture that existed at the time. During a TV talk show, James E. Burke, CEO of J&J during the Tylenol crisis, explained that the widespread disposition to view Johnson & Johnson favourably was a result of the high level of public trust built up and handed down as a legacy of previous managers. Asked to explain his company's handing of the crisis and the remarkable recovery that followed, Burke simply answered: 'I think the answers come down from the value system ... What's right works. It really does. The cynics will tell you it doesn't, but they're wrong.'[37]

Questions:

1. What is your reaction to J&J's Credo and, more specifically, to the first article: 'Our first responsibility is to the doctors, nurses and patients ... '?

2. What specific purpose did J&J's Credo serve in the Tylenol affair?

3. What lessons can be learned from this?

Sources: Johnson & Johnson corporate website: 'Our Credo Values': http://www.jnj.com/connect/about-jnj/jnj-credo/; Wikipedia: '1982 Chicago Tylenol Murders'; R. F. Harley, 'Johnson & Johnson Scare: The Classic Example of Responsible Crisis Management', in R. F. Harley (ed.), *Business Ethics: Mistakes and Successes* (Hoboken, NJ: Wiley, 2005): 303–14; M. S. Schwartz, 'Tylenol Tampering', in R. W. Kolb, *Encyclopedia of Business Ethics and Society* (Los Angeles: Sage, 2008): 2128–9.

Dilemma 1

A petroleum refinery plant in a Southern European country was proud of the low level of labour accidents they had and, for that reason, paid bonuses to its employees. Nevertheless, over the years, safety standards began to fall, especially among workers who were not employees of the company but, rather, employees of subcontracted companies. These workers mainly carried out maintenance tasks under the supervision of the chief maintenance engineer from the refinery or one of his technicians. They received minimum instruction for each assigned task.

One day, in the course of usual maintenance operations, work was due on the atmospheric distillation tower. It was necessary to replace a heat exchanger, a delicate operation that requires rapid execution in order to avoid gas leaks. The head of the maintenance department chose two employees from a subcontracted company who had previously carried out routine operations but had never replaced a heat exchanger. After a short training session that same morning, and accompanied by a supervisor, the operation began. In the course of the substitution, they unwittingly altered the positioning of a pipe connection, which resulted in the pipe sliding and the violent emission of the liquid that flowed through it, producing a 'blow torch effect' that burned both workers and caused superficial wounds to the supervisor. One of the workers died instantly, the second a few hours later in hospital.

It was necessary to deal with journalists who were awaiting information on the causes and other details of the explosion. The general manager of the refinery knew that journalists could either assuage an incident or stoke a climate of hostility towards the company.

Questions:

1. What ethical issues can you find in this case?

2. Who bears responsibility for this incident?

(cont'd)

3. What would you do if you were the general manager of this plant, regarding the official statement?
4. How could such accidents be avoided in the future?

Summary

Ethics, developed by classic Greek philosophers over 2,500 years ago, provided a rational basis for morality. Rational ethics (or simply 'ethics') differs from moral judgements, personal and social values, religious ethics and moral theology.

Since the 1970s, a movement in favour of business ethics has been emerging. One of its causes was increasing social pressure regarding corporate ethical behaviour in response to business scandals. Another important factor was a greater awareness that ethics is associated with business itself, and is linked to long-term results associated with the trust that ethical behaviour generates.

Business ethics can be defined as a guide for seeking human excellence in business organizations, or simply as a guideline for human quality in business.

We can distinguish four constitutive aspects of business ethics: (1) individual business ethics; (2) management ethics; (3) organizational ethics; and (4) societal business ethics.

Business ethics deals with three courses of action: (1) ethical issues – unacceptable actions; (2) dilemmas – situations in which it is not clear what is acceptable; and (3) improvements – situations in which human excellence can be improved.

Several reasons trigger the introduction of ethical practices and programmes to business organizations, including: (1) image recovery after business scandals; (2) avoiding the risk of losing a favourable image or being sued for misconduct; (3) building corporate reputation; (4) enhancing stakeholder relationships; and (5) acting with genuine ethical commitment.

In practice, some companies show a real commitment and ethical behaviour, while others use ethics as 'window dressing'. However, a growing number of companies agree that, to a greater or lesser extent, ethics must be taken into account.

... a great deal of economic life depends for its viability on a certain limited degree of ethical commitment. Purely selfish behavior of the individual is really incompatible with any kind of settled economic life.[1]

Kenneth Arrow (1921–)
Nobel Laureate in Economics in 1972

Chapter Aims

This chapter will allow you to:

- become more familiar with the human and social dimensions of business
- discuss the role of the state in the regulation of the economic system
- gain an understanding of the prospects and problems of the free market
- discuss under what conditions, if any, capitalism is ethically acceptable
- discuss the role of business laws and other regulations and their limitations
- distinguish between legality and morality, and discover some practical implications of the difference
- gain an understanding of 'soft regulation' from civil society
- discuss the necessity of ethics and business ethics beyond market and laws.

Key terms

Asymmetrical information
Capitalism
Civil society
Competition
Externalities
Fair competition
Freedom
Government intervention
Hard regulations

Laissez-faire
Law
Legality
Market
Market economy
Mass media
Monopoly
Monopsony
Oligopoly

Perfect market
Rationality
Regulations
Shareholder activism
Sociability
Society
Soft regulations

Business in Society: Are the Market and Regulations Sufficient?

INTRODUCTORY CASE 2:

THE ENRON COLLAPSE

Enron was established in 1985 as a traditional pipeline company distributing natural gas during the early years of the liberalization of energy markets in the USA. Energy liberalization offered new business opportunities in which Enron, under the leadership of its CEO Ken Lay, took on a new role.

Seeing the opportunity, Enron decided to turn itself into a company trading commodities, buying and selling natural gas. As deregulation caused disparities in gas prices, Enron guaranteed long-term supply at a fixed price to its clients. By 1995, Enron had become the leading company in its sector. Shortly afterwards, Enron took a step further as an intermediary and began to act as a broker. Enron began to assume the mediation risks previously borne by the clients, who took out insurance to protect themselves against risks such as interest rate movements, unpaid credits, meteorological conditions and so on.

Enron relied directly on buyers and sellers, and demanded quick access to credit markets. However, as Enron rarely had liquidity, it was obliged to turn to the banks.

The turnover of Enron rose so impressively that, at the end of 2000, it became one of the largest companies in North America in terms of sales. But, behind this facade, its debt was also soaring, and seemed disproportionate in relation to its equity. Given that Enron already had high debt levels on its balance sheets, it needed to maintain a good credit rating.

In 1997, Enron began to explore new markets, as it believed that the solution to its debt problem was to invest abroad in power plants, Internet companies, fibre optics and so on. However, many of these investments did not live up to their expectations. The lack of success of these new businesses and the negative development of energy markets affected profits and growth. This made it difficult to maintain a good credit rating and share price.

It was then that some Enron senior managers decided to manipulate its books to deliver the elusive earnings growth. The operation was headed by Andrew Fastow, Enron's executive vice president and chief financial officer. To maintain growth in earnings, Enron introduced a number of dubious practices. One of these was in using a technique called 'Mark-to-market accounting', which is permitted by American law; however, the application of this made by Enron is more than questionable, since contracts were made on a long-term basis (for as long as 20 years), and no one can foresee the price of raw materials and other basic commodities over such a long period.

In addition, Andrew Fastow set up a complex network of supposedly independent partnerships known as 'special purpose entities' (SPE) to hedge the value of certain assets, to take on some current and future debts, and to carry out transactions – especially asset sales – in a very covert way. Enron indirectly controlled most of these SPEs, which turned out to number some 3,000. The parent company (Enron) avoided consolidation of the SPEs due to a loophole in the accounting rules that say that consolidation is not required as long as there is an outside party with an equity investment at risk in the SPEs equal to 3 per cent of total assets. This happened to be so in Enron's case. As a consequence, the financial situation given by Enron's balance sheets was far from the real picture.

This made it impossible to have a correct estimate of the profits that would be received as a consequence of the assets. In addition, under pressure to find new contracts, especially at the end of each trimester, the strain on the traders became almost unbearable.

The bursting of the Internet bubble in the middle of 2000 led to a tumbling in Enron's stock price. In February 2001, Jeff Skilling, who joined Enron in 1990 as chairman and CEO of Enron Capital & Trade Resources, was appointed CEO of Enron; however, in August of that year, he suddenly resigned and Ken Lay took over as CEO.

In October 2001, Enron revealed third quarter losses of $618 million and announced the reduction in shareholder equity to $1.2 billion. This caused the price of Enron shares to drop further. Finally, the real situation came to light and Enron's stock price fell to about $0.30. Unable to pay the loans, Enron went to court to file for bankruptcy protection on 2 December 2001.

After the Enron bankruptcy, multiple investigations were opened. As of July 2005 there had been 16 guilty pleas and six convictions, only one of which was thrown out.

Enron had a detailed 64-page 'Code of Ethics' and a set of corporate values, which included respect, integrity, communication and excellence. However, in practice, the bottom line was the supreme value, and the climate in Enron was characterized by attitudes of arrogance, greed, corruption and ruthlessness.

After the fall of Enron and an intense public debate, the Sabanes–Oxley Act was promulgated in the USA in 2002. The Sabanes–Oxley Act contains stringent measures to avoid situations such as those of Enron. It was the most significant change in US security laws since the early 1930s. Although the Sabanes–Oxley Act introduces more transparency in corporate accounting practices, some complain that compliance with it is very costly for companies, including small and medium-sized enterprises.

Questions:

1. What do you think about the strategies of the CFO, Andrew Fastow, to maintain the credit rating and the share price?

2. Who is responsible for the Enron scandal? Top executives, the board of directors, auditors, banks, lawyers, analysts ...?

3. Do you think that the Enron scandal was due exclusively to the insufficiency of US laws?

4. Why might corporate values and the 'Code of Ethics' not have prevented Enron's fall?

Sources: *Financial Times*, issues from October 2001 to February 2002; F. Peñalva, 'Learning from a Crisis', *IESE Alumni Magazine*, 87 (2002); D. Windsor, 'Enron Corporation', in R. W. Kolb, *Encyclopedia of Business and Society* (Los Angeles: Sage, 2008): 716–19.

BUSINESS: A HUMAN AND SOCIAL REALITY

A sound development of business ethics should not forget an obvious and important consideration: business is about human activity that is carried out by individuals within organizations. These organizations are a social reality, and the fact is that business is a part of society.

Thus, arriving at a correct view of the human being and society seems somewhat relevant for business ethics. Actually, it is not an easy task to acquire it; a long philosophical debate has taken place concerning both concepts. However, it seems clear that the view of the human being and society adopted by some particular sciences is a reductionism. This is the case of most current economic theories that consider a model of man, termed *homo oeconomicus* (economic man), with only interests and preferences, which one tries to maximize. This model can be useful for developing certain economic theories, but many would agree that the human being is much more than a *homo oeconomicus*.

In spite of these conceptual difficulties, something can be said on the human being that might be useful for business ethics. Philosophers usually emphasize a number of features that characterize human beings.[2] A very concise review of these features is the following:

Human rationality

Rationality is the quality or state of being rational; that is, having intellectual understanding. Rationality gives capacity for abstraction, which goes beyond empirical data received by the senses, and the capacity to deliver judgements. In addition, humans can know or consider universal concepts, such as beauty, peace and wisdom. Moreover, humans are capable of reasoning not only about external things, but also about themselves.

Freedom and emotions

Humans also have emotions, sentiments and bodily needs, which stimulate desires. However, we have the capability to deliberate on such desires and decide whether or not we want to follow them. Thus, human action is not determined by automatic stimulus response, or by physical or biophysical laws, but by free choice. Freedom or self-determination permits one to decide whether or not to respond to a stimulus, or to choose among several alternative courses of action. Although, sometimes, human behaviour is not especially reflective, we have autonomy to decide whether or not to act, or to do one thing or another, by means of a conscious process.

Inner privacy and rich language

Through self-reflection, each human individual realizes that one has an inner privacy, a 'self-possessed "I"', which confers a rich interior life upon the person. Human individuals can share their own intimacy with others and establish with them intentional and friendly links, which can bring about strong forms of unity and friendship. Human language provides a rich way to communicate thoughts, feelings and projects, and can foster the forming of mutual links.

Sociability and capacity for friendship

Humans are social beings, inclined by nature to companionship with other persons. Human relations can also have special features embedded in rationality. Although human relationships can be violent – and, as a matter of fact, sometimes they are so – humans have found ways to collaborate and achieve common goals or to find concurrent interests in civilized ways. What is more, human relations are not always purely utilitarian: they can be based on a sense of service and on friendship.

Openness to human growth

Human beings can undergo physical development, which has a limit, but also, and above all, are open to unlimited moral self-development by acquiring what reinforces the noblest human capacities. These capacities are related to the searching for truth and with loving and doing what one understands to be truly good.

Uniqueness

Finally, a human being is not a mere exemplar of an animal species but, rather, someone unique, irreplaceable by any other human being, except perhaps for the execution of certain mechanical tasks. Rationality and free choices shape our character and our own particular biography.

Humans live in *society*, from the Latin *societas*, which means a 'friendly association with others'. It is related to another Latin word, *socius*, meaning 'companion, associate, comrade, or business partner'. In practice, society usually refers to an association of people. There are societies of which one is a natural member, such as the family into which one is born or the political community to which one belongs. Many other societies, however, are organized, voluntary associations of people.

The term 'society' addresses a number of important existential issues. Society is not a mere abstract or linguistic concept. Many social phenomena cannot be reduced to individual behaviours. Explaining certain situations requires a view of something 'greater than the sum of its parts'. Society is more comprehensive than the people who make it up, who are only a part of it. Moreover, societies often endure beyond the lifespan of their individual members.

There is no complete agreement on the origin and nature of society. There are two extreme positions, *individualism* and *collectivism*, which are often criticized. Individualism conceives every form of human community as a set of individuals united by free agreements or contracts. Far from this atomistic vision of the society is collectivism, which takes an ordered organism as a model for society.

In the Aristotelian tradition, especially in the later proposals, both individuals and the whole are considered. Society is understood as a consequence of the human capacity to establish friendly association with others. It is therefore very close to the previously mentioned etymological meaning of society. Some Eastern traditions are quite in line with this approach, which considers that the whole is greater than the parts. However, another relevant Western tradition is based on an individualistic approach, seeing society as a set of individuals united exclusively by common interests through hypothetical social contracts. These different views have important consequences for understanding the social reality of the business enterprise. We will consider this point later on.[3]

BUSINESS WITHIN THE MARKET ECONOMY

No one can understand business ethics without a firm grasp of the social environment in which firms operate. Business is born within society and functions there, and it is from society that any firm obtains its permission to operate. Business is involved in the structure, organization and functions of society, in its social and cultural context, and maintains a rich network of societal relationships.

Business cannot operate in the absence of an appropriate social and political context. The ground for business activity and economic development is not well prepared when a country lacks political stability, or there is inefficiency in public administration, corruption or insufficient juridical guarantees. Business needs all of these, along with respect for individual freedom and private property.

It is within society that the market system enables a business to interchange products and services with others and create wealth. Most countries maintain a free market economy system (usually we simply say 'market economy'), based on private property and freedom of enterprise and contract, in which decisions are coordinated through free competition and agreements between buyers and suppliers. The price, determined by the abundance of supply and demand, gives 'market signals' of what to produce, when buyers are willing to pay a relatively high price in comparison with the product cost, or which products are no longer viable because their price fails to outweigh their cost. In a free market, the 'price mechanism' provides most of the relevant information for making efficient marketplace decisions,[4] whereas in a controlled market it is the government that, directly or indirectly, regulates prices or supplies, distorting the 'market signals'.[5]

A free market offers business the opportunity to buy and sell goods and services, and to make a profit. But the market also presents threats: a firm can lose clients to a competitor, or even be eliminated from the marketplace altogether, if its rivals offer more desirable products, services or working conditions.

From a social perspective, a free market provides incentives for economic dynamism:

- It stimulates the production of saleable goods or services, which prevents the squandering of resources on undesired products
- It fosters an efficient assignment of people and resources in order to lower costs; consequently, prices tend to decrease and quality to increase
- A free market motivates innovation and a productive use of available resources.

Apart from fostering economic dynamism, the market economy makes economic goods of ever greater quality accessible to more and more people. In addition, it respects people's freedom of exchange and choice through market transactions.

Economists have developed the idea of a 'perfect market'. They suppose that all actors in the market – buyers and sellers – try to maximize the actor's utility (economic rationality). Among a long list of criteria for a perfect market, three are critical:[6]

- *Perfect competition*, which is when there is a sufficiently large number of participants such that no individual can affect the market
- *Complete information*, which is where all people who participate in the market have complete information about product and price, and neither information costs nor taxes exist
- *No externalities*, which is where there is no impact on any party not directly involved in an economic decision.

However, in real markets:

- *Competition is not perfect.* On the contrary some actors, including business firms, have 'market power'; that is, the capability to adjust the market price of a good or service. Market power permits participants to appropriate more benefits for themselves while providing fewer benefits and transferring more cost to others. An extreme case of market power is when there is only one seller (*monopoly*) or one buyer (*monopsony*) of a certain product or service, so that an individual or company has a disproportionate voice in the terms on which other individuals or business enterprises have access to it (if there is a lack of viable substitute goods).

- *Information is asymmetrical.* Information is asymmetrically distributed between the buyer and seller or producer and consumer, apart from many other possible types of incomplete information.

- *There are externalities.* Externalities incur costs for a third party (for instance, pollution) and so escape the market pricing mechanism.

These conditions, in which market allocation is not the most desirable way, along with other situations termed 'market failures' do not lead to social welfare enhancement.[7] Apart from this, the free market has other negative aspects:

- *Risk of abuses.* A free market brings about competitive pressures to reduce costs. While this certainly has its positive side, such pressure can result in the exploitation of workers, or the abuse of the good faith or ignorance of consumers through misleading information or fraud.

- *Lack of equity.* A free market, for all its efficiency in the assignment of resources, remains very ineffective in terms of equity. It does not simply reward work: its results are also conditioned by the relationship of supply and demand.

- *Lack of moral concern on the product.* The market itself is blind to the content of the transaction, caring nothing for the distinction between wheat and cocaine.

- *Not all legitimate demands are satisfied.* A free market only responds to the demands of those consumers with sufficient funds to purchase its products. The market cannot satisfy basic needs, such as nutrition and health, if people are too poor to buy products conducive to physical well-being, if they cannot afford medicines or even basic foods. In that case, satisfaction of needs requires other means, such as solidarity or social policies, different from the logic of exchange characteristic of the market.

Some of these limitations can be resolved by an appropriate legal framework and with appropriate governmental policies, apart from corporate social responsibility[8] and private action of solidarity. A pure free market system, operating without interference from government or other non-market institutions, does not exist. In every country, businesses operate within a modified free market system, constrained by more or less broad governmental or supra-governmental regulations.

Insight 2:

Is capitalism ethically acceptable?

A frequently asked question is whether capitalism is ethically acceptable. The quick answer is: It depends on what capitalism you are talking about. The system of economic organization called capitalism presents a wide variety of manifestations, although all of them are based on a free market.[9] Current examples of capitalism are the Anglo-Saxon model and European Continental Capitalism. The former is less regulated and more market oriented, while the latter is more concerned with the rights of all stakeholders and includes many social regulations and policies. Japanese capitalism, although this is now changing, used to include close coordination between the government and the policies of major companies, with well-established social networks, including banks and suppliers, and stable industrial relations.

Actually, every form of capitalism has an institutional and societal framework within which the market operates. Laws and social control can maintain a market under an appropriate level of control by society and the state in order to avoid abuses and to guarantee that the basic needs of the whole of society are satisfied. If such a framework respects and protects people and the environment, and prevents abuses, the resulting capitalism based on private property, free enterprise and social participation is ethically acceptable, since it respects human dignity and contributes to the common good, two crucial ethical references that will be discussed later.[10]

However, capitalism is not acceptable if economic freedom is exercised without considering other aspects of human freedom and a sense of moral responsibility, or when the institutional framework does not respect human rights sufficiently. In this sense, some talk of 'savage capitalism' in those forms of capitalism in which the accumulation of capital becomes a supreme criterion; profits are obtained at any cost, and people, in practice, are reduced to a state of quasi-servitude, or the environment is not respected.[11]

GOVERNMENT INTERVENTION AND FAIR COMPETITION

Government intervention on market flaws is carried out through regulations, taxes and subsidies. Explaining these actions is beyond our purpose here, other than to briefly mention regulations.

A government provides a framework to the market through laws and by creating institutions of control; courts are in charge of applying the laws. A minimal framework for markets is the model known as *laissez-faire* ('let do'), which confines government intervention to occasions of market failure; maintaining private property rights and social order; enforcing compliance with contract law; and very few other business regulations, such as those that establish the ground rules of free market competition. This form of capitalism was practised in Europe during the Industrial Revolution and in the United States before the Great Depression of 1929. Today, very few countries practise strictly *laissez-faire* capitalism. On the contrary, the state tends to play a prominent role in the capitalist system: most countries have abundant regulations regarding labour, consumer and the environment.

A limited number of strategically crafted regulations can favour market and business activity, and contribute to a good society – if they enjoy a sound ethical basis. Too many regulations, though, can strangle the advantages of the free market. Moreover, there are not only business failures; there are also 'government failures', which occur when a government intervention causes a more inefficient allocation of goods and resources than the market, if left to itself, would have brought about.

Sometimes government takes action on the economy in order to control the economic situation when this is believed necessary, especially in crises. A recent and striking case was the intervention of the governments in the face of the *subprime mortgage crisis* in 2008, in which liquidity in the global credit markets and banking system contracted dramatically.

A key issue in market economy is maintaining fair competition – which is based on price, quality and service, not on whatever abuse of market power a company might be able to get away with. Fair competition permits the attainment of the advantages of a market economy.

Competition collapses when there are monopolies or monopsonies. However, monopolies are not necessarily detrimental to consumers. There are 'natural monopolies', in which a company becomes the sole supplier of a product or service because the nature of that product or service makes a single supplier more efficient than two or more in competition. Some monopolies are legally sanctioned by the state, often to provide an incentive to invest in a risky venture or enrich a domestic constituency.

Apart from a few cases of acceptable monopoly or monopsony, competition under fair conditions is preferable for bringing about the optimal conditions for trade. That is why most countries have laws that seek to prevent abuses derived from monopolies, monopolistic practices or situations that restrict competition (antitrust laws, in the USA; competition law in the EU) and governmental agencies to act against companies involved in such practices. These laws cover three groups of business practices:

- *Agreements among business firms that restrict competition.* The most common case is an agreement known as a 'cartel'. In industries where cartels exist, usually those that are oligopolistic, companies agree to restrict free trade and competition through price fixing, agreements on market shares, allocation of customers or of territory, establishment of common sales agencies, division of profits and so on. One particular form of illegal agreement among firms is 'bid-rigging', which can occur where contracts (for example, government construction contracts) are determined by a call for bids. In a bid-rigging exercise, one group of bidders will be designated to win the bid with the agreement that others will have their turn in future bidding.

- *Abusive business practices.* These are generally related to cases of unfair pricing, such as price gouging, predatory pricing or dumping, abusive manners or 'refusal to deal'. The latter refers to agreements to restrict the supply of goods with the intention of lessening competition in a certain market.[12]
- *Threats to competition derived from mergers and acquisitions of large corporations.* Some such mergers and acquisitions and even some joint ventures can restrict competition. For this reason there are laws establishing that such operations must be carried out under the supervision of public authorities. In order to reduce threats to the competitive process, authorities do not allow mergers or acquisitions under certain circumstances, or they impose certain conditions to protect competition (for instance, divesting part of the merged business).

Fair competition also excludes 'competitor bashing', including making false claims and accusations against a competitor's reputation in order to drive away business (tortious interference with business) and using 'tort' (a wrongful act) to interfere in a mutual contract between two parties (tortious interference of contract).

Other unfair business practices generally prohibited by law are bribery, fraud, misrepresentation, trademark infringement and misappropriation of trade secrets, among others, which will be discussed later.[13]

ARE LAWS ENOUGH?

Direct state intervention in economic affairs can occur when a state run business seems truly necessary on national security grounds, but also for less justifiable reasons. Such interventions can often be problematic, introducing the inefficiency typical of government into business management, and fostering an entrenched habit of passivity about economic initiatives. Besides, state interventions in economic affairs can discourage citizens and corporations from undertaking business projects with freedom and an entrepreneurial spirit. Thus, the state must not prevent free exercise of economic activity. On the contrary, it ought to be creating the conditions that foster initiative.

Market and laws might seem sufficient to maintain the system and contribute to a good society. This is the vision, for example, of the economist Milton Friedman.[14] Certainly, as noted, a free market provides an efficient mechanism for the assignment of resources in accordance with consumer desires; and laws provide the necessary ground rules – such as respecting private property, honouring contracts and acting without deception or fraud, and doing what is necessary to avoid or minimize market failures. However, laws have a number of limitations:

- *Laws generally come late.* Only in the aftermath of problems and scandals are new laws promulgated with an eye to preventing similar scenarios. However, experience shows that novel ways of evading the law continually emerge.

- *Laws only provide minimal standards.* Laws are insufficient to cover the whole field of human activity. They cannot regulate every action: such is not their purpose.

- *There is a risk of ineffectiveness in the application of business laws.* It is very difficult – probably impossible – to achieve a 'perfect law'. Laws have loopholes, and those who disregard ethics can exploit these so as to escape the spirit of any law. Moreover, some countries lack the means for law enforcement that incentivize effective application; or, what is worse, corruption might prevent the consistent application of laws, rendering them ineffective.

- *Informal constraints are also relevant.* As Nobel Laureate Kenneth Arrow has argued, informal constraints such as trust and morality must be assumed to operate in advanced market economies, since formal constraints alone (legal rules and other external regulations) could not stem force or fraud.[15]

- *Organizational life is richer than market and laws.* However, management entails much more than following the market and complying with the laws.

CIVIL SOCIETY DEMANDS ON BUSINESS AND ITS 'SOFT REGULATIONS'

Business does not operate exclusively between the twin poles of market and government. Civil society also plays a prominent and increasing role in conditioning business activity. The notion of *civil society* is complex. It generally refers to civic and social movements, organizations and institutions based on voluntary associations, distinct from state structure and commercial institutions.[16] Civil society embraces social movements defending particular goals: non-governmental organizations (NGOs), trade unions, professional and business associations, community groups, churches and faith-based organizations, universities, research think tanks, family associations, coalitions and advocacy groups, registered charities and so on. Such groups form the fabric of any society.

Historically, the influence of civil society on business has taken place through social activists and movements, and associations created for particular ends. The first action to change business behaviour was focused on working conditions. The demands came from the labour movement (which started in Europe during the Industrial Revolution), together with religious voices and political groups. Labour activists and associated working people formed trade unions or labour unions. They organized campaigns, demonstrations and strikes to pressure their employers – and, above all, governments – to implement laws to regulate labour relations and protect workers' rights. After decades of fighting, these laws were promulgated in many countries. In addition, after the First World War the International Labour Organization (ILO) was created as an agency of the League of Nations (it is now an agency of the UN) with a tripartite structure (employers, employees and governments) to defend labour, and to protect unions and rights related to labour.

Another highly significant social movement for business relates to 'consumer advocacy', which began in the USA at the beginning of the twentieth century to confront unethical practices in selling, advertising and usage of products, mainly in the food industry. In the 1930s, consumer pressure grew and as a result the US Food and Drug Administration was established. A law was introduced that allowed the government to inspect seafood processing plants. In the 1960s, the consumer movement came to its height, its campaigning for regulations covering the safety of products, labelling and advertising, leading to more new legislation in these areas. The European governments were even quicker to recognize their responsibilities to consumers.

In the 1960s, other social movements emerged, such as the civil rights movement (mainly in the USA) against racist practices; the movement for women's rights, which campaigned against the historical and traditional bias in the rights enjoyed by women; the conservation movement, which was especially concerned about chemical pesticides; and the ecology movement, which was stimulated by a widespread acknowledgement of the ecological crisis on our planet.

Other social groups can also wield influence by creating public opinion that pressures both governments and businesses to make decisions aligned with their proposals. Universities and research centres, along with experts in particular subjects, can contribute to shaping public opinion, especially if the mass media help to spread their ideas and findings.

More recent movements arising within civil society are related to problems associated with globalization, including social inequality and poverty, human rights in developing countries and international trade. Some groups focus on specific issues, such as working conditions in sweatshops, or child labour. These social movements can act informally or through associations, commonly under the form of non-governmental organizations (NGOs).[17]

Among the tactics employed by NGOs to pressure businesses or governments to promote certain social or public policies, the following are most common:

- Litigation against companies
- Organizing boycotts of certain products or brands
- Demonstrations
- Publicizing reports attacking corporations
- Acting through coalitions of NGOs
- A variety of direct actions that damage a company's interests, or even the interests of third parties. It is well known that some direct actions against environmental destruction are carried out by the environmental organization Greenpeace.
- Other tactics include acquiring shares to participate in shareholder meetings with the intention of exerting influence to change corporate practices, such as divestment from particular countries where human rights are disrespected, adoption of environmentally friendly policies and so on (*shareholder activism*).

The *mass media*, understood as being any means of public communication reaching a large audience, have a great role in shaping public opinion, with a subsequent influence on civil society. 'Mass media' includes newspapers, magazines, television, radio broadcasting and Internet media (videos, personal or organizational webpages, blogs, podcasts and so on). These sometimes belong to governmental agencies and sometimes function as commercial enterprises, but Internet media have become part of civil society.

Civil society exerts indirect influence on business by pressuring and lobbying governments to implement laws and regulations and to establish agencies of governmental control. This has been the traditional influence of civil society on businesses. But it can also exert a direct influence, something more and more frequent nowadays. Civil society thus imposes on business what has been called 'soft regulation'.[18] Companies, to some extent, take this soft regulation into account in order to avoid risks (losing clients, perhaps being targeted for boycotts), and to achieve the reputation of being a responsible business.

LEGALITY AND MORALITY

Some ethical norms, laws and other legal regulations do overlap: they all prohibit theft and injury to others, for example. Ethics is related to law, but the scope of the former is much broader. Unlike laws, which only cover certain aspects of economic activity with minimal standards, ethics covers every aspect of human activity. In other words, legality and morality are distinct, but related.

Laws can sometimes be unethical; that is, contrary to ethical standards. For instance, some labour legislation shows insufficient respect for human rights. Thus, we can find business issues that are obligatory both ethically and legally; others that are required by ethics, but not by law; and still others compulsory from a legal perspective, but not ethically licit. The third possibility presents the dilemma of what to do when law obliges unethical action. This was the case of companies in South Africa during apartheid. They were obliged to follow racist practices, which generated great controversy, and eventually some companies opted to divest and leave the country.

Ethics comes first. Ethics precedes the law and gives it moral legitimacy. In order to contribute to building a just society, laws must be consistent with ethics, and must articulate sound specifications of general ethical principles. However, frequently, legislative changes occur due to social pressures and the introduction of new cultural views. Ethics, by contrast, does not follow social demands, although ethical reflection is sensitive to social problems. Nevertheless, such problems are viewed through the lens of timeless ethical principles, such as the intrinsic value of every human being.

Furthermore, when a company faces contradictory laws, ethics provides the criteria by which to discern the proper course. This is especially relevant in a global context: a company can meet with different laws in different countries. Laws in one country might promote great respect and excellent work conditions, while somewhere else a lack of respect for people could result in sub-human conditions.[19] Ethics, by contrast, considers the equal dignity and human rights of all, seeing beyond ethically questionable, soft, local laws.

The previous reflection does not mean that the law has no moral significance, neither, by any means, that there is no moral obligation to obey the law: this is only true of laws contrary to human rights and other ethical duties. Acting in compliance with just laws is an ethical requirement for social life derived from the necessity of an authority's governance of a community. In addition, most ethical values and principles are very generic and stand in need of specification. In issues related to public life, these values and principles are specified by laws. For instance, laws provide specific and reasonable rules for respecting the right to life and health in the workplace. Such rules should be followed, not only for fear of legal coercion, but also out of moral obligation.[20]

Similarly, 'soft regulation' can be related to ethics, but social demands are not an intrinsic ethical requirement. Social demands depend on the culture (or cultures) of each society, which change over time. Thus, some decades ago, a new sensitivity to the natural environment was awakened in response to massive destruction of resources and increasing pollution. Fears of global warming and pollution are currently widespread, along with the need to prevent abuse of labourers in various countries, with some groups demanding that major companies take responsibility when such violations occur in their supply chain.

Rational ethics deals with social demands, trying to discover business ethics issues in new social sensibilities. Thus, in the last few decades, sensitivity to the environment has provoked serious reflection on these issues, which led to the formulation of rational principles regarding the environment and its protection. Similarly, business ethics considers demands concerning labour abuse in some countries in the light of human dignity, human rights and other ethical principles or standards, and analyses to what extent a company is responsible for abuses in its supply chain.

BEYOND MARKET AND REGULATIONS

In summary, business faces the requirements of the market, derived from competition, laws, or 'hard regulations' from government or governmental agencies and 'soft regulations' in the form of significant social demands. These are interrelated (see Figure 2.1). Abusive situations within a market stimulate social movements, and civil society pressures corporations and governments, which in turn promulgate new laws, and these condition the market. The question arises: Is there room for business ethics? Where do they fit in? As noted above, laws cannot cover everything. Neither can social demands. Whereas ethics applies to every action, legality covers only what is necessary to avoid abuse, and to ensure a fair and peaceful society and a civilized framework for the economic system. In addition, as noted, laws generally come later. By contrasting, ethics precedes the law, and it provides principles applicable to all manner of human and social problems.

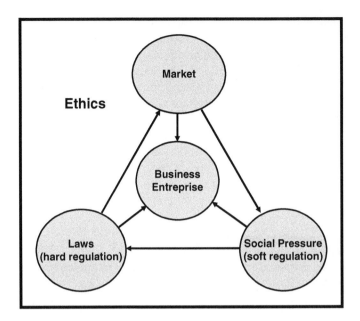

Figure 2.1   Pressures and constraints on the business enterprise

Another argument is that coercion and control imposed by laws are not always sufficient. Although laws are generally effective for coercing proper behaviour, coercion is not the only way to foster it. People can be motivated both extrinsically (via rewards and punishments) and intrinsically (through the intrinsic value of their action). When someone perceives the moral value of an action, this can motivate a particular behaviour regardless of punishment dictated by laws and other regulations.

There are ethical values, principles and norms beyond both hard and soft regulations. However, it would be erroneous to conclude that ethics is only a set of those rules not included in the content of regulations. Regulations can, and should, be inspired by ethical values and principles, and can contain ethical norms. Ethics is beyond the market and its regulations. Through the lens of ethics, we can evaluate the market; besides, ethics provides guidelines for people involved in regulations and in business enterprises.

Also, business organizations involve other formalities besides laws and others' external regulations. Business has internal norms, processes and systems for implementing business strategies, and business ethics provides guidelines for designing these corporate rules with attention to appropriate moral norms.

Furthermore, in business organizations not everything is formalized. Spontaneous interactions among co-workers and all other varieties of human relations within an organization create interlocking relations that bring about what is called an 'informal organization'. These links encourage cooperation, commitment and a sense of belonging to a group or team.

It is ultimately people who are at the centre of business organizations and, within them, people can and should work toward their personal development. As Llano wrote: 'The business organization should personalize the individual, and certainly not depersonalize as does the State, nor impersonalize as does the market.'[21] Ethics plays a role in promoting moral links – a lack thereof usually works to the detriment of cooperation, the essence of any organization – and in personalizing the individual.

Last, but not least, human life is not limited to economic and legal systems. Economics is not everything. Economics and the laws that regulate it are instrumental for life, but do not constitute its entirety. Human and social life is not exhausted by the economic system; neither can the market meet every variety of human need – only those involving economic transactions.

Business ethics in practice 2:

Cummins Engine Corp. – Ethical training and compliance with law

The history of Cummins Engine Corp. started with Clessie Cummins, a professional chauffeur, who believed he could improve Rudolph Diesel's engine and adapt this engine for use in transportation. After some work that confirmed his ideas, in 1919 Cummins founded an engine company bearing his name. Cummins Engine Corp. began by producing mobile diesel engines in an era where incumbent truck manufacturers were reluctant to change from gas to diesel engines.

The beginnings of the company were shaky, Cummins having to overcome threats of bankruptcy, but eventually his invention won through. Cummins mounted a diesel engine in a used Packard limousine and, at Christmas 1929, he took W. G. Irwin for a ride in America's first diesel powered automobile. With a new infusion of Irwin capital, Cummins started popularizing the notion of the automotive diesel.[22] During the Second World War, most of the company's output went to the US War and Navy Departments. Cummins products endured harsh conditions, from the tropics to the sub-Arctic. The American convoys that supplied allied forces in Europe, Africa and elsewhere were powered, in part, by Cummins engines.

The postwar efforts during 1946–56 turned out to be a business catalyst for the diesel engine in trucks. The company sales grew from $20 million to $60 million, and international expansion started for good. However, in the meantime, a new task and challenges appeared. In 1970, the US government passed the Clean Air Act, which set tough new standards for diesel engine emissions. Nevertheless, that was not an obstacle for Cummins as, thanks to its advanced research, the company could meet those new standards. It improved the fuel economy and reliability of its engines. In the 1980s, Cummins confronted global competition and, in response to this challenge, it launched a massive restructuring programme, investing $1.3 billion in new plant and equipment, and in new engine designs.

Business ethics in practice 2: (cont'd)

In the early 1990s, this international effort moved ahead with major manufacturing ventures in Japan, China and India. Since that time, Cummins has been a global company, currently employing 28,000 people, serving customers in over 160 countries. It has a network of 550 company owned distributor facilities and over 5,000 dealer locations. In 2007, Cummins reported net income of $739 million on sales of $13.05 billion.[23]

For all those years the company grew successfully, showing a great concern for business ethics. It initiated a training programme on ethics and management in the early 1990s to improve its ethical business conduct.[24] For Cummins, ethics rests on a fundamental belief in people's dignity and decency.[25] Therefore, it elaborated a code of business conduct, with detailed guidelines on such topics as import and export control, antitrust compliances, dealings with government contracts, payments to officials, terms of contracts, meals and gift discounts, diversity and equal opportunity employment, financial record keeping and document retentions.[26]

Nevertheless, in 1998, Cummins had to pay the largest civil penalty ever for violation of environmental law. The US Department of Justice and the Environmental Protection Agency (EPA)[27] handed down an $83.4 million penalty against diesel engine manufacturers for their fuel emissions. Under this settlement, seven major manufacturers of diesel engines, including Cummins, would spend more than $1 billion to resolve claims concerning the installation of computer devices in heavy-duty diesel engines that resulted in illegal amounts of air polluting emissions.[28] Without admission of guilt, Cummins paid a $25 million fine and an additional $35 million as a contribution to environmental programmes. The penalty, accompanied by media fallout, shook the company and changed its long-term vision.

Cummins learned its lesson. A reinforcement of the ethical vision came with a new CEO, Tim Solso, who introduced sustainability reports and also instigated greater financial transparency, as well as reiterating the company's commitment to fundamental ethical values. Currently, there is a permanent dialogue between employees and managers about ethical standards. At a designated time of the year, each head of group, division and department reviews the ethical practices together with their staff, and consider whether revisions or additions are appropriate.[29]

Now, as a result of all those changes, Cummins is not only a world leader in emission reduction, but also a leading company in launching and practising various ethical programmes. Its 'mission' underlines such goals as motivating people to act like owners working together, exceeding customer expectations by always being first to market with the best products, partnering with customers to make sure that they succeed, creating wealth for all stakeholders, and demanding that everything the company does leads to a cleaner, healthier, safer environment.[30]

Business ethics in practice 2: (cont'd)

Currently, Cummins management oversees strategies and programmes, and encourages community involvement and responsible citizenship. Its Community Involvement Teams, among many projects, deliver books to schools in China and build schools in Brazil. In addition, there is the Cummins Foundation, which is one of the oldest corporate charitable foundations in the United States.[31]

In 2007, *Corporate Responsibility Officer* ranked Cummins Engine Corp. in position 35 among the 100 Best Corporate Citizens.[32] Since 1999, it has been included among the '100 Best Corporate Citizens'.[33]

Questions:

1. How could Cummins, despite its strong concern for business ethics, break the environmental law through exceeding emissions levels?
2. Why could Cummins now go beyond the law?

Dilemma 2

A construction company based in Europe is planning a project to build a road in an Asian country. Managers realize that the safety standards required by law in this country are not as strict as those in Europe. Applying European standards would increase the cost by 0.75 per cent. The company's public works engineers recommend applying the standards commonly used by the company in Europe, since they believe that the standards of the Asian country are insufficient and human lives are at risk. However, the competitors might have different criteria and the company might lose the public competition to obtain the project when the government agency of that country evaluates the bids from several companies.

Questions:

1. What is your evaluation of the situation described?
2. What observations would you give to managers if your opinion were sought?
3. Would you suggest any alternative to obtain the contract and prevent accidents?

Summary

Business cannot operate without an appropriate social and political context. It needs political stability, efficiency and uncorrupted public administration, as well as adequate juridical guarantees.

The free market system is very efficient in the assignment of resources but much less so in terms of equity. A key issue in market economy is maintaining fair competition. Moreover, the market cannot satisfy human needs when those in need lack sufficient funds to participate. Such cases require social approaches that go beyond the market mechanism.

Capitalism based on private property, free enterprise and social participation is ethically acceptable if it functions within a legal framework in which abuses are prevented, and respect and protection for people and the environment are guaranteed.

The market presents certain limitations that require a legal framework. Among these are 'market failures', the possibility of exploitative situations of workers or abuse of the good faith or the ignorance of consumers.

Government intervention on market flaws is carried out through regulations, taxes and subsidies.

Market and law are not sufficient to guarantee sound economic activity. Laws generally come late and only provide minimal standards. Coercion and control are sometimes insufficient, and the application of the law is sometimes inconsistent.

Besides, informal constraints are also relevant to economic activity, and organizational life is richer than market and laws: it requires cooperation, commitment and a sense of belonging. Furthermore, the economy is instrumental for human life: market and law, therefore, are not sufficient for a completely good life.

Apart from laws and governmental regulations, there is the 'soft regulation' required by civil society.

Market and laws are not enough for a sound corporate life. Organizations have their own norms, beyond governmental regulations and social demands. Furthermore, in business organizations not everything is formalized. An informal organization and informal interconnection encourage cooperation, commitment and a sense of belonging.

Ethics provides a guideline with which to evaluate the morality of the market, laws and social demands, and to motivate for a right behaviour in economic activity.

Whereas recognition of the inherent dignity and of the equal and inalienable rights of all members of the human family is the foundation of freedom, justice and peace in the world.

UN Universal Declaration of Human Rights (1948),
Preamble

Chapter Aims

This chapter will allow you to:

- gain an understanding of cultural diversity and its challenges for business
- give arguments for and against cultural relativism
- recognize common values despite cultural diversity
- comprehend the social and ethical standards proposed for international organizations as worldwide business guidelines
- obtain an overview of how the most influential religions view business ethics.

Key term:

Buddhism	Culture	Judaism
Christianity	Diversity	Masculinity
Collectivism	Ethical universals	*Shintō*
Confucianism	Femininity	Taoism
Cultural diversity	Hinduism	Uncertainty avoidance
Cultural imperialism	Individualism	
Cultural relativism	Islam	

Cultural Diversity, Common Values and International Standards

INTRODUCTORY CASE 3:

**SELLING IN A DIFFERENT CULTURAL CONTEXT –
DO ETHICAL STANDARDS CHANGE?**

In 1990, Manville Corp. was still recovering from the asbestos crisis that had led to its filing for bankruptcy protection in 1982. At the end of 1988, Manville was emerging from Chapter 11 of the United States Bankruptcy Code. The company was getting back on its feet, but there were still plenty of problems to be tackled. At the same time, other problems had arisen, one being a controversy in Japan over the growing fibreglass business on which Manville had staked its future.

The crisis that led to the filing for bankruptcy was caused by mounting asbestos lawsuits – asbestos having been Manville's primary business for more than a century. Manville employees and asbestos installers filed a host of suits against the company, alleging failure to give timely warning of the dangers of asbestos when the company already knew of its harmful effects, and concealment of the results of medical tests undergone by employees.

The courts ruled against the company and Manville was forced to pay out large sums of money. In view of the sheer number of pending or foreseeable future lawsuits (asbestos related diseases had a latency period of several years), and considering that federal accounting rules required a company to set aside funds as a reserve against anticipated claims, Manville filed for Chapter 11 and tried to rebuild.

Strictly speaking, Manville had acted within the law, as the regulation was patchy and voluntary at the time its workers inhaled asbestos fibres. However, by failing to give employees and users timely information about the dangers of the work, the company had shown a lack of respect for certain human rights. Moreover, medical information about employees' health had been concealed from those concerned and the company had failed to make the necessary investments to protect its workers from asbestos hazards. As a consequence, large numbers of workers had inhaled asbestos fibres, leading to illness and death.

In 1982, the asbestos business accounted for 42 per cent of Manville's turnover, but in view of the situation, management decided to dispose of the group's asbestos assets and concentrate on its other businesses, one of which was the production of fibreglass and associated products.

Fibreglass is made by forcing molten glass through a nozzle like a fine sieve. On solidifying, the glass forms a flexible, acid-inert, heat-resistant and highly insulating fibre. This low cost fibre is used in textiles, as a reinforcing agent in some plastics, in thermal and acoustic insulation materials, and in other industrial applications.

At the beginning of the 1990s, Manville was the world's largest producer of non-woven fibreglass, the second largest in fibreglass for insulation and the third largest of continuous fibre.

Fibreglass manufacture in the United States was subject to certain recommendations and requirements. In 1977, the National Institute for Occupational Safety and Health (NIOSH) recommended a limit on workplace concentrations of air-borne fibres of three fibres per cubic centimetre, so as to avoid irritation to the eyes and respiratory tract. Meanwhile, the Occupational Safety and Health Administration (OHSA) classified any suspension of fibreglass particles in the air as an 'irritating dust' and provided a guide for anyone exposed to it.

In addition, since 1976 companies had been obliged by law to notify the Environmental Protection Agency (EPA) within 15 days of any new (previously unknown) information they might acquire about the dangers of fibreglass. Manville scrupulously followed all of these recommendations and, though not required to do so by law, published a wide range of reports on health and safety in the handling of fibreglass products, giving precise instructions for protection.

To general surprise, in 1987 a report was published questioning the safety of fibreglass. The report came from a highly respected body in the field of cancer, the International Agency for Research on Cancer (IARC). IARC suggested that fibreglass should be classified as 'possibly carcinogenic to humans'. The main study cited in the report was one in which glass fibres had been implanted in the lungs of animals using surgical techniques in laboratory tests.

Manville reacted immediately. From October 1987, all of Manville's fibreglass products carried a label warning of the possible risk of cancer from handling them. The label was clearly visible. It was placed on the front of the packaging and printed in a large font size to make it noticeable.

The legal obligation to place such warning labels about the dangers of fibreglass was not at all clear, and implementing them was left largely to each company's discretion. Under US law, a cancer warning had to be given on a label if evidence of the dangers were substantial. The rule was stated in general terms and merely said that companies must formulate a hazard warning that was appropriate to each case.

John Martonik, deputy director of the US Occupational Safety and Health Administration (OSHA), thought that the 1987 IARC report should oblige all fibreglass manufacturers to put warning labels on their products. However, this was just an opinion, not a legal obligation. In fact, very few of Manville's competitors put labels on their products.

Having learned a painful lesson about the concealment of information affecting human health, Manville was especially sensitive to the need to disclose details and show concern for health, safety and the environment. To put that concern into practical effect, a health, safety and environment committee had been created, with the same rank as the audit committee and reporting to the Board of Directors (not the President). Mr Stephens, Manville's CEO, remarked: 'We acknowledge that we have been in serious trouble and, for that reason, we should demand more of ourselves than any other company.'

Manville had many fibreglass customers in Japan. Previously, it had also had a fair number of asbestos customers. From October 1987, all Manville fibreglass products shipped to Japan carried warning labels, albeit only in English. To ensure the warning was understood, from 1990 a Japanese translation was added. The text of the warning was of the same font size as the word Manville. That was when the problems started.

For the Japanese, even today the word 'cancer' calls up images of the terrible events at Hiroshima in 1945, when the atomic bomb not only flattened the city, but also released radiation that spread cancer for miles around. Most Japanese were only too familiar with the horrific stories and photographs of skin cancer and other types of disease. They even referred to cancer as 'C', so as not to have to say the word. It was hardly surprising, therefore, that any product described as possibly carcinogenic should be met with immediate rejection.

In Japan, it was not mandatory to use such labels, neither was it recommended. On the contrary, some Japanese government officials advised the avoidance of any warning about 'C', so as not to cause alarm. Manville's clients did not want to scare their employees. Architects were worried in case the label caught the attention of lawyers, who might sue them for using possibly carcinogenic materials in their buildings. As an alternative, they suggested that they could give any necessary explanations; there was no need to put a label on the product.

But Manville decided to keep its warning label. That decision had a significant impact on the fibreglass division's income statement: it lost $25 million in sales. Some Manville senior managers wondered whether they should stand by their decision, or, if not, what alternatives were open to them. 'Do we have an obligation to tell our customers everything we know about the products we supply?', they asked themselves.

Questions:

1. In cases like this, operating in a different cultural context, do you think that fundamental ethical principles change or merely have a different application?

2. Do you think Manville should maintain such labels in Japan?

3. What would you recommend to Manville management?

Source: Abridged version of the case study 'Manville in Japan: The Warning Labels Controversy (A)', D. Melé (Barcelona: IESE Publishing, 2005). Published with permission.

CULTURAL DIVERSITY AND BUSINESS ETHICS

A major issue in business ethics is cultural diversity, especially with regard to morality and religion. Other aspects of cultural diversity – such as language, clothing, traditions, and ways of interacting with one another and with the environment – can be important for managing diversity, and might also be indirectly relevant for business ethics to the extent that these aspects might condition human and environmental relations.

Business can find cultural diversity within the various arenas of its activity. First, in the workplace, since it is populated by men and women, people of different generations and diverse professional and cultural backgrounds, and, what is more, people of different ethnicities, religions and races. This latter is particularly significant in countries with increasing immigration. Second, a business that operates in several countries faces cultural diversity, in both the workplace and the marketplace, not to mention in dealing with local governments and the social environment. There are obviously significant variations among countries in terms of customs, beliefs, history, tradition and social organization.

Understanding the distinctive characteristics of various cultures is essential to enable a company to attend to demands and foresee possible reactions. Although different cultures might exist within a single country, some scholars have found certain relevant characteristics common to a number of national cultures. A popular classification is that of Hofstede, using five basic dimensions[1] (see Table 3.1): power versus distance (small versus large), individualism versus collectivism, masculinity versus femininity, uncertainty avoidance, and long- versus short-term orientation.

An important element of every culture is religion. Religions present beliefs, values and practices with some effect on behaviour within the business context. They might even stipulate specific precepts regarding business (see an overview of religious approaches to business ethics in the Appendix to this chapter). Apart from this, other influences and personal values and habits lead to different moral evaluations of business situations and issues. Even within the same country or geopolitical area, cultural diversity can be evident and posits challenges for business.

Cultural differences can also arise from mergers and acquisitions of business organizations with conspicuous cultural differences. Since cultural diversity exerts significant influence on operations and management, increasing attention has been focused on this phenomenon, along with how it ought to be managed. Although cultural diversity creates some problems and challenges, it can also enrich the organization in manifold ways. Several strategies have been considered.[2] Some defend options in which the cultural diversity is in some way accepted (inclusion, assimilation, toleration, fostering mutual adaptation or building relationships based on communication and collaboration). Others follow a different course, adopting strategies of exclusion, suppression or even denial of the differences.

Table 3.1   Dimensions of national cultures

Dimensions	Meaning
Small vs large power distance	The extent to which power is distributed unequally and the degree to which this situation is expected and accepted. In societies of large power distance (for example, China or India) subordinates acknowledge the power of others simply based on where they are situated in certain formal, hierarchical positions. The contrary occurs in countries where there is small power distance, such as in most Northern European countries.
Individualism vs collectivism	The degree to which people act with autonomy and choose their own affiliations, or else act predominantly as a member of a life-long group or organization. The USA is among the most individualistic countries (note that, in this sense, individualism does not mean lack of generosity), while Latin American, African and Asian countries are among the least individualistic.
Masculinity vs femininity	Conventionally, 'masculine' or 'quantity of life' refers to values such as competitiveness, assertiveness, ambition, and the accumulation of wealth and material possessions, whereas 'feminine' or 'quality of life' emphasizes people and relationships.
Uncertainty avoidance	The degree to which people prefer rules, structured proceedings and remaining in the same situation for a long time in order to avoid anxiety and uncertainty. Japan is very high in this category, while Mediterranean countries are at the other extreme, with more emphasis on improvisation than on rules.
Long- vs short- term orientation	The importance attached to the future versus the past and present. Traditions, reciprocity, gifts, favours and perseverance are valued more in long-term oriented societies, such as China and India.

Source: Adapted from Hofstede, 2003, 2004.

Cultural diversity challenges business ethics when moral or religious beliefs and values, at a personal or social level, clash with the dominant culture of the workplace, or when a company operates in a cultural environment in which the local values and the values of the company are different or even in tension. Which values or practices should prevail?

If we formulate an example of an expatriate manager who comes across certain questionable local customs, such as discrimination against women or minorities, for example, or evident lack of respect to people or environment. Should the manager apply universal principles or adopt the saying: 'When in Rome, do as the Romans do'?

Some respect cultural diversity, even considering it as enrichment in some aspects, but also accept the existence of universal ethical values and principles higher than cultural values and standards of morality. Contrastingly, others propose forgetting about universal ethical principles and adopting what is called *cultural ethical relativism* (or simply *cultural relativism*).

Defenders of cultural relativism argue that everyone should follow the predominant morality of the cultural environment or society in which they find themselves. Consequently, they reject any *ethical universal* (universal values and principles), except, of course, the principle that mandates cultural relativism.

None doubt cultural diversity; it is a matter of fact. But, what about cultural relativism? Does cultural relativism follow from the fact of cultural diversity? These are sensible questions that deserve discussion.

CULTURAL RELATIVISM AND ETHICAL UNIVERSALS

Cultural relativists note, first, that different cultures have different moral codes, and that certain conduct is considered moral in some cultures and immoral in others. This fact leads them to affirm that there are no ethical universal principles or any ethical universal. They hold that any culture is superior to others and urge us not to judge the moral codes of other cultures by our own. Imposing one's own culture over that of others would be *cultural imperialism,* which obviously they reject.

Similarly, cultural relativists argue that we cannot judge moral behaviours of other historical periods on the basis of our current moral codes. This includes practices such as slavery, infanticide, torture, human sacrifices and burning a widow along with the corpse of her husband, which most would now describe as degrading or inhuman.

Perhaps those who committed these acts believed they were doing the right thing, but that is not the point. The question is whether we can analyse cultural or historical practices from the Archimedean point of trans-cultural ethical principles – by criteria such as human dignity or the 'Golden Rule',[3] which is common to the vast majority of religions and wisdom traditions.

Several criticisms have been levelled against cultural relativism.[4] They include:

- *The existence of cultural diversity does not prove the truth of cultural relativism.* Nobody denies the fact of cultural diversity – the actual variety of behaviour and cultural moral codes. However, rational ethics differs from cultural values, as noted in Chapter 1 (p. 16). People's behaviour is a matter for sociology or cultural anthropology to investigate, but what people do is not necessarily the right thing. We must remember that ethics comes from rational reflection about good and bad. Rejecting such reflection would mean substituting sociology for ethics.

- *The moral judgement of cultural groups might be influenced by historical and social conditions and by false beliefs.* Cultural moral codes usually address concrete practices, not generic principles, and numerous factors, including beliefs, can influence their formulation. Many writers[5] refer to the tribal custom whereby after a certain age, parents are put to death by their children. This fact appears to constitute an excellent argument for cultural relativism, since a moral principle as universal as the duty to love, honour and care for one's parents is violated. However, the reason for the killing is the cultural belief that people exist in the afterlife in the same physical condition in which they departed the earth. Thus, precisely the principle that mandates caring for one's parents led people of this culture to kill them, since it would be cruel to have them existing eternally in an unhealthy state. In business, too, we can also discern the influence of various moral perceptions and judgements.

- *Cultural diversity can include basic common values and universal principles.* Comparing Russian and American judgement regarding certain issues of business ethics in the early 1990s, Puffer and McCarthy suggested that Russians, but not Americans, found ethically acceptable such practices as personal favouritism, grease payments, price fixing, manipulation of data, and ignoring senseless laws and regulations.[6] These differences could be due to the culture created in Russia in the wake of 70 years of a communist regime. In contrast, Americans, but not Russians, found the following practices ethically acceptable: maximizing profits, exorbitant salary differentials, lay-offs, and whistle-blowing. Again, the culture of equality that developed in Russia, as opposed to the capitalistic culture of America, can provide one explanation. Despite their differences, it is noteworthy that both countries agree that some business actions must be considered ethical: for instance, keeping one's word, maintaining trust, fair competition, and rewards commensurate with performance. Similarly, both groups disapprove of certain unethical practices: gangsterism, racketeering, extortion, black market operations, price gouging and refusal to pay debts.

  In comparing the moral judgements of managers from different cultures, similar conclusions can be inferred. Thus, comparing managers from America and China – two quite different cultural contexts – Whitcomb *et al.* found great agreement regarding disapproval of the following: revealing trade secrets, exceeding pollution standards, publishing a book with sufficient information to produce an atomic bomb, and refraining from whistle-blowing regarding a car that might cause serious or even fatal accidents.[7]

  In contrast, they disagree on the morality of paying a foreign business person to obtain an important contract. Such different judgements can be due to numerous circumstance and local customs, which can vary greatly according to cultural context. It could, of course, also be due to the personal ethical training of the subjects, rather than basic principles. Their agreements are merely based on the universal principle 'Do not injure anyone for the sake of one's own interest.'

- *Some cultural practices are objectively better than others.* If we take cultural relativism seriously, we will hold that a culture that allows dictatorship or tyranny would be perfectly acceptable, as would genital mutilation of little girls, or cutting off the hand of a thief, if required by the local moral code. But such practices are contrary to the common moral sense of most people. In the business world, there are few who doubt that some cultures can be qualified as better than others in matters of business ethics: some are more sensitive, for instance, to fair transactions, or to serious respect for human rights and environmental issues.

- *It is problematic to make the moral code of one's own society synonymous with right behaviour.* In cultural relativism, the guarantee of rightness arises from the fact of belonging to a group. But if the measure of right and wrong is one's own society or cultural group, what guarantee can there be that one's own behaviour is right? The mere social fact of belonging to a group? Are we not rational beings equipped with a conscience that impels us to seek the truth in moral matters? Another problem arises as well: one usually belongs to several groups or communities, each with its own culture (neighbourhood, town, society at large, an ethnic or religious group, a business corporation and so on). Which of these groups, then, should I follow in preference to others, if I have no superior criterion?

- *Cultural values can be manipulated.* Cultural values are sometimes modified by the influence of powerful economic groups that manipulate public opinion. This seems an especially serious objection in our society, in which some values, customs and behaviours seem born of the powerful influence of the ubiquitous mass media, supported by sophisticated communications technology. There is a risk of passing off the ideologies of the elite as ethical principle.

- *Cultural relativism prevents any moral progress.* Moral reformers who have historically sought to improve moral custom would have very little opportunity to act within cultural relativism. Everything is fine as it is: why work for change if no culture can be deemed superior to any other? The 'defence of human rights' makes no sense if a given culture's acceptance of their violation makes that violation acceptable.

Contrary to cultural relativism, objective ethical values and principles provide a permanent reference point for business management and, in the midst of cultural change, for distinguishing passing fashions or demagogic demands.

Although cultural differences are repeatedly emphasized, we hear far less about the values common to countless cultures. However, common values in different cultures exist (see Insight 3). This is made clear if you consider religions and wisdom traditions, which are significant elements of cultural diversity (see Table 3.2).

The existence of some basic common values and norms makes business activity possible. Indeed, some values and norms are indispensable for sustained business relationships. De George has suggested that ethical norms provide the basis for rules of conduct that should be abided by and that

Table 3.2   Tentative list of values common to most great world religions and wisdom traditions

Values	Meaning
Respect for persons (Golden Rule)	Treat others as you would want to be treated.
Following one's conscience	Do what you know to be good; avoid wrongdoing.
Beneficence/avoidance of malice	Be kind to others and hurt no one.
Justice, equity, trustworthiness	Give to everyone what is due; act in good faith; fulfil commitments and keep promises; be guided by the spirit of the law more than its letter.
Truthfulness, honesty	Speak the truth and do not conceal it.
Caring, compassion	Show effective concern and empathy for others, especially for those who share special bonds or who are intimate (parents, children, friends, neighbours).
Mercy, generosity	Give to the poor, give from the heart, and give without thought of return.
Hospitality	Give a cordial and generous reception to strangers.
Peace	Live with others in harmony: 'As you sow, so shall you reap.'
Unity of humanity	Consider all people as a single family.
Stewardship	Preserve the earth and water; take only what you need.
Wealth sharing	Wealth is a blessing that anyone can share.
Magnanimity	Be great of mind and heart; be willing and courageous enough to take actions for a noble purpose.
Moderation	Practice moderation in all things.

Sources: Re-elaboration from Moses (2001) and Lewis (1987).

contract, life and truth must always be respected. He adds that violating these norms constitutes not only immoral behaviour, but also a serious erosion of business.[8]

Many would agree that, without some basic moral rules, markets fail.[9] This is why the market system functions within a legal framework that reflects such rules. More specifically, Quinn and Jones highlight two principles generally acknowledged as part of the implicit morality of the market: honouring agreements and avoiding lies.[10] These basic rules are necessary in business, but ethics is broader than this, and the need for ethics in business includes making business more human, promoting trust and maintaining the sustainability of our planet. These latter goals lead to the need for universal business ethics standards.

Insight 3:

Are there common values in different religions and cultures?

Moses and Lewis have taken note of some values common to most great world religions and wisdom traditions. A tentative list of such values can be gleaned from their respective works[11] (see Table 3.2):

Similarly, the Interfaith Declaration, created in the capital of Jordan by theologians, academics and prominent business figures in 1993, indicates four key concepts or principles presented in Judaism, Christianity and Islam:

- Justice (fairness)
- Mutual respect (love and consideration)
- Stewardship (trusteeship)
- Honesty (truthfulness).[12]

In addition, Dalla Costa[13] suggests that five core values emerge from two other religious declarations – 'The Declaration of the Parliament of the World's Religions' (1993) and 'The Tie That Bids' (1991):

- Respect life
- Be fair
- Be honest
- Strive for justice
- Honour the environment.

Surveying people 'of conscience' of different religions, a number of relatively common values are salient. Thus, a study based on interviews with 24 such subjects from different cultures revealed that eight values were shared:

- Love
- Truthfulness
- Fairness
- Freedom
- Unity (fraternity, solidarity, cooperation, community, group allegiance, oneness)
- Tolerance
- Responsibility
- Respect for life.[14]

Similar results were found in a meeting with 30 representatives of teachers' unions, faith communities, ethics centres and family support organizations,[15] with the goal of creating a list of core ethical values, acceptable to almost everyone. They found the following:

- Trustworthiness (honesty, candour, integrity, reliability and loyalty)
- Respect (civility, autonomy, tolerance)

> **Insight 3: (cont'd)**
>
> - Responsibility (accountability, excellence, self-restraint)
> - Fairness (fair process, impartiality, equity)
> - Caring (concern for the welfare of others, benevolence)
> - Citizenship (respecting the law and protecting the environment).
>
> They agreed that these core values 'transcend cultural, religious, and socioeconomic differences'.[16]

INTERNATIONAL ETHICAL STANDARDS FOR BUSINESS

In line with the call for the introduction of universal principles and standards in business, prominent international organizations have made certain proposals. Some of these refer to labour rights, such as the Declaration of Fundamental Principles and Rights at Work, adopted by the International Labour Organization (ILO)[17] in 1998, or the Workplace Code of Conduct[18] of the Fair Labor Association (FLA). The latter emerged in late 1990, in response to the invitation by former US president Bill Clinton, and to public indignation at labour abuses committed by multinational companies in developing countries, especially in the textile industry.

Other texts advocate respect for the environment and sustainability, such as a set of principles developed by the Coalition for Environmentally Responsible Economies (CERES),[19] as well as the Business Charter for Sustainable Development, prepared by the International Chamber of Commerce (ICC)[20] and the Rio Declaration on Environment and Development, which emerged from the UN conference on environment and development held in Rio de Janeiro in 1992. There are, besides, several well-known international standards covering a wide variety of concerns, including human and labour rights, the environment and sustainability, and the fight against corruption. Among them are the UN Global Compact, The CRT Principle for Responsible Business and the OECD Guidelines for Multinational Enterprises.

UN Global Compact[21]

This is probably the most widely recognized international code for business conduct. The UN Global Compact was launched in 1999 by the then Secretary General of the United Nations, Kofi Annan, at the World Economic Forum. The UN Global Compact proposes ten principles inspired by earlier UN documents, notably:

- The Universal Declaration of Human Rights (1948)[22]
- The International Labour Organization's Declaration on Fundamental Principles and Rights at Work (1998)[23]
- The Rio Declaration on Environment and Development (1992)[24]
- The United Nations Convention against Corruption (2003).[25]

These principles cover four areas: (1) human rights, (2) labour, (3) the environment, and (4) anti-corruption (Table 3.3).

The Global Compact is not a regulatory instrument but, rather, a forum for discussion and the networking of companies, labour and civil society, along with UN agencies. Its aim is to encourage businesses worldwide to adopt sustainable and socially responsible policies, and to report on their implementation. It relies on public accountability, transparency and commitment to initiate and share substantive action in pursuing the principles upon which the Global Compact is based. The Global Compact has a responsive, functional structure, with two complementary goals:

- To mainstream the 10 principles in business activities around the world
- To catalyse actions in support of UN goals.

Table 3.3   UN Global Compact Principles

Scope	Principles	Content
Human rights	Principle 1	Businesses should support and respect the protection of internationally proclaimed human rights; and
	Principle 2	Make sure that they are not complicit in human rights violations.
Labour	Principle 3	Businesses should uphold the freedom of association and the effective recognition of the right to collective bargaining;
	Principle 4	The elimination of all forms of forced and compulsory labour;
	Principle 5	The effective abolition of child labour; and
	Principle 6	The elimination of discrimination with regard to employment and occupation.
Environment	Principle 7	Businesses should support a precautionary approach to environmental challenges;
	Principle 8	Undertake initiatives to promote greater environmental responsibility; and
	Principle 9	Encourage the development and diffusion of environmentally friendly technologies.
Anti-corruption	Principle 10	Businesses should work against corruption in all its forms, including extortion and bribery.

These goals are to be achieved through policy dialogue, learning, country/ regional networks, and partnership projects.

Companies that decide to participate undertake to cite the Global Compact in their corporate communications and annual reports, to disclose specific examples of actions taken to implement the ten principles and to work in partnership with the UN on projects in support of the principles.

The Global Compact does not have any effective monitoring or enforcement provisions, and this is probably its main weakness. In addition, there is also the danger that some companies will take advantage of the oversight and the lack of compulsion and use it simply to burnish their image. However, currently, the Global Compact is the world's largest initiative to promote business responsibility, and a starting point for further initiatives. The 10 Global Compact Principles, as we will discuss in other chapters, provide a set of elemental but basic points to implement business ethics into business worldwide.

The Principles for Responsible Business[26]

In 1986, a group of senior European, Japanese and US business leaders founded the Caux Round Table in order to join forces and reduce escalating trade tensions. They met annually in the Swiss city of Caux. In 1992, they concluded that they needed to agree on a set of ethical and moral principles specifically applicable to the world of business and firms. The Principles for Business were first published in 1994, based on the Japanese concept of *kyosei*, which means 'living and working together for the common good enabling cooperation and mutual prosperity to coexist with healthy and fair competition', and on *human dignity*, which refers 'to the sacredness or value of each personas an end, not simply as a means to the fulfillment of others' purposes or even majority prescription.' In 2009, these Principles were updated and published with the name of 'The CRT for Responsible Business' (see Table 3.4). They are rooted in three ethical foundations, namely:

- Responsible stewardship
- Living and working for mutual advantage
- The respect and protection of human dignity.

A detailed Stakeholder Management Guidelines accompanies these principles for helping their implementation, considering the following stakeholders: customers, employees, shareholders, suppliers, competitors, and communities.

OECD Guidelines for Multinational Enterprises[27]

The main goal of the Organization for Economic Cooperation and Development (OECD), founded in 1961, is to promote policies contributing to economic growth and development. It currently has 30 member countries in Europe and North America. The Guidelines for Multinational Enterprises, last revised in 2000, are part of the Declaration on International Investment and Multinational Enterprises. The Guidelines include recommendations, voluntary principles and

Table 3.4   The Caux Round Table Principles for Responsible Business

Principle 1 – Respect Stakeholders beyond Shareholders

- A responsible business acknowledges its duty to contribute value to society through the wealth and employment it creates and the products and services it provides to consumers.
- A responsible business maintains its economic health and viability not just for shareholders, but also for other stakeholders.
- A responsible business respects the interests of, and acts with honesty and fairness towards, its customers, employees, suppliers, competitors, and the broader community.

Principle 2 – Contribute to Economic, Social and Environmental Development

- A responsible business recognizes that business cannot sustainably prosper in societies that are failing or lacking in economic development.
- A responsible business therefore contributes to the economic, social and environmental development of the communities in which it operates, in order to sustain its essential 'operating' capital – financial, social, environmental, and all forms of goodwill.
- A responsible business enhances society through effective and prudent use of resources, free and fair competition, and innovation in technology and business practices.

Principle 3 – Respect the Letter and the Spirit of the Law

- A responsible business recognizes that some business behaviors, although legal, can nevertheless have adverse consequences for stakeholders.
- A responsible business therefore adheres to the spirit and intent behind the law, as well as the letter of the law, which requires conduct that goes beyond minimum legal obligations.
- A responsible business always operates with candour, truthfulness, and transparency, and keeps its promises.

Principle 4 –Respect Rules and Conventions

- A responsible business respects the local cultures and traditions in the communities in which it operates, consistent with fundamental principles of fairness and equality.
- A responsible business, everywhere it operates, respects all applicable national and international laws, regulations and conventions, while trading fairly and competitively.

Principle 5 – Support Responsible Globalisation

- A responsible business, as a participant in the global marketplace, supports open and fair multilateral trade.
- A responsible business supports reform of domestic rules and regulations where they unreasonably hinder global commerce.

Principle 6 – Respect the Environment

- A responsible business protects and, where possible, improves the environment, and avoids wasteful use of resources.
- A responsible business ensures that its operations comply with best environmental management practices consistent with meeting the needs of today without compromising the needs of future generations.

Principle 7 – Avoid Illicit Activities

- A responsible business does not participate in, or condone, corrupt practices, bribery, money laundering, or other illicit activities.
- A responsible business does not participate in or facilitate transactions linked to or supporting terrorist activities, drug trafficking or any other illicit activity.
- A responsible business actively supports the reduction and prevention of all such illegal and illicit activities.

standards addressed by governments to multinational enterprises to achieve four overarching goals:

- To ensure that the operations of these enterprises are in harmony with government policies
- To strengthen the basis of mutual confidence between enterprises and the societies in which they operate
- To help improve the foreign investment climate
- To enhance the contribution to sustainable development made by multinational enterprises.

These goals are to be achieved, first, through general policies, such as the obligation to make disclosures to governments and unions, to collaborate with the local community, to abstain from improper involvement in political activities, not to interfere unduly in government policy making, and not to offer or accept bribes. Second, they relate to financial policies in matters such as the balance of payments, abuse of market power, taxation, and transfer pricing. A third section deals with various aspects of employment and industrial relations. A fourth section concerns the environment and addresses issues such as the use of natural resources, company location, health risks and proper waste treatment. Lastly, companies are called upon to contribute to science and technology by diffusing technologies and know-how, and making them available to the community.

APPENDIX: RELIGIOUS APPROACHES TO BUSINESS ETHICS

Religions have a profound influence on many people. They involve values, principles, norms or virtues useful for business ethics.

It is noteworthy that adherents of the three major monotheistic religions (Judaism, Christianity and Islam) have a commitment to their own faith and consider it unacceptable to follow more than one. Adherents of ancient Asian religions (Hinduism, Buddhism, Confucianism, Taoism and *Shintō*), by contrast, often accept syncretism. One can thus be a follower of Confucianism, Taoism and Buddhism simultaneously; one religion does not exclude others.

We will outline the approaches to business ethics in the largest world religions, without any claim to exhaustiveness.[28]

The greatest monotheistic religions
Judaism

Judaism has a long business ethics tradition and a well-defined perspective.[29] The main authoritative source for understanding the foundation of Jewish business ethics is the *Torah* or Written Law (the five books of Moses that make up the Pentateuch). The *Talmud,* Judaism's vast compendium of normative teachings, is also significant. The latter examines numerous aspects of human life, including commercial relationships, and gives normative instructions on how to live in this world.

According to Judaism, the legitimacy of business activity and profit, conducted within a framework of religious and ethical norms, is one of the guiding principles of business ethics. In Judaism, there is no mistrust of material goods, although several texts warn against greed.[30]

An essential part of the *Torah* that is shared by Christians is the *Ten Commandments* or *Decalogue*. It contains several precepts that can be applied to business: the prohibitions on working on the Lord's Day (the *Sabbath*), on murder, theft, bearing false witness against one's neighbour and coveting one's neighbour's goods. 'You shall not murder' includes not causing injury, and 'You shall not bear false witness against your neighbour' includes not lying. 'You shall not steal' does not merely prohibit theft and fraud. Sellers must be honest, offer fair prices, and avoid adulteration of products, falsification of measures, concealment of flaws and deceptiveness about quality.

The protection and preservation of human life have clear primacy among conflicting interests. Any serious suffering is also to be prevented. In a business context, this means promoting safety in the workplace and, in a products context, being considerate with workers and the welfare of strangers, helping indigents and avoiding activities that could cause pollution and damage human health.[31] A Talmudic perspective can also be applied to lay-offs and downsizing.[32]

Jewish business ethics also contains a set of relevant values and norms for marketing.[33] One of these values specifies that all consumers are entitled to protection. Jewish law does not accept the Roman concept of *caveat emptor* ('Let the buyer beware'), by which the buyer takes all the risk. On the contrary, the vendor must prevent damage and loss to the consumer by disclosing relevant information.

Christianity

Christianity is a universal religion able to be integrated into a great variety of cultures. Christians believe that Jesus of Nazareth is God who became a man, and is thus the fulfilment of God's revelation to humankind. Christian ethics, consists of following and imitating Jesus in his love. This includes both virtues and precepts. Jesus summarized all moral precepts in the double commandment of love: Love God, and your neighbour as yourself.

Loving one's neighbour requires justice, a sense of justice in business includes keeping promises, respecting contracts, acting justly in exchanges avoiding appropriation of the property of others, observing regulations issued by legitimate authority, paying taxes, respecting personal reputation, avoiding rash judgement and attitudes of flattery or adulation.

Jesus mentioned several businessmen in his parables, exhibiting both good and evil behaviour, and stressed the necessity of the good use of one's talents.

Business is not evil in itself, but Jesus warns against greed – the temptation to serve money rather than God. In Christianity, as in Judaism, man's dominion over other beings (animals, plants, minerals) is not absolute, but, rather, is limited by concern for the quality of life of his neighbour, including generations to come. Man's role is to be a cooperator with God.

Since the end of the nineteenth century, the Roman Catholic Church, the largest branch of Christianity, has developed a corpus of business and economic ethics in several documents ('encyclicals'), known as Catholic social teaching.[34] The Christian Orthodox Church also has social teachings, although with little development on economic and business ethics.[35] The Lutheran tradition focuses on 'covenantal' love and justice in the biblical sense.[36] The Evangelical community emphasizes piety, witnessing, tithing and neighbourliness. These values are important foundations in their model for business ethics.[37] Other Christian churches also apply biblical teachings to ethical issues in economics and business.

In Catholic social teaching, as well as in other Christian traditions, the centrality of the human person and his or her personal vocation are generally emphasized. The teaching also stresses that human labour, expended in the production and exchange of goods or in the performance of economic services, stands superior to other elements of economic life. The rights of workers and employee participation in corporate life are highlighted as well. Similarly, there is concern for environmental responsibility and for the phenomenon of consumerism: it encourages developing appropriate consumer attitudes and lifestyles, educating consumers in the responsible use of their power of choice, and forming a strong sense of responsibility among producers, mass media and public authorities.

A free market with an appropriate legal and ethical framework is fully acceptable.[38] The right to private ownership is proclaimed, but it must be subordinated to the universal destination of material goods. All property has a social function. Profits are understood as a regulator of business life, but other human and moral factors must be considered as well. Consequently, any theory that makes profit the exclusive norm and ultimate end of economic activity is deemed morally unacceptable.

Islam

The central moral concept of Islam is *tawhid* or unity with God. Business is not outside this comprehensive worldview, and any business activity should be run according to the laws of nature dictated by God. Islam does encourage business practices and trading. Prosperity is desirable, although it is not a goal in itself. The right to property is recognized but not unlimited. As in Judaism and Christianity, those who possess wealth must be aware that they are not the true owners, but only trustees. This is related to the concept of *zakah* (alms), one of the five pillars of Islam, by which the needs of the poor are met. Islamic institutions understand *zakah* as a compulsory wealth tax for the benefit of especially needy groups in society. Once the tax is paid, there is no impediment to people enjoying their remaining riches, as long as they do so without ostentatious consumption.

Islam accepts the market system but adds that the price mechanism should be complemented by some device for minimizing unnecessary claims on resources. The Islamic perspective encourages a societal and welfare approach rather than decisions based on the maximization of profit.

No one is allowed to destroy or waste God-given resources: these are to be used in such a way as to avoid impeding anyone's well-being – this also means refraining both from doing harm to others and also practising leniency, which includes politeness, forgiveness and removal of hardship.

Justice is central in business transactions. This has several manifestations: fulfilment of promises, pacts and contracts both oral and written; and sincerity and honesty. Lying and cheating are strongly condemned; exactness in weights and measures is demanded, as is consideration of merits and competence in the selection and employment of workers. Fairness in contract negotiations and other agreements is required as well. Islam also contains specific prescriptions regarding several aspects of marketing.

Islamic banks are considered to have an ethical identity, as the foundation of their business philosophy is tied to the Islamic religion. Islamic banks must avoid investing in or financing activities that could be abhorrent to Islam, or that appear to constitute speculation – such as investments in the futures market – as the consequences of such actions are unknown. Moreover, parties of the contract cannot predetermine a guaranteed profit: thus, in the Islamic Banks' annual reports, information on any involvement in any permissible activity must appear and, if this has proved profitable, the report must include the percentage of profit from such activities together with information on how such profits have been managed.[39]

Islam considers interest (*riba*) illegitimate, holding that to lend money with a predetermined profit is a form of injustice and exploitation (usury). In Islamic countries where *riba* is forbidden, money lending is not conducted as the conventional debt-based operation. Instead, depositors of a bank become investors in projects to which this bank lends money. In this way, depositors share the risks of these projects, as well as any profits or losses.

Asian religions

Hinduism

This is an ancient Indian tradition, without any prophet or founder, with scriptures and a wide range of beliefs but no source of authority. The closest thing in Hinduism to a concept of ethics is the idea of *dharma,* which means 'that which upholds or supports'. *Dharma* is an all-important principle of cosmic and social action, significant for the norms for proper ritual and social behaviour. It refers to the underlying order in nature and life, which makes possible the cosmos, the harmonious complexity of the natural world. It can also be understood as the right way of living or moral law. Another important concept is *karma,* which refers to the culminating value of all of one's life actions, good and bad, which together determine one's next rebirth and death. *Dharma* and *karma* provide the basic structure of Hindu morality.

Hinduism provides a way of understanding everyday life. It contains politically, socially, culturally and even racially interwoven elements. One of these is the caste system, determined by *karma*, which ranks society according to class. By doing good or evil, every individual can attain a superior or inferior caste. Respect for life, from plant life to human life, is guided by the same principles of rebirth and *karma*.

Pursuing prosperity is one of the aims of life. Thus, Hinduism has a positive attitude towards business and wealth creation. In particular, there is great esteem for wealth based on agriculture and trade, and the owner of an enterprise should create conditions wherein families can be effectively productive. However, wealth is not the supreme goal. It is subordinate to *dharma* and, above all, to *moksha* ('salvation'). On the other hand, Hinduism gives higher honour to the ascetic who renounces material goods for the sake of spiritual realization. Hinduism strongly condemns such sins as lying, fraud, violence, cheating, laying traps for others, being evil-minded and arrogance, whereas it praises truthfulness, generosity and selfless, disinterested actions.

It has been suggested that Vedic (Hindu) philosophy could provide sound bases for models of excellence in business.[40]

Buddhism

This religious tradition focuses on the cessation of all suffering through training of the mind. Since Buddhist precepts are not based on any higher deity, breaking those precepts does not amount to an offence to the Creator. Buddhism considers Four Noble Truths:

- The universal existence of suffering
- Its causes (the craving for pleasures of the senses, success, prosperity, happiness)
- The ending of suffering (by eliminating the causes)
- The way that leads to the cessation of suffering (which is the Eightfold Path).

The objective of the Eightfold Path is to reach *nirvana*, where the spirit merges with eternal harmony. This includes:

- The right view (which involves accepting the Four Noble Truths)
- Right aspiration (or avoiding pleasures of sensual desire)
- Right speech (which advises the shunning of gossip, harsh words and foolish talk)
- Right conduct (which forbids killing, stealing, lying, adultery, abuse and drug use)
- Right livelihood (meaning one must not earn money in a way that harms others – Buddhism thus stands against companies that neglect the welfare of the environment or animals)

- Right effort (which teaches how to acquire good qualities)
- Right mindfulness (or being observant, free of desire and sorrow)
- Right concentration (which leads to meditation).

Buddhism is opposed to hedonism and prescribes ascetic practices, although not in extreme measure. The Buddhist is expected to lead a life of service and loving kindness, with compassion not only for humans, but also for any sentient being. This, then, should be a Buddhist's main motivation in business, not simply profits. According to Schumacher, the driving principle of a 'Buddhist Economics' is a production system in which only necessary material goods are produced, and only in harmony with the environment and its resources, using modern technology selectively rather than being used by it in the service of selfish interests.[41]

Confucianism

This could be viewed as a religion and a philosophy, but, above all, it is a path to moral wisdom, emphasizing certain virtues, moral conduct, and proper hierarchical relationships. The individual is never perceived as an isolated being but, rather, as a part of overlapping social networks.

The core of Confucian ethics[42] comprises three elements – *ren*, *yi*, and *li* – that define what is morally acceptable in human society.

- *Ren* is a capacity for compassion for or benevolence towards fellow humans. The quintessence of *ren* is *zhong shu*, which can be considered as the Confucian formulation of the Golden Rule. *Zhong shu* has two senses:
  - A weak sense: people should not do to others things that they do not want others to do to them
  - A strong sense: one is obligated to help others to develop morally in the process of developing one's moral self, which is seen as a major life goal of a person.
- *Yi* is a capacity to discern appropriateness and the right direction in acts, relationships, and other human matters.
- *Li* represents the many etiquettes, norms, and protocols in both personal and institutional lives. The legitimacy of *li* is based on *ren* and *yi*, and only in the presence of *ren* and *yi* are people obligated to follow *li*. It means that people do not have the obligation to observe a *li* that violates *ren*. Though *li* is not, in itself, a virtue, observing *li* is a basic virtue.

Ren and *yi* often work in unison to define morality and to guide actions. Both *ren* and *yi* are Confucian mega-virtues. They include others virtues such as: righteousness, diligence, acting before speaking, prudence, action in keeping with words, demonstrating filial piety to parents, displaying brotherly respect for brothers, associating with men of moral principles, loving learning, loving others, being broad-minded and non-partisan, goodwill towards others, being accommodating, having a sense of dignity but not being proud, courageousness, steadfastness, self-reflection, self-motivation, fair-mindedness, and others.

For Confucianism, the nature of a person's self is defined by and comprises the bundles of his or her social relationships in the world. Social relationships and their harmony are of utmost importance in human society. Collective values and interests are over and above individual values and interests.

Regarding business, Confucianism maintains the superiority of right over profits. Promptness in practice, slowness to speak and maximum loyalty are crucial virtues in business.

The family is the prototype of all social relations, presumably within the business firm as well. Within the family, members restrain their own individualism to create a harmonious group that works effectively. This brings about a certain familial collectivism.[43]

Confucius' ideal is a well-ordered society based on good governance. Rulers must be moral role models for society. Extrapolating this view to apply to management and corporate governance, one could infer that Confucianism demands moral leadership in business and elsewhere. Education for a good society should be focused not only on acquiring knowledge or the skills of a particular profession, but on growth in moral judgement and self-improvement. Confucianism focuses on trust, reciprocity and mutual benefit in relationships.[44]

Some widespread attitudes in China, Japan, South Korea, and other Asian countries – such as the importance of personal relationships (*guanxi*), or saving face (*mianzi*) – are strongly associated with Confucianism.

According to Romar, Confucianism is a compelling managerial ethic for several reasons:[45]

- It is compatible with accepted managerial practices
- It requires individuals and organizations to make a positive contribution to society
- It recognizes hierarchy as an important organizational principle and demands managerial moral leadership
- The Confucian 'Golden Rule' (*Zhong shu*) and virtues provide a moral basis for the hierarchical and cooperative relationships critical to organizational success.

However, according to Ip, Confucianism can be problematic in the corporate context, due to its familial collectivism and certain practices that contrast with some international standards and which emphasize concern for individual interests and human rights.[46]

Taoism

This is present in China as well as in other Asian countries. It is a philosophy, ethics and religion in one. *Tao* ('path' or 'way') is the First Cause of the universe, but is not a personal being like God. The most basic ethical principle of Taoism, perhaps, is living in harmony with the *Tao*.

Regarding business, one can deduce from Taoism that business, as with any other human activity, is a part of the whole, and must be run in harmony with the *Tao*. Corporations centred on the *Tao* should take care of their people (employees, shareholders and other stakeholders) and not interfere unfairly with competitors.

The motivation for business should not be personal success or gain, but the common good. Taoism praises moderation in money making, avoiding frenzied work, and not worrying about the opinions of others. That is to say, do not chase money, security or human approval. Honesty, compassion, humility, detachment and self-esteem are other virtues included in Taoist philosophy.

Self-esteem is presented as a means to inner peace and to harmony in dealings with others. As to action, Taoism invites reflection before making any decision and following the art of *wu wei* (literally, non-action), since there is no sense in trying to control everything. Taoism emphasizes virtues such as tolerance, compassion, following the will of the people and humility.

According to Taoism, ethics has to be discovered from nature rather than by searching for ethical norms from rational principles or social perceptions; society is natural and not the result of a social contract. Harmony with ethics, not the accumulation of wealth, is the supreme end of business.

Shintō

Shintō has been heavily influential in shaping the cultural context of Japanese business. It has no formal dogma, no holy writings, and no body of religious law. However, it entails several beliefs with a direct influence on ethics and business. The first is that morality and uprightness are related to *Kami* (god). Nature is considered sacred. *Shintō* emphasizes the group and the benefit to one's own group. The foundational group is the family, highly valued by *Shintō* as the locus of the preservation of traditions. This behaviour includes that of individuals within a company, from whom right practices, diligent work, sacrifice, sensitivity and a positive attitude are expected.

Considering individual–group relationships, there are several *Shintō*-related notions that exert a heavy influence on Japanese business organizations:

- *Joge* refers to the relationship between superior and inferior, which must be strong and includes the link between employer and employee and between companies and the nation
- *Honne* is related to honest communication of one's perceptions and beliefs, which is balanced with *tatemae* (things as they are made to appear), meaning face-saving
- *Haji* is the shame felt when objectives are not achieved or norms not observed.

Shintō can explain certain differences in the behaviour of Japanese and American executives.[47]

Business ethics in practice 3:

Canon and the *kyosei* concept – Working together for the common good

Canon is one of the largest manufacturers of printers, cameras and computer peripherals for home and office use. It has operations in Asia, the USA, Europe, Africa, the Middle East and Oceania. Its headquarters is in Tokyo, Japan and it employed over 24,000 people worldwide in 2007.

Canon was set up in 1937, when Saburo Uchinda and Garo Yoshinda founded the Precision Optical Instruments Laboratory in Tokyo to develop cameras. In 1947, this company was renamed Canon Camera Inc. after its successful brand of Kwanon cameras. In 1949, Canon got its shares listed in the Tokyo Stock Exchange and, as it entered international markets, it faced many business challenges.

Although Canon has been practising its cooperative spirit since 1937, its management only formally conceptualized the *kyosei* principle in 1988 and committed itself to a set of related principles.

Kyosei is a concept with Confucian roots that has been applied in a variety of ways for many generations in Japan. It can best be defined as 'living and working together for the common good', but Canon broadens the definition of this notion to: 'All people, regardless of race, religion or culture, harmoniously living and working together into the future.' It tries to achieve harmonious relationships between the customers, suppliers, competitors and governments with which it deals.

Kyosei is deeply embedded in Canon's core purpose and is the principle that guides Canon in achieving its goals.

Canon is characterized by sustainable prosperity and devotes effort not only to growing and developing as a company, but also to such areas as environmental assurance, compliance and personnel development.

The principle of *kyosei,* together with the principle of human dignity, was taken as a base for the first formulation (1994) of the Caux Round Table Principles (see p. 55) in order to formulate a set the ethical standards for business worldwide.

Questions:

1. What do you think about *kyosei* as corporate philosophy in Canon? What human and economic advantages or disadvantages might it promote?

2. Do you think that the *kyosei* principle, perhaps in other terms, could be appropriate for other companies?

Sources: R. Kaku, 'The Path of Kyosei', *Harvard Business Review,* 75 (1997): 55–62; 'The Journey to Kyosei: Reminiscences of Ryuzaburo Kaku', *Harvard Business Review,* 75 (1997): 58–9; C. M. Boardman, 'The Confucian Roots of Business Kyosei', *Journal of Business Ethics,* 48 (2003): 317–33; and Canon corporate website: www.canon.com

---

Dilemma 3

Carlos had been appointed general manager of a company based in Spain that owned a chain of hotels located in this country and in Latin America. One of the hotels was in a beautiful resort on a Caribbean island. On his first trip to pay a visit to this hotel, Carlos was surprised at how they selected cleaning staff – which, in the vast majority of cases, comprised women. Apart from other requirements, the hotel management asked candidates for a medical report on their health along with a test regarding pregnancy. Apparently, this practice was legal or, at least, nobody had created trouble because of it.

The wages of these women were about $95 a month but, in spite of this low amount, numerous people were interested in working at the hotel. Carlos asked if this was not an undue intrusion into people's privacy and whether requiring the pregnancy test might lead to some women having an abortion to get a job. 'Well, I don't know,' answered the hotel manager. 'But what I can tell you is that this information is very relevant for us and what they might do is a personal matter for them, not my problem.'

Questions:

1. What do you think about this practice for selecting cleaning staff? Is it ethical?
2. What would you recommend to Carlos?

Summary

Cultural diversity posits the existence of a variety of people, with their behaviours, values and beliefs. Managing businesses in cultural diversity presents the challenge of either respecting cultural diversity but remaining constant to higher, universal ethical principles, or else adopting whatever moral values and standards prevail in the countries or socio-cultural environments where the company operates.

Cultural relativism, which holds that ethics should be taken from culture, does not follow from the fact of cultural diversity, and many criticisms of this relativism can be found.

Although cultural differences are repeatedly emphasized, there are values common to most great world religions and wisdom traditions, such as the Golden Rule.

Well-known international organizations have proposed standards for business worldwide. Among them, the UN Global Compact, the Caux Round Table Principles for Business and the OECD Guidelines for Multinational Enterprises. In their documents – which try to promote business responsibility – human dignity and human rights are a crucial reference point.

Religions are a key element in cultural diversity. They present precepts, values and virtues for business. In spite of their many differences, some common values can be also found among them. Most insist on the acceptability of business activity but also urge the avoidance of greed.

Part II
The Individual within the Organization

I do not think we have psychological, ethical and economic problems. We have human problems with psychological, ethical and economic aspects.[1]

Mary Parker Follett (1868–1933)
Pioneer in management thought

Chapter Aims

This chapter will allow you to:

- gain an understanding of certain key ethical concepts: values and goods, principles and norms, and virtues
- acquire an idea of the mainstream theories used in business ethics
- discuss how ethics is at the core of every human action, including business actions
- distinguish between real goods and apparent goods, and to know how practical rationality permits us to identify certain basic human goods
- provide information about the universality of the basic ethical principle known as the Golden Rule
- discuss the human dignity of every person and how such dignity serves as a proper foundation for human rights
- be familiar with the most relevant elements of two key ethical principles: the Personalist Principle and the Principle of the Common Good
- understand and discuss the four fundamental human virtues.

Key term:

Act utilitarianism
Apparent goods
Cardinal virtues
Civic friendship
Common good
Courage
Deontologism
Discursive ethics theory
Ethical principles
Ethical values
Ethics of care
Friendship
Flourishing
Golden Rule
Human dignity

Human flourishing
Human good
Human needs
Human rights
Human virtues
Integrative social contract
Justice
Kantianism
Moderation
Moral character
Natural Rights Theory
Norms (rules)
Person
Personalist Principle
Practical rationality

Practical wisdom
Principle of the Common Good
Principles
Rawls' Theory of Justice
Real goods
Rights
Rule utilitarianism
Social contract
Utilitarianism
Values
Virtue
Virtue ethics

Ethics, at the Core of Human Action

INTRODUCTORY CASE 4:

EASY MONEY ON WALL STREET

A great number of mergers and acquisitions took place in the United States during the 1980s. Some individuals exploited the situation to make money easily by taking advantage of market conditions. They targeted companies in soon-to-be announced mergers and acquisitions before the news was made public. As a result of the merger or the acquisitions, these stocks would increase in value the moment such operations were announced. One such individual was Dennis Levine.

Dennis's parents were immigrants and had to work hard to raise and give a university education to their children. Dennis studied business administration and then applied for a part-time MBA programme in New York. He is remembered as a good student with great ambition. He used to say: 'I will be millionaire when I am 30.' According to one of his professors, all his interests were focused on finance and on easy money-making.

After obtaining his MBA degree in 1978, Dennis started to work in Citibank Corp. in Manhattan. From 1979 to 1985, he worked in the merger and acquisitions department of Smith and Barney, Harris Uphan & Co., a firm of stockbrokers and investment analysts. There, he obtained information about mergers and acquisitions before they were made public and became effective on the New York Stock Exchange (NYSE). Then, he bought and sold stock through the Bank Leu of Nassau, Bahamas, where he opened an account under the name of 'Diamond'.

In addition, Dennis contacted people he knew from previous jobs who were working in law firms and investment banks, and persuaded them to pass him confidential information related to mergers and acquisitions projects. In exchange, Levine rewarded them with substantial financial compensation. Thus, Levine was able to predict the movement of certain stocks of the market with more certainty.

In February 1985, Dennis Levine was hired by Drexel Burnham Lambert, a well-known investment bank, as one of its managers, receiving an annual pay package of over one million dollars. In addition to his new post, he continued operating on the stock markets using information obtained from his work and from the network of informants he had established. It was then that Levine contacted Ivan Boesky, a well-known broker for the NYSE, whose stock trading activity was followed by many. They agreed to work together: Levine would supply information to Boesky and, if the trading were successful, Levine would receive 5 per cent of the profits that Boesky had earned by buying stocks.

The biggest deal that Levine and Boesky pulled off was from the merger between Nabisco Brands and R. J. Reynolds. To finance this operation, these companies contracted the services of Drexel Burnham. Before the merger was made public, Boesky had been informed of it through Levine and, in a span of seven days, he bought 377,000 shares of Nabisco at a price between $65–75 per share. Levine himself bought 150,000 shares. After the merger was announced, Boesky sold his shares at $80 per share. The benefits obtained by Boesky in that one week's work amounted to $4 million. Levine sold for a $2.7 million profit.

In 1985, the Securities and Exchange Commission (SEC), in charge of monitoring stock movements, detected some important irregularities that had their origin in the Bank Leu of Nassau, an entity that Levine used to make some of his stock trades. Petitioned by the SEC, the government of the Bahamas gave permission to investigate. The inquiries soon revealed Levine's activities, as well as those of Boesky and the informants. After news about the arrest of Levine and Boesky came out, the Dow Jones Index fell 43.31 points, around 2.33 per cent. It was the biggest drop in two months.

Dennis Levine was charged and sentenced to two years in prison and to a fine of $362,000 for 'insider trading' – the technical name for using unpublished information which can be pricing-sensitive and is obtained from people through their work in a firm. Many believed that the punishment was not proportionate to the $11.5 million that he had gained during his six years of operations in the stock exchange through the Bank Leu in the Bahamas, nor to the loss of trust in the stock system through corrupt practices in the market. The reason for the light punishment was an agreement by which the penalty would be less if Dennis incriminated Boesky, who had long been suspected of irregular practices, although the SEC could find no proof. Finally, Boesky was sentenced to three years' detention and fined $100 million, half of which was to be destined to compensate the damages suffered by the investors.

In March 1990, Dennis Levine made a declaration in *Fortune Magazine*, in which he affirmed:

> I have had four years to reflect on the events leading up to my arrest. It's been hard, but finally you take it on the chin. Unfortunately, my family also had to endure the trauma of humiliation, disgrace, and loss of privacy – and they did nothing to deserve it...I will regret my mistakes for ever. I blame only myself for my actions and accept full responsibility for what I have done...People always ask, 'Why would somebody who's making over $1 million a year start trading on inside information?' Here's

what I thought at the time, misguided as I was: When I started trading on non-public information in 1978, I wasn't making a million. I was a 25-year-old trainee at Citibank with a $19,000 annual salary. I was wet behind the ears, impatient, burning with ambition. In those days people didn't think about insider trading the way they do now: You'd call it 'a hot stock tip'.[2]

Some wondered why Dennis did not mention what he wanted to do with the $11.5 million he gained through insider trading activities.

Questions:

1. What questionable actions or wrongdoings can you find in this case?

2. What motivations can you identify in the behaviour of the characters mentioned in this case?

3. What do you think about the Dennis Levine's declarations in *Fortune Magazine?*

Source: Abridged case study: 'Storm in Wall Street (A)' by D. Melé (Barcelona: IESE Publishing, 1989). Published with permission.

VALUES, PRINCIPLES AND VIRTUES IN HUMAN ACTION

This chapter seeks to provide a solid foundation for business ethics. Let us begin by reviewing a few key concepts used in ethics.

Values and goods

'Value' comes from Latin *valere*, 'to be of worth'. Thus, etymologically, value means a quality intrinsically worthy or desirable. This is one of the word's most common meanings. However, value is an equivocal term: we can speak of personal values, social values, corporate values, human values and also ethical values. Ethical values are often understood as synonymous with human values: these refer to moral excellence in human beings.

Ethical values are closely related to goods. Early in his *Nicomachean Ethics* (I, 1), Aristotle defined 'good' as an aim that can motivate an action. In other words, goods show the end to which an action is oriented. A good can be perceived as something valuable or desirable – a value – and thus become a motive for acting. As we will see below, friendship is a human good and, because it is a good, can be taken as a value; that is, as a motive for acting (doing something for the sake of friendship).

Some goods are appropriate for perfecting the agent *qua* human being. These kinds of goods are called *human goods* or *moral goods* (in ethics they are also referred to simply as 'goods') and the corresponding values or motives are called *ethical values* or *human values.* Other goods and values are also desirable because they are perceived as useful for some purpose (for example, money); these are *useful goods*; or by reason of the pleasure they bring about (for example, a delectable ice-cream sundae); these are *pleasant goods*. Useful and pleasant goods are desirable but do not improve people as human beings.

Principles and norms

Principles are propositions taken as fundamental norms for directing behaviour.[3] Principles serve as a starting point for deducing and inferring specific norms. Both principles and norms express the moral duty to behave rightly. Principles are not proven or demonstrated; they are considered self-evident (axioms) or taken for granted. In some way, any ethical theory includes one or more axioms as a starting point. From these, other principles can be deduced. Some ethical theories are based on principles and norms that give guidelines for evaluating alternatives, discerning the correct course of action, establishing priorities, and discovering the correct relationship between ends and means.

Virtues

By this term, we mean good character traits. Virtues (from the Latin *virtus*, meaning 'strength') contribute to a better perception of ethical values and reinforce the will for good behaviour. Virtues are acquired by the repetition of good actions.

Aristotle already realized that actions create the 'moral learning' that shapes character. In this regard, he wrote:

> the virtues we get by first exercising them, as also happens in the case of the arts. For the things we have to learn before we can do them, we learn by doing them; for example, men become builders by building and lyre-players by playing the lyre; so too we become just by doing just acts, temperate by doing temperate acts, brave by doing brave acts.[4]

Notice that values belong to the cognitive sphere, whereas virtues refer to character. Recognizing an ethical value is not equivalent to having acquired the corresponding virtue. For instance, the understanding that being generous is praiseworthy is a value, but the recognition of this value does not make one a generous person. Nevertheless, the recognition of values is important, since it can motivate one to acquire virtues.

Evaluation of a business action

Human actions are those decided freely and rationally: the agent considers whether such action is an appropriate means to a given end. It is also logical for the agent to consider the action's possible effects: external, such as obtaining a product, making money, achieving power or reputation; as well as internal, on the agent, such as satisfaction and learning (acquisition of knowledge, skills and habits). Both means and ends can be evaluated in light of appropriate values and norms.

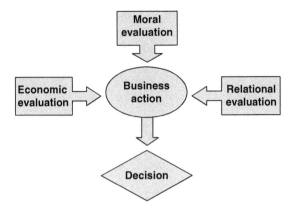

Figure 4.1   Evaluative dimensions of a business action

In a business action, three types of evaluations are generally relevant for decid-ing a business action (Figure 4.1):

- *The economic evaluation*: the action's economic value and the norms to calcu-late it (cost–benefit analysis is crucial).

- *The relational evaluation*: the reaction of the social environment to the action and its consequences for futures relationships and social cohesion. This requires taking into account people and groups affected by the action, as well as social values and social norms, both written and unwritten, including laws and other formal regulations, customs and generally accepted practices.

- *The moral evaluation*: the action's 'moral quality'. This requires making a moral judgement about the action, bearing in mind ethical values along with norms. Moral judgements thus introduce ethics into the evaluation of the business action through values and norms.

When any of these evaluative dimensions is not considered, the evaluation is incomplete because every human action – and, consequently, a business action – entails economic, relational and moral aspects.

The ethical evaluation requires, first of all, moral thinking about the action, and moral thinking is an essential capability for effective managers and organizational leaders.[5] Ethical values and norms have their role, but they are not sufficient. According to Aristotle[6], a sound ethical evaluation can only come from a virtuous person, this is, a person 'habituated to desire to do what is good and noble'.[7]

Virtues, as mentioned, contribute to an enhanced perception of ethical values and a more potent will to act rightly.

In sum, goods (values), principles (norms), and virtues are integral to human action and should therefore be basic categories of a sound theory of ethics.

- *Human goods* provide motives for acting ethically, and *human values* are such motives.

- *Principles and norms* provide guidelines, especially to those whose virtues are weak, for determining what is morally unacceptable, for resolving ethical dilemmas and for acting as a guide to human excellence – but principles and norms are not sufficient for making moral judgements. Every situation is unique, and some are too complex to be settled by the mechanical application of a rule. Virtues, and particularly practical wisdom (see p. 87), are also required, although sound advice from people possessed of practical wisdom and the study of wisdom traditions can compensate for an individual's personal lack of it.

- *Virtues* help to identify the good in each situation, and to apply principles and norms correctly, as well as facilitating moral reasoning and decision-making. What is more, virtues bestow interior strength for good behaviour.

A PERSON-CENTRED APPROACH

Several theories have been proposed as a basis for business ethics (an overview of the mainstream theories can be found in the Appendix of this chapter). Some focus on virtues, others on principles, and still others on values. However, as Koslowski affirms, 'ethical theory aims at the theory of virtues, the theory of goods and the theory of duties'.[8] Similarly, Polo writes 'A complete ethics has to include goods, norms and virtues',[9] and MacIntyre adds that virtues, rules and goods have to be understood in their mutual relationship.[10] As noted, all of these elements – goods (values), principles (norms) and virtues – are at the core of human action.

In accordance with these ideas, this book follows what can be called a person-centred approach' (PCA), seeking the consistent integration of goods, ethical principles, and virtues with human nature as the reference point. This approach, basically, is conducted within the Aristotelian tradition, which emphasizes virtues but also includes goods and principles. It focuses on human persons – in their individual and social dimensions – stressing human dignity, human rights, benevolence and caring for people, along with the common good of human communities. The particular circumstances and consequences of each action are also taken into account for making moral judgements.[11]

The PCA is in line with the primitive idea of understanding ethics as a guide to human excellence[12] – or, as some authors would now say, directing actions towards 'human flourishing'[13] – which is constituted, according to Aristotle, not by honour, wealth or power but by positive qualities of character called virtues, and over the course of one's whole life.[14]

Although different people might have various visions of what constitutes human flourishing, these differences appear slight in light of certain fundamental aspects of human excellence. Most would say that being responsible, generous, a good friend and a person of integrity, even at great cost, are aspects of human excellence. Similarly, few would recognize human flourishing in someone addicted to drugs, a completely egoistical person or someone lacking in moderation. The recognition of the presence or absence of human qualities such as these shows us that, generally, we can arrive at a common understanding of what human excellence is, at least in its fundamentals. Furthermore, an authentically ethical attitude leads one not to resign oneself to mediocrity but, rather, to seek that which is noblest in human nature for the highest standards of morality. In this way, learning from the best ethical traditions, along with a sincere dialogue, can help to discover human excellence to guide both one's own conduct and that of others.

PRACTICAL RATIONALITY AND HUMAN GOODS

Human actions begin when an individual perceives some aim and considers it attractive or interesting for some reason. This good becomes a motive for action. A reflective person will move beyond the attraction of a good and question whether the aim of their action will really be good for him- or herself. As MacIntyre points out, this question about the good of one's action leads to a rational inquiry: 'What is really good for me, as a human being and beyond my desires?'. This in turn leads to a more philosophical question: 'What is the good as such for a human being as such?'[15]

Beneath the search for what is really good for me as a human being – a good that contributes to my human flourishing – lies the concern that not everything one might desire would, indeed, be good. In other words, some aims that drive human actions are 'real goods' (or simply 'goods'), but others are only 'apparent goods'. For instance, the aim of obtaining money through fraud is an apparent good: it is attractive in some way, but not a real good because the agent is eroded as a human being, becoming a worse person.

Everyone has a moral sense that moves him or her to act in accordance with the reason that discerns between good and bad, between real and apparent goods. The whole ethical problem is acting in accordance with the real good, in spite of the attraction that an apparent good might exert. In doing so, an agent prefers 'being better' to 'having more' (money, power, pleasure and so on).

Real goods present themselves to human reason as aims that are worthy of pursuit; apparent goods reveal themselves as deserving of avoidance. In the Aristotelian tradition, this human capacity for moral sense is called 'practical reason', which brings about practical rationality.

Practical rationality, very simply put, is the intellectual capacity of the human person to direct conduct towards the most appropriate aim by use of the right means. It differs from the concept of rationality used in economics, which refers to an action's evaluation in terms of its effectiveness or efficiency for obtaining a given goal, termed 'instrumental or calculative rationality'. Both instrumental and practical rationality are action oriented, but in different ways. They consider respectively the 'technical' and 'ethical' aspects of the action. Instrumental rationality can help us, for instance, to build an effective and efficient weapon. Practical rationality inquires whether it is right to produce, sell or employ such a weapon.

The philosophical theory of goods uses practical reason to discover human goods from the knowledge of human needs that psychology provides. While the philosophical theory focuses on aims, and reflects on their nature and their contribution to human excellence, the psychological theory of need focuses on

> **Insight 4:**
>
> ### Are there some universal basic human needs?
>
> Probably the best-known work on human needs is that of the psychologist Abraham Maslow (1908–70), based on clinical observations. Although his work has some limitations, many of Maslow's insights are still valid. He first presented a pyramid with five basic human needs: (1) physiological needs; (2) needs for safety or security; (3) the need for love ('sense of belonging'); (4) the need for esteem; and (5) the need for self-actualization.[16] Later, he added two more types of needs at the top of the pyramid: (6) cognitive needs; and (7) aesthetic needs.[17] These needs are common to all, although in different manifestations.
>
> Maslow suggested that needs can be ranked hierarchically, and posited that the basic needs of survival and safety must be gratified before the higher needs, love and esteem, etc. come into play. Although the needs at the base of the pyramid are usually more compelling than those at the top, many have questioned his idea that as long as 'inferior' needs are not satisfied, 'superior' needs do not require any attention. Apart from this, Maslow's list of human needs is still widely accepted.
>
> Alderfer suggested a simpler list of human needs: (1) existence; (2) relatedness; and (3) growth.[18]
>
> Another proposal was offered by Max-Neef, who distinguished between desires or 'wants', (which are usually presented as 'needs' by economists) and 'fundamental human needs'.[19] The latter are not individual desires but, rather, needs flowing from human nature that are universal. Unlike 'wants', which are innumerable, fundamental human needs are limited and constant through all human cultures and across historical time, although their *specific* content changes with cultures and over time. On this point, Max-Neef agreed with Maslow, but disagreed that human needs are hierarchical. Instead, he suggested that fundamental human needs are interrelated and interactive. He classified the fundamental human needs as (1) subsistence; (2) protection; (3) affection; (4) understanding; (5) participation; (6) recreation (in the sense of leisure, time to reflect and so on); (7) creation; (8) identity; and (9) freedom. He added that poverty is a lack of satisfaction of any of these needs, not merely of subsistence (material needs).

the individuals, trying to discern their needs by understanding which features move a being to act towards a goal and which give purpose and direction to certain behaviours. Well-known physiologists have outlined a list of universal basic human needs (see Insight 4). Some correspondence can be found between lists provided by several authors. Considering such basic human needs, practical rationality can discover a set of basic human goods as shown in Table 4.1. Let us briefly describe these goods:[20]

Table 4.1   Basic Human Needs and Basic Human Goods

Basic Human Needs			Basic Human Goods
(Maslow, 1954, 1970)	(Alderfer, 1969)	(Max-Neef, 1991)	
Cognitive		Understanding	**Truth**
Aesthetic	Growth		**Beauty**
Self-actualization		Creation Identity	**Work**
Esteem		Affection	**Friendship**
Love and Belonging	Relatedness	Participation Freedom	**Religion (transcendence)**
Safety		Protection	**Life**
Physiological	Existence	Subsistence Recreation	

Truth

The need to acquire knowledge and to understand it responds to the human good of truth,[21] not only for utilitarian purposes, but to understand more fully the world, oneself and the whole meaning of human existence. It is not always easy to learn or confront the truth, but the pursuit of human excellence requires knowing it so that it can guide our lives.

Beauty

Humans need aesthetic experience. This need might be satisfied by creating things of beauty or by experiencing harmony, balanced structures and magnificent forms, including the material and the spiritual. Thus, beauty can be counted a component of human well-being.

Work

Work, understood in a board sense as any human purposeful activity which develops capabilities and can contribute to better conditions of life, can be seen as a basic human good. It satisfies the needs of self-actualization and personal growth, and gives an opportunity to create new things and to build a personal identity.

Friendship

The need of esteem requires self-respect and enjoying good reputation of others. The need for 'love and belonging' includes a sense of membership in groups, sharing warm dealings, receiving and giving love, enjoying peace, harmony and appreciation from others. From these needs, practical rationality can recognize friendship as a basic human good.

The basic good of 'friendship' includes two meanings:

- In a weak sense, friendship means respect for people, and living in peace and harmony with one another, and within community. It could be called 'civic friendship'.
- In a strong sense, friendship involves acting for the sake of one's friend's purposes and well-being. This is the more common sense of friendship, which does not need further qualification.

Religion (transcendence)

The need for belonging (Maslow) or relatedness (Alderfer) also concerns the cosmos, and even reality beyond it; a sort of Absolute or 'sublime principle' of the cosmos. Religion is, in a broad sense, concerned with such an Absolute. Most people are religious and follow some faith: they worship, pray or otherwise have dealings with God or divinity. Others, who are agnostics or atheists, can possess some sense of transcendence or appreciate the awe inspiring complexity of the universe, or somehow search for an absolute meaning of their lives. Religion or transcendence is an aim that bestows the ultimate meaning upon human existence. Searching for this final significance (God, transcendence) and establishing the corresponding relationship is a good for human beings.

Life

Human persons need air, food, water, shelter, clothing, rest, exercise, recreation and other 'commodities' related to the body. We also need protection against hunger and violence, confidence, bodily security, stable employment, sufficient resources, security for one's family, reliable health care, protection of property and so on. The existence of these physiological and safety-related needs lead us to discover life as a human good – indeed, the most basic human good, because without life no other goods exist.

Life is much more than simple biological existence. It is a healthy and integrated existence lived under humane conditions. Numerous goods are included in the basic good of life, such as a healthy diet, housing and proper exercise. Along these lines, the good of life also includes issues such as avoiding undue stress, overwork and so on. The opportunity to have a livelihood, and adequate protection and safety are instrumental goods that contribute to the basic good of life.

All of these are involved in human flourishing, but there is a hierarchy among them. While life is the most basic, truth, friendship and religion (driven by truth), are the highest, since they refer to the noblest, specifically human characteristics: intellectual knowledge and free will.

In business, it is particularly pertinent to speak of the basic human good of friendship, even in its lower form – mutual respect and living with others in harmony, order and peace. The majority of the most appreciated human values are to do with this good: for instance, the values of respect, equity, truthfulness, honesty, caring, mercy, generosity, gratitude and loyalty.

THE GOLDEN RULE: A GLOBAL ETHICAL PRINCIPLE

Human goods present themselves as normative; that is, as principles for action, from which ethical norms are derived. In human relationships, and particularly in business ethics, the human good of friendship is crucial.

There is a principle known as the Golden Rule, which presents us with a fundamental way of living on friendly terms with others. It can be formulated in simple terms by saying: 'Treat others as you would like to be treated.' A more accurate articulation might read: 'Treat others only as you would be willing to be treated in an identical situation.' For instance, if you are a salesperson, consider how you would like to be treated as the buyer; if you are the supervisor, put yourself in the shoes of your subordinate and so on. The Golden Rule stimulates one to know others and to develop the moral imagination to know, and do, the right thing.

One encounters the Golden Rule in most of the great religious and wisdom traditions, although its formulation varies. These traditions include Ancient Egyptian, Zoroastrianism, Greek philosophers (Pittacus, Diogenes, Sextus, Isocrates and Epictetus), Judaism, Christianity, Islam, Sufism, Hinduism, Jainism, Sikhism, Confucianism, Taoism, Buddhism, *Shintō*, Secular Humanism, Native American Spirituality, the Baha'i Faith and African proverbs, among others.[22] Sometimes the Golden Rule is presented negatively, sometimes positively. 'Never impose on others what you would not choose for yourself' (Confucius) is an example of the former. A positive formulation is this: 'Whatever you wish that men would do to you, do so to them' (Jesus Christ).

It is worthy of note that the Golden Rule was formulated by people belonging to different cultures, and most probably without any cross-cultural influence. This shows the capacity of human rationality to discover such a basic principle of morality as this, which permits people to live together in harmony and peace.

The Golden Rule, because of its wide cultural acceptance, is considered to be a global ethical principle, constituting an excellent meeting point among different cultures. However, its application relies on other developments that specify how others should be treated. We will consider this in the next section.

HUMAN DIGNITY AND THE PERSONALIST PRINCIPLE

Recognizable human features and identity is crucial for treating people correctly, beyond the insights provided by the Golden Rule. Such recognition entails the knowledge of what the human individual is as such, and not only how useful he or she might be for me. Although it is not easy to answer what a human individual is, some crucial features can be outlined, as already offered (see pp. 25–6) – among them: rationality, freedom, self-consciousness, and the uniqueness of every human being. Every individual is 'someone' unique, unrepeatable and of immense value – in a certain sense 'absolute'. A human being is not 'something' interchangeable with other individuals of the same species, but 'someone'.[23] Each individual not only has biology, but also a biography, a unique history that each one keeps in his or her intimacy. Such features allow us to introduce the crucial concept of human dignity.

Human dignity means that the human person is intrinsically worthy in a certain absolute sense (only subordinated to the Absoluteness of God, as the ultimate foundation of such dignity). Human dignity is at the root of most international documents on human rights and standards for corporate responsibility.[24] Many religions and wisdom traditions also consider human dignity at least indirectly.

Human dignity is 'constitutive'. This means that every human being has an intrinsic value, regardless of race, age, sex or any other particular condition and also independent of any legal recognition (or lack thereof). Other types of dignity associated with a role might be lost (for example, a judge) for corrupt conduct while acting in a particular role, but human dignity can never be lost because it is inherent in the human condition.

The recognition of human dignity is a starting point for ethics: many consider it axiomatic. Indeed, several philosophical and theological traditions converge in their acknowledgement of human dignity. Kant considers it to be a consequence of human autonomy and freedom. Aristotle, although not adhering to the concept of human dignity as such, recognizes that human beings are superior because of their rational nature. Thomas Aquinas agrees with Aristotle and adds that the supreme dignity of human beings lies in their being directed towards the good by themselves and not by others.[25] In the Judeo-Christian tradition, the human dignity of every individual is especially emphasized, as a being created in the image of God.[26]

There is a term coined centuries ago to express the dignity of every human individual: 'person'. This word denotes dignity[27] and is synonymous with being rational and conscious, the owner of his or her acts (at least, potentially), with strict uniqueness and one's own identity. As Kant pointed out, things have a price; persons have dignity. Human dignity – being a person – is therefore an essential ethical value that demands an appropriate response. That response is presented in the Personalist Principle.

An initial formulation of the 'Personalist Principle' was made by the German philosopher Immanuel Kant (1724–1804). His ethical theory (see Appendix) is based on a self-evident categorical imperative that can be formulated in three different ways. In the second formulation, the categorical imperative focuses upon the necessity of unconditional respect for the human individual. He wrote: 'Act in such a way that you treat humanity, whether in your own person or in the person of any other, always as an end and never simply as a means'.[28]

This categorical imperative points to the dignity of the person that always deserves respect. This is usually presented as a constraint in dealing with people. It can also be seen as a basic norm of strict justice, meaning the duty of giving to each his or her right, understanding that a right is a prerogative possessed by a person – something to which one has a just claim.

Duties of justice has been the cornerstone in prevalent Western ethics for only the last few centuries. However, other ethics systems are wider. In Aristotelian ethics, not only justice, but also friendship is very significant. For its part, Christian ethics refers to care and neighbourly love. Other traditions emphasize some shared human values beyond duties of justice. Some postmodern ethical approaches also stress responsibility and care for others.[29]

Recognizing that every person has an absolute worth, one might wonder whether what is due to each person is only the minimum required by justice (respect for rights), or whether it also extends to benevolence and care, considering people's needs, especially the needs of those closest to one. An affirmative answer leads one to understand that the ethics of dealing with people includes both aspects: justice and care. An alternative could be to define 'justice' in a broader sense, covering strict justice (respecting rights) and also care (concern and help in persons' needs).

These considerations are consistent with the wider reformulation of the second Kantian imperative proposed by Wojtyla, which includes concern and love for people and not only respect. Wojtyla called his proposal the 'Personalist Norm' or 'Personalist Principle'.[30] He distinguishes two aspects: one negative, closely related to the Kantian categorical imperative, and one positive. The former *proscribes* using people as a mere means to an end, while the latter *prescribes* an attitude of love towards persons.[31] In a broader formulation, the Personalist Principle can be expressed as follows:

Negative formulation: *Human beings should never be treated as a mere means to an end.*

Positive formulation: *Persons should be treated not only with respect but also benevolence and care.*

In its negative formulation the Personalist Principle uses the adjective 'mere'. This is essential, since people can be means or resources to obtain certain ends. Workers are human resources or assets in the production process, and customers are the means by which to obtain incomes. However, both workers and customers are much more than this; they are persons, and consequently deserve to be treated with respect and never as 'mere' resources or simple means but, rather, in a respectful way.

The negative formulation of the Personalist Principle is very relevant to business ethics, as we will see in the following chapters. It prohibits:

- *Making any attempt an human life.* Taking any action directly oriented to killing people or any attempt against human life or physical integrity is not allowed.

- *Slavery, exploitation and manipulation.* People can never be considered or treated as objects of property (slavery) or used for selfish purposes (exploitation). Neither is using people as inanimate objects (manipulation) ethically acceptable.

- *Mistreatment of persons or groups.* It is unacceptable to insult, humiliate, slander, blackmail or injure people in any way. Neither can they be coerced to act against their conscience.

- *Breaking one's own word.* People trust in one's word, and not honouring one's own word means not giving due consideration to the other. Consequently, it is not ethically acceptable to breach legitimate contracts and morally just agreements.

- *Lying.* It is not acceptable to act with deception by telling lies, making false promises, creating unfounded expectations, or persuading people through false propositions.

- *Theft.* Usurping another's property against the reasonable will of the owner is also forbidden. Property is sometimes external to the person, but when sometimes it belongs to a person, it is, in a certain sense, like an extension of the person, and deserves to be respected.

The positive formulation of the Personalist Principle demands more than simply respect for people. It encourages solicitude for others, especially those around one, with an attitude of service, emphasizing solidarity, caring for one's relationships and for the common interests of communities of which one is a member. This also entails sympathizing with others and acknowledging their sufferings, as well as a sense of collaboration, a willingness to participate in joint efforts for common purposes.

The specific requirements of the Personalist Principle in its positive formulation are very open, and can hardly be expressed in terms of rigid norms. They depend upon circumstances, including specific links that unite people, capacities of the subject, types of relationships and even the social context. Practical wisdom (see pp. 87) is essential in order to determine the best course of action in each situation.

HUMAN RIGHTS

Dealing with justice and rights requires, first, identifying who is the *subject* of a right and what is the *object* of that right; that is, the thing to which a person has a claim. This can be material or immaterial. Examples of objects of rights are a house (a property right), an invention (an intellectual property right), and one's own life (a personal right). The existence of a right is derived from the existence of a *title*; that is, a reason that justifies a person's claim to the object of his or her rights. A right differs from a demand precisely in that a right is supported by a title, which imposes a duty of justice on somebody else (the term of a right).

There are legal rights, specified by law, such as rights deriving from citizenship. Other rights are acquired – for example, by signing a contract; still others are *natural rights*, also called *human rights*, because we possess them simply by virtue of being human.

Human dignity and the Personalist Principle, along with human goods, provide a sound basis for human rights.[32] The recognition of human beings as persons includes recognizing whatever the person possesses as a part of his or her human condition: life, body, reputation, property or freedom of movement, and anything else related to human goods. This supports the belief in the existence of certain innate prerogatives of every human being: human rights. Human rights are intrinsic to every human being and previous to any legal formulation. They remain inviolable and inalienable, even when dismissed or trampled on by governments or by a community.

Two kinds of rights can be distinguished: negative and positive. The former refers to individual rights that must be respected by everybody, including public authorities: for instance, the right to life and security of the person; equality before the law and the right to due process; freedom of religion, speech and association. Positive human rights refer to those rights necessary for life and for human growth that ought to be protected and provided by society and public authority (the state). These include, for instance, the right to education, health care and a livelihood. Human rights are older than the modern declarations that refer to them.

The formulation of human rights has a long history.[33] At present, the best known and most influential document on the subject is probably the Universal Declaration of Human Rights (UDHR) approved by the General Assembly of the United Nations in 1948, shortly after the Second World War and the notorious Nazi human rights violations. This Declaration is centred on the recognition of the universal dignity and the essential equality of every human being – regardless of gender, race, creed or religion – and includes both negative and positive rights. Since 1948, other significant international declarations have been promulgated, reinforcing and developing the UDHR. Most of them take human rights as a crucial reference point.

Currently, a worldwide consensus on human rights exists, but critics can be found as well. One objection is that human rights theories have generally been developed within Western civilization, and appear to be a secular version of the Judeo-Christian tradition; hence, they should be not applicable to countries with different cultural or religious traditions. Granted, human rights theories grew up within the humanism of Western civilization, with its profound Judeo-Christian roots. Christianity strongly emphasized human dignity, and human rights can be found implicitly in the Judeo-Christian Ten Commandments: 'Thou shalt not kill' means the right to life, 'Thou shalt not steal', the right to private property and so on. However, similar prohibitions are also found in other religious or wisdom traditions. Basic human rights can be found in ancient civilizations – such as the Persian Empire in the sixth century BC under Cyrus the Great, in the Maurya Empire of ancient India in the third century BC, and in the Early Islamic Caliphate in the seventh century AD – although without the label 'human rights'.[34] Asian democratic societies, such as those of the Hindus, have a long tradition of respect for individual rights.[35] Besides, let us not forget that the Universal Declaration of Human Rights was approved by the General Assembly of the United Nations without a single 'nay' vote from the more than one hundred countries represented.

THE PRINCIPLE OF THE COMMON GOOD

Human beings are not isolated; we live together within a complex set of interdependences. We are able to associate through voluntary connections based on agreements of mutual interest or friendship, or through interactions based on personal generosity.

In many areas of human life one can discover collaboration and cooperation. Sometimes this is instrumental: entered into with the aim of achieving one's own interests in food, shelter, transportation, health care, cultural goods and so on; or else to achieve reputation, power and other goals related to public recognition. The achievement of such goals very often requires certain actions by other people. However, living in society and, more specifically, in relationships with other people does not always come about due to purely utilitarian interests. Collaborating and cooperating with others, and even helping people, can be regarded as an end in itself. The latter is characteristic of authentic friendship.

Hannah Arendt (1906–75), one of the twentieth century's most influential political philosophers, claimed that, although the ties of intimacy and warmth can never become political, in the public sphere civic friendship is possible. Moreover, she held that the only truly political ties are those of civic friendship and solidarity, since they make political demands and preserve reference to the world.[36] Friendship, civic friendship and solidarity have their roots in human sociability, which is also expressed in other communities, such as families, churches, schools, hospitals, universities and other human associations.

The concept of the common good appears precisely upon considering the social dimension of the person and how people live and act in a collaborative manner within communities, establishing more or less lasting ties.[37] It refers to goods shared by those who are united in some way or belong to a community.

In communities, people are united by common goals and share goods associated with membership. The common good is different from the 'total good' or sum of all the particular goods of all community members. The common good is not a sum but, rather, the result of the interacting of all goods for the sake of a common goal. The common good is indivisible and is potentially participated in by all community members, but nobody is its owner. In a political community, neither any individual citizen nor the state owns the common good.

Some examples might clarify this important concept. A society without epidemics, with unpolluted air, living in a peaceful manner, with social cohesion, a good educational system is a society enjoying goods from which all can benefit. If we consider a small society, such as the family, we can recognize shared goods, such as having an atmosphere of harmony, mutual respect, understanding and concern for one another. In business firms, common goods are, for example, having a culture of commitment and cooperation, and a good work climate. At an international level, neighbourly relations among nations, free-flowing communications and agreements on sustainable global development are also expressions of shared goods.

Common good is sometimes identified with 'the public interest' or 'the common welfare'. This is not far wrong, but the common good is broader than this, since it includes everything that can contribute to authentic human flourishing.

One way to make the common good practical is by referring to the external conditions of a community that foster the flourishing of its members – but such flourishing has to be achieved freely by each person, in accordance with both basic human goods and individual preferences. In this regard, Finnis states that the common good includes 'such an ensemble of conditions which enhance the opportunity of flourishing for all members of a community'.[38]

The concept of the common good also differs from the interest of the majority, sometimes called the 'general interest'. This arises from individual interests – whatever they might be, whereas the common good respects human dignity, human rights and human development. In a certain society, the interest of the majority might justify, for instance, sacrificing the inalienable rights of a single individual, while the common good cannot, since it is good for everybody to live in a society where human rights are respected and even favoured.

Four types of external conditions can be distinguished as aspects of the common good:

- *Socio-cultural values*, which include full respect for human dignity and human rights, freedom, safety, order, peace and justice, which permit living together respectfully and foster a sense of tolerance and cooperation.
- *Organizational conditions*, which permit access to health, educational, cultural and religious goods, as well as respect for human freedom, truth, justice and solidarity, including prevention of corruption, fair laws and other regulations, and guarantees of fair trials and procedures.
- *Economic conditions*, which can favour human growth in such a way that everyone can enjoy a reasonable level of well-being. Economic growth is instrumental and subordinated to people, not the contrary.
- *Environmental conditions*, regarding maintenance of an appropriate human habitat for current and future generations.

Each human community (family, business, religious associations, sports clubs, political groups and so on) has a specific common good that can be recognized as such. According to Aristotle, the political community has a more complete common good than do smaller communities. In the current global world, in which people are highly interconnected, there is also a universal common good.

The specific determination of what contributes to the common good in each community depends on circumstances, and it must be discovered with practical wisdom and also, frequently, through sincere social dialogue. Within a community, the final decision on particular aspects of the common good is the job of those who rule the community, but it must always respect human dignity and human rights.

The principle of the common good arises by considering that it is created by cooperation among community members. Each person or group that forms part of a community is interdependent with the whole. The common good is fostered when members of a community are receptive to ways of contributing to the community's improvement, to the benefit of everyone, including themselves.

Those who take advantage of social cooperation for personal interest without any contribution (this is what is called the 'free rider problem') are seen as exhibiting incorrect behaviour.

Since collaboration is necessary for social life, it is rational to hold that ethics requires as a duty that every member of a community collaborate in the common good, and never damage it. However, the specific contribution required is not equal for everybody. It depends on the capacities and concurrent circumstances of each member.

The principle of the common good can be formulated as follows:

In acting in a social context, both individual and social institutions must contribute to the common good of the community in accordance with the concurrent circumstances and their respective capacities, and must harmonize or subordinate their own interests to the common good.

While the Personalist Principle guides interpersonal relationships, the Principle of the Common Good provides orientation for relationships between the individual and society. The common good appears as a higher criterion by which to judge particular interests that might conflict. This means, for instance, that a CEO's particular interests in amassing more power by making acquisitions of other companies has to be subordinated to the good of the company as a whole.

A correct interpretation of the Principle of the Common Good can never exclude respect for human dignity and rights to the benefit of any supposed 'higher' common interest. As noted above, respect for every human being is always an absolute moral. In other words, both the Personalist Principle and the Principle of the Common Good should be considered together.

The positive requirement is 'contributing to the common good of the community in accordance with concurrent circumstances and individual capacities'. This is what happens in a company when managers and employees try to do whatever is necessary to contribute to the situational needs and goals of an organization, or of a part of it.

Management literature has coined the expression 'organizational citizenship behaviour', which is very close to the positive principle of the common good. It is defined as a type of individual behaviour beneficial to the organization and is discretionary; that is, not directly or explicitly recognized by the formal reward system.[39] The common good principle does not exclude, however, that some of its requirements might also be formalized and even rewarded.

MORAL CHARACTER AND FUNDAMENTAL HUMAN VIRTUES

The PCA considers human virtues as a key element. Notice that we talk of 'human virtues'. This differs from other approaches in which virtues are seen only as means with which to enhance efficiency or because, in a particular social context, certain character traits ('contextual virtues') are valued.[40] Here, virtues take human nature as reference, and they can therefore be called 'human virtues'. Human virtues shape moral character and human flourishing.

Virtues are an essential element of human behaviour. People, in their goal-directed behaviour, experience motivations; that is, internal forces that actuate a behavioural pattern. These motivations are supported by a set of natural inclinations that dispose us to act in a certain way. Under a certain stimulus, such natural inclinations are activated, and motivations spontaneously appear. The resulting motivation is a want or desire that drives one to act.

Such 'spontaneous motivations' can play an important role in human action. Very often, spontaneous motivations are accompanied by physical or emotional sensations. However, we do not necessarily follow such motivations. We have to decide whether or not to do so.

Practical rationality acts along with spontaneous motivations and emotions, evaluating the appropriateness for the subject of following such motivations, and how to resolve situations with conflicting spontaneous motivations.

Rationality can prevail against spontaneous motivations, but this is not always the case. The existence of 'irrational' behaviours that follow spontaneous rather than rational motivation is well known. Sometimes, the spontaneous motivation to make money at any cost is very strong, but it can be controlled by the rational motivation of acting with integrity. Exercising practical rationality generates a virtue called 'practical wisdom'.

Practical wisdom

Practical wisdom (*prudence*, in classic nomenclature) therefore aids practical rationality in identifying the right thing to do in each situation, and in resolving conflicts between spontaneous motivations and also in providing rational motivations. Practical wisdom, as with any other virtue, is developed by repetition and by avoiding its opposite.[41]

Practical wisdom is crucial for good behaviour, but it is not sufficient. To act rightly, we need both practical wisdom and operative virtues, which provide us with the interior strength to act well.[42] These operative virtues have traditionally been called by three names: justice, courage (or fortitude) and moderation (or temperance). These virtues are related to three basic natural inclinations that require self-regulation in order to avoid behaviours that would be far from human excellence:

Justice (friendship)

This virtue governs our relationships with others. Specifically, it denotes a sustained or constant willingness. Treat everyone – fellow human beings and the divinity – in an appropriate way, in accordance with their respective identity. Justice regulates the inclination to possess and also to give or share what one has with others. Justice is currently understood in a narrow sense, which refers to the strict respecting of others' rights. Among other duties, it precludes taking things without respecting the rights of others, and renders others their due. At the same time, justice leads to distributing joint or shared property with equity. It also entails contributing what is due to society as a whole, in order to provide appropriate social conditions for the human development of all. This is generally called 'social justice'. Indirectly, justice also refers to the natural environment, the habitat of human beings, including future generations. In particular, animals should be treated without cruelty, even with kindness and respect for their own identity.[43]

'Justice' also has a broader sense, which refers to benevolence and care for the good of others. In this broad sense, justice is close to 'neighbourly love' and 'friendship'. It comprises all of the virtues related to human relations, including honesty, loyalty, gratitude, generosity and solidarity.[44]

Courage

This virtue (*fortitude*, in classical nomenclature) regulates the inclination to overcome hindrances and obstacles to doing good. Thus, what is characteristic of this virtue is persevering or pursuing what is good in spite of obstacles. It can appear as fear, on the one hand, or aggressiveness, on the other. The fear leads to a blockage when facing a hardship or a problem, without struggling to achieve something valuable. Hindrances, by contrast, can be dealt with violently, having recourse to unmeasured aggressiveness. Courage allows one to overcome fear and to strive to attain goals essential to a human way of life. Courage also restrains aggressiveness, encouraging us to reach valuable goals in an appropriate way.

Moderation

This virtue (*temperance*, in classical nomenclature) regulates the human inclination towards pleasure, providing self-mastery and avoiding immoderate attachments. The search for pleasure can turn out to be unrestrained, an obstacle to other valuable activities, less pleasant but much more conducive to human excellence. Addiction is an extreme case of a lack of self-mastery. The search for pleasure can, in some cases, be very strong; in others, too weak, with an unreasonable lack of sensitivity for pleasurable things. Self-moderation helps to avoid both extremes.

All of these virtues provide for the most effective compromise between two vicious extremes.[45] Thus, courage negates cowardice as a consequence of fear and also precludes excessive aggressiveness and temerity. In practice, these virtues require the determination of the 'golden mean' between two extremes. In other words, to become moderate, courageous and just it is necessary to know what 'the moderate', 'the courageous' and 'the just' are in every particular circumstance. This requires an intimate knowledge of each situation and a sense of the human goods acquired by previous actions. This is precisely the role of practical wisdom, which helps us to find the golden mean of the operative moral virtues and, consequently, the right thing to do in each situation. Practical wisdom therefore has a driving role among the operative moral virtues. It is an intellectual virtue because it belongs to the cognitive sphere, but also a moral virtue because it is essential for moral life.

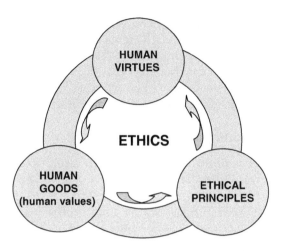

Figure 4.2   Interconnection between goods, principles and virtues

Traditionally, these four virtues have been considered the fundamental human virtues: they are not generated by human nature but acquired by repetitions of acts. Human nature, however, gives us the capacity to receive them. These virtues are called 'cardinal virtues' (from the Latin *cardo*, 'hinge') because they are like the hinge upon which the door of human excellence swings, and other human virtues, which contribute to human excellence, can be regarded as being included within these four.

The cardinal virtues were first introduced by Plato.[46] The Bible also mentions them.[47] The Roman emperor-philosopher Marcus Aurelius emphasized them and stressed their comprehensive character.[48] Subsequently, the cardinal virtues were also adopted by Christian authors, such as St Ambrose, St Augustine of Hippo and St Thomas Aquinas.[49] Virtues described in other traditions might also be related to the cardinal virtues.[50] Contemporary scholars have also emphasized and developed some aspects of these four virtues.[51]

As we have seen, human goods (values) entail principles and norms (rules) and, acting in accordance with such norms, the agent acquires human virtues, which in turn favour the discovery of goods and the interior strength to obtain them. This interrelationship among goods, principles and virtues is shown in Figure 4.2.

APPENDIX: AN OVERVIEW OF MAINSTREAM ETHICAL THEORIES FOR BUSINESS ETHICS

There are several significant ethical theories that have been applied to business ethics, and particularly to decision-making. One set of theories is deontological. These focus on ethical duties or obligations. A second group focuses on an action's consequences. Utilitarianism is the most popular theory of this group.

Other theories place special emphasis on the social context and are rooted in political traditions. Integrative Social Contract Theory has gained popularity since the 1990s, especially in the United States. In Europe, especially in Germany, some insights of so-called discursive ethics have been applied to business ethics. Finally, there are virtue-ethics approaches, which follow the Aristotelian tradition and focus on the agent and his or her moral character.[52]

Deontologism (deontological theories)

Deontological theories present duties for human action based on rationalistic principles. We will address two main theories: Kantianism and the Natural Rights Theory.

Immanuel Kant (1724–1804) is the paramount representative of the classical, rationalistic, deontological approach. A central concept in Kant's ethical theory is the 'categorical imperative', from which all moral duties and obligations derive.[53] Kant distinguishes the categorical imperative from the hypothetical imperative. 'I ought not to lie (never, no matter what circumstance I might encounter)' is a categorical statement. 'If I want to gain his trust, I ought not to lie', is hypothetical. According to Kant, the categorical imperative discloses itself as a supreme, unconditional moral law: an absolute requirement for every human action.

Kant presented three different formulations of his categorical imperative. The first, which is probably the best known,[54] states: 'Act only according to that maxim whereby you can at the same time will that it should become a universal law'.[55] This formulation expresses the idea of 'moral maxims' that are universal and impartial, without connection with any specific physical details surrounding the proposition. For instance, the proposition 'to commit a murder is wrong' can be derived from the categorical imperative because it could be applied to any rational being.

In Kantian theory, there are only formal statements (called 'maxims') for the guidance of actions. It considers neither values, nor virtues, nor consequences, focusing instead on the action and on the agent's goodwill regarding fulfilment of the moral law. Goodwill is developed by acting rationally in accordance with the principles laid down by the categorical imperative.

For Kant, the only pure or legitimate reason to fulfil a duty is for the sake of the duty itself, not for any further requirement (developing moral excellence, for instance). The only answer to the question 'Why should I do my duty' is 'Because it is your duty'. Consequently, in the Kantian view, behaviours deserve moral esteem if they are carried out for the sake of moral duty. In business, for instance, a behaviour aimed at obtaining reputation would deserve no moral esteem at all. According to Kant, we should act neither for the sake of an action's consequences nor out of natural inclinations. Thus, 'Refrain from lying, because you want to gain his trust' is not moral; one does not lie because that is one's duty, the right thing to do.

A crucial concept in Kantian theory is the autonomy of the agent. The agent's interests are limited only by moral law, which is made by the rational agent in accordance with impartiality and universal criteria. This is quite different from Aristotle and, above all, from Aquinas, who would say that human reason exercises its autonomy in discovering laws given to human beings by God through their rational nature, not in making the moral law. In contrast, for Kant, God is no longer the moral legislator, as he was for Aquinas. It is human autonomy that gives rise to moral law, a moral law apparently applicable to everybody.

Although a Kantian theory of ethics might seem problematic to some, it contains some interesting elements, such as its respect for persons. In practice, the Kantian approach has been employed for business ethics as one possible basis for ethical reasoning in decision-making,[56] and has even been used to develop textbooks on business ethics and management ethics.[57]

Another deontological theory, and one sometimes employed in business ethics, is based on *natural rights*. This entails the recognition of self-evident human rights and freedoms, with no further justification. In this view, human rights are inalienable entitlements that deserve to be respected in interactions with others. The British philosopher John Locke (1632–1704) conceptualized the notion of the 'human right',[58] although its components were already implicit in previous thinkers and even the Bible, as has been mentioned.

At the centre of Locke's argument is the claim that individuals possess natural rights, independent of the political recognition granted to them (or not) by the state.[59] Initially, human rights and freedoms included the right to life and liberty, and freedom to use one's property as one chose. Later, the list of human rights was extended to include freedom of thought and expression, equality before the law, the right to privacy, freedom of conscience and so on. Currently, the Universal Declaration of Human Rights contains many additional human rights.

Utilitarianism

In contrast to deontological approaches, utilitarianism states that what determines an action's rightness is not duties but the consequences of that action, and specifically the sum of its contribution to overall utility (happiness, understood as pleasure or satisfaction) for all persons affected by it.

Basically, this theory considers only one principle, which is usually formulated as 'the greatest happiness for the greatest number'.[60] The main representatives of utilitarianism are Jeremy Bentham (1748–1832) and John Stuart Mill (1806–73). According to the former, who took a completely hedonistic approach, a right action is one that equals the greatest sum of pleasure and the least sum of pain in those affected by the action.[61] Mill also followed a utilitarian principle but presented a wider vision about the goods to be evaluated. In Mill's view, higher pleasures are associated with the mind and lower ones with the body. All of these must be considered and evaluated.[62]

Thus, a right decision comes down to a problem of evaluation of pleasure and pain, and then an arithmetical calculation before applying the utilitarian principle. This presents the serious difficulty of measuring something as subjective as pleasure and pain. In the face of this difficulty, and to make utilitarianism easier to apply, a different approach was suggested, consisting of replacing the analysis of each act (*act utilitarianism*) with a set of rules (*rule utilitarianism*). These rules are determined by considering that certain actions are never conducive to general happiness (for example, slavery or child labour).

Another criticism of utilitarianism is its lack of respect for minorities and for human rights. Even the fundamental human rights of a few people can be violated if you show that the pleasure of the majority is greater than pain caused to the minority. While a deontological approach advocates for human rights, applying utilitarian theory in a society that is racist in its majority, for instance, can lead to violations of human rights of an ethnic minority, for this would amount to the greatest happiness (satisfaction) for the greatest number.[63]

In a business context, utilitarianism poses difficult questions. How should we evaluate right action regarding safety in the workplace? How can we compare the value of human life with economic costs? Is human life measurable only in economic terms?

Theories rooted in political traditions

Contractualist tradition dates from the seventeenth and eighteenth centuries.[64] This tradition assumes a model based on a hypothetical 'social contract' among those who belong to any human community. Related to this tradition is the proposal of the American philosopher John Rawls (1921–2002), who presented a particular *theory of justice*.[65] Rawls understands justice as impartiality. His theory combines liberalism and egalitarianism, and has enjoyed great popularity in the USA, as well as other countries.

Underlying the social contract theories is a strong individualistic vision of society. In essence, proponents of the social contract hold that society is made up of individuals with conflicting interests who need a hypothetical 'social contract' for living together in peace. Thus, society is organized according to implicit agreements between people and government: people give up certain rights to a government in order to receive social order. In the business context, the social contract relates to the idea that the norms that ought to govern business have to be created by an agreement between relevant parties involved in each business.

The best-known application of social contract theory to business ethics is in Donaldson and Dunfee.[66] Their approach, called *Integrative Social Contract Theory*, considers two kinds of norms: 'hypernorms' and 'authentic norms'. Hypernorms are widely recognized as ethical standards. They are consistent with the findings of universal human values, with precepts of major religions and philosophies, with norms proposed by prominent non-governmental organizations. Authentic norms come from 'microcontracts' for a given community (firms, departments within firms, national economic organizations and so on) grounded in informed consent and buttressed by the right to exist. In order to be binding, a microsocial contract norm must be compatible with hypernorms.

The *Discursive Ethics Theory* does not provide substantive norms, only norms for following a rational process to reach a consensus. This is based on the theory of communicative action proposed by Jürgen Habermas.[67] Discursive ethics focuses on a dialogical method as a means to a peaceful settlement of social conflicts. Basically, it consists of gathering all those involved in a conflict and engaging them in discourse, in which each party presents its best arguments to convince the others, all working towards the end of eventually obtaining a solution acceptable to everybody.

This approach presents a set of procedural norms ('presuppositions of communication and argumentation') which foster impartiality and non-coactive actions, among other guarantees for fruitful discourse. In business ethics, for instance, it can be applied to the elaboration of a code of conduct or to settle conflicts between groups with a stake in the firms. This procedural theory has been applied to business ethics by some scholars.[68]

Although the idea of resolving conflicts rationally is certainly unobjectionable, there are at least three problems with discursive ethics. First, there is a practical difficulty in harmonizing completely different visions through procedural norms. Second, there is no guarantee that the consensus arrived at will be ethically acceptable simply by virtue of being based on procedural norms. Third, business ethics is here reduced to a tool for solving problems arising from conflicts.

In spite of some interesting insights contained in normative political theories, their application to business ethics is controversial. Some scholars believe them applicable to business, as are other political theories, arguing that although businesses differ from states, the difference is one of degree, not kind. Others[69] find it problematic to apply political theories to business, regarding it as an altogether different reality. Another serious objection is whether we can accept as an ethical norm an agreement between relevant parties even though it offers no guarantee of moral quality.

Virtue ethics

In the past few decades, Aristotelian ethics has grown in popularity,[70] and several scholars have presented Neo-Aristotelian approaches to business ethics,[71] such as the 'virtue ethics' approach, which emphasizes the role of rationality and character in making sound decisions.[72]

The Aristotelian tradition centres on how to live to attain the 'good life' or 'human flourishing'. They also refer to the 'happiness' associated with the good life (*eudaimonia*, in Greek) – not happiness in the sense of pleasure, but the joy that comes of acting honestly, helping others, or being aware that one's work is contributing to the well-being of others.

An objection to the Aristotelian approach would be that the concept of the good life could be different for different people, rendering it an inappropriate ethical reference point. Aristotelians would probably respond that, although each individual can undoubtedly have a particular view of the good life, there are some views of human flourishing that are common to every human being (integrity, concern for others, justice and so on).

Another common objection to this tradition is that virtues do not provide clear principles or norms that can be formalized in an ethical code. This is not completely true, since Aristotle's writings provide some basic ethical standards and some followers, such as Thomas Aquinas, did develop specific norms.[73] On the other hand, considering ethics as a simple set of well-defined norms or codes is also problematic, inasmuch as not everything could be included, and the role of character is forgotten. Particular situations are diverse and complex: practical wisdom seems essential for resolving dilemmas and remaining conscious of the ethical dimension of each situation.

The Aristotelian tradition also considers justice in a social context: that of the 'natural law'. Natural law theory was outlined by Aristotle in its basic dimensions, and by other ancient philosophers, such as Cicero.[74] In the Middle Ages, Aquinas developed a realistic theory of natural law as a framework for a proper social order. Natural law theory was used in business ethics in an international context in Europe from the fifteenth to the seventeenth century, when adherents of three different religions were present – namely, Catholics, Protestants and Muslims.[75] Currently, natural law theory, although it is not a dominant theory in business ethics, has been applied to the analysis of several contemporary ethical issues, with the argument that this theory provides a more useful and more insightful basis for evaluating the ethics of business practices than do other more popular theories.[76]

In addition to these theories, others have emerged in the twentieth century within the philosophical stream of thought called Postmodernism. Postmodernism emphasizes particular situations rather than universal principles. In business ethics, the 'ethics of care' has gained popularity. Both Gilligan and Slote, for example, see the individual as deeply embedded in a net of interpersonal relations, and emphasize the responsibility of individuals for maintaining the interconnectivity of the network members.[77] Another stream of thought that could be relevant to business ethics is Personalism.[78] Authors of this school, though varying in many aspects of their thinking, agree on stressing the centrality and intrinsic value of the person.[79]

Business ethics in practice 4:

François Michelin – A person-centred vision of a business leader

The French company Michelin was founded in 1889 by two partners, Aristide Barbier and Nicolas Edouard Daubrée, whose families formed a union by both marriage and business. Everything started when an English cyclist came to Clermont-Ferrand, a French village, looking for a rubber patch to repair a tyre. Jules Michelin made the repairs in two hours, and then suddenly thought about the need for tyres in general. Six months later, he invented the tyre that could be disassembled and changed in a few minutes.

Many years later, there was another great innovation in Michelin, the radial tyre. It was born out of the difficulties experienced with the standard tyre, with which cars could go no faster than eighty miles an hour without the tyre blowing up. The radial tyre gives three times more mileage than a conventional tyre, allows for a reduction in fuel consumption and gives a more comfortable ride. Its invention was thanks to Marius Mignol, a Michelin employee who had joined the company as a typist in the printing department. Within the company, Mignol's creativity and talent were appreciated and he was promoted to technical functions.

Today, Michelin Group is a worldwide company. Its mission is 'to contribute in a sustainable way to progress in the mobility of people and goods by constantly making travelling safer, easier, more enjoyable, more economical and more respectful of people and the environment'.[80] They manufacture and sell tyres for all kinds of vehicles in more than 170 countries, and account for 70 per cent of the replacement tyre market. Behind the success of the radial wheel, which has established Michelin as the most important tyre producer in the world, constant innovation and development is always in focus. One of the latest advances of Michelin were tyres integrated to digital systems, or development of a complete coherent tyre pressure monitoring system – the EnTire Solution.

According to Mr. Michel Rollier, Managing General Partner of Michelin, 'a company's performance is not assessed only in terms of its economic results. It is also measured by its ability to develop its employees and to take its place harmoniously in the communities and Society around it.'[81] This is in line with the five Michelin values on which they base their development: (1) respect for customers; (2) respect for people; (3) respect for shareholders; (4) respect for the environment; and (5) respect for facts.[82] Decision-making is taken in the light of these values.

François Michelin, the great-grandson of Jules Michelin, was at the helm of Michelin for over half a century and he then became honorary president of the company. François Michelin has a particular 'business philosophy' – inherited, in part, from his family. He likes to use the word 'factory' instead of 'company' and he explains that the word factory 'conjures up notions of machines, things that are produced, and, most importantly, men and women who are employees, customers and shareholders.'[83] Moreover, he states that property is theft, when it is not at the service of people.[84]

François' vision is that every human being is unique and unrepeatable. It is not his or her job or job title but being a person that determines who he or she is. He thinks that a manager must treat all of his workers individually and with great respect, just as his grandfather used to do, addressing a worker as 'Sir'.[85] François underlines that 'the most important aspect of the human being is that he is self-teachable'.[86]

François Michelin has great confidence in the human person:

All that man asks for is to be allowed to surpass himself and become what he is. As soon as you give him the means to do so, you acknowledge all the glorious splendour of his humanity. Any man that you can look at straight in the face, regarding him as a unique individual who is free and responsible, blazes forth like a light as dazzling as the sun. When I think of everything that could be accomplished if one could release all the energy found in human beings![87]

Meanwhile, every action in business remains a reflection of the freedom and responsibility of the person who performs it. Michelin reminds us of the Golden Rule, according to which one should not do to others what one would not want done to oneself. Being a Christian, Michelin often also remembers that human beings have been created in the image and likeness of God, which provides every individual with an incomparable dignity; the dignity of being a person. This is why one of the elements that differentiate the company is the emphasis on individual treatment of workers, listening to them and to their deepest motivations,

---

Business ethics in practice 4: (cont'd)

giving them the possibility to develop talents inside and outside the plant. He highlights that people have all the means to better themselves or to destroy themselves,[88] and believes that work gives to each person not only the opportunity to build certain goods, but also to grow themselves as human beings.

One of the company's characteristics is also fair treatment for the customer. Transactions between a producer and buyer have to respect a code of ethics. A person has no right to lie – François underlines – and if you are not always asking yourself if what you are doing is good, you slip.[89] 'Truth is greater than you are.'[90] Although it is not only the task of acting on the truth, but also loving and accepting another person as he or she is.[91] Passing that message on to the generations to come is one of the Michelin's objectives.

Questions:

1. What are the main features of François Michelin's vision?

2. Which aspects of the vision stand out for you?

3. Do you think Marius Mignol's invention has anything to do with the corporate mission and 'philosophy' of Michelin?

Sources: J. Couretas, 'Philosopher on the Factory Floor: The Sacramental Entrepreneurship of François Michelin', Acton Institute, 2003: http://www.acton.org/commentary/commentary_138.php; F. Michelin, *And Why Not? Morality and Business* (Maryland: Lexington Books, 2003); Michelin Corporate website: www.michelin.com

---

Dilemma 4

Paula worked as assistant of the Chief Executive Officer of XYZ, a listed company. Some weeks ago, Paula and her husband went for dinner with William and Anna. The latter was a close friend of Paula from their childhood; her husband William, aged 34, worked for an important investment bank. During the animated conversation that accompanied dinner, William explained that he had very high expectations of promotion. Nevertheless, he felt himself unsatisfied since he did not have the houses, cars and watches that some of his companions had. Speaking about their respective jobs, William asked Paula if the results of XYZ were going to be good in the present year. Paula wanted to make an impression, and gave him an extended answer. XYZ's results were going to be excellent for a number of reasons, which she went on to explain in detail. During the following days, Paula and William met at different events. William took advantage of any occasion to question her about XYZ. One day, when Paula was in her office, William called her, but this time he did not ask any questions. Instead, he made her a proposition. His bank offered her a substantial amount of money to obtain, in advance, the monthly results of XYZ.

Questions:

1. What traits do the characters of this case show?
2. Is there anything wrong in Paula's behaviour when she provided William with information about XYZ?
3. What would you recommend Paula to do about the offer?
4. Would you offer her any advice about her future behaviour?

Summary

Ethics is at the core of human action. Principle and norms, values (goods) and virtues have a role in evaluating the morality of a human action (ethical evaluation).

The person-centred approach (PCA) to business ethics proposed here takes as its main points of reference human excellence or flourishing, which requires human virtues.

Apart from virtues, the PCA includes considering human goods and principles and their corresponding norms.

Truth, beauty, friendship, religion (transcendence) and life are fundamental human goods.

Dealing with people requires, first, the recognition that humans have a constitutive dignity; that is, an intrinsic value, regardless of race, age, gender or any other particular condition, and also one that is independent of any legal recognition.

The Personalist Principle derives from the intrinsic worth of the human being. This principle states that 'every human being should never be treated as a mere means to an end' (negative formulation). Persons should be treated not only with respect, but also with compassion, a sense of collaboration and 'neighbourly love' (positive formulation).

Human dignity, together with the Personalist Principle and human goods, provides a sound foundation for human rights, and has a wide application in business ethics.

The common good is a good potentially shared by all members of a community. It can be understood as the external conditions of a community (socio-cultural, organizational and economic) that foster the personal development of its members.

The principle of the common good states that: 'In acting in a social context, both individual and social institutions have to contribute to the common good in accordance with the concurrent circumstances and their respective capacities and harmonize or subordinate their own interests to the common good.'

There are four fundamental human virtues: (1) practical wisdom; (2) justice (understood in a broad sense); (3) courage; and (4) self-control. These virtues include all other virtues necessary for human excellence.

The mainstream theories applied to business ethics, and particularly to decision-making, include Deontologism (Kantianism and Natural Rights Theory); Utilitarianism; theories rooted in political traditions, such as the Integrative Social Contract Theory and Discursive Ethics; and theories that follow the Aristotelian tradition. The latter focus on the agent and his or her moral character (virtue ethics).

The first sign of corruption in a society that is still alive is that the end justifies the means.[1]

Georges Bernanos (1888–1948)
French writer.

Chapter Aims

This chapter will allow you to:

- become familiar with different meanings of responsibility and to distinguish between responsibility, accountability and liability
- discuss for what, and to whom, we are responsible
- gain an understanding of the criteria for ascribing responsibility
- consider to what extent individuals within an organization bear responsibility for their actions
- distinguish four forms of the moral responsibility of an individual within an organization
- discuss what is actually the responsibility of an individual within an organization
- distinguish between direct and indirect intentionality, and to gain an understanding of responsibility for the consequences of one's actions
- understand more thoroughly how to formulate moral judgements – in particular, when an action brings about both good and bad effects, including actions of cooperation with bad effects.

Key terms:

Accountability	Intentionality	Responsibility for commission
Action directly voluntary	Invincible ignorance	Responsibility for cooperation
Action indirectly voluntary	Judgements of conscience	Responsibility for induction
Antecedent responsibility	Legal responsibility	Responsibility for omission
Collateral effects	Liability	Role model
Congruent responsibility	Material cooperation	Scandal
Consent of the will	Milgram's experiment	Secondary effects
Consequent responsibility	Moral certainty	Side effects
Direct intentionality	Moral conscience	Social responsibility
Doctrinal advice	Moral responsibility	Transcendent responsibility
Formal cooperation	Negligence	Triple Font Theory
Good example	Persuasion	Vincible ignorance
Impulsive advice	Principle of Double Effect	Voluntariness
Indirect intentionality	Recklessness	Voluntary in the cause
Intentional ignorance	Responsibility	

Individual Responsibility and Moral Judgements in Business

INTRODUCTORY CASE 5:

WORLDCOM – THE DILEMMA OF CYNTHIA F. COOPER

In 2002, WorldCom (now MCI Inc.) was the second largest long-distance telephone company in the USA, with 20 million customers and over 80,000 employees in 100 countries. Surprisingly, this company had been set up only 16 years earlier, when Bernard (Bernie) Ebbers and several other local investors founded Long Distance Discount Services (LDDS), which changed its name to WorldCom in 1989. In the 1990s, WorldCom acquired dozens of companies, including MCI, three times the size of WorldCom. This growth required a series of sophisticated financial operations. Scott Sullivan, WorldCom's chief financial officer (CFO), was a key person in such growth.

The Enron scandal, at the end of 2001, was very recent, and WorldCom had Arthur Andersen as an external auditor, as had Enron. In March 2002, the Stock Exchange Commission (SEC) extended its investigation to WorldCom. At this time, the stock had dropped below $5 and the credit problem became more and more serious. In April 2002, the board of directors forced Ebbers to resign, but he received a severance package of $1.5 million a year for the rest of his life, in addition to other lavish perks.

Simultaneously, Cynthia F. Cooper, Vice President of Internal Auditing at WorldCom, began to be concerned about suspicious financial transactions and accounting. The concern started when a senior line manager complained to her that her boss, CFO Scott Sullivan, had usurped a $400 million reserve account he had set aside as a hedge against anticipated revenue losses. Cynthia had a great dilemma to resolve, since she did not know what to do with such information, and feared being involved in the cover up of a fraud. In addition, she had no clear evidence with which to probe what had happened.

She decided to talk about the issue with WorldCom's CFO Scott Sullivan, but this turned out to place her in direct conflict with him, as well as the company's auditor, Arthur Andersen. However, Cynthia did not give up and decided to keep on investigating in secret, often late at night. Helped by an expert in information technology, she accessed WorldCom's computerized accounting information system. Thus, she obtained evidence that fraud was being committed. Her investigation revealed that the company was trying to represent operation costs as capital expenditures to make the company appear to have more profits.

When Sullivan found out about her investigation, he asked Cooper to delay her work until the third quarter. She decided otherwise and, in June 2002, informed the audit committee of WorldCom's board of directors that the company had covered up $3.8 billion in losses through suspect accounting practices. The company immediately announced this accounting fraud and Sullivan was fired. When these facts became known, WorldCom shares fell 76 per cent in after hours trading. This incident led to the biggest stock market crash of the time. Almost simultaneously, it was announced that WorldCom would cut 17,000 jobs.

In July 2002, only one month after Cynthia had blown the whistle, WorldCom declared bankruptcy and reappeared in 2004 with the name of MCI Inc. It was the biggest bankruptcy in US corporate history. The company had to restate finances, reorganize and settle the debt. It was a monumental task to revive the company, which took over 500 WorldCom employees, plus 800 from two consulting firms. The real WorldCom accounting fraud involved over $11 billion and the accumulated debt rose to around $365 million.

In 2003, a special investigative committee of the Board of Directors of WorldCom, reported that 'from the first quarter of 2001 through the first quarter of 2002, WorldCom improperly capitalized approximately $3.5 billion of operating line costs in violation of well-established accounting standards and WorldCom's own capitalization policy. Various employees indicated that Sullivan decided the amounts WorldCom would capitalize'.[2] This report added:

> Ebbers was autocratic in his dealings with the Board, and the Board permitted it. With limited exceptions, the members of the Board were reluctant to challenge Ebbers even when they disagreed with him. They, like most observers, were impressed with the company's growth and Ebbers' reputation, although they were in some cases mystified or perplexed by his style. This was Ebbers' company. Several members of the Board were sophisticated, yet the members of the Board were deferential to Ebbers and passive in their oversight until April 2002.[3]

Sullivan acknowledged his leading role in WorldCom's accounting fraud. He recognized that from 1999 until May 2002, WorldCom, under his direction, manipulated the books and oversaw billions of dollars of company expenses in order to hide its declining financial condition. Actually, in 1999 Ebbers had said to Sullivan that he must do everything necessary to present excellent quarterly figures and to pay off the company's burdensome acquisition debts.

In 2005, Sullivan was sentenced to five years in prison – a fifth of what sentencing guidelines suggested. He regretted his actions: 'Every day I regret what happened at WorldCom', he told Judge Jones. 'I violated the trust placed in me. My actions are inexcusable ... I chose the wrong road and in the face of intense pressure I turned away from the truth.' WorldCom's former CEO, Ebbers, received a 25-year prison sentence for the fraud.

Cynthia Cooper was named as Person of the Year (one of three) by *Time Magazine* in 2002. In 2003, she received the Accounting Exemplar Award for people of high professionalism and ethics in accounting practices or education. Since then, she has been travelling extensively, giving talks to students and business leaders. In 2008, she published a book explaining her experiences.[4]

Questions:

1. What do you think about the decisions taken by Scott Sullivan? Is he fully responsible for them?

2. Would Cynthia Cooper have borne any responsibility for Sullivan's fraud if she had done nothing?

3. What is your moral judgement on Cynthia Cooper's decision to conduct a secret investigation of the corporate accounts with the help of the information systems technician?

4. What about Cynthia Cooper's decision to inform the board's audit committee about possible irregularities carried out by her boss, Scott Sullivan?

5. What do you think about the award given to Cynthia Cooper?

Sources: D. Collins, 'WorldCom', in R.W. Kolb (ed.), *Encyclopedia of Business Ethics and Society* (Los Angeles: Sage, 2008): 2275–6; C. Cooper, *Extraordinary Circumstances: The Journey of a Corporate Whistleblower* (Hoboken, NJ: Willey, 2008); K. Crawford, 'Ex - WorldCom CEO Ebbers Guilty', *CNN/Money*, 15 March (2005): http://www.money.cnn.com/2005/03/15/news/newsmakers/ebbers/index.htm; R. Lacayo and A. Ripley, 'Persons of the Year', *Time*, 22 December (2002); J. D. Moberg and E. Romar, 'WorldCom', Markkula Center for Applied Ethics, Santa Clara University, (2003), http://www.scu.edu/ethics/dialogue/candc/cases/worldcom.html; S. C. Pandey and P. Verma, 'From WorldCom to MCI", *Decision* 33 (2006): 141–90; 'WorldCom Bigs indicted', *CBS*, 2 March (2004), http://www.cbsnews.com/stories/2004/03/03/national/main603749.shtml; Wikipedia (WorldCom); BBC report: http://www.news.bbc.co.uk/2/hi/business/2077838.stm: Time report: http://www.time.com/time/subscriber/personoftheyear/2002/poycooper.html

RESPONSIBILITY, ACCOUNTABILITY AND LIABILITY

The whole idea of responsibility is associated with the capability of answering for one's own acts. The word 'responsibility' is derived from the Latin *respondere*, meaning 'to respond'. It refers to the human ability to undertake acts due to one's own free will. Therefore, responsibility presupposes freedom; that is, that individuals who act are in control of their actions: they are not mere mechanisms in which 'behaviour' occurs automatically due to external stimulus.[5] This had already been noted by Aristotle, who affirmed that 'a man is the origin of his action'.[6]

In business, as in other ambits, responsibility has different meanings, but each of these has to do with giving answers or with being answerable for actions.

Responsibility as a virtue

When we call someone a 'responsible person' or remark that he 'conducts himself responsibly', we refer to a positive character trait. A responsible person is one who acts with deliberation about his deeds and their consequences. Being responsible is a sign of moral maturity and is closely related to trustworthiness.

Responsibility as obligation

In this case, responsibility involves a certain activity entrusted or assigned, or a duty or job inherent in a position. This is the meaning, for instance, if we say: 'She is responsible for logistics.' Within organizations, managers and employees bear certain responsibilities and have to answer for compliance with them. In a broad sense, this duty can also be understood as self-assumed in response to one's awareness of the needs of one's peers, and of how such needs might be met.

Responsibility as attribution

This refers to the cause or condition of the ascription or imputation of an action, or of its consequences. We attribute responsibility when we say: 'He is responsible for this fraud,' or 'He is responsible on account of his negligence.' Similarly, this meaning of responsibility indicates who is required to compensate for damages due to misbehaviour.

Responsibility, in the sense of attribution or imputation of an action or its consequences to an agent, is especially relevant to both ethics and legal studies. However, in the legal field, responsibility is only mentioned in connection with offences or crimes to determine guilt,[7] whereas in ethics it refers to all manner of human actions, good or bad, and therefore meritorious or blameworthy. In ethics, it is known as 'moral responsibility'.

Accountability

This is related to responsibility but with a narrower meaning, although especially significant in the business world. It can be defined as being open to judgement by one's peers or, indeed, by the entire society, on the basis of the implicit or explicit expectations or rights of those forming the judgement. Accountability can take the form of written or verbal explanations or justifications for one's activities.

While accountability seeks to explain actions performed, individually or collectively, responsibility focuses on being the author of actions. Although the terms can sometimes be used synonymously, they are quite distinct. For instance, managers can delegate responsibilities, and those who accept them ought to answer for fulfilling the associated duties. However, managers who delegate do not renounce accountability for the tasks they have delegated. Similarly, one can argue over who is responsible for a fraud within a company, but the company as a whole must be accountable.

Liability

This refers to the responsibility of fulfilling one's legal obligations and the demands of equity. For instance, in business, we speak of 'product liability' and 'accounting liability'. Product liability is the responsibility for any injuries one's products might cause. This responsibility is borne by those who make a product available to the public (manufacturers, distributors, suppliers and retailers). 'Accounting liability' is defined as obligations arising from past transactions or events, the settlement of which might result in the transfer or use of assets, provision of services or other yields of economic benefits in the future.[8]

FOR WHAT AND TO WHOM ARE WE RESPONSIBLE?

Human freedom has two main features: self-possession and self-determination.[9] *Self-possession* means that the human individual is the owner of his or her acts. *Self-determination* expresses the human capacity to make choices, which includes deciding to act or not, or to follow one course of action or another. Both elements are fundamental to individual responsibility. Every individual is responsible for his or her truly free acts; that is, all acts over which one has dominion. In other words, I am answerable for the acts that depend on me, acts of which I am conscious and that I wish to perform. This leads to the concept of *voluntariness*, meaning that human action proceeds from one's own choice and free will.

Some people speak as if one were only responsible for the consequences of an action, but this is simplistic. Carlos Llano identified four forms of responsibility: antecedent, consequent, congruent and transcendent.[10]

Antecedent responsibility

Responsibility includes, first of all, the action itself. It would be irresponsible to lack sound reasons for one's action. Thus there is an antecedent responsibility that consists of acting only after possessing proper justification.

Consequent responsibility

It would also be irresponsible to fail to own up to the consequences of one's actions, seeking to attribute them to someone else. The question arises: For which consequences is one responsible? Is the agent responsible only for the immediate consequence of the action? Is there responsibility only for clearly foreseeable consequences, or also for possible but improbable consequences? Is one responsible for every effect of an action, including those that were impossible to foresee? To what extent is one responsible for a chain of events derived from an action when other causes might also have contributed? These are questions we try to answer in this chapter.

Congruent responsibility

There are two more forms of responsibility that, though not often reflected upon, are important at the personal level. One, which can be called congruent responsibility, is present when one is faced with a situation in which one sees the need for congruency, or consistency, of the action contemplated and one's vision of life.[11] This 'congruent responsibility' refers to a 'vital' attitude of acting in harmony with what one is (or would like to be). This could happen under the pressure of circumstances which requires one to adopt a certain attitude. For instance, awaking to the reality of being surrounded by people in need, or noticing a chance to contribute to solving important problems, or perhaps a political or social situation that requires the making of a commitment. In business, this could happen, for instance, in the case of critical situations in which a manager is especially indispensable to a firm's survival.

Transcendent responsibility

There is also a responsibility derived from discovering a personal calling or 'vocation' to carry out a certain mission on the world. This includes, first, personal growth as a human being. Let us not forget that human actions have internal effects on the subjects who perform them. Agents develop themselves, acquiring virtues and vices through their actions. There is a more specific sense of professional vocation. It might be strong in doctors, nurses or teachers, but, in a certain sense, any noble human work, including management, amounts to a calling.[12] Frequently, this calling and the responsibility to follow it, is connected with transcendence and divinity: thus, it is called a *transcendent* responsibility.

In this book, there is insufficient space to deal with these latter two forms of responsibility, which posit complex philosophical questions.

Regarding the question: 'For what and to whom are we responsible?', we can distinguish at least three types of responsibilities:

Legal responsibility

By virtue of living in society, we acquire legal responsibility, which entails answering to public authorities, including to courts, regarding our compliance with or infringement of the law.

Social responsibility

This is related to social expectations and to the impact of actions on society. One aspect of this response is the impact of our actions on the natural environment. (In this sense, we can speak of *environmental responsibility*.)

Moral responsibility

This regards ethical requirements. This responsibility can be judged by the people around us, but everyone also has 'an internal judge' known as *moral conscience*, which applauds or reproaches one's actions and can even produce inner joy or deep remorse. Some philosophers – and, of course, many religions – add that we are, above all, responsible to God, the author of the moral law and the supreme judge of all. In this sense, moral responsibility is responsibility to God.

Aristotle was probably the first in initiating a reflection on moral responsibility.[13] Since then, philosophical reflection on moral responsibility has had a long history. Our aim here is only to provide a few basic but useful insights for business ethics.

MORAL RESPONSIBILITY AND ITS MODIFIERS

Voluntariness – when an action proceeds from one's own choice and free will – entails rational knowledge of the action, together with the aim that guides it, and the agent's inner consent to performing it. These two elements determine moral responsibility for a human action. Thus, establishing the degree to which an action can be ascribed to an agent requires that we consider both the *intellect's knowledge* and the *will's consent*: in other words, to what extent an act proceeds from the agent's own understanding and free decision.

Voluntariness is complete or perfect if the agent has full knowledge and full consent when performing an action. If knowledge or consent is for some reason diminished, the voluntariness is incomplete, and the responsibility partial. The following presents a few factors that can modify the degree of an agent's responsibility.

Modifiers of knowledge

The agent might suffer from a lack of knowledge of some material or ethical aspect of the action. A simple example should suffice: one who pays for something with counterfeit currency is most probably aware that it is wrong to do so (knowledge of the ethical norm): however, the person might not realize that the currency is false (ignorance of a relevant material aspect).

We can distinguish three aspects of ignorance or lack of awareness: the invincible, the vincible and the intentional:

- *Invincible ignorance*: This is when ignorance cannot be overcome by reasonable means (a relatively easy investigation, asking an expert when there is a suspicion that something is wrong and so on). Invincible ignorance or lack of awareness eliminates the voluntariness of an action. Therefore, an action preceded by invincible ignorance or lack of awareness is not morally ascribable to the agent.

- *Vincible ignorance*: Vincible ignorance originates in a person's negligence or lack of interest in personal training, in the failure to ask for advice, or in the failure to pay close enough attention. When ignorance or lack of awareness is avoidable (vincible), these actions are morally imputable. Guilt increases in proportion to negligence, recklessness or the demonstrable lack of concern about an action's seriousness.

- *Intentional ignorance*: In some cases, the ignorance or lack of awareness is studied or purposeful. This occurs when someone wilfully avoids finding out what his or her responsibilities are, or overlooks them in order to evade them. This attitude leads to the intentional avoidance of knowing those things one is obliged to know. It might be due to a particular interest (generally economic). Purposeful ignorance is not only ascribable to the agent, but is also morally more serious than avoidable ignorance, because it is the consequence not merely of convenience or negligence, but also of a lack of moral rectitude.

Modifiers of consent of the will

Some situations can lack voluntariness because of an absence, to some degree, of consent of the will. It is worth noting that *feeling* and *giving consent* are not the same thing. Feelings arise spontaneously or in response to external stimuli, but consent does not exist until these feelings are freely accepted or 'owned'. For example, an action against our interests can cause feelings of aversion or hatred toward the person who harmed us. But this is different from *wanting* to hate, which is a deliberate and free act that transforms the felt hatred into consented to or accepted hatred.

Several factors can affect the voluntary nature of an action, causing a partial or even a complete absence of consent:

- *Mental illness or physical factors.* The use of reason can be affected by various causes, including mental illness and other diseases. In such cases, voluntariness can be limited or even non-existent. Acting under the effects of inebriation or drugs also decreases the will's role, although one might have initially willed to be under the influence.

- *Existence of force*: This is when violence or any physical coercion is used to make someone do something against his or her will. The victim of force has no responsibility if he or she does not internally consent. If the victim consents reluctantly, responsibility is reduced, though not erased.

- *Strong emotions.* Emotions are a mental and physiological state associated with a wide variety of feelings, thoughts and behaviour. They can bring about great intensity in the performance of an action. Anger or rage can be relevant in some situations, as can strong fear. 'He was blinded with anger', or 'She fell into a fit of rage' are expressions that denote acting under the influence of strong emotions. The moral responsibility of a person affected by anger depends on the extent to which it was willed. One can act moved by spontaneous anger when insulted. In this case, the voluntariness lessens and so, too, does the responsibility. In some cases, strong emotion causes a complete loss of control. Very violent, spontaneous emotion might preclude any moral responsibility. However, this is rarely the case.

  One can become angry voluntarily; for example, by brooding over insults, humiliations or other bad experiences from the past. Such emotions can entail more voluntariness in subsequent actions, even more than if the emotions were absent – emotion here does not lessen responsibility and could even increase it.

- *Intellectual fear.* An understanding of a possible evil and a movement of the will to avoid it by rationally devised means. Intellectual fear can appear, for instance, when someone fakes a document for fear of losing a job, or when telling a lie for fear of being disgraced. Intellectual fear is different from emotional fear. The former occurs when one acts *from* fear; the latter when one acts *with* fear. Although intellectual fear can be accompanied by emotional fear, it is conceptually different. Intellectual fear does not eliminate voluntariness, though it can diminish it and, with it, the corresponding moral responsibility.

- *Habits*: Prevailing dispositions of character give a settled tendency or usual manner of behaviour, for good and for ill. Habits are acquired by repetition of similar acts, and they influence performance. Acts done out of habit are done easily, with little or no deliberation. Thus, for instance, some people lie frequently and almost without awareness or forethought, having acquired the habit early in life. Others are reluctant to fulfil certain duties because of sheer laziness – another habit. There is responsibility in the voluntary acquisition of habits, however. In performing a particular action, the voluntariness depends on the degree of awareness with which the act is performed, as well as the amount of effort expended to free oneself from the pattern.

- *Sociological factors*: These factors are related to the cultural and social environment, customs and, sometimes, genuine pressures from an organization or from the immediate work environment. To some extent, these can also diminish responsibility. However, it is difficult to say to what extent sociological factors can do so.

Detailed analyses of the factors that can modify the consent of the will are beyond the scope of the present work. In fact, each situation has its own elements and, in some cases, specific knowledge from experts might be needed.

FORMS OF INDIVIDUAL RESPONSIBILITY

Four forms of moral responsibility can be distinguished; two due to individual actions themselves, and two by virtue of contributions to the actions of others (see Figure 5.1):

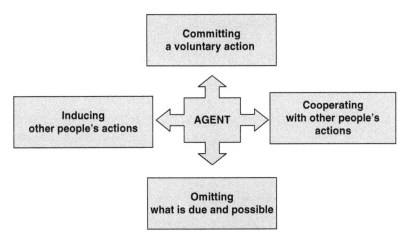

Figure 5.1   Forms of individual responsibility

Performing a voluntary action

Responsibility for performing a voluntary action is commonplace (for example, selling a product, requesting or approving an advertising campaign, committing fraud and so on). Every directly voluntary act is ascribable to its author or agents, since it is the result of deliberation and free choice. As noted, when someone performs an act, he or she becomes personally responsible for it and for its reasonably foreseeable and avoidable consequences.

Omitting what is both due and possible

An omission, in the ethical sense, takes place when one fails to perform a feasible action, despite an obligation to do so. For example, the failure to establish the necessary rules to protect worker health, or to provide the necessary resources for safety and hygiene in the workplace, would be acts of omission by the manager. Consequently, to the extent that an action could and should have been carried out, the individual is guilty of omission.

An omission can be fully deliberate; that is, with direct intentionality. This occurs when someone omits something knowingly while being perfectly aware of the obligation to act – when one can act but does not. Full responsibility attaches to such conscious omission. This responsibility or guilt can be greater if the omission was premeditated or done with real malice.

There are others types of omissions, more frequent in business life, that do not involve direct intentionality. These occur when someone fails to perform a feasible action due to lack of awareness of the situation or lack of consciousness of the obligation. These omissions can fall under the headings of negligence or recklessness:

- *Negligence* entails a failure to act with the prudence that a reasonable person would exercise under the same circumstances. For instance, maintaining obsolete equipment through lack of interest in staying abreast of technological innovations, or losing a contract due to lack of attention to the correct preparation of a tender.
- *Recklessness* is conduct characterized by a conscious and dangerous disregard of others' safety or well-being, resulting in the creation of an obvious and substantial risk of harm (safety in industrial facilities, in driving and so on).[14] Recklessness can also be present in behaviours driven by an intemperate activism, for example, or running excessive risks without carrying out a serious study or seeking adequate advice.

Responsibility increases in proportion to the degree of negligence, recklessness or lack of concern demonstrated and the seriousness of the omission (for example, the responsibility is greater when human lives are at stake, as opposed to material goods).

Inducing other people to action

In acting or in failing to act, one can induce others to act similarly. Faced with the inducement of their managers, subordinates are still responsible for their own actions, but they are often largely conditioned by the actions of their managers and co-workers.

One way to induce people to act is by *persuasion*. This can be done in various ways, including *giving advice* and *praising* or *criticizing* one's decisions and actions. People whose position or profession gives them special influence over an action have an added responsibility. Consultants, lawyers and others with experience or prestige fall into this category.

Inducement to wrongdoing can take the form of advice with no moral consideration whatsoever (*impulsive advice*) or advice that denies the immorality of the act and persuades the person that the act is actually good (*doctrinal advice*), which is even more serious. Those who induce others in wrongdoing through advice or persuasion are responsible for the action regardless of whether they acted in bad faith, with invincible ignorance, or with serious negligence.

Acting as a *role model* is another means of influence. Managers can be role models for people in their organization. Someone who behaves well sets an example. People who behave poorly set a bad example. It is well known that people are influenced by the expressed thoughts and actions of others in their social environment, even in the absence of explicit advice or attempts at persuasion. We have a natural tendency to try to emulate the achievements of others and to imitate some aspects of their lives. We often adopt certain people as role models of conduct. The responsibility for setting a good or bad example depends largely on the level of recognition or authority of the one who influences and on the personality of the 'influence'.

Any inducement to misbehaviour in others is termed '*scandal*' (in a moral sense) – etymologically, 'stumbling block'. In its common language sense, scandal usually means an apparent violation of morality or propriety; in a moral sense, it is closer to its original meaning, in that it leads one to stumble and fall. It could be defined as an attitude or behaviour that leads others into wrongdoing, or an impediment that prevents others from improvement.

Sometimes both good examples and scandals are *direct*; that is, deliberate and intentional attempts to influence others. Sometimes, however, they are *indirect*; their purpose is not to induce others to act, though some imitation might be foreseen. In direct scandal, there is full guilt.

However, an indirect scandal is not always imputable, since it could be an unavoidable effect of a just action. This occurs, for example, when someone follows the example of another in the belief that a company has secured government contracts through peddling influence, when in fact this is not the case. When it can be foreseen that indirect scandal might occur, reasonable means should be taken to prevent it (in the influence-peddling example, the circumstances should be explained in order to prevent misinterpretations).

Cooperating with the actions of others

In business, people often perform actions in cooperation with others. Manufacturers cooperate with salespeople and vice versa, designers cooperate with manufacturers, investors cooperate with the enterprises in which they invest, suppliers cooperate with the activity of their clients through the products or services they provide, buyers cooperate with the activity of the company that sells to them, advertising agencies cooperate by providing economic support to the media in which their advertisements are placed and so on. Ethical issues can arise in certain cases of cooperation. For instance, when a manager gives in to the wishes of a corrupt politician or civil servant who asks for a commission to 'speed up' matters, or when someone acts as a supplier to a company that carries out questionable activities, or when someone in a company decides to sponsor depraved television programmes.

In cooperating with others' actions, one shares in them – including in their morality – to some extent. This form of responsibility is termed *complicity* when one participates in a wrongful act. Complicity can be by not disclosing or not hindering wrong actions when one has an obligation to do so, or by covering up for those who have committed a crime. Cooperation with good actions should be fostered, and cooperation in wrongdoing avoided. However, sometimes people are under heavy pressure to participate. This often presents delicate situations, requiring a rigorous analysis. We will return to this point later, but let us first consider the following findings on individuals within organizations.

> **Insight 5:**
>
> **Milgram's experiment**
>
> At the beginning of the 1960s, the psychologist Stanley Milgram (1933–84)[15] carried out an experiment on obedience to authority. He tried to answer a question that arose after the Second World War: Could someone turn into an Adolf Eichmann?[16] First, Milgram gathered 40 people, asking them to participate voluntarily in an experiment on learning. He asked a professional actor to play the role of the student (the victim), while the volunteers were the teachers. The 'experimental scientist' – the authority figure – was played by an impressive man dressed in a white coat. Each 'teacher' in his turn was placed in a separate room from the 'student' so that they could communicate but could not see each other. The teacher was given an electroshock generator, ranging up to 450 volts, and a list of word pairs that he was to teach the student. If the answer were incorrect, the teacher would give the student a shock, increasing the voltage for each wrong answer. After a number of increases, the actor started to bang on the wall; finally, after several episodes of banging and complaining about his heart condition, all responses by the student would cease. If, at any time, the subject indicated his desire to halt the experiment, the scientist firmly ordered him to continue.
>
> The most amazing thing to note is that 65 per cent of the subjects administered shocks in excess of 400 volts, while the rest stopped the experiment. Milgram performed variations of the experiment and obtained similar results, the interpretation of which is controversial. The agent cedes control to an authority, but are the 'Milgram subjects' responsible for their cruelty of wilfully injuring an innocent and defenceless person?

RESPONSIBILITY OF INDIVIDUALS WITHIN ORGANIZATIONS

Individuals within organizations are involved in formal and informal structures and can experience powerful pressure to meet corporate goals or objectives. They can be constrained or even coerced by others' power – which presents no problems if the action in question is good, but that is not always so. As to the responsibility of individuals within an organization, some social psychologists stress the influence of the organizational context on personal behaviour to such an extent that people in an organization are regarded as automatons: apparently their character and personal traits are irrelevant in explaining their behaviours.[17] To support this argument, Milgram's experiment on the reaction of people under authority is frequently cited (see Insight 5).

There are other laboratory experiments that offer some support to the Milgram experiment.[18] A frequent conclusion of social psychologists is that a relatively high percentage of people obey orders, whatever they might be, ignoring their own conscience. Nevertheless, strong objections can be marshalled. The first comes from personality psychologists who tend to acknowledge relevant personal freedom and personality traits even in the organizational context and to criticize the laboratory experiences of many social psychologists as being far removed from the real world.[19]

Other objection comes from considering that, even in the context of the Milgram experiments, not 100 per cent of the participants obeyed orders. People with stronger character and greater ethical sensitivity will be less likely to obey an order that runs contrary to conscience.

In spite of many limitations, Milgram and related experiments make it clear that social conditions can have a real influence on personal behaviours, which underlines the importance of the organization in misbehaviours. Such experiments also illustrate the difficulties of identifying the extent to which actions are voluntary within hierarchical organizations when strong pressures exist.

In practice, different people exhibit varying degrees of susceptibility to situational pressure from their organizations, which makes moral conduct more or less difficult for each individual.[20] Indeed, organizational pressure is one of the sociological factors mentioned earlier (p. 107) that can decrease voluntariness and blame in an employee who is obliged to commit wrongdoing, especially if one is in a position with little decision-making authority, where refusing to follow an order or suggestion could have serious consequences.

However, in general, it is not true that an individual within an organization can do nothing except obey when he or she is pressured to misbehave. In many cases, the employee will be able to report negative pressures to superiors, or even to external entities with the power and, presumably, the willingness to take corrective action (*whistle-blowing*).[21] Under other circumstances, a manager or employee pressured to act unethically or to cooperate in wrongdoing might proclaim an objection of conscience or, as a last resort, leave the firm. In other situations, the cooperation of an individual with the action of others within an organization can be a 'material cooperation with wrongdoing' that might be acceptable under certain conditions, as we will discuss below.

MORAL JUDGEMENTS: THE TRIPLE FONT OF MORALITY THEORY

In any human action one can evaluate both the responsibility of the agent (blameworthy or praiseworthy) and the objective morality of the action. The latter requires sound moral judgement.

A judgement of an action's morality, according to a theory termed 'Triple Font of Morality' (or simply Triple Font Theory)[22] should consider three elements:

- The *intention* of the agent; that is, the aim of performing an action evaluated in moral terms.

- The *moral object* (or simply *object*) of the action: This is the action chosen as a means to achieve the aim with regard to its morality. When we describe a transaction as a fair deal or a swindle, or when we say that a theft or murder has occurred, we are talking about the 'moral object' of certain human actions. Notice that the object is different from a 'neutral' description of the action. Thus, killing a man is the empirical fact, but might describe an assassination or an act of self-defence – two very different occurrences, morally speaking (different *objects*).

- *Circumstances.* Circumstances include relevant aspects of the situation, including the socio-cultural context where the action takes place and the consequences (*consequent circumstances*) arising from the action. Circumstance can aggravate or attenuate the moral seriousness of a decision. Some circumstances can also change the moral object (for example, acting in self-defence when facing an unjust aggressor).

The justification for including the first two elements (intention and object) is that, in performing an action, we choose an end and elect a means. Since both elements are *intentional*, we are responsible for both in any human act. Actually, in the mind of a decision-maker, intention and object form a unit. In other words, they are two aspects of a single voluntary human act. The inseparable unity of the intention and object leads to the conclusion that, for a human action to be good (ethically correct), both the intention and the object must be good, since a thing is good only when all its parts are good. This point leads us to enunciate the following principle:

For a decision to be morally good, both the intention and the object must be good.

Consequently:

- *Choosing a wrong object corrupts the decision*, even if the intention is good. For example, committing a fraud to save the company from bankruptcy is bad, not because of the intention, but because of the morality of the chosen action (object).

- *A wrong intention makes the decision, as a whole, wrong*, even if the object is good. This is so, for instance, when a person gives to charity (object) purely out of vanity (intention), or if a boss deals kindly with subordinates (object) in order to manipulate them (intention).

In simpler terms, 'the end does not justify the means' or, more explicitly: 'a good end does not justify morally wrong means'.

It is therefore unacceptable to do wrong in the hope that some good will come of it. Applying it to some common business situations, one would conclude that it is not ethically acceptable, for instance, to 'cook the (accounting) books' to secure a loan that would be crucial to a company's survival; or to deceive clients about product quality to maintain even badly needed income, or to offer a bribe to obtain an important contract.

Consequently, to make a sound moral judgement, correct identification of the intention and object is crucial. In some cases, apparently 'dirty' means are not actually 'bad means' because, considering all relevant elements of an action, it is reasonable to think that the object of such action is morally acceptable. This is the case, for instance, of giving money to an extortionist in extreme situations in order to obtain a legitimate right.[23] However, there are some objects that are never acceptable (intrinsically wrong actions). We will consider this point below in dealing with the morality of the object (pp. 113–14) and with the principle of double effect (pp. 117–20).

Morality of the end (intention)

An intention is good if it is directed towards a human good.[24] The moral quality of the intention can range from merely acceptable to excellent, depending on the purpose for which the action is performed. The more valuable the end of a decision, the better the intention and, therefore, the higher the moral quality of the decision.

For instance, acting to earn money honestly is a good intention, but the moral quality of the intention will be greater to the extent that the one who acts gives others the same consideration as him- or herself. In other words, dealing with people and respecting their dignity and rights is sufficient for a good intention, but the intention is better if one tries to serve people in the best possible manner.

Morality of the means (object)

The morality of the means is determined by reference to ethical values (human goods) and the corresponding ethical principles. The Golden Rule, the Personalist Principle and the Principle of the Common Good are particularly relevant.[25] Practical rationality, as well as the intention and relevant circumstances, is essential for determining the objects, as we will discuss (pp. 114–15).

An means is not ethically acceptable (licit) if one of the following obtains:

- *The action is intrinsically wrong.* Certain actions are directly contrary to human dignity, and to other moral absolutes included in the negative formulation of the Personalist Principle, or actions directly oriented to erode the common good. These actions are ethically unacceptable whatever the intention and circumstances. For example, falsely reporting employee misbehaviour is always unacceptable.

- *The action is wrong under certain circumstances.* There are actions that are always wrong; others are wrong only in a particular situation, depending on the circumstances. For instance, reporting real misbehaviour of an employee to those who have a right to know is acceptable, sometimes even compulsory.

However, it is wrong to make such misbehaviour public among people who have no right to know of it.

- *An action is reasonably disproportionate to its consequences.* This would be the case of a disproportionate punishment of an employee for an act of insubordination, or a sanction so severe that it would bring about effects worse than the good aimed at (for instance, the negative effect of employing coercion to discourage misbehaviour for the sake of the positive aim of maintaining discipline). Another example would be undertaking a dangerous task involving a risk to life or health that was disproportionate in comparison with the necessity of such work, or with the benefit it would secure.

- *The action is forbidden by a just law.* Just laws produce moral obligation. Acting in compliance with fair laws is an ethical duty for social life derived from the necessity of an authority's governance of a community. Indeed, some ethical values are specified by laws. For instance, laws provide specific and reasonable rules for respecting the right to life and health in the workplace. Such rules should be followed, not only for fear of legal coercion but also out of moral obligation. However, unjust laws do not give rise to any moral obligation. Laws are unjust, for instance, when they are contrary to human rights.

Aggravating and attenuating circumstances

Intention and object are the primary fonts of morality, but also circumstances can sometimes be relevant for arriving at an accurate moral judgement. As noted (p. 112), certain circumstances can aggravate or attenuate the moral seriousness of a decision. Consequences are circumstances which present a special problematic, which will be considered below (pp. 115–7). An example of relevant circumstances would be the misappropriation of corporate funds by an employee. Whatever the intention, the object is a theft (withdrawing money without the reasonable will of its owner), which is not right. The amount of money stolen is a circumstance that makes the decision more or less serious from a moral, and even legal, point of view. However, the amount of money stolen does not change the object of the decision (theft), but only 'adjusts' the culpability of such a decision, and subsequent action.

PRACTICAL WISDOM IN MAKING MORAL JUDGEMENTS

Practical wisdom is crucial for formulating moral judgements, because these refer to particular situations that are in some respects unique. As has been explained in Chapter 4 (p. 87), practical wisdom is a virtue that reinforces practical rationality, through which we make moral judgements.

Principles and norms aid in making moral judgements, especially for those whose practical wisdom is not well developed. Principles, norms and other ethical standards usually gather conclusions of practical wisdom accumulated through the ages. They help especially through a set of negative duties, which point to actions that should never be committed – such as stealing, lying or committing slander – and signal certain universally accepted minimum standards.

Principles and norms also provide positive duties and signal a direction but have no upper limit. Their specific contents can be determined by considering, with the help of practical wisdom, the particular circumstances of a given situation.

Moral judgements are also called 'judgements of conscience' because compliance with them is revealed in each person's conscience as obligatory. Frequently, judgements of conscience provide a personal conviction that an action is indubitably right, based on the certainty of a conclusion formed after sincere and rigorous deliberation. This type of certainty is known as *prudential* or *moral certainty*. Most people agree that a sincere and honest judgement should be followed since, for every individual, his or her judgement of conscience is the immediate norm of morality.

In some situations, the decision-maker might feel certain of making a right judgement, when in fact that judgement is flawed because, although he or she was acting in good faith and seeking reasonable means for arriving at a sound judgement, some essential element has escaped consideration. In this case, the subject acts with invincible ignorance and consequently bears no responsibility, as has been noted (p. 105).

In other words, following one's own conscience is right, if the moral judgement has been made with sincerity and honestly seeks the right thing. That is why every effort must be made to avoid error in making judgements of conscience. This includes:

- Adopting a *sincere attitude* of seeking what is good, and avoiding the temptation to justify one's own interests by false rationalizations

- Applying *basic ethical principles* – first, the Golden Rule, which requires putting oneself in another's shoes and reflecting on how one would like to be treated

- Achieving a serious *ethical training*, particularly in topics related to one's own field

- Seeking *advice* from competent people of proven moral solvency in doubtful cases.

RESPONSIBILITY FOR CONSEQUENCES: THE PROBLEM OF SECONDARY EFFECTS

Returning to the question of the consequences for which we are responsible, two extreme positions can be encountered:

- *Over-attributed*. It is argued that since people continually interact with others and we are all in a state of global interdependence, we all are responsible for everything that happens in the world.

- *Over-restricted*. This is the position that one bears responsibility only for the immediate and intentional (wanted) consequences of an action, while undesired consequences would be beyond one's responsibility. This would be the case of a company not assuming the responsibility for consequences in a neighbourhood of a factory that produces foul odours, noise and dust, or a manager who does not consider the consequences of selling weapons to a terrorist group.

Historically, the former example portrays a common misbehaviour in many businesses. Fortunately, many people are now increasingly aware of these unintended but foreseeable 'secondary effects', as they are usually termed. When an individual or institution does not bear the full consequences of its actions we talk of *moral hazard*.

In order to analyse the responsibility for consequences, we will begin by distinguishing between direct and indirect intentionality:

- *Direct intentionality.* An action with direct intentionality is one in which someone decides to perform or not perform it in order to achieve something desired, or as a means to an end. These actions are termed 'directly voluntary'. Many business actions are undertaken with direct intentionality, as when a manager settles upon a strategy, expands a business, knowingly omits certain workplace safety measures, forges a commercial document, consciously fails to make a payment and so on.

- *Indirect intentionality.* This occurs when someone consciously, on his or her own initiative, carries out an action (or allows an omission) that causes something undesired but foreseeable (at least, vaguely) and also avoidable. In other words, the intentionality is 'indirect' when one knows that a particular event might occur in consequence of a given act, or when any foreseeable damage might happen through negligence or recklessness. Actions with indirect intentionality are termed 'indirectly voluntary' or 'voluntary in the cause'.

A classic example of an *indirectly voluntary* action is a driver who runs over someone when intoxicated. In business, an illustrative example would be an employee injured when failing to take reasonable precautions, or an accident involving a consumer due to an inappropriate use of a product when the manufacturer has not given proper instructions. In these cases, there is no present consent of the will, but there is consent to the cause that provokes such accidents.[26]

Having made this distinction, we can better deal with the question of foreseen but undesired consequences, or 'secondary effects'. Agents are seeking certain goals, but normally those goals are achieved along with other consequences, known as *secondary effects*, *side effects* or *collateral effects*. This terminology seems appropriate because these are associated with the main effects – the goal or goals sought. The term 'secondary effects' does not imply unimportance but, rather, that the intention to achieve them is indirect or secondary.

The responsibility for secondary effects therefore depends on the capacity to *foresee* and *avoid* them. There are others factors too, such as the seriousness of the wrongdoing in which the agent cooperates and the causal proximity of the action to its consequences. A set of criteria can develop this point, which provides help to determine responsibility for an action's consequences:

- *An agent is responsible for reasonably predictable consequences of an action that can be avoided.* There is indirect voluntariness for such predictable consequences for people and the environment because the agent knows they might be associated with the action. Such predictable consequences are determined through one's own experience, by seeking appropriate advice, and by considering what usually occurs in similar situations. Managerial decisions must therefore take into account predictable secondary effects, which are avoidable to a greater or lesser extent. This brings about ethical questions, especially when the secondary effects are negative. We will discuss this point later (pp. 118–19).

- *The greater the capacity to avoid negative secondary effects of an action, the greater the responsibility to avoid them.* Some medicines produce side effects. If these can be avoided or minimized by introducing another ingredient, one has a responsibility to do so. Similarly, in mining and construction, with its long experience of industrial accidents, one has the responsibility to profit by such experience and to introduce preventative measures, including proper training, specific precautions for each job, appropriate monitoring, prohibiting alcoholic beverages in the workplace and so on. The responsibility would be diminished for accidents in sectors with limited experience, or when accidents are very difficult to avoid.

- *The more serious the consequences of an event, the greater the responsibility to take appropriate measures, even if the consequences are only remotely likely.* For example, a machinery manufacturer should foresee possible injuries to those who will handle the machines and introduce safety measures to avoid them. If lives are at stake, the measures will be stringent. Another example would be the responsibility for food quality when consumers' health is at risk. This responsibility for quality is higher in products related to health.

- *The greater the causal proximity of the action and its consequences, the greater the responsibility.* Consequences beget further consequences, and these lead to yet others, and so on. Responsibility is not measured equally for the immediate and remote consequences of an action. The more remote the consequence, the less causal connection it has to the action, since it depends on actions that are beyond the control of the original agent, and on decisions made by other people. For example, there is close proximity between an industrial accident and a lack of adequate precautions, whereas the causal proximity between a traffic accident and those who produced the beer that made the driver drunk is practically non-existent. However, a closer causal proximity with accidents would exist if the manufacturer used persuasive advertising inducing people to drink.

THE PRINCIPLE OF DOUBLE EFFECT

Closely connected with the responsibility for secondary effects is the Principle of Double Effect, highly relevant in various business situations. Many human actions simultaneously give rise to a good effect (or even several) that is specifically intended as a goal, and a bad effect (or effects). An example of such actions is a factory that produces a useful product, creates wealth and provides jobs, but pollutes.

Sometimes one finds an alternative with no bad effects, but this is not always possible. Sometimes one must choose between doing nothing and an alternative that is not wrong in itself (the object is licit), but which gives rise to bad secondary effects, together with one or more good primary ones. Other illustrative examples could be a corporate downsizing that is judged necessary to maintain a firm's competitiveness or even survival, and the corresponding lay-offs. The risk of industrial accidents in production can also be considered a potential bad effect in an otherwise beneficial production process.

A traditional situation used to discuss actions of double effect is the case of killing in legitimate defence. The principal (good) effect of an action of legitimate defence is to save one's own life or the life of a third party, but a further consequence is the death of the assailant (bad effect). However, killing the assailant to save a life would not be strictly necessary in certain situations. If it were possible to subdue the aggressor without lethal measures, then taking his life would not be reasonable, and such an action would forfeit its legitimacy.

This example shows us intuitively how bad side effects are tolerable if, and only if, there is a proportionately grave reason for permitting them, and if the action itself is not intrinsically wrong. If the negative effects are out of proportion to the need to perform the action, it could be rendered ethically unacceptable.

Actions of double effect have long been a matter of study and debate and the doctrine or theory of double effect has been developed to provide guidelines for making moral judgements under vexing circumstances.[27] Here, we will present a simple approach, keeping in mind what we have just said regarding responsibility for secondary effects.

A number of conditions can be specified to determine whether an action with a negative side effect is ethically licit.[28] To explain this, it might be useful to pick a case of double effect in business – for instance, the restructuring of a company with any lay-offs – and see how these criteria can be applied.

- *There is no better acceptable alternative*: It would not be wise to inquire into the lawfulness of one alternative without having first deliberated sufficiently upon other possible solutions. Very often, with a little creativity and professional competence, one can come up with a better alternative than 'do this' or 'do nothing'. (Is the restructuring with lay-offs the only possible solution to a problem of economic viability?)

- *There is a just cause for this action*: If not, it lacks uprightness of intention. Practical wisdom helps to evaluate whether a just cause is present. (What does the decision-maker really want in restructuring: to keep the firm competitive and economically viable, or only to gain desorbitated profits?)

- *The action itself is not intrinsically wrong*: The object chosen as a means should be licit, since it is never permissible to do wrong directly. The good effect must be produced directly by the action, not by the bad effect; otherwise, the bad effect would, in fact, be the object of the action. In other words, the side effects should be genuine side effects. For example, it is not reasonable to say that cheating the buyers of second-hand vehicles is a side effect of the used-car business. To cheat is an act with a specific object, which is intrinsically wrong. A negative consequence can only be tolerated when it is an inevitable effect of action that, in itself, is good or neutral. (A restructuring with a lay-off is not intrinsically wrong.)

- *The bad effects are proportionate to the necessity of the action*: Responsibility for consequences (bad effects) has to do with their seriousness and with the proximity of their cause (action), as noted above. The moral evaluation of the proportionality between the need to perform the action and its bad effects should be made through prudential judgement; that is, considering with practical wisdom how the action affects people from an ethical perspective (human good) in both its good and its bad effects. (What would be the probable psychological and economic consequences for those who face being laid off? What about the morale of employees who survive this round of lay-offs? What will the social impact on the community be? Is all this proportional to the need to implement the lay-off?)

Often this point is the most difficult. Here, practical wisdom is essential for a sound prudential judgement. Note that a prudential judgement – in the ethical sense, this is one with practical wisdom – is not a matter of weighing up the pros and cons, based on physical or economic goods, as in a cost–benefit analysis. Neither is it a question of weighing up advantages and disadvantages in any utilitarian fashion but, rather, it is a question of prudentially weighing the human goods sought by the action and the indirect consequences of the action against such human goods.

The challenge is to judge impartially, without letting one's own interests induce one to rationalize selfishness. The Golden Rule aids in such decisions: putting oneself in the other's position, and recalling that human good is common to the one who decides and those upon whom the effects fall.

When in doubt, as noted (p. 115), practical wisdom demands that one seek advice from honest and level-headed experts. One will thus be able to secure an independent, qualified opinion, avoiding the disadvantages that arise when an interested party must be the one to judge.

- *Reasonable means will be employed to minimize negative secondary effects*: One is responsible for reasonably predictable and preventable consequences, as noted (p. 116). One must do whatever is practical to avoid, or at least minimize, these effects – take measures to avoid pollution, to prevent labour accidents, and other such secondary effects. (In our lay-off example, this could mean aiding those who will lose their jobs; for example, helping them through outplacement, granting economic compensation or possibly transferring them to a different branch and so on.)

- *The purpose of monitoring and evaluating the situation periodically*: Circumstances can change and, inasmuch as there are negative effects, practical wisdom requires periodic monitoring and evaluation to establish whether the situation has persisted and to ensure that the means to minimize negative effects are being implemented correctly, or whether they might be enhanced, perhaps, by technological updates. This makes sense, for instance, in problems such as pollution and hazardous products.

- *Take steps to find some alternative that avoids actions with double effects in the future*: As mentioned above (p. 118), the first condition for accepting as licit an action with a double effect is that there be no better acceptable alternative. However, in many situations, a decision with a double effect is implemented and brings about a new and relatively permanent situation. Integrity requires exploring new alternatives with fewer or no negative side effects that can replace the problematic decision as soon as possible. For years, DDT was the most widely used pesticide in the world. However, in 1960 it was discovered that DDT was preventing many fish-eating birds from reproducing, a serious threat for human food and to biodiversity. These side effects led to the search for alternative products to replace DDT as an insecticide, and DDT is now banned in many countries.

The preceding considerations have immediate implications for how to resolve conflicting duties and other dilemmas, and to discuss the acceptability of cooperation of others' wrongdoing with an action whose object is good or indifferent. This latter is the topic of the last section of this chapter.

COOPERATION IN WRONGDOING

How can we determine responsibility in cases of cooperation with the intrinsically wrong actions of another (the principal agent) when performing a good action out of serious necessity? To address this problem, it is crucial to begin to distinguish between formal and material cooperation in wrongdoing:

- *Formal cooperation in wrongdoing*: This occurs when a person explicitly approves of another's action or shares the principal agent's intention, either for its own sake or as a means to some other goal. This is what happens, for instance, when a manager agrees to a fraud proposed by his boss and cooperates in carrying it out. Formal cooperation in wrongdoing involves guilt; complete voluntariness is present. It is therefore never acceptable.
- *Material cooperation in wrongdoing*: This form of cooperation is present when one disapproves of the other's action but cooperates because of a real necessity (for instance, to avoid being fired). The first responsibility here is to seek to avoid such cooperation. In some situations, the agent might even be persuaded to switch to an acceptable course of action, one in which the agent could collaborate without misgivings. If the agent might be open to such a change, the first responsibility is to try to instigate it.[29]

With material cooperation in wrongdoing, there is voluntariness in the cause but not in the effects. The agent tolerates or suffers undesirable consequences associated with the action because of the need to obtain a good or avoid harm.

Material cooperation in gravely wrong action is never acceptable; for instance, any cooperation in actions in which the right to life is violated. In lesser cases, the points noted above regarding responsibility for secondary effects must be kept in mind. This includes considering the degree of the necessity to cooperate, the proportion between the necessity to cooperate and the seriousness of the action. The causal proximity of the action is also relevant. Regarding the latter, it might be useful to distinguish between two situations: immediate and non-immediate material cooperation:

- *Immediate material cooperation* occurs when the participation of the cooperator has great causal proximity to the action of the principal agent, and when the action could not be carried out without such cooperation – for example, an accountant who, pressured by his boss, collaborates in preparing a misleading financial report, although without falsifying any documents. Another case is a sales manager who pays a 'commission' on sales to a client's head of purchasing because the latter had threatened to buy from a competitor otherwise. In this way, the sales manager cooperates with the illicit action of the head of purchasing.

  Immediate material cooperation in wrongdoing could involve guilt due to causal proximity. However, according to the criteria on responsibility for consequences listed previously (pp. 116–17), extreme situations are possible in which some immediate material cooperation could be temporarily licit (while other alternatives are explored), if there is a serious need to cooperate (for instance, maintaining one's job, or the firm's survival) and the cooperation does not involve very serious matters.

- *Non-immediate material cooperation in wrongdoing* occurs when the cooperator not only disapproves of the principal agent's actions, but the cooperation has little causal proximity, or when the action with which one cooperates could easily occur without that cooperation. For example, a clerk who, compelled by his boss, is working to search for documents that will be used to prepare a misleading report. In the example of paying a 'commission' to the head of purchasing, the employee who, following orders, prepares the money involved is another example of someone engaging in remote cooperation with an illicit action.

  Non-immediate material cooperation in wrongdoing is more acceptable than immediate cooperation, although it, too, should be avoided if possible.

In sum, material cooperation in wrongdoing might be justifiable and not involve guilt under the following conditions:

- There are *no viable alternatives* to cooperation. This includes being convinced that there is no way to persuade the wrongdoer to switch to an ethically acceptable action.
- The cooperator's action is *not intrinsically wrong*. Otherwise, it would be not only cooperation but also reprehensible in itself.
- There is *no approval* of the principal agent's action. This is the condition for material, not formal, cooperation.
- There is a *proportionately serious reason* for the cooperation: to protect an important good or avoid a greater harm. The graver the wrongdoing, the more serious a reason required for the cooperation.
- The importance of the reason for cooperation must be proportionate to the *causal proximity* of the cooperator's action to the principal agent's action.

The closer the cooperator's causal proximity, the closer this cooperation is to an immediate cooperation.

In addition,

- Measures should be taken to *avoid misunderstandings*, such as explaining the reasons why one is cooperating in wrongdoing when it is necessary.
- *Periodic review* is necessary to check whether other alternatives are possible, if the situation is ongoing.

Business ethics in practice 5:

Danone – The decision to close biscuit plants

The Groupe Danone is a French food product company, with headquarters in Paris and almost one hundred years of history. It was founded by the family of Antoine Riboud after the Second World War. His son, Franck Riboud, took over the company in 1996, and started a new stage in its history through a series of international mergers and acquisitions, focusing on fresh dairy products, biscuits and beverages. Nowadays, among its brands are various mineral waters (Evian, Volvic, Badoit, Aqua, Naya), Lu biscuits, and food products bearing the labels Danone, Royal Numico, Actimel, Activia and Blédina baby food brands.

Danone has had a business and social responsibility policy since the 1970s. It was based on a speech given by Antoine Riboud in 1972 that has been called 'The Marseille Speech'. He underlined four fundamental values: openness, enthusiasm, humanism and proximity. These values, which have not changed, include other values:

- *Openness* exists when the company pays attention to safety and respects the environment and cultural diversity. Openness also underlines curiosity, agility and simplicity.
- *Enthusiasm* is characterized by boldness, passion and an appetite for challenge.
- *Humanism* is understood as the attention paid to individuals – consumers, employees or citizens. It should be the heart of all decisions. Danone emphasized sharing, an approach to dialogue, transparency, teamwork and responsibility.
- *Proximity* regards being close to each person – colleagues, consumers, clients, suppliers, stockholders and society – and to becoming a part of their everyday lives.

Danone also has a guide for its management, called the 'Danone Way' launched in 2001, which focuses on management care for employee development, reducing the use of water and energy, and respecting the local people and environment. It was a new approach and an attempt to help business units to integrate social responsibility and sustainable development in their day-to-day management. Briefly, it is an attempt to build a bridge between the business and society.

Business ethics in practice 5: (cont'd)

In 1996, due to overcapacity, Danone closed a factory in Ultzama, Spain, which was an important source of labour and everyday products for the local people. In Ultzama, there were 175 employees, the average age of whom was over 41 years. The Director of Human Relations of Danone in Spain, Francesc Martínez Rius, assured that the closing of the Ultzama plant was done with concern for all employees, on the basis of social and individual solutions, personalized for every worker, and based also on the governmental plan of reindustrialization. Danone eliminated 175 jobs at the Ultzama plant; however, about 450 jobs were created in the area surrounding Ultzama. Many recognized that it was an exemplary way of closing the plant. The 1998 Danone Social Report explained the Danone policy in closing plants: 'No employee should be left alone to deal with a job problem and jobs must be created wherever they are destroyed.'

The occasion to put that slogan into action appeared on 29 March 2001, when Danone announced the reorganization of its biscuit business in Europe, closing down six of the 36 factories: two in France, one in each of Hungary, Italy, Belgium and Holland. That decision was due to the fact that the company needed to resolve excessive production capacity. The average use of its competitors' factories was at 70 per cent as opposed to 43 per cent for Danone during that time. The announcement caused great alarm, as the action affected 1,200 jobs, most of them in France. Many workers manifested their disapproval and the press had no hesitation in criticizing the company, which had previously enjoyed a strong reputation for social responsibility.

During its reorganization, Danone took measures to minimize the undesirable consequences of the decision. The lay-offs were accompanied by actions beyond legal obligation. In each factory, a team was dedicated to supporting the laid-off employees in finding a new job. The company also favoured other internal solutions such as the mobility incentive, compensation in the case of salary decrease and exploratory trips to the new host city in cases of worker relocation. They also had some external solutions such as reassignment in local companies or helping to create new businesses. Finally, 95 per cent of the workers were successfully reassigned.

The decision to close several biscuit plants to optimize production capacity was accompanied by several measures to improve the nutritional profile of the products, and by stepping up marketing and advertising efforts on the nutritional value of biscuits. Such policies seem to be a key to Danone's success in the biscuit division in the subsequent years.

In that time, the biscuit division grew. The biscuit line posted growth topping 3 per cent in 2006, up from 1.5 per cent in 2005. In July 2007, this division of Danone had 15,000 employees. Danone was in second position worldwide as a biscuits producer and in first place in 75 per cent of the countries where it did business. Over 80.4 per cent of biscuit production was destined for European markets, and 19 per cent for Asian markets – the new challenge for Danone Biscuits.

Questions:

1. Analyse the positive and negative consequences of closing Danone's biscuit plants.

2. What do you think about the decision taken by Danone regarding the closing of biscuit plants and how the decision was implemented?

Sources: Danone corporate website: http://www.danone.com/en/company/history.html; http://www. danone.com/images/pdf/dan_envsocperfindic06.pdf; Groupe Danone 2007 Year Final Results, http://www.phx. corporate-ir. net/phoenix.zhtml?c=95168&p=irol-newsArticle&ID=1108139: http://www.danone.com/en/news/ media/download-center.html; Select Recursos Humanos, ETT, S.A. (1997), http://www/select.es/actualidad/ index.asp?fuseaction=entrevistas_ficha&opc=9; Wikipedia: http://www.en.wikipedia.org/wiki/Groupe_Danone; A. Blytch, 'Corporate responsibility at Danone', *Ethical Corporation*, 17 December (2003); C. Frade, 'Danone anuncia que clausurará seis fábricas en Europa', *El Mundo*, 30 March (2001); 'Cierre de la fábrica de Ulzama de Danone, SA.', IPES-ESADE, http://www.uca.edu.sv/facultad/clases/eco/m100203/doc7.doc; J. Tagliabue, 'Cookie Maker Cuts Back', *New York Times*, 30 March (2001), http://www.nytimes.com/2001/03/30/business/30FOBR. html?ex=1204952400&en=d8fd1a2d6862b95a&ei=5070

Dilemma 5

Petra is the director of the branch of a bank in a small city. She has a good reputation as a professional and many people ask her for advice on how to use their savings profitably. Petra had been heavily pressured by her boss to generate investors urgently for a listed company. The 'order' came from the board of directors of the bank. Due to her experience and perspicacity, she understood that the company must be in a weak financial situation and that her bank must have important interests in it. An injection of capital from small investors would probably be crucial in maintaining the market value of the company. After receiving the 'recommendation' from her boss, she was approached by Mrs Blythe, a middle class widow aged 70, seeking advice from Petra, as usual. She wished to invest $30,000 without a high risk. Petra knew that, after Mrs Blythe, other clients might also ask her similar questions. She did not know what to answer.

Questions:

1. What is Petra's problem?

2. To what extent is Petra responsible for the advice she might give to Mrs Blythe?

3. What would you do if you were Petra?

Summary

It is because persons are conscious, free beings that responsibility can be ascribed to them. This entails the idea that we must answer for those actions that are under our own dominion. Accountability – a related but not identical concept – refers to being open to the judgement of others. Liability refers to legal responsibility, often regarding products.

Responsibility has at least three different meanings: (1) a virtue (being a responsible person); (2) an obligation (bearing responsibility); and (3) an attribution (being responsible – guilty – for an accident).

A person is responsible for his or her actions, having considered the reasons for acting (antecedent responsibility) and the consequences (consequent responsibility). In addition, there is a responsibility that arises from certain vital engagements (congruent responsibility), or from the acknowledgement of a personal calling (transcendent responsibility).

Responsibility can refer to legality (legal responsibility), social expectations (social responsibility) or moral principles (moral responsibility).

To determine the degree to which an action or its consequences can be ascribed to an agent, one must consider both what knowledge the agent had, or should have had, and to what degree the will consented.

Performing or omitting an action to achieve something desired as an end in itself, or as a means, is a directly voluntary action. By contrast, it is indirectly voluntary when the agent can foresee an action's possible consequences but does not will them as a direct aim. An agent bears responsibility for an action's secondary effects if they are foreseeable and avoidable.

There are four basic forms of responsibility: (1) performing a voluntary action (commission); (2) omitting what is due and possible (omission – deliberate or through negligence or recklessness); (3) fostering other peoples' actions or behaviours (induction); and (4) cooperating with others' actions, through intentional actions or omissions (cooperation).

Intention, object and circumstances are the components of the 'Triple Font Theory' of morality. A moral judgement evaluates the morality of a decision. It is principally directed at the evaluation of the morality of the chosen end (intention) and the chosen action (object). For a decision to be morally good, both the intention (end) and the object (means) must be good. There are circumstances that can aggravate or attenuate the morality of a decision.

Principles and norms aid in making moral judgements through presenting negative duties and the subsequent unacceptable actions. Formulating sound moral judgements also requires practical wisdom.

Certain business actions bring about unintended secondary effects that have to be included in moral judgements insofar as they are predictable and avoidable. An action with positive primary effects and negative secondary effects (double effect) would be acceptable under certain conditions discussed in this chapter.

Formal cooperation in wrongdoing (when it includes approval of the wrong action) involves guilt. Generally, an immediate material cooperation in wrongdoing (without approval) also involves guilt, although in some extreme cases it can be acceptable. Remote material cooperation in wrongdoing can be justified under certain conditions.

Right living, living the good life, means first and foremost ordering one's priorities into a correct hierarchy ... The fox and the hare do not argue with one another about the right way to live; they both go about their own way or one eats the other.[1]

Robert Spaemann (1927–)
German philosopher

Chapter Aims

This chapter will allow you to:

- gain an understanding of business contracts and ethical issues related to them
- discuss some forms of misappropriation, industrial espionage and fraud
- consider issues regarding trade secrets and conflicts of interest
- distinguish between tax evasion and tax avoidance and the morality of each
- become more familiar with insider trading and the major arguments about the morality of the practice
- discuss the practice of whistle-blowing and the conditions for its moral acceptability
- distinguish different forms of corruption and questionable payments, including bribery, extortion, kickbacks, blackmail and facilitating payments
- read a brief note on restitution and compensatory damages.

Key terms:

Bankruptcy
Blackmail
Breach of contract
Bribery
Business contracts
Confidential information
Compensatory damages
Conflicts of interest
Contract
Copyright infringement
Corruption
Counterfeit
Embezzlement

Extortion
Facilitating payments
Fair agreement
Fraud
Fraudulent conveyance
Gifts-giving
Good faith
Industrial espionage
Insider trading
Intellectual propriety
Kickbacks
Misappropriation
Misrepresentation

Patent infringement
Private information
Professional secrecy
Professional secret
Restitution
Substantial errors
Tax avoidance
Tax evasion
Trade secrets
Trademark infringement
Whistle-blowing

Frequent Ethical Issues in Business

INTRODUCTORY CASE 6:

SIEMENS – SEVERAL BRIBES HIT THE COMPANY

Siemens has been a world leader in electronic engineering and electronics for over 150 years and is one of the outstanding German multinational companies. The company began in 1847, when Werner von Siemens created seamless insulation for copper wire. Currently, Siemens covers a wide variety of products and fields, including automation and control, lighting, medical diagnostic procedures, generation, transmission and distribution of power, financial services, rail transportation, technological support to airports, and water technology, among others. Siemens gives employment to 450,000 people and is present in 190 countries. It is known as a company that offers high quality products.

At the turn of the current century, and even before, Siemens began to be hit with accusations of bribery. At the end of 2006, a former employee of Siemens explained that secret accounts outside Germany existed and were used to pay bribes for contracts. After an investigation, five Siemens employees were taken into custody. Siemens recognized that some of its employees were engaged in fraud involving between €10– €30 million.

Soon it was reported that Siemens had diverted around €100 million to Dubai. Then those funds were channelled through different companies in the Caribbean into Swiss accounts. The investigators suspected that this money was to ensure that Siemens was awarded attractive contracts for the 2004 Olympic Games in Athens.

Another problem involving Siemens surfaced in 2006 through IG Metall, one of the dominant metalworkers' unions in Germany. They affirmed that Siemens had tried to pay a bribe to AUB, a small union, to gain support for its policies, since in Germany, in large corporations, union representatives take part in corporate governance.

In March 2007, German prosecutors arrested one of the most senior executives of Siemens, bringing about the 'black money' scandal. German authorities ordered the company to pay fines and taxes of about €380 million and Siemens was alleged to have been using the network of 'black accounts' for bribery for years.

In May 2007, two Siemens managers were convicted by a German court for bribery and corruption. The trial revealed a system of 'slush funds' in the German conglomerate; that is, an auxiliary monetary account or reserve fund generally used for illegal payments. They were accused of paying kickbacks to two officials at the state-owned Italian energy company Enel between 1999 and 2002. They admitted that the money was paid in order to secure a €450 million deal for Siemens-made gas turbines, but justified themselves by saying that Enel employees had asked for money in return for the contract. They did not act for personal gain but in the best interests of their company. The auditors also discovered more than 20 unknown recipients from across the globe, to which €100 million were paid. A Cyprus based company, IBF Business Service Ltd, received €29.4 million. Millions were also transferred to accounts in the United Arab Emirates, Indonesia and Sudan. Apparently, there was no other way to win contracts in some countries abroad where bribing for contracts was a common practice.

Again, Siemens was fined €201 million by the Munich court on 4 October 2007. This court named several former Nigerian telecommunications ministers as well as other officials of Russia and Libya between 2001 and 2004. The payments were made to win lucrative contracts for telecommunications equipment. The company accepted responsibility for the misconduct and agreed to pay the fine. Later, it was announced that five ex-ministers and other senior officials named as recipients of €10 million in bribes from Siemens would be investigated in Nigeria.

It was also reported that the Siemens corruption scandal involved a slush fund of €420 million, paid to the consultants for over seven years, which was much higher than previously thought. The company admitted that it faced investigation in several countries. In its former communications department, a number of payments were discovered where neither the recipients nor the cause for payment were clear.

Many German investors had lost confidence in Siemens's Chief Executive Officer, Klaus Kleinfeld, and not only on account of these scandals, in which he was not directly implicated. Less than one third of investors believed that the current CEO was able to increase the company's value. Finally, in April 2007, the Siemens CEO stepped down from his post, along with the chairman of Siemens' supervisory board, and on 1 July a new CEO was appointed. The new board chairman stated that the change in leadership meant a clean break from the past.

In the following months, other scandals from the past emerged. In December 2007, the Norwegian division of Germany's Siemens AG announced a shake-up of its board, because the company was suspected of having provided illegal trips to military officials. After hitting its operations in Germany, Switzerland, Italy, Greece, Norway, the United States and Russia, the scandals spread to its operations in China.

Questions:

1. What might have motivated some Siemens executives to become involved in such practices?

2. What short-term and long-term consequences can bribery bring about?

3. How would you recommend that the new Siemens CEO should face such scandals?

Sources: BBC: http://www.news.bbc.co.uk/2/hi/africa/7105582.stm; *Business Week,* http://www.businessweek.com/globaliz/content/mar2007/gb20070314_175589.htm?campaign_id=rss_daily; *Der Spiegel,* http://www.spiegel.de/international/0,1518,462954,00.html; *Dw-World. De:* http://www/dw-world.de/dw/article/0,2144,2249977,00.html; *The Guardian,* http://www.guardian.co.uk/business/2006/dec/14/germany.internationalnews; 'Nigeria to Investigate Siemens Bribes Scandal', F. Rajiv and B. K. Bellakonda, 'The Bribery Scandals at Siemens AG', ICFAI Center for Management Research, distributed by ECCH (www.ecch.com); *Reuters,* 19 November (2007), http://www.reuters.com/article/companyNewsAndPR/idUSL193502420071119; Siemens website, http://w4.siemens.de/archiv/en/index.html; C. Taylor, 'Siemens Faces $538M in Taxes, Fines for "Black Money" Scandal', *Electronic News,* 53 (43) (2007): 10–22; *All Business,* http://www.allbusiness.com/government/government-bodies-offices-government/6245961-1.html; *Timesonline:* http://www.business.timesonline.co.uk/tol/business/industry_sectors/engineering/article2881841.ece; *Wall Street Journal,* http://www.online.wsj.com/public/article/SB119749893893424887.html

---

BUSINESS CONTRACTS

A contract is an agreement or exchange of promises between two or more parties (individuals or groups) by which the parties commit themselves to some course of action.[2] In business, the subject matter of a contract is usually an exchange of products (raw materials, facilities, funds or other goods or services) for money. This is the case of trade (purchase–sale) contracts, rental contracts and labour contracts. The latter deserves special consideration because work is an activity of the person and not a mere commodity.[3]

Contracts are the skeletons of business relationships: honouring them is crucial for the entire field of economic activity. The obligation to honour a contract is based on the fact that everyone is responsible for their own commitments. It is a part of the Personalist Principle and the human good of friendship, the minimum requirement of which is to live together in justice and harmony.[4]

In line with this requirement, a vast amount of legislation on contracts has been developed from ancient Roman Law, which established a general principle that 'pacts must be kept' (*pacta sunt servanda*). Legislation on contracts enforces the fulfilment of legitimate ones and provides remedies for breach of contract.

A contract includes three key elements:

- The *object* or matter of the contract, which includes the specific commitments assumed
- The *agreement* reached by the will of each party, which produces a certain link between them
- The *contractual duties* and rights derived from the agreement.

The validity of a contract, and the consequent moral duty, require three conditions:

- *Capacity of the parties*: Since the agreement has to be reached through a deliberate and free decision of each party, a valid contract requires the capacity of parties and, first, sufficient mental discernment. Legislation can add particular formal requirements regarding the capacities of the parties. A contract has to be possible: the parties must have the capacity or power to do what is established.
- *Appropriate matter*: A contract without licit matter is not legitimate; that is, a commitment to carry out wrongdoing is not morally acceptable. This would be the case of a contract for industrial espionage, or for causing harm to somebody. Such contracts should not be executed; however, if they are, the party who has agreed to pay is obliged to do so. The matter should also include a delimitation of obligations to avoid possible misinterpretations insofar as possible.
- *Fair agreement*: This requires acting in good faith; that is, with honest conviction about the truth or falsehood of any proposition, without duress or intimidation, and seeking equitable agreements. A fair agreement also requires mutual and external acceptance of duties, without misrepresentations or any wording likely to lead to mistakes.

Law requires certain formalities for the legal validity of contracts, such as being written and being signed in the presence of a notary. These legal formalities vary in accordance with the type of contract. However, the ethical perspective is wider. Both oral and written contracts oblige ethically, if consciously entered into and meeting the other conditions of validity mentioned above.

A number of ethical issues regarding contracts are worth highlighting. Among others are:

- *Breaching a legitimate contract*: To commit breach of contract is to fail voluntarily to do what was undertaken, with damage to one's counterpart. Justice requires appropriate compensation for such damages. Sometimes it is impossible to fulfil a contract for involuntary reasons. This is the case of certain business or personal situations in which, acting in good faith, a business is not sufficiently profitable to pay debts (to suppliers, financial creditors and so on). If the agent is, for some reason, not responsible for the problem, the breach is not formally contrary to justice. However, the situation created is not acceptable, and debts should be paid according to the terms agreed upon as soon as possible.

A particular situation is *bankruptcy*, that is, legally declared inability of an organization (or an individual) to pay their creditors. In this case and similar predicaments, debts can be partially or completely dismissed in accordance with the law and judgements of the court. This is a known risk that is an implicit element of the trade contract. However, it is not ethically acceptable to mislead creditors or to abuse one's power when facing a probable bankruptcy by favouring oneself, or by giving one creditor unlawful preference to the detriment of another. This is an ethical issue, generally included in legislation, called *fraudulent conveyance.*

- *Making illicit or illegal agreements*: This includes any commitment contrary to ethical principles or involving contractually unlawful obligations. Contracts with such matter are illegitimate and do not oblige in any way.

- *Entering into a contract with misrepresentation and lack of good faith*: *Misrepresentation* is false statements made by one party that induce the other party to enter into the contract. This occurs, for instance, when a purchase decision is made and executed based on a seller's false statement or promise regarding the quality or nature of the good or post-sales service.

  In a contract, there is lack of *good faith* if one of the parties entered with the intention of defrauding the other. Lack of good faith can lead not only to misrepresentation but also to taking advantage of the ignorance or lack of awareness of the counterparty in some substantial aspect of a contract, when the information necessary for consciously consenting is not possible for the counterparty to attain through reasonable means. This could be, for instance, the case of a company purchasing on credit if, unbeknownst to the seller, this company suffers from such serious debt that it will be practically impossible to pay in full. This could occur when the seller has no reasonable means of discovering the financial situation of the purchaser and assumes that payment will proceed as usual.

- *Contracting with substantial errors*: One or both parties might make mistakes about the object of the contract (for example, understanding a donation instead of a sale) or can err in some substantial aspect of the contract's content (derivative financial products for stock obligations). An incorrect understanding of an essential point in a contract can invalidate it, because this would indicate a lack of real will to do something to rectify the contract. When a claim about mistakes in a contract has to be decided by a court, numerous aspects are examined to avoid abuse.

- *Acting with duress and undue influence*: Using intimidation or threats to compel a person to reach an agreement or to sign a contract is unjust and, if significant duress or undue influence is present, the agreement or contract is invalid. There is a special risk of undue influence in contracts when one party is in a position of power over the other.

MISAPPROPRIATION AND FRAUD

There are a number of well-known ethical issues in which the right to private property is violated. In essence, all of these are forms of *theft*; that is, appropriating personal property without the reasonable will of the owner.

Misappropriation

Misappropriation is a kind of theft, and consists of an intentional usurpation of the property or funds of another for one's own use or another unauthorized purpose. This is the case, for instance, of the appropriation for private use of the goods of a company where one works, including material goods and intellectual property. Claiming excessive expenses or making inefficient *use of resources* would also fall under the heading of misappropriation. Artificial price manipulation through unlawful monopolies and other abusive commercial practices is also a form of misappropriation; these matters will be considered later in this volume.[5]

Infringement of intellectual property

Misappropriation also covers several kinds of infringement of intellectual property rights. Among them are:

- *Copyright infringement*: Using, and especially trading, material without the permission of the copyright holder, even when no formal copyright exists.
- *Trademark infringement*: The violation of the exclusive right attached to a registered trademark (a distinctive sign of some kind, used by an organization to distinguish its products from those of others) without the authorization of the trademark owner or any licensee (provided that such authorization was within the scope of the licence).
- *Patent infringement*: Another important case of misappropriation of intellectual property. It occurs when someone utilizes an invention protected by a patent without the permission of the patent proprietor. This is so because a patent allows its proprietor the right to exclude others from utilizing the invention in question. However, occasionally there are controversial issues, such as patents regarding certain pharmaceuticals for developing countries, in which the right to life, morally speaking, takes priority over the right to patent property. However, pharmaceutical companies argue that patents are necessary to incentivize expensive research into new drugs. This is an ongoing controversy.[6]

Industrial or corporate espionage

This is a brazen misappropriation of intellectual property. In industrial espionage, someone tries to obtain secret or confidential information for commercial purposes, without the permission of the firm that owns it. In fact, it is a type of theft. The object of the industrial espionage might be anything that can benefit the usurper or a third party.

Fraud

Fraud is theft by means of deception. It takes place when deception is deliberately practised in order to secure unjust gain.[7] In business, fraud can appear in a great variety of forms: deception over the quality or weight of products; forgery of cheques or invoices, as well as a request for funds from an individual or firm when no obligation to pay exists (*false billing*).

Counterfeit

One specific type of fraud is a *counterfeit* or imitation, usually produced with the intent to represent the content or origins of a product deceptively. In business, this generally occurs with goods such as clothing, watches, software, pharmaceuticals, or any other manufactured item. Counterfeiting generally includes patent or trademark infringements.

Embezzlement

There is a form of misappropriation called *embezzlement,* which is a fraudulent theft of funds or property by a trustee (one who holds property on behalf of a beneficiary) or by a person with the responsibility to care for and protect another's assets (for example, managers and treasurers). This form of misappropriation is contrary not only to justice and truthfulness, but also to the fiduciary duty of someone entrusted with something owned by another.

TRADE SECRETS

People working for a firm have access to information that others do not. The firm owns this information, unless it is easily (and legitimately) obtainable by people external to it. Some information is explicitly defined as confidential or a trade secret; other information might not be explicitly so labelled but is obviously so by its nature.[8]

Confidential information regarding trade might be complete or might consist of essential details on new products, inventions, technologies or innovations in the manufacturing process, market research, studies of competitors, key information about clients or customers, new business ideas or business plans and so on. Generating this information might have required costly investment, and its disclosure can provoke a loss of competitive advantage or otherwise damage the firm.

Facilitating a competitor's access to this information, directly or indirectly, without an institutional agreement, is not only a great disloyalty to one's own firm but also a clear misappropriation of intellectual propriety.

In this context, *trade secrets* can be defined as any formula, pattern, design, instrument, process or compliance of information used in a business and not known to people outside the firm that provides a benefit to the holder or an advantage over competitors or customers.

Apart from the moral duty to keep trade secrets, many companies protect confidential information by requiring employees to sign agreements containing the specific commitment to non-disclosure of such information. The law generally also protects trade secrets, and courts have developed a rich jurisprudence with a number of criteria for determining the seriousness of violations of such secrets.[9]

A delicate situation can result when an *employee leaves a firm* and is hired by a competitor. Trade secrets should also be kept in this situation. However, one can use his or her personal skills to obtain information in the new job, since skills belong to each person. In practice, the new employee could well suffer serious pressure to disclose trade secrets of the former firm, and embarrassing situations might arise. In order to avoid possible prejudices, managers or employees who manage sensitive confidential information are often required, under a non-competition contract, not to work for a competitor for a certain period (perhaps two or three years) if they leave the firm.

Another issue arises when someone in marketing has personal contacts or even a particular friendship with the firm's customers. Do these connections belong to the firm or to the employee? On one hand, many of these contacts have probably been made by the employee while working for the firm and, in economic terms, this has required an investment by the firm. In some ways, loyal customers form part of a firm's assets. However, on the other hand, the employee has achieved these relations with customers, which is a completely personal matter. A prudential solution could be not to take customer records from one's former firm, but the employee is free to inform customers that he or she is now working for a different firm. Obviously, customers are not anybody's property and, with this information, they can freely decide to maintain their loyalty to the original firm or move to the employee's new firm.

CONFLICTS OF INTEREST

In business ethics, as well as in the legal context, a conflict of interest is understood as a situation in which the private interests and the official responsibilities of a person in a position of trust are in conflict, or when someone who ought to be serving people has competing interests. A typically illustrative example is an attorney or a law firm that simultaneously represents two opposed clients.

In business, a conflict of interest can arise when an employee, an executive or a director of a firm has interests that compete personally or professionally with the duty to serve his or her firm with loyalty (fiduciary duty). There are many cases in which a conflict of interest can take place. For instance:

- A person responsible for purchases having an interest in some supplier, either directly or through a close relative (spouse, child and so on)
- An official of a governmental institution with interests in a firm that offers goods or services to such institutions
- Working for a competitor or taking on any outside employment in which the interests of one job contradict those of another

- A director of a large company who, as a member of the board of directors, has voted on whether to buy a small firm for a certain price, if he is one of the owners of that firm

- Auditing and providing consultancy services to the same company, which impedes auditing with independence and impartiality (as happened with Arthur Andersen in Enron).

The existence of a conflict of interest does not mean that the agent will necessarily act against his or her fiduciary duties to the firm by exploiting a professional or official capacity for personal benefit. However, when conflicts of interest exist it is difficult to act impartially, avoiding the undue favouring of any of the conflicting interests. In addition, if a conflict of interest becomes public, confidence towards a person, group, firm or another institution might be eroded. Such conflicts are therefore best avoided. Transparency about conflicts of interest in organizations is highly recommended.

In fact, corporate codes usually prohibit situations with employees or managers with conflicts of interest, or else oblige one to reveal such information to a superior officer. Even if the company's code does not require it, a person of good sense would reveal the existence of such a conflict in order to avoid making decisions involving the subject of the conflict. Some companies also take measures to prevent people from making decisions over issues in which such a conflict could exist.

TAX EVASION AND TAX AVOIDANCE

Tax evasion refers to avoiding the payment of taxes lawfully due. This differs from *tax avoidance* or *tax mitigation,* which is making use of legal methods to one's own advantage in order to reduce the amount payable.

Taxation is a means of distributing benefits and burdens among citizens. Tax collection uses different mechanisms, including tax on personal and corporate income (usually the most substantial), tax on consumption, donations and wealth transfer, special taxes on products such as tobacco and alcoholic beverages, and so forth. Taxes are used for provisioning public services such as public institutions (courts, government, parliament and the like), defence, public safety and so on. In most countries, health care, education, public transport and some infrastructures are also supported by public funds derived from taxation.

Taxation is an instrument of both economic and social policy. Governments can grant incentives or disincentives for economic activity by decreasing or increasing taxation on a particular industry or on all economic activity. Simultaneously, governments can develop social policies favouring social equity in tax collection or the assignment of funds to subsidize those with special needs – such as pensioners, the unemployed, large families and through a variety of social services.

Taxation posits a number of ethical, economic and political questions regarding property rights and their social function, personal freedom and solidarity, efficiency in the allocation of resources collected, economic productivity, efficiency of the economic system and equity. The latter questions touch on the degree to which taxation should be proportional to incomes or to real economic capacity (being single or with a large family, for example) and, if progressivity on the wealthy is acceptable, to what degree.

The rate of taxation is also controversial. Some defend a low rate of taxation, arguing for the rights of private property (high taxes can be like a sacking, in extreme cases), the minimal role delegated to government for the provision of public services, and the favourable effects of low taxation on investment and wealth creation, which can bring about even higher global income from taxation. Others, however, are in favour of higher taxes, arguing in favour of social justice, which requires that society ensure basic social conditions that allow everybody to live in accordance with their dignity and need for human development (heath care, education, shelter and so forth).

The discussion of these topics never ends. The debates include ethical aspects of distributive justice and a respect for human dignity, but also extend to economic, and even ideological, issues.

The ethical justification of taxation is its presumed contribution to the common good, which includes using objective and fair criteria (distributive justice), and the authority of those who govern society, and determine the rate and mechanisms of taxation.

In practice, taxation is determined by specific legislation, and the law should be followed, unless it clearly violates human rights or other fundamental ethical standards. This rejection would require wide support from sensible and upright people. It should be noted that, in general, there is a moral obligation to pay taxes as defined by law. Consequently, tax evasion is not only illegal, but also ethically wrong.

Tax evasion can include other ethical issues, such as failing to report income, faking expenses, or reporting financial statements inaccurately. Since governments impose strict and serious penalties for tax evasion, those who evade paying taxes are also at risk of harming themselves or their organization.

Taxpayers are morally obligated to be truthful about their financial status. However, they can take advantage of the tax avoidance foreseen by those who make the law, following the spirit and the letter of the law, without exploiting loopholes. The latter requires good reason for not paying more than is justly required but also prudence in not acting against the spirit of the law.

Another point regarding tax evasion involves making use of foreign tax havens – countries that have a lower tax rate and more confidential banking procedures than those in one's own nation. This is the case, for example, for the Cayman Islands, and the Republic of Seychelles. Using a tax haven is not necessarily illegal or unethical, although it might often be so. Global finance frequently uses offshore mechanisms to avoid the taxes and restrictions associated with the national financial market.[10]

Companies that register in tax havens can pay taxes in their own country when they repatriate foreign earnings through dividends, or by other means. However, frequently using a tax haven involves frauds, unfair exploitation of legal loopholes and lack of solidarity with one's home country, which provides the business with the infrastructure, educated people and social environment where business can take place.

INSIDER TRADING

Insider trading is the trading of stocks or other securities of a firm or corporation, such as bonds or stock options,[11] using internal information that has not been disclosed to the public that, if and when it were disclosed, could substantially influence the price of such stocks or securities. The prior knowledge that a company's profits or losses were far higher than anticipated would be an example of insider information, as would the discovery or launch of a new product expected to be very profitable, knowledge of a very promising research project or changes at top-level management, capital increases, or plans to merge or take over another company.

A typical case of insider trading is when someone takes advantage of insider information about impending mergers or takeovers to buy stocks in the companies in question before others know of the change. Then, a few days or even hours later, he or she could sell the stocks at a tremendous profit. This is different from forecasts made on the basis of analysis of public information, including information coming from highly specialized publications, longstanding experience or other forms of professional expertise, which is fully legitimate.

Considering insider trading, two questions arise: (1) why is insider trading wrong? and (2) who is guilty for trading with inside information?

Morality of insider trading

Some economists[12] argue that insider trading produces two adverse effects for market competitiveness: (1) it dissuades others from acquiring information and participating in the market (if just a few insiders are going to have all the advantages, it is safer to put funds into some more profitable venture); (2) it distorts the information provided by market operators and received by other investors. If insider trading were licit, the massive sale of a company's stocks could be interpreted as the economically rational decision of an executive with inside information. However, other economists disagree.[13] But, whether or not insider trading contributes to the efficiency of stock market pricing, there are several ethical arguments that conclude that insider trading is not ethically acceptable:[14]

- *It is an act of unfair competition.* Present-day stock markets are regulated according to the principle of transparency of transactions and of fundamental information provided. This means that companies, generally issuers of negotiable securities, must provide the entire market with the information needed for investment decisions. This amounts to a public commitment consisting of not buying or selling securities on the basis of inside information. Insider trading is therefore a form of unfair competition, because it does not comply with the explicit or tacit commitments required of all participants in the stock market.

• *It erodes the trust that the securities market needs to operate.* Insider trading reduces investors' trust, and trust is widely acknowledged to be fundamental for the proper operation of any market, including the securities markets. Investors must be guaranteed equal opportunity and protection from illicit trading, which affords advantages to inside investors to the detriment of others. Insider trading also affects companies and other economic agents, since the secondary securities market plays an important role in securing financing for economic agents, and in channelling savings and achieving returns on them, thus benefiting society as a whole. Therefore, there are economic, social and ethical reasons for wanting the stock market to work well.[15]

• *It is a violation of fiduciary duty and a breach of professional secrecy.* Among the responsibilities inherent in a management or professional post is the obligation of loyalty to the explicit and implicit commitments assumed when accepting the post. This includes respecting the secrecy of all matters that are known due to one's professional work and which, owing to their content, must be considered confidential. A company's managers and employees enjoy a relationship of trust with the firm and are consequently obliged to practise loyalty. They are hired to work for the company, for which they are suitably paid, and not to take advantage of their positions for their own personal benefit, to the detriment of others.

  Another clear commitment of managers and employees is to look after the legitimate interests of the company. These interests could be affected if it becomes known that someone in the company is making use of inside information. The damage might be even more serious for firms that act as advisers to issuers of securities. If it comes to light that the employees of a law firm or an investment bank were using the information obtained to trade on the stock market before that information were made public, the firm would lose clients and its image would be badly tarnished.

• *It is an act of misappropriation of private information.* Information generated in economic and business activities is an intangible asset, often one of great economic value. Information obtained through a management decision, or knowledge about company operations, when it is a direct consequence of the position a person holds in the organization, cannot be considered the private property of that person. The fact that managers and employees have this sort of information does not give them the right to benefit from it. And it is clearer still that the professionals working on the plans for a future takeover are not the 'owners' of the knowledge about the takeover.

Until it is publicly disclosed, all information belongs to the company. Even so, it is a very peculiar type of asset in that its use must be carefully restricted.

This information is held 'in trust' rather than owned. When a company is listed on the stock exchange, neither the company nor its stockholders are the absolute owners of any information that can affect stock prices, since both present and future stockholders have 'ownership' rights. It is therefore illicit for officers to use inside information, even in the hypothetical case of having the stakeholders' consent to do so.

Insider trading is a form of theft, given that profits are obtained by those who use this information to the detriment of those who have no access to it but who do have a right to know everything of public interest to investors.

Responsibility for insider trading

We have to consider, first, that inside information might come from the companies themselves (obtained from an occupant of an executive position in the company), from service companies (for example, law firms or investment banks preparing a takeover) or from public institutions. These sources of information are accessible to people involved in the firm where the information is generated. This includes institution partners, board members, managers and employees of the company. There are also other types of people who have access to the information through their work, profession or position, such as consultants, auditors, members of law firms, banks and even journalists or printers who receive the news for publishing beforehand. Both groups of people are guilty of trading with inside information because all of them have the duty of professional secrecy. The people who extract information from anyone in such groups are also guilty.

However, the responsibility is not borne by those who obtain information without being certain that it is, in fact, inside information, or by those who are not even sure the information is accurate (because it has been passed on by word of mouth or obtained by spying on an expert who usually makes successful deals and is known to be an inside trader).

Those who come upon information accidentally, either through someone's indiscretion or by chance, should proceed as if they had found lost property. It is not licit to keep or use lost property. It must be returned to its rightful owner or left at a 'lost and found' desk. In this case, it is not apparent who the owner is, but there clearly is one. Appropriating such information and trading with it also means appropriating the earnings obtained. The correct procedure is not to use it (leave it in the 'lost and found') so that its rightful owner can do so (the fact that it could be picked up by chance and used by someone else does not justify the first person's use of it).

Another possibility is that of third parties who obtain the information through someone's lack of discretion (relatives, friends, colleagues in other departments of the company and so on), either directly or with the recommendation to buy or sell securities. This group could include people who come by the information accidentally (unintentionally overhearing a conversation, accessing the data by chance on the computer and so on).

WHISTLE-BLOWING

The term 'whistle-blowing' has its origins in the practice of English metropolitan police (bobbies) who would blow their whistles when they observed a crime. In business ethics, whistle-blowing means the reporting of an organization's unethical practices by a current or former employee, either within the organization ('internal whistle-blowing') or publicly ('external whistle-blowing').[16] The wrongdoing might have to do with corrupt practices, adulteration of foods, health/safety violations, blatantly unlawful conduct, fraud and so on, which circumstances generally have a considerable effect on the public interest.

Whistle-blowing, as with any other ethical action, requires, first of all, rectitude. This means that one needs to be revealing the wrongdoing on moral grounds and not, for instance, for revenge.

External whistle-blowing reports conduct contrary to the common good or public interest to people or entities that have the power and, presumably, the willingness to take corrective action. These entities might be governmental or watchdog agencies, local authorities or law enforcement agencies. Sometimes, the mass media can also be an appropriate channel for whistle-blowing.

Internal whistle-blowing can include similar issues or any other irregularity. Some companies have institutionalized channels to report misconduct, with the opportunity for anonymity. These channels can include ombudsmen, ethical or compliance officers, and complaint hotlines.

Whistle-blowing has its ethical justification in the moral duty to avoid wrongdoing and to contribute to the common good. Covering up wrongdoing when it could be prevented entails responsibility for cooperation – by omission – in wrongdoing.[17]

Some people bear more responsibility than others due to their organizational position or role, or expertise on a topic. For instance, a company physician has more responsibility for whistle-blowing about a lack of protection of workers' health than does a financial officer, who also knows the facts.

Because of its negative effects, whistle-blowing should be the last resort. These effects include personal inconvenience, risk of retaliation against the whistle-blower and possibly loss of the organization's reputation.

The following are several criteria for analysing the extent to which one might be obliged to become a whistle-blower:

- Whistle-blowing should be done with *uprightness*, never as an act of revenge or with the intention of damaging a person or the organization to which one belongs or has belonged.

- Whistle-blowing should relate to an issue of *sufficient moral importance*. For instance, when covering up an issue would affect people's health or bring about serious economic damages.

- One should possess *relevant information* before blowing the whistle. This does not mean possessing absolute certainty, as if one were proving a crime at a trial, but at least sufficient clues to initiate an investigation.

- One should explore all *ordinary channels* within the organization for dealing with misconduct and exhaust all possibilities before undertaking any external whistle-blowing, which could damage the organization. However, in some cases, such as a real risk of retaliation against the whistle-blower, or urgency, public whistle-blowing could be recommended.

- One should have *reasonable grounds* for believing whistle-blowing would be effective. This requires foreseeing that those charged with preventing or punishing misconduct will act effectively.

- Finally, one should choose *the best way* to blow the whistle. Having recourse to appropriate agencies is often preferable to going to the media. A controversial point is whether whistle-blowing is in conflict with the employee's duties of loyalty to the firm.[18]

Few would deny that employees bear duties of loyalty in serving the legitimate interests of their firm and in keeping the secrets and confidential information that they know by virtue of working there. However, loyalty is not a virtue if it means adherence to illegitimate interests or faithfulness to illegitimate commitments.[19] Whistle-blowing favours the common good and does not work against any legitimate commitment. A whistle-blower who acts uprightly is being loyal to the moral good as well as to his or her employer.

In order to protect higher goods and avoid retaliation, whistle-blowers should be protected, but they must also be aware that false accusations can also be levelled via established proceedings for whistle-blowing.

BRIBERY, EXTORTION AND OTHER IRREGULAR PAYMENTS

Bribery

An action in which someone gives cash, a gift or some other benefit such as an emolument or privilege, to obtain an unjust judgement, a vote or some type of behaviour by someone in a position of trust. One might seek to obtain a favourable but unjust sentence from a judge, a public contract or a privilege from a civil servant or politician, or a favourable decision from a purchase manager. Those who receive a bribe take advantage of their position for personal benefit (or for the benefit of their political party or other organization) and act against the duties of their position; that is, to give a fair sentence or judgement, or to pursue the best interest of the institution for which they are working.

Extortion

This takes place when someone (the extortionist) demands money, or some other gift to which he or she is not entitled, through intimidation or undue exercise of authority. In business, extortion can come from an extortionist who proposes accepting a bribe, or in 'exchange' for doing what one is obliged to do, or perhaps for granting favourable treatment to the disadvantage of others with the same right. Extortion occurs, for instance, when a politician demands money for bypassing the usual process and giving a contract to a chosen company, or when a purchase manager demands money or a gift for his or her personal benefit (not a discount for the company) under the threat that otherwise the company will buy from a competitor. Extortion comes, therefore, from those with decision-making power over something that affects the victim of the extortion, or can exert influence on such a decision.

Extortion is sometimes, but not always, quite blatant (*explicit extortion*). It might be subtly insinuated, without explicit demands, where it is known to be general practice (*tacit extortion*). In the latter case, it might appear to be a bribe but is actually extortion.

Blackmail

Blackmail is a particular form of extortion It occurs when a person threatens to expose discreditable information about someone unless the victim gives money or some other thing of value to the blackmailer.

Kickbacks

Kickbacks is a colloquial term that refers to the return of a percentage of a sum of a contract received by a civil servant, politician or some other person who selects such a contract. From an ethical perspective, a kickback is a form of bribery or extortion, depending on whether it is offered (bribery) or required (extortion).

Facilitating payments

Facilitating payments, sometimes also called 'grease payments', consist of giving some moderate amount of money to public officials (or to employees of a private company) for actions such as processing papers, issuing permits and so on, in order to expedite performance of duties of a non-discretionary nature; that is, duties they are already bound to perform. These payments are not intended to influence the outcome of the official's action, merely its timing. Thus, facilitating payment is not bribery – just a little tacit extortion.

Gifts and business considerations

Giving small gifts in a business context can be a sign of hospitality or gratitude, or an expression of regular business considerations, practised by an entire industry, or in a certain country. However, certain gifts and business considerations are actually elaborately disguised bribes, or serve as a way to ensure that the bribes go unnoticed. 'Business consideration' might appear in the form of invitations to restaurants to discuss business, or trips to visit facilities related to a possible sale. But sometimes business considerations include luxury lunches in fashionable restaurants, tickets to operas or shows, visits to facilities in far-off places with short vacations included in the same package, training courses with or without a per diem allowance and so on.

Practical wisdom helps determine how far one can go, depending on the circumstances. In each environment and situation, one should distinguish between permissible and impermissible gifts. Some companies, in their codes of business conduct, even give very precise guidelines on the subject, including the maximum value of a gift one can accept. People offering business considerations must take into account the local customs of the country, the usual practices within the industry and – above all – common sense.

To distinguish ordinary business considerations associated with a purchase transaction from another comparable to a bribe, there are two sensible guidelines:

- Do not accept any consideration that seems excessive
- Do not let any considerations received hamper your freedom and independence to choose what you deem best for the company you represent.

Insight 6:

Fighting against corruption

Corruption, basically bribery and extortion, is often mentioned among the causes that greatly contribute to underdevelopment and poverty. It destroys trust, prevents the smooth functioning of economic and political institutions, and introduces a lack of transparency into crucial aspects of business and social life. When corruption enters the political arena, the role of representative institutions is distorted. Corruption runs against the basic common good of *legality*, which entails respect for rules.

To fight against corruption, a number of laws, international conventions and other documents have been published. Some national laws against corruption include regulations regarding transactions and business activities in foreign countries. This is the case of the *Foreign Corrupt Practices Act* promulgated in the US in 1977, after the Watergate scandal and certain other affairs involving business corporations.[20] This was a praiseworthy initiative; however, some American companies complained because this measure left them at a competitive disadvantage.

A more international initiative was undertaken by the OECD. This organization launched the *OECD Anti-Bribery Convention* in 1997.[21] The 37 countries that have ratified it have made the commitment to monitor and follow up on bribery within their scope of responsibility.

In 2003, another convention was approved by the General Assembly of the United Nations[22] under the title *UN Convention Against Corruption*. This is a comprehensive set of standards and measures to promote international cooperation to fight against corruption worldwide. Approximately 140 countries have signed it.[23]

An admirable initiative to fight corruption at the international level is *Transparency International* (TI), a global civil society organization.[24] Among other

Insight 6: (cont'd)

activities, since 1995, TI has compiled the annual *Corruption Perceptions Index*. This index, which has become very popular, ranks 180 countries by their perceived levels of corruption, as determined by expert assessments and opinion surveys.

All these measures can aid in fighting bribery and other forms of corruption. However, we should not forget individual corporations.[25] Business can easily accept and perpetuate corruption in organizations or, on the contrary, they can act efficiently to prevent it. Corruption spreads within the organization through processes of rationalization (people try to justify it) and socialization (increasing numbers of people participate in it). A culture of honesty and transparency is a good means with which to fight against corruption. Top management serve as ethical role models in either fostering or preventing corruption.[26]

MORALITY OF BRIBERY AND EXTORTION

Both offering and accepting a bribe are morally illicit, as is extortion, for a number of reasons:

- First, those who receive a bribe or who practise extortion act against justice, and those who offer bribes *cause injustice*. A job or position does not entitle its holder to accept money, so taking advantage of this position for personal profit is an abuse of power. Moreover, injustice might be done to the company or the public institution itself if it has to pay a higher price (contract, product purchased and so on), perhaps to compensate for the amount of the bribe. In addition, injustice might be done to those suppliers who 'play clean' and could offer a better product than those who pay bribes.

- Second, accepting a bribe is an act of *disloyalty* to the company in which a person is employed (in the case of purchasing managers) or to the society served (in the case of civil servants and politicians). The duties of loyalty inherent in the job of purchasing manager basically consist of buying what is best for the company. The same could be said of a civil servant or a politician working in public administration.

- Third, these actions contribute to the *spreading of a culture of corruption*. Furthermore, they encourage others to participate in underhanded dealings to the detriment of professionalism and authentic service (better prices, quality products and service), which works against the common good.

Seeking human excellence requires serious efforts to fight against corruption. However, certain situations can present difficult problems for business. While giving or accepting a bribe or extorting is never acceptable, *giving in to extortion* can be acceptable in some difficult circumstances.

Giving in to extortion to obtain something wrong in itself (for example an unjust decision) is always ethically unacceptable, since this is an intrinsically wrong action. However, giving in to extortion could be acceptable when the victim has a right to something and can only obtain it by giving in to the extortionist.

Those subjected to extortion do not provoke or approve of the extortionist's behaviour. Indeed, they are victims and have no choice but to pay. This falls under the heading of double effect, and can be acceptable in some cases, for a just and proportionate cause. The corresponding responsibility is a material cooperation in wrongdoing. Following the guidelines established for these kinds of actions,[27] the following criteria can help to determine whether it is ethically acceptable to give money to an extortionist in order to obtain a legitimate right:

- *Resisting extortion*: This is the first thing to do. There are a number of steps that can be taken, including reporting the affair to the appropriate legal authority, presenting a formal complaint to the company or institution that employs the would-be extortionist, reporting the extortion to the media and so on. These can be effective in some situations and can contribute to changing corrupt environments.

- *Seeking alternatives*: If the problem cannot be solved by resisting extortion, some other alternative should be explored. There are companies that systematically refuse to give in to extortion and, if it is not possible to avoid extortion, they look for clients who do fair business. This is the right thing to do when possible, even if it brings great inconvenience. But unfortunately, it is not always possible. There are highly regrettable situations in which corruption is deep-rooted and companies cannot do any business without paying off a powerful extortionist.

- *Being honest*: This means acting with uprightness, without deceiving oneself about the situation. One should strive to exercise legitimate rights (for example, participating in fair commercial competition). This also requires that the payment does not directly put another competitor at an unjust disadvantage. Another aspect of honesty is avoiding rationalizing ones actions. For instance, it would not be acceptable to argue that there is no alternative if alternatives had not already been sought and considered.

- *Having just and proportionate causes*: An action with a double effect is only licit if there are just and proportionate moral reasons to tolerate negative effects. The latter can include, for example, the degree of illicit enrichment of the extortionist and the introduction of a dangerous practice into the company itself, and a possible increase in the amount of corruption in the environment.

- *Avoiding scandal*: Giving in to an extortionist can cause moral scandal in those unfamiliar with all aspects of the case. Consequently, it is advisable to explain the personal opposition of the person succumbing to the pressure, and the moral and business reasons for accepting the extortion.

Reflecting on these criteria requires practical wisdom. In complex situations, or when in doubt, it is advisable to seek help from impartial, upright and capable people. In this respect, it is worth keeping in mind the difficulty of being a judge and an interested party at the same time.

Regarding facilitating payments, these can be a common practice in some environments and some laws might even tolerate this practice if it is common in a country where a company operates. However, this is not a strong enough ethical argument to justify such payments. In practice, facilitating payments have a pernicious effect on the function of public and private administrations. All too often they are the slippery slope to more serious forms of corruption: they impose additional costs on companies and citizens and, in the long run, they sap the ethical foundations of organizations. Thus, business firms should, as much as possible, avoid both facilitating payments and payments under explicit extortion. [28]

RESTITUTION AND COMPENSATORY DAMAGES

Misappropriation brings about a permanent state of injustice. Someone has taken something that belongs to someone else. Thus, justice requires *restitution;* that is, the return of anything misappropriated or a due compensation for damage unjustly caused. Restitution is also required for embezzlement of the assets of others (even if the parties harmed are unknown to the embezzler), and for any profits obtained through insider trading. When the damaged parties are anonymous, the money should go to charitable or benevolent institutions.

The obligation of restitution can be delayed when the debtor has not returned the goods or money in question but, as soon as it becomes possible, it must be made. However, this obligation can cease for certain reasons, such as if the debt is written off by the creditor, or other situations contemplated by the law.

One form of injustice is that which comes from actual injury or economic loss unfairly caused. To overcome such situations of injustice, some kind of compensation is required to restore the injured party in the position he or she enjoyed prior to the injury. *Compensatory damages* are paid to compensate for such injuries or loss, and refer to harm caused to a person's property, personal well-being or financial interests (for example, physical injuries, torts, breach of contract, wrongful termination). Frequently, it is a court that will determine how to reimburse an injured party for the harm caused by another's actions.

Business ethics in practice 6:

General Motors – Sullivan Principles and gift-giving policy

General Motors Corporation (GM), nowadays the world's largest car producer, employs around 700,000 people in 33 countries throughout the world.

For a long time, Leon H. Sullivan (1922–2001) was Board Member of GM. Dr Sullivan was a Baptist minister and a civil rights leader. He is famous for a set of principles known as the *Sullivan Principles,* published in 1977 to apply economic pressure on the apartheid policy of South Africa. The policy was updated in 1999, with a global perspective launching the *Global Sullivan*

Business ethics in practice 6: (cont'd)

Principles (GSP). These principles were incorporated by GM's Public Policy Center, and also adopted by many corporations based in the United States.

In GM, the following GSP are especially relevant:

Principle 1: We will express our support for universal human rights and, particularly, those of our employees, the communities within which we operate and parties with whom we do business.

Principle 2: We will promote equal opportunity for our employees at all levels of the company with respect to issues such as color, race, gender, age, ethnicity or religious beliefs, and operate without unacceptable worker treatment such as the exploitation of children, physical punishment, female abuse, involuntary servitude or other forms of abuse.

Principle 6: We will promote fair competition including respect for intellectual and other property rights, and not offer, pay or accept bribes.

Principle 8: We will promote the application of these Principles by those with whom we do business.

In accordance with Principle 6, in 1996 GM revised its policy on gifts, entertainment and gratuities, adopting strict measures.

Until then, entertainment and gift-giving in the automotive industry had been historically an acceptable business practice. GM itself had received a storm of media releases on the company's gratuities policy. But with the new policy, the situation changed. The new policy stated that employees must keep their integrity and restrain from offering, paying and accepting bribes. Exactly the same rules were applied to employees of all levels. The company prohibited its employees from accepting most gifts from dealers. Only items valued less than 25 dollars were permitted, inexpensive mementoes such as logo pens or cups.

The *GM Vision and Gift Policy* states that the best course is to decline any gift, entertainment or gratuity from a supplier. Gifts from anyone who might be seeking to influence GM's decision-making should be politely declined. Entertainment – such as a sporting event, theatre event or golf – can be accepted if offered by a non-supplier on condition that this is not lavish or frequent, and does not create a sense of obligation to the host. Dinners should be paid for by employees, and only awards dinners can be accepted. With the exception of 'official' gifts or entertainment, it is not appropriate to receive any gratuities from government or union officials.

Finally, even in limited situations, no gratuity should be offered unless it is legal, complies with the customers' and GM's policies, is justified by a legitimate and evident business interest pertaining to GM, is reasonable in light of prevailing local business custom and is infrequent.[29]

GM has continued with its gift policy, which is considered to be one of the strictest of that type in the car market.

Questions:

1. What effects might GM's policy on gifts and entertainments have in practice?
2. Do you think that GM's policy on gifts and entertainments is too strict?

Sources: V. Alonzo, 'GM has 'Zero Tolerance' for Free Subscriptions', Incentive, 170, 10 (1996): 14; 'GSP in Action' (General Motors), http://www.thesullivanfoundation.org/gsp/inAction/inAction%20-%20GM/default. asp; Global Sullivan Principles of Social Responsibility, www.thesullivanfoundation.org/foundation/; http://www. thesullivanfoundation.org/gsp/default.asp; J. Schmelz, 'Under General Motors Code, is Dealer Preview a Bribe?', Automotive News, 71 (1996): 14.

Dilemma 6

Peter, Bill, Dave and Fernando had just finished their first MBA year in a Spanish business school and now they were undergoing a project for a Belgian company as a requirement for a practical project during the summer term. This Belgian company was interested in entering the Spanish and German markets to provide a certain financial service. The four peers were hired to investigate these markets and to find possible business opportunities in which the Belgian company could become involved. They decided to divide the project into two: Bill and Fernando would take care of investigating the Spanish market, and Peter and Dave would investigate the German market. The information on the Spanish market was acquired with speed and efficiency thanks to some of Fernando's personal contacts. However, this was not the case for Peter and Dave. Time passed and the two still came up with nothing. When they presented their study to Brussels, their boss told them that if they could not produce data for Germany, the company would limit itself to the study done in Spain. This meant that they would be paid half the amount of the proposed project. Nevertheless, the four peers insisted on the initial offer and promised to do whatever was possible to gather the necessary data on the German market.

Peter contacted Mr Jones, a well-known broker in the City, through his brother who was working in London. Mr Jones had in his possession complete and valuable information about the German finance market. On the other hand, his information regarding the Spanish finance market was limited. Mr Jones made Peter a proposition: if Peter would agree to send him the report made on the Spanish market, on his part, Mr Jones would give Peter the study of the German market. Peter agreed.

When the report from Mr Jones of the German finance market arrived, amidst the euphoria of the other three of having the necessary data, Peter presented to them the deal that he had struck with Mr Jones. Bill and Fernando were opposed to what Peter had done since they were bound to confidentiality by the Belgian company. They drove home the point to Peter that his

Dilemma 6 (cont'd)

agreement with Mr Jones was a purely personal matter and that they did not have authority to send him the report on the Spanish market.

Dave tried to mediate between the two factions. He suggested that it was not necessary to send the entire report – specifically, the market opportunities and the methods of exploiting the opportunities – but they could limit the report to the data about the market accessible to anybody who investigated the same area.

Bill was entirely against this proposition. He stressed the idea that the data that they gathered was the fruit of long hours of research, a number of trips and other expenses, of which all costs were assumed by the Belgian company that had hired them. It was also agreed that all information acquired during the preparation of the project should be kept under strict confidentiality. Dave and Peter insisted on their position, arguing that in the UK this exchange of information was legal and frequently practised.

Questions:

1. What do you think about Peter's agreement with Mr Jones? Was it ethical?
2. Is Dave's recommendation acceptable?
3. Do you agree with Bill?
4. What would you recommend they do?

Summary

Contracts should be honoured if made and executed in good faith, if they were freely accepted and if the commitments made are morally just.

Misappropriation consists of an intentional usurpation of property – including material goods and intellectual property, or another's funds – for one's own use or for some other unauthorized purpose. There are several kinds of infringement of intellectual property rights, including infringement of copyright, trademark and patent. Industrial espionage is also a form of misappropriation.

A fraud is a theft via deception deliberately practised in order to secure unfair gain. A great variety of frauds exists. Some common forms include deception on quality or weight of products, forgery of cheques or invoices, counterfeiting, false billing, and giving a solid guarantee to pay for a product when one knows this would very probably be impossible.

(cont'd)

Embezzlement is the fraudulent appropriation of funds or property, which is especially serious because it is committed by a person with a responsibility to care for and protect another's assets, such as a manager or treasurer.

Trade secrets and confidential information must not be revealed, even when a manager or employee leaves their company.

Conflict of interest arises in situations in which the private interests and the official responsibilities of a person in a position of trust are opposed. When conflicts of interest exist, it is difficult to act impartially. They should thus be avoided. Transparency about conflicts of interest is highly recommended.

Tax evasion refers to avoiding the payment of lawfully due taxes. This differs from tax avoidance or tax mitigation, which is making use of legal methods to one's own advantage in order to reduce the amount of tax payable. There is an obligation to pay fair taxes, and the existence of unfair taxes should be proved beyond doubt.

Insider trading uses internal information that has not been disclosed to the public for the trading of stocks or other securities of a firm or corporation, and could substantially influence the price of said stocks or securities. Insider trading is unfair because it entails unfair competition, erodes trust in the securities market, is a violation of fiduciary duty and a breach of professional secrecy, and a misappropriation of private information.

Whistle-blowing refers to the reporting of a corporation's unethical practices by a current or former employee, either within the organization ('internal whistle-blowing') or publicly ('external whistle-blowing'). Since whistle-blowing entails both good and bad effects, a careful analysis is necessary before deciding to blow the whistle. In order to protect higher goods and to avoid retaliation, whistle-blowers should be protected, but it is also necessary to be aware that false accusations, using an established procedure for whistle-blowing, can also occur.

Corruption includes practices such as bribery, extortion, blackmail, kickbacks, questionable gifts and entertainment, and facilitating payments. Offering and accepting a bribe are both morally illicit, as is extorting. However, giving in to extortion can be acceptable in certain situations if the need is extreme.

When an injustice has been committed, it requires restitution. Similarly, injury or unjustly caused economic loss requires payment of compensatory damages.

Part III
Managerial Ethics

Free enterprise cannot be justified as being good for business; it can be justified only as being good for society.[1]

Peter Drucker (1909–2005)
Management guru

Chapter Aims

This chapter will allow you to:

- discuss why the purpose of the firm is relevant to business ethics
- consider the concept of 'corporate mission' and its difference from 'corporate vision', as well as the notion of 'mission-driven management'
- gain an understanding of conventional views of the business corporation and its historical antecedents
- discuss three different proposals about the conception and purpose of the firm in society
- gain an understanding of the view of the firm as a community of persons and the multi-ends of the firm
- discuss three models for corporate governance from an ethical perspective.

Key terms:

Agency theory
Community
Corporate governance
Corporate mission
Corporate vision
Corporation
Fiduciary duties

Firm's multi-ends
Homo oeconomicus
Management performance
Mission-driven management
Property rights
Purpose of business
Stakeholder approach

Sustainable corporation
Shareholder approach
The common good approach
Theory of the firm
Visionary companies
Wealth creation

The Purpose of the Firm and Mission-Driven Management

INTRODUCTORY CASE 7:

WAL-MART – AN INNOVATIVE STRATEGY WITH QUESTIONABLE PRACTICES

Wal-Mart is the largest public corporation in the world in terms of revenue. It is also the world's most important privately controlled economic institution, and has no rivals in influencing wage rates, prices and economies on a local, national and global scale.

The American company runs a chain of supermarkets in the USA and in other countries, having over 1.9 million employees. Its history began in 1940, when Sam Walton, a businessman from Arkansas, after beginning with a few retail outlets, opened his Walton's Five and Dime Store.

In 1962, his first Wal-Mart Discount City store appeared. The success of Wal-Mart's formula, which fanatically emphasizes cheap shopping, led Walton to open several new stores in the rural American South and gain high profits. In 1985, with just 1,000 stores, Walton was named by *Forbes* as the richest man in the USA.

With its slogan 'Always low prices. Always', Wal-Mart has grown to be one of the most admired companies in the world for its innovative strategy. Wal-Mart had been a huge company in terms of job creation (though at the cost of the disappearance of small retailers) and made it possible for consumers from poorer areas of the States and some other countries to save, on average, $600 per individual per year at the checkout counter.

In addition, Wal-Mart has taken some social initiatives. A well-known example was its action after hurricane Katrina in 2005. This hurricane was one of the deadliest ever recorded when it hit the southern coast of the United States. Wal-Mart immediately sent 1,900 trucks of water and other supplies to the afflicted areas. It contributed $17 million to the relief effort, and over $3 million in merchandise.

Although the immediate focus was on helping Wal-Mart's employees (who are called 'associates') and to facilitate the re-opening of their affected stores, they also supplied provisions to other victims whom governmental agencies could barely relieve.

In 1992, Walton passed away. Since then the expansion of the company has accelerated. Two factors contribute to the enlargement of Wal-Mart, logistics supported by information systems and globalization. Wal-Mart's management also decided to develop a more urban strategy. Along with this, pushing low prices on everything consequently shaped an aggressive culture, hostile to outsiders. At the turn of the century, after half a century of commercial success and social recognition for its low prices, the corporate reputation of this company dramatically decreased because of certain questionable practices with employees and suppliers. In 2004, precisely the year in which Wal-Mart reached the top of the *Fortune 500* list, Lee Scott, CEO of the company, suggested to investors that the company's poor reputation posed a threat to the continued growth of the business.

A centralized system gave Wal-Mart enormous power over suppliers. Critics say that Wal-Mart cut the suppliers' profit margins to the bone. This was apparently the case with Vlasic, one of Wal-Mart's suppliers. According to the executives of Vlasic, this company went bankrupt as a consequence of the treatment received from Wal-Mart.

Wal-Mart adopted a set of standards for suppliers in 1992, which included issues such as compliance with applicable laws and practices, reasonable hours of labour, no child labour, freedom of association (union) and others. However, critics said that the company had never taken these standards seriously.

A documentary entitled *Wal-Mart. The High Cost of Low Prices* listed a number of employees' rights violations. One of them was with regard to labour unions. Wal-Mart had traditionally been opposed to unions in the USA, though it negotiated with unions in Britain and some other countries. In the Philippines, Wal-Mart once dismissed 116 workers on strike. Wal-Mart was also accused of refusing to pay a basic minimum wage and of forcing employees to work overtime.

In December 2005, a Californian court ordered Wal-Mart to pay $172 million in damages for failing to provide meal breaks (as required under state law) to nearly 116,000 hourly workers. The company appealed the case. Further allegations referred to the illegal immigrants in the USA who were used as cheap labour. In 2005, Wal-Mart paid $135,540 to settle labour charges for allowing minors to operate hazardous machinery.

Wal-Mart was said to put tremendous pressure on store managers to control labour costs, resulting in underpaid employees in Bangladesh, Indonesia and China, and also in America. Furthermore, the numerous class-action lawsuits involved allegations of sex-based discrimination in pay, promotions, job transfers, training, job assignments and health-care coverage. The latter was given to less than 50 per cent of all employees. Wal-Mart also faced numerous cases of sexual harassment.

Wal-Mart wanted to change its reputation but, meanwhile, the lawsuits continued.

Questions:

1. In whose interest is Wal-Mart managed?

2. Do you think that these possible violations of workers' rights are actually a consequence of the philosophy and strategy of Wal-Mart?

3. What would you recommend to improve ethical behaviour and to change the negative image of Wal-Mart?

Sources: R. Berner, 'My Year at Wal-Mart', *BusinessWeek*, 12 February (2007); R. E. Freeman, 'The Wal-Mart Effect and Business, Ethics, and Society', *Academy of Management Perspectives*, 20 (2006): 38–40; C. Fishman, 'The Wal-Mart Effect and a Decent Society: Who Knew Shopping Was So Important?', *Academy of Management Perspectives*, 20 (2006): 6–25; R. Greenwald, *Wal-Mart. The High Cost at Low Price* (film), http://www.walmartmovie.com/; R. Slater, *The Wal-Mart Triumph: Inside the World #1 Company* (New York, Portfolio, 2003); 'Wal-Mart and a Union Unite, at least on Health Policy', *New York Times*, 7 February (2007).

RELEVANCE OF THE PURPOSE OF BUSINESS

Determining the purpose of business in society is highly relevant for business ethics, and for management ethics in particular. Many assume that business exists for the purpose of making money. Actually, this is a subjective motive for undertaking or managing a business, and one that is very relevant. Nevertheless, the purpose of the firm as an institution within society is more complex than the subjective motivation to make money.[2]

By the purpose of business, we mean the role of business in society and its social and ethical justification. To understand the purpose of business, we need to recognize that business benefits several groups of people, and that various factors must be present for a business to survive.

The existence of a business requires several groups of people whose subjective motivations for taking part perhaps differ, although they might also have shared goals. A firm needs capital to build its business, customers with an interest in the products or services it offers, managers and employees to contribute with their work, suppliers of raw materials, loans and services. Society – primarily, the local community – is also necessary: it provides infrastructure and supports the business. Society receives from business both benefits (for instance, products, jobs and taxes) and inconveniences (noise, waste, odours, increases in traffic and so on). The various constituent groups have different motives for acting in business (wages, products, income, personal development and the like), but all have an interest in its existence. Therefore, business performs several functions and appears to be a purposeful activity that benefits various parties and, through them, society at large.

The question of the purpose of business is important for at least two reasons. First, it determines whether an organization's activities are appropriate. Consequently, the purpose of a business gives us criteria with which to evaluate whether it is succeeding. A business has a different purpose than an NGO, but their respective purposes give us criteria to evaluate them and to justify their existence. Second, the purpose is important because it furnishes criteria for evaluating whether an entity is well designed and well managed. Whether a firm is successful and well managed will be defined in accordance with the purpose of business.[3]

Business ethics is concerned with both the morality of the activities derived from the purpose of the firm, and also with criteria to evaluate whether the firm is well designed and well managed from a moral point of view. Thus, understanding the purpose of the firm is very relevant to business ethics.

MISSION-DRIVEN MANAGEMENT

A defined purpose of business in society allows for the evaluation of the 'mission' chosen by each specific firm. Etymologically, 'mission' is from the Latin *missum*, or 'sent'. Many companies, including most *Fortune 500* corporations, have a written mission statement, which announces what the organization intends to do. Sometimes, the corporate mission is less than explicit, but many companies are managed according to a certain idea about what justifies their existence.

Some corporate mission statements contain only one objective, often related to the product and the client. This is the case of IKEA, a furniture company based in Sweden: 'IKEA's mission is to offer a wide range of home furnishing items of good design and function, excellent quality and durability, at prices so low that the majority of people can afford to buy them.'[4]

Others focus on several stakeholders. Thus, Merck, a well-known pharmaceutical company, states: 'The mission of Merck is to provide society with superior products and services by developing innovations and solutions that improve the quality of life and satisfy customers' needs, and to provide employees with meaningful work and advancement opportunities, and investors with a superior rate of return.'[5]

A third group includes several conceptual aspects in their mission statements. One example of this is Ben & Jerry's, whose mission statement includes three interrelated missions: (1) product mission; (2) economic mission; and (3) social mission.[6]

Related to corporate mission is the 'corporate vision'. Corporate vision defines what the organization intends to be in the future. It reflects the view of the organization's desired characteristics, what it would like to achieve in the mid-term or long term. In this sense, we talk of 'visionary companies' – when their future is focused on magnanimity, or presented though original ideas or innovative perspectives. Corporate vision is therefore different from mission, although there is often confusion between the two. While mission explains what the organization is doing now, vision is an aspirational description.

Corporate vision is frequently presented through a few challenging and easily remembered concepts to encourage people within the organization to advance towards a certain desirable form of conduct. Thus, Procter & Gamble, a well-known manufacturer of a wide range of consumer products, defines its vision as: 'Be, and be recognized as, the best consumer products and services company in the world.' [7]

In spite of the proliferation of mission and vision statements, not all companies use them as a management tool. Others, though, take them seriously as a compass for every corporate activity. Mission-driven management refers to the approach of managers who seek to adjust their managerial actions to the corporate mission.

Corporate mission is, then, the basis for the formulation of business strategy by which a company selects its long-term goals and decides upon the allocation of resources. Strategy is generally related to meeting market needs and stakeholder expectations, and to obtaining a competitive advantage. This can include a set of multi-year programmes that are subsequently developed and entail objectives, policies, plans, organizational structure and the corresponding implementation. Some have suggested that any area of responsibility within an organization should have its own mission in addition to the corporate mission.[8]

After this brief introduction, let us now examine the purpose of business. First, though, it is worth considering a few selected views of the firm. This will help us to comprehend the varying proposals about the purpose of business in society.

Insight 7:

The business corporation – An historical overview

A famous legal definition of the corporation was given at the beginning of the nineteenth century by United States Chief Justice John Marshall. In his words, 'A corporation is an artificial being, invisible, intangible, and existing only in contemplation of law. Being a mere creature of law it possesses only those properties which the charter of its creation confers upon it.'[9] This view has long prevailed. Its roots are to be found in the concession given by monarchs, and later by states, through a charter that allowed someone to create and run a business. This perspective still serves as a useful legal construct to facilitate juridical considerations. Even today, in legal studies, the business corporation (frequently taken as synonymous with 'firm')[10] is generally considered as a legal or 'fictitious person', an artificial entity, to whom specified rights and duties are ascribed. However, the idea that a corporation is only a legal fiction has been the target of severe criticism due to its high degree of abstraction and lack of realism.

Another view of the firm also emerged in the nineteenth century. Influenced by a strong ideological individualism that emphasized individual freedom, many theorists saw business firms as a *mere aggregate of individuals*. In fact, it was beyond argument that, at that time, firms were no longer created by concession but by free agreement between the parties.

With the emergence of large-scale enterprises and huge bureaucracies, a collectivistic view of the firm was fostered. Considering the compact and highly

Insight 7: (cont'd)

depersonalized structure of many companies, along with the influence of collectivistic ideology, the organization was increasingly seen as a single entity, and individuals were frequently regarded as almost completely subordinate to the organization. The whole was what mattered, and the individuals all but disappeared within it.

From this perspective it was easy to argue that corporations had not only a personhood, but also had to be dealt with as if they were a 'corporate person'. This view was initially proposed in Germany, and then in the USA, more than a hundred years ago. Today, some firms are still run according to this vision.[11] When a firm is seen as a compact structure, rules, procedures, policies and orders tend to eliminate any initiative on the employees' part, and to constrain individual decision-making autonomy within the organization. Individuals are 'diluted' within the system as passive elements of the production process, being treated as cogs in a machine. Many talents, skills and capabilities of people within the organizations also go to waste. A related view is to understand the corporation as analogous to a *living organism* with a body, mind and will. As with any organism, corporations have to adapt to their environment, and everything they do has to correspond to this purpose. If the firm is like an organism, people working within it are its 'organs', with little personal autonomy – mere passive elements of the system.

IS THE FIRM ONLY A SET OF CONTRACTS OR A MERE SYSTEM OF INTERESTS?

In the nineteenth and at the beginning of the twentieth centuries, two dominant views of the firm emerged (see Insight 7) that are still relevant today: the aggregate entity and collectivist views of the firm. But, beyond them, the firm can be seen as a community of persons, as will be explained later. From this perspective, the firm is considered a real entity created by an enduring union of persons who have a common goal but do not lose their autonomy, freedom and dignity; neither are they passive elements of the system. However, there are other views of the firm.

Neoclassical economics takes as its starting point the view of the firm as a mere aggregate of individuals united by a set of contracts. It adopts the *homo oeconomicus* model, in which individuals have interests and preferences, and act exclusively for self-interest, seeking merely to maximize their utility. This view also holds that individuals are united exclusively for reasons of power and advantage, and that the corporation is an artificial and fictitious entity. The 'collective' is merely the sum of individual interactions.

The view of the firm as a *set of contracts* is actually a hypothesis for economic theory, which helps in the understanding of empirical facts and the making of predictions. However, this view is reductionist, since it overlooks the possibility that individuals might establish links beyond the 'logic of interchange'. In addition, one can observe that, apart from contracts, other human relationships do exist within the firm, and real human behaviour does not always correspond to the *homo oeconomicus* model.[12]

Another view presents the firm as a *system of interests*. From this perspective, the firm is also an abstract and fictitious entity,[13] but stakeholders (owners, employees, customers, suppliers, the local community and possibly others) and their respective interests are essential. The corporation is seen, basically, as a centre of coordination of stakeholder interests or as 'a clearinghouse or nexus of activity where stakeholders satisfy their desires'.[14] One way to understand how the corporation works to coordinate interests is by considering that organizations have 'social contracts' with stakeholders, an idea borrowed from political theory.[15]

Understanding the firm as a mere social mechanism and social contract network also appears to be a narrow view. It presents an individualistic approach, which leads to viewing human relationships as based on mere hypothetical social contracts for converging mutual interests.

In a firm, one might encounter real commitment and willingness to cooperate in common purposes, although people might also have individual motives for working together. Cooperation to meet common goals is commonly accepted as an essential characteristic of organizations.[16]

People within a corporation carry out activities in cooperation, and the result cannot be attributed to anyone in particular but is attributable, rather, to the corporation as a whole, or to a group within the corporation. Common language also attributes actions or activities to corporations as a whole. Firms have a culture, a history and an accumulative learning; this remains even when individuals, who can join and leave the firm, have gone. In addition, firms interact, as a whole, with other social groups or institutions. Finally, from a philosophical perspective, we can argue that the whole, created by a principle of unity, is more than the sum of its parts.

All these arguments lead to the conclusion that a firm is a real entity (although very particular); that is, something more than the sum of the individuals who make it up. However, this entity does not cancel out its parts; on the contrary, it depends completely on the individuals that comprise it, and on the relationships between them. As pointed out earlier (Insight 7), this differs from the vision of the corporation as a living organism or as a 'corporate person', into which individuals practically disappear.

THE FIRM AS A COMMUNITY OF PERSONS

A third view of the firm is that which sees it as a human community, more specifically a 'community of persons', emphasizing the fact that those who form it are individuals with intrinsic dignity and open to personal development. This view is compatible with holding that a firm includes a set of contracts and a constellation of stakeholder interests, both convergent and conflicting. However, this view adds that persons are social beings; not only individuals with interests, but also with the ability to cooperate and contribute with a sense of service, to act with reciprocity and 'civic friendship'[17].

A community is generally understood as an enduring unity of persons involved in a common action for a shared purpose, although personal motivations can vary.[18] This is the case of a firm that includes a set of people united by various relationships, involved in a common action with the shared purpose of producing goods and services. Links that unite people within and around the firm can be very complex. First, there are contractual links or relationships based on mutual interests. Other links can also be very relevant, however. There are emotional links (a shared sense of belonging, affection for one's work in the corporation) and moral links (commitment, moral loyalty, willingness to work for the common good of the firm and so on). As Solomon pointed out, people who join a corporation find themselves, once hired, members of a social collective. In addition, frequently 'there is a conscientious effort to become a member, to internalize the appropriate shared attitude'.[19]

Firms are formed by individuals, their respective relationships and the resulting unity. Therefore, the firm is not an artificial entity or mere human construct. Neither is it a compact entity in which the individual fades to unimportance. Instead, the firm is a community of persons; that is, free and autonomous individuals who voluntarily undertake a corporate activity, working together to attain both individual and common goals.

FOR WHOSE BENEFIT SHOULD A COMPANY BE MANAGED?

Returning to the starting point, there is a question that is frequently posed as an alternative way to inquire into the purpose of business: For whose benefit should a company be managed? Two main answers are often given to this question. One is 'for the benefit of the stockholders (or shareholders)'; the other, 'for the benefit of all stakeholders, (including stockholders)'. These two positions, and the respective arguments to justify them, deserve some discussion.

The shareholder approach

The first position holds that the purpose of the business firm is to maximize shareholder wealth. This refers not only to current profits, but also to market assessment of a firm's economic value, which includes expectations about future profits.[20] Neoclassical economics accepts this position, along with the view of the firm as a mere set of contracts. Many companies, especially in the Anglo-Saxon world, follow this proposal. Several arguments are used to defend this position, but they have not met with universal approval. The arguments for and against it can be categorized into five groups:

- *Fiduciary duties.* Managers are agents of shareholders, who are the principals. Thus, they bear fiduciary duties to shareholders and have to serve their best interests, understood as maximizing their wealth. These fiduciary duties have, as a constraint, legislation, the rules of the free market and perhaps certain ethical customs.[21] Certainly, managers must not put their personal interests before their fiduciary duties, and must not profit from their position as fiduciaries, unless the principal consents. However, it is not ethical to serve the principal's interests at the cost of unethical behaviour towards others. In other words, fiduciary duties are not absolute; they are limited by other moral obligations.

- *Legality.* Legality in many countries, especially those of Anglo-Saxon influence, supports the idea that a corporate behaviour is right when it seeks to maximize profits and wrong when it does not.

  Against the 'legal argument', it is argued that not all countries have laws defining the purpose of the firm as maximizing profits or maximizing value creation for shareholders. Some countries, including continental Europe and Japan, are not as strict as the USA and other countries in demanding that all corporate decisions and behaviours be focused on the principle of maximizing profits or shareholder value. Europe and Japan are more in line with the idea that business functions are not only economic but also social, and that corporations ought to practise sustainable management.

- *Property rights.* Another argument for this view regards property rights. Property is something owned by an individual or group and entitles them to exclusive rights. The right of ownership entitles one to dispose of the property, to use it or not, to prevent others from using it, or to transfer ownership. Based on property rights, defenders of maximization of shareholder value usually recall that those who own a corporation (shareholders) have a right to decide how to use their property. From this premise, it can be assumed that shareholders want the corporation to maximize its profits, and consequently that managers should seek to do so.

  The arguments of property rights are also criticized by the stakeholder approach. Many might accept that the property right is real but not absolute. Property, they point out, has inherent limits.[22]

- *Wealth creation.* In a free-market system, focusing business activity on maximization of shareholder value is an effective path to wealth creation, since it incentivizes cost-cutting and profitable innovations, along with economic stimulus to open new markets. This argument is related to the 'invisible hand' metaphor of Adam Smith. Smith argued that when, in a free market, individuals pursue their own self-interest, this also tends to promote the good of their community as a whole. It is as though an 'invisible hand' were doing so. Thus, it is desirable that each firm seek to maximize revenue for itself, because in this way it maximizes the total revenue of society as a whole. Proponents of this vision[23] stress that social welfare is maximized when all firms in an economy maximize total firm value.

  Efficiency in wealth creation is a strong argument in favour of the maximization of shareholder value, although there are exceptions. However, wealth creation for shareholders cannot be the supreme argument to justify the purpose of business within society, wealth creation being only one aspect of a good social order. Wealth can be created at the price of maintaining subhuman conditions in the workplace, or without respect for human rights, or by overexploitation of natural resources and lack of concern about waste or pollution. Wealth can also be generated by selling products that are dangerous, harmful or have a negative impact on human flourishing.

- *Management performance.* Finally, it is argued that considering maximization of shareholder value introduces clarity and simplicity into management and serves as a strict control on managers to avoid opportunistic behaviours.[24] In addition, maximization of shareholder value presents a single, valuable objective to which one can refer everything else. This permits mathematical formulation of an objective function, with certain constraints and a variable to maximize. True enough, formulating a theoretical objective function to maximize shareholder value makes brilliant mathematical developments possible and simplifies matters enormously, but managing a corporation requires attentiveness to manifold aspects that cannot be quantified and introduced into an objective calculation.

    Apart from this, as Herbert Simon pointed out many years ago, managers do not always know how to maximize profits due to a lack of complete information in managerial decision-making.[25]

The stakeholder approach

This second proposal is closely related to the stakeholder view of the firm previously mentioned (pp. 159), which considers each company as a constellation of stakeholder interests. According to Evans and Freeman, the purpose of the firm is 'to serve as a vehicle for coordinating stakeholder interests' and management must balance all stakeholder interest.[26] As they affirm:

> the corporation ought to be managed for the benefit of its stakeholders: its customers, suppliers, owners, employees and local communities. The rights of these groups must be ensured, and, further, the groups must participate, in some sense, in decisions that substantially affect their welfare ... [Management] must act in the interests of the stakeholders as their agent, and it must act in the interest of the corporation to ensure the survival of the firm, safeguarding the long-term stakes of each group.[27]

Some authors introduce variations on understanding the purpose of the firm within the stakeholder approach. Clarkson holds that the purpose of the firm is to create wealth or value for its stakeholders by converting their stakes into goods and services. He argues that this is necessary for the survival and continuing profitability of the corporation.[28]

The stakeholder approach also presents arguments regarding fiduciary duties, legality, property rights, wealth creation and management performance:

- *Fiduciary duties.* Proponents of the stakeholder approach, such as Evans and Freeman, argue that managers bear fiduciary duty not only to shareholders, but also to all stakeholders.[29] In some way, stakeholders take on a manager as the agent of their respective interests. Not everybody accepts this argument: thus, as an alternative, other proponents of the stakeholder approach do not speak of fiduciary duties to stakeholders but, rather, of obligations of managers to stakeholders derived from their legitimate interests and relationships with the firm.[30]

- *Legality.* Laws change over time, and no two countries have identical legislation. Even in countries with a strong Anglo-Saxon influence, courts, in their interpretation, have evolved from a narrow view to one that considers long-term profits rather than immediate rewards. This permits managers and boards of directors to incur expenses or to invest in actions that are not directly related to short-term profits, including social donations, if such expenses or investments can contribute to maximizing long-term profits and shareholder value. Furthermore, numerous laws have been introduced in recent decades to bestow rights upon employees, consumers, local communities and other stakeholders (or reaffirm rights) that oblige corporations to pay more attention to stakeholders.

- *Propriety rights.* Donaldson and Preston argue in favour of the stakeholder approach, that property rights should be based upon an underlying principle of distributive justice. They also contend that all the critical characteristics underlying the classical theories of distributive justice are present in stakeholder theories.[31]

- *Wealth creation.* Freeman and others defend the position that the firm's long-term wealth creation is better served by considering the interests of stakeholders. In Freeman's words 'to maximize shareholder value over an uncertain time frame, managers ought to pay attention to key stakeholder relationships'.[32] Some research favours this thesis, and many managers agree with it, although more empirical evidence would be needed to prove or disprove it.[33] In any case, it is now commonly accepted that under certain conditions the satisfaction of the interests of stakeholders contributes to long-term value maximization. Thus, the stakeholder approach can converge with the shareholder approach in the long term. Jensen, an outstanding proponent of the shareholder approach, accepts considering stakeholders interests if they contribute to shareholder value maximization in the long term. He interprets this as 'enlightened value maximization'.[34]

- *Management performance.* A stakeholder approach precludes an objective function for evaluating business actions, and there is a risk of managers justifying self-serving behaviour by appealing to the interests of stakeholders. However, this risk could exist in any model. In addition, under certain conditions, managerial accountability to stakeholder groups can be promoted to deter misbehaviours.[35]

THE PURPOSE OF THE FIRM

Instead of asking for whose sake a company should be managed, we can go directly to the point and enquire as to the purpose of business, or, if one prefers, what justifies the existence of business within society.

At the beginning of this chapter, we highlighted that, according to Peter Drucker, business can be justified only as being good for society. Being good for society can be related to the concept of the common good – something potentially participated in by all members of a community.[36]

Different social groups (families, churches, schools, media and so on) are communities within the larger community. Each has its own common good. The particular common good of a group or institution is acceptable to the extent that it would contribute to the common good of society at large. Business corporations also have their own good, which contributes to society's common good in various ways.

If the purpose of the firm is to achieve the common good of both itself and society, one might inquire, how exactly it can do this. The firm performs several functions with their corresponding ends, which we can consider in light of their contribution to the common good. The firm can become a contributor to the common good in the following ways:[37]

- *Creating added economic value with justice and distributing it with equity.* The supply of useful goods and services is driven by the 'profit motive' in any business firm. Profits and the corresponding wealth creation contribute to the common good if it has been generated with justice and if, afterwards, it is equitably distributed among constituencies who have contributed to its creation: management, shareholders, workers and society (taxes and voluntary corporate donations). Indirectly, firms can also contribute to wealth creation through suppliers and customers.

- *Supplying useful goods and services efficiently and fairly.* The firm contributes to the common good by an efficient production and/or promotion and sale of goods and services that are genuinely useful for people, and by offering and selling them under fair conditions. Business activity provides access to goods and services for a greater number of people than would be the case if there were no business firms.

- *Providing jobs, opportunities and organizational conditions in accordance with human dignity and human rights.* People involved in the organization can gain their livelihood, develop their talents, acquire knowledge and skills, and flourish as human beings. These opportunities include training and learning, and the possibility of establishing human relations and cooperating in common actions. In this way, firms also contribute to the common good.

- *Promoting the necessary relationships between the firm and its constitutive stakeholders, fostering reciprocity, collaboration and cooperation among them.* Maintaining links with constitutive or primary stakeholders (basically employees, shareholders, clients/customers, suppliers and communities) is crucial for the life, and even for the survival, of a business firm. Ethics and, more specifically, the common good require that these links are based on reciprocity, following the Golden Rule, and cooperation, instead of relations of domination and abuse of power.

- *Striving for the continuity and sustainability of the firm.* This end entails maintaining the firm's existence and competitive ability over time. It makes the other ends possible. Such an end requires proficient management that does not forfeit a favourable position in the market and that knows how to manage a sustainable corporation.[38]

- *Being a good corporate citizen.* The business firm contributes to the common good beyond its core activities, acting as a good citizen; that is, being an agent for good within society.[39] This entails compliance with the law; paying taxes; avoiding negative impacts on people and the environment; and indirectly favouring the activity of other companies, institutions or communities that benefit the activity of the corporation. Business can also contribute to the common good through specific actions for solving social problems together with other social groups or institutions and the government, in accordance with the firm's capabilities and without damaging its own mission.

Along with these positive effects, business activity can also erode the common good in different ways; for instance, supplying harmful goods or services, creating wealth unfairly, or maintaining jobs and work conditions in which human dignity is not sufficiently respected or human flourishing is prevented. The common good can also be eroded through an abusive consumption of natural resources, pollution, inappropriate waste disposal and so on, and by lack of an appropriate balance between work and private or family life.

Therefore, the purpose of the firm contains manifold ends that derive from the firm's functions, oriented to the common good. These multi-ends, which define the purpose of the firm, should be included in the corporate mission, at least implicitly. This leads us to define the purpose of the firm as the *common good through its multi-ends.*

These multi-ends are different but interdependent. Procter & Gamble presents some of the mentioned ends in its mission statement (called 'Our Purpose') which points out its interdependence: 'We will provide branded products and services of superior quality and value that improve the lives of the world's consumers, now and for generations to come. As a result, consumers will reward us with leadership sales, profit and value creation, allowing our people, our shareholders and the communities in which we live and work to the common good to prosper.'[40]

The common good approach

The previous considerations about the purpose of the firm suggest a new approach about the fundamental orientation of management, wider than shareholder and stakeholder approaches, derived from considering the firm as a community within a larger community. This could be termed 'the common good approach' or 'multi-ends approach'. The arguments discussed for both the shareholder and stakeholder approaches can be considered in this approach:

- *Fiduciary duties.* It is argued that the primary fiduciary duty of those who manage the corporation is to the corporation itself. According to Koslowski, 'fiduciary duty entails something more than agency, something more than merely acting in the interest of one's principal. It is a duty to act for the good of the whole institution, the entity for which one has been authorized to act by the principals'.[41]

- *Legality.* This approach also considers that legality does not have a strong stock-holder orientation in all countries. Moreover, laws are not in themselves a moral justification. Ethics comes first [42]. 'Whatever the legality may be, a corporation is a member of the larger community, which is inconceivable without it.'[43]

- *Property rights.* It is emphasized that ownership, although it confers rights, also has a social function, and the means of production (property) performs a social function, too.[44] Besides, a corporation is not merely material property – such as a plot of land or a car – but, rather, a human reality. In a corporation, owners hold shares and risk funds, but workers contribute with their personal work to the goals of the corporation and risk their employment. In business, nowadays, knowledge is crucial and, in many companies, human capital is more important than financial capital.

  The language of business often suggests that people are mere 'human resources', and corporations simply a matter of ownership that is bought and sold, sometimes without acknowledgement that the corporation is made up of persons. As the celebrated management writer Charles Handy wrote:

  > the idea of a corporation as the property of the current holders of its shares is confusing because it does not make clear where power is. It is an affront to natural justice in that it gives inadequate recognition to the people who work in the corporation and who are, increasingly, its principal assets. It might even be considered immoral for people to talk of owning other people, as shareholders implicitly do.[45]

- *Wealth creation.* Wealth creation is crucial for business and, when carried out with justice, is an integral part of the common good of the firm and society; it must therefore be pursued as a primordial goal. The mission-driven orientation to the common good includes both seeking fair profits and coordinating legitimate stakeholders' interests. In the long term, the common good orientation will probably contribute to excellent results in terms of wealth creation, as proponents of the stakeholder approach contend. But this approach stresses that profits, while doubtless important, are not ends in themselves. They are instrumental; their function is maintaining and improving the firm in the long term in such a way that the company can achieve its aims and contribute to societal well-being and the development of people.

  Here, it is worth underlining that profits are not the end of business but the means. People are the end. In the words of Handy:

  > Profits are the lifeblood of any business, but life consists of more than keeping the blood flowing; otherwise, it would not be worth living. As more corporations realize this truth, they will become increasingly interested in enriching the lives of the people who work in them. In time, the laws governing corporations will change to reflect the new reality. First, however, we need a language to explain this new theory – a language of community and citizenship, not of property.[46]

- *Management performance.* In this approach, management performance requires a sense of stewardship, which leads to a careful and responsible administration of assets entrusted to one's care, and to developing the best strategies, being aware of one's social function and moral responsibility. Practical wisdom is also required to specify the contents of the common good in every situation and to deal with stakeholders' interests. As with the stakeholder approach, the manager needs integrity. In addition, certain control systems are necessary to avoid the risk of managerial opportunism, in case of managers with less integrity.

IMPLICATIONS OF THE FIRM'S PURPOSE FOR CORPORATE GOVERNANCE

At the beginning of the twentieth century, when companies became greater in size, owners were no longer able to control their business as they had done previously. In many cases, those who owned the business stock would never have been in the company factories or known most aspects of how the company was being managed. The problem created by the separation of ownership and managerial control was pointed out by Berle and Means.[47] They warned of the concentration of economic power brought about by the emergence of a powerful class of professional managers, insulated from the pressure of stockholders and without any public control. In order to deal with this problem, business firms and corporations established what we now call 'corporate governance' with the duty of supervising management and to direct the corporation.

Facing the problem of the separation of ownership and control in the modern corporation, several models have been proposed to prescribe how to use power in corporate governance and how this can control managerial power. They are closely related to how the firm and its purpose are viewed (see Table 7.1). Three proposals for the purpose of the firm bring about three models of corporate governance: (1) the shareholder model; (2) the stakeholder model; and (3) the mission-driven model.

The shareholder model

This model assumes that the purpose of the firm is maximizing shareholder wealth. This is closely related to agency theory, which considers managers as agents and shareholders as the principal.[48] Although managers should do their best to serve shareholder interests, an exclusive focus on them might leave managers disinclined to fulfil their fiduciary duties; they might take advantage of opportunities to benefit themselves or others at the expense of stockholders. In order to avoid this problem, corporate governance should be oriented to aligning the manager's economic interests with those of the shareholder. Bonds related to profits or share value, as well as stock options, are used to this end, frequently with very high executive compensations.[49]

This model can help prevent opportunistic managerial behaviours and the associated unfair conduct towards shareholders. However, looking exclusively at

Table 7.1   Models of identity and purpose of the firm and the corresponding models for corporate governance

	View of the firm	Purpose of the firm	Corporate governance model
Contractual approach	A fictitious person and a set of contracts	Maximizing shareholder wealth	*Shareholder model* Orientation to maximize shareholder value (there is a tendency to be more tolerant in considering the interests of other stakeholders).
Stakeholder approach	A system of stakeholder interests	Coordinating stakeholder interests	*Stakeholder model* Orientation to stakeholder interests, creating value for the stakeholders and maintaining the survival of the firm.
Common good approach	A community of persons producing goods and services	Achieving the multi-ends of the firm in accordance with the common good of the society	*Mission-driven model* Orientation toward the good of the firm, defined by its multi-ends in accordance with the common good of society through the firm's mission (legitimate stakeholder interests are also considered).

fiduciary duties towards shareholders can incentivize decisions and actions that do not respect the rights of other stakeholders. In addition, control can hardly be absolute. The agent usually has more information about his actions or intentions than the principal does, because the principal usually cannot monitor the agent with perfect effectiveness. The agent might have an incentive to act inappropriately (to the principal's mind) if the interests of the agent and the principal are not aligned.

Another difficulty is that this model looks more easily to short-term horizons than to long-term horizons, and this can be contrary to the common good of the firm by damaging the firm's long-term sustainability.

Finally, this model contains grounds for anthropological and ethical reservations. The anthropological hypothesis that managers' actions seek to benefit their own self-interest and damage that of others needs further enquiry. It would doubtless be naïve not to acknowledge that managers might adopt opportunistic behaviour, but it should not be forgotten that they can also be very responsible, discharging their duty in the best interests of the company. Strong incentives to align managers with shareholder economic interests can foster egoistical tendencies and bring to pass what have been called 'self-fulfilling prophecies'[50] – that egoistical managerial behaviour will be fostered by applying the theory. From an ethical perspective, this model does not ensure ethical behaviour towards stakeholders other than shareholders. As noted above, this model can promote injustices towards stakeholders for the sake of maximization of shareholder value.

Although this paradigm is still dominant in many US and UK companies, as well as in other countries, it is nonetheless controversial.[51] There is currently a tendency to be more tolerant in considering the interests of other stakeholders and in including them in corporate governance, but the main principle of maximization of shareholder value remains.

The stakeholder model

According to this model, corporate governance and management should be oriented to the legitimate interests of all the relevant stakeholders of the firm, seeking to create value for them. Thus, contributors of capital, including stockholders and bondholders, should receive a rate of return sufficient to induce them to contribute their capital to the enterprise. At the same time, employees should receive appropriate compensation and meaningful employment opportunities; the customers should receive the products they want at a reasonable price and so on.

This approach presents some limitations. One of these regards the determination of which interests to satisfy, and the challenge of choosing a sound ethical theory to resolve conflicting stakeholder interests. Although the viability of the firm as a whole is also considered by some authors, in stakeholder theory the attention is basically focused on balancing interests rather than on the firm. There is the risk that such balance might not always be in the firm's own best interests and, if it is not, all stakeholders will ultimately be harmed.

The mission-driven model

This focuses on governing the firm as a whole, considering it as a human community or, more precisely, as a community of persons within society.

An analogy can be established between this model of corporate governance and the government of a country: the rulers of a country and those who govern a firm. Suitable political action should be oriented to the public interest and not to the interests of politicians or those of their electors. Similarly, directors of a board or others who take part in corporate governance should seek the common good of the firm over and above the interest of any stakeholder.

This model is therefore based on the idea that the purpose of the firm is achieving multi-ends in accordance with the good of the firm and the common good of society through mission-driven management. The long-term results are crucial, but short-term results can only be forgotten at the peril of the firm's survival. Management needs to balance both short- and long-term results with practical wisdom.

Business ethics in practice 7:

Medtronic – A mission-driven company

Medtronic Inc. is a leading global medical technology company, based in Minneapolis. It was founded in 1949 as a very small company repairing medical equipment, but was soon modifying equipment and producing new devices needed for special tests. In 1957, they invented the first wearable pacemaker in the world. In the following years, the company grew with innovative high-tech products and with entrance into new markets. By the end of the 1970s, the company stock was listed on the New York Stock Exchange.

In 1962, Earl Bakken, the founder of Medtronic, wrote the Medtronic Mission. This was not conjectural, but a milestone for Medtronic. They have never changed it. Since then, Medtronic leadership has continued the mission and made serious efforts to implement it. This is the Medtronic Mission:

> To contribute to human welfare by application of biomedical engineering in the research, design, manufacture, and sale of instruments or appliances that alleviate pain, restore health, and extend life.

> To direct our growth in the areas of biomedical engineering where we display maximum strength and ability; to gather people and facilities that tend to augment these areas; to continuously build on these areas through education and knowledge assimilation; to avoid participation in areas where we cannot make unique and worthy contributions.

> To strive without reserve for the greatest possible reliability and quality in our products; to be the unsurpassed standard of comparison and to be recognized as a company of dedication, honesty, integrity, and service.

> To make a fair profit on current operations to meet our obligations, sustain our growth, and reach our goals.

> To recognize the personal worth of employees by providing an employment framework that allows personal satisfaction in work accomplished, security, advancement opportunity, and means to share in the company's success.

> To maintain good citizenship as a company.

A survey showed that 92 per cent of all Medtronic employees claimed that the work they did supported the Medtronic mission, 90 per cent had a clear understanding of its mission, for 84 per cent Medtronic's mission was consistent with their personal values, and 84 per cent felt proud to work for Medtronic.

In 2000, Medtronic's CEO, William George, received the Distinguished Executive of the Year Award at the Academy of Management's annual conference in Washington, DC, for his leadership, 'which exemplifies the highest ideals and values'.

At that time, Medtronic had 26,000 employees and was worth $63 billion. It had $5 billion in sales coming from a variety of devices that did everything from controlling pain to reducing the tremors of Parkinson's disease. The *Economist* described Medtronic as the most innovative firm in the medical-device industry and a *Fortune Magazine* cover story named Medtronic as the 'Microsoft of the medical device industry'.

Business ethics in practice 7: (cont'd)

Between 1985 and 2001, Medtronic's revenues grew from $363 million to $5.5 billion, an 18 per cent compound growth rate. Earnings per share grew from $0.04 per share in 1985 to $1.05 in 2001. This was a compound growth of 23 per cent per annum. The rates of growth of revenues and earnings were very consistent, looking back over this period. In George's speech, given when he received his Distinguished Executive of the Year Award, he affirmed that these results were a real test of Medtronic philosophies.

'My basic premise', he said, 'was that those companies that devote themselves to maximizing shareholder value as their primary purpose will ultimately fail to do so in the long run.' Moreover, he claimed that it was a big mistake to make decisions just to increase short-term shareholder value. He called it 'selling a soul'. According to George, when the leadership sells its own soul to gain personal advantage and to abandon long-held values or its mission, the trust is broken and it will never be regained.

He assured that 'there is a better way to increase long-term shareholder value, but this cannot be the primary objective'. In his own words, 'It is my belief that corporations are created for a purpose beyond making money. Sustained growth in shareholder value may be the end result, but it cannot be the sole purpose.' He added: 'The real bottom line of the corporation is not earnings per share, but service to humankind. To achieve sustained success, a corporation that thinks about its long-term best interest must lead with its values – from top to bottom.' George believed that one of the greatest contemporary business challenges was creating a values-centred and performance-driven organizational culture.

Following Medtronic's experience, George suggested three necessary conditions for long-term growth in shareholder value:

• A mission-driven company

• A values-centred organization

• An adaptable business strategy.

According to George, a mission-driven company and a values-centred organization yields sustainable increases in shareholder value, as is shown in Figure 7.1. George agreed with the concept of serving everyone who had a stake in the organization, in the following order: (1) customers; (2) employees; (3) shareholders; (4) suppliers; (5) communities. Nevertheless, these are not independent but interrelated.

He claimed that 'in mission-driven companies, employee motivation comes from believing in the purpose of the work and being part of creating something worthwhile'. George knew that employees are seeking meaning in work, as they spend more time at work than anywhere else in their lives. Thus, they have a right to a meaningful job. Fair compensation is not enough. A purpose to their work and a consistent set of values – such as serving customers, quality or integrity – should be remembered by them every day.

The third necessary condition for sustainable growth in shareholder value is a sound business strategy that is adaptable to changing business conditions.

Business ethics in practice 7: (cont'd)

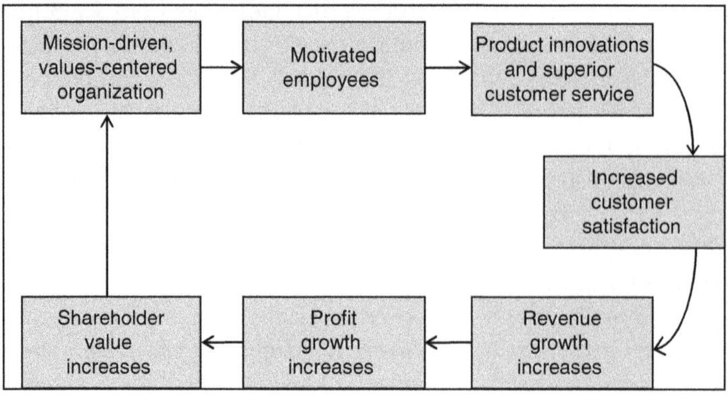

Figure 7.1   From corporate mission and values to shareholder value increase

Source: Adapted from the speech given by W. W. George at the Academy of Management in 2000 (see van de Ven, 2001, in sources for this case).

Regarding corporate values, George stated that certain values must be highlighted by the company, in order to gain the employees' trust and belief in the purpose of their work. He stressed: serving customers, quality, integrity in business dealings, respect for employees, and good citizenship. For him, integrity is paramount. It appears as the value that is required in every authentic leader. George noted that integrity is not just the absence of lying, but telling the whole truth, as painful as it might be. He underlined: 'if you don't exercise complete integrity in your interactions, no one can trust you. If they cannot trust you, why would they ever follow you?'[52]

In the following years, Medtronic has continued its successes, under its mission and values, and accompanied by a strong research and development, proximity to clients and innovative technologies.

Questions:

1. What aspects of Medtronic's mission do you find outstanding?

2. What do you think of Bill George's vision about the corporation's purpose and his order of priorities among stakeholders?

Sources: Abridged version of the case study Medtronic Inc.: From Corporate Mission to Organizational Culture (A) by D. Melé and A. Corrales', IESE Publishing, Barcelona, Spain, 2005 (published with permission), extended with information from the following sources: W. W. George, Leading With Your Values, (Center for Ethical Business Cultures, 1993); W. W. George, Authentic Leadership: Rediscovering the Secrets to Creating Lasting Value (San Francisco: Jossey-Bass, 2003); W. W. George, True North. Discover your Authentic Leadership (San Francisco: Jossey-Bass, 2007); Medtronic Official Website: www.medtronic.com/corporate/history.htm; A. H. van de Ven, 'Medtronic's Chairman William George on how Mission-driven Companies create Long-term Shareholder Value', Academy of Management Executive, 15 (2001): 39–47.

Dilemma 7

Borgani is a Chinese company that produces screens for televisions, computers and video games. Its chain manufacturing system has allowed successive progress, year-on-year, in terms of productivity. Recently, a new process of production has been adopted and, for that reason, the people in charge of this process were modifying the workflows. Although most of the operations are automated, the production system required a human intervention to carry out diverse checks throughout the production chain.

Xiang, who has been working as a quality manager for more than 15 years, has seen how the working conditions have changed over time and how they have become harder. He, as most workers, thinks that wages are too low and the working conditions are poor. Management only reward the increase in productivity.

If, in a certain month, the production has increased – mainly because there were fewer test failures – in the following month, production was expected to reach this higher level. However, in practice, it was difficult to surpass the previous flows.

On the other hand, the production manager observed that within the control systems it was necessary to consider a threshold of failures that would be fixed as a 'floor'. Particularly, it was in the last days of each month that a greater number of failures took place.

One day, Xiang observed that one of the workers conducted an incorrect operation on one of the screens, rendering it unusable. Although it could have been an involuntary error, he wondered if it might have been done deliberately.

Wei, the general manager of this factory, was very rough in dealing with people, as were the supervisors. He justified himself, saying that this was the only way to act and to obtain as much profit as possible, which is the main interest of the company owners, and necessary to secure his annual profit related bonus.

Workers were unhappy and the turnover of personnel was higher than in other similar factories. Xiang was in favour of abandoning the system of premiums and, instead, of implementing a more humane way of work. But what could he do? One option was to talk with Wei about the factory problems. On other occasions, Wei had shown himself receptive to ideas and had appreciated some suggestions from Xiang to improve the production system.

Questions:

1. What do you think about Wei's view of the company and the management role?

2. What would you suggest to Wei, if you were Xiang?

Summary

The purpose of business has to do with the role of business in society, and its social and ethical justification. With this purpose in mind, one can determine whether its activities are appropriate. The purpose furnishes criteria for determining whether the firm is well designed and well managed.

The business corporation or firm is frequently seen in legal studies as a fictitious person. Neoliberal economics usually considers the firm to be a set of contracts. Others view it as a living organism, a compact entity, or a vehicle for coordinating the interests of those with a 'stake' in the firm (stakeholders).

The model of the business firm as a community of persons emphasizes that the firm is made up of free and rational individuals, with an enduring unity, a common action and a shared purpose. This view is compatible with recognizing that a firm *includes* a set of contracts and a constellation of stakeholder interests, both convergent and conflicting.

Three major purposes of the firm have been proposed: (1) maximizing shareholder value; (2) coordinating the firm's stakeholder interests; and (3) achieving multi-ends in accordance with the good of the firm and the common good of society. Proponents of these proposals base their arguments on their own understanding of managerial fiduciary duties, the applicable legal framework, property rights, and the firm's contribution to wealth creation and managerial performance.

The multi-ends of the firm include:

- Supplying useful goods and services efficiently
- Creating added value fairly and proceeding to its equitable distribution among constituencies who have contributed to its creation
- Providing jobs, opportunities and organizational conditions for personal development of those involved in the organization
- Promoting the necessary relationships between the firm and its constitutive stakeholders, fostering reciprocity, collaboration and cooperation among them
- Striving for the continuity of the firm under competitive conditions
- Being a good corporate citizen.

According to how the purpose of the firm is understood, these are three different models for corporate governance: (1) the shareholder model; (2) the stakeholder model; and (3) the mission-driven model. The latter is consistent with seeing the firm as a community of persons and defining its purpose as achieving its multi-ends in accordance with the common good.

Justice and power must be brought together, so that whatever is just may be powerful, and whatever is powerful may be just.[1]

Blaise Pascal (1623–62)
French thinker, mathematician and scientist.

Chapter Aims

This chapter will allow you to:

- gain an understanding of different types of power to be found within the business corporation
- discuss why a right use of power requires justice
- distinguish different forms of justice
- discuss some common problems of justice in management
- reflect on excessive executive compensation and whether this entails an injustice
- consider how truthfulness is a crucial ethical requirement for communications and to discuss some related problems
- acquire information about OECD guidelines for corporate governance
- be familiar with a set of ethically good practices for corporate governance.

Key terms:

Coercive power
Communication
Commutative justice
Concealment of the truth
Distributive justice
Earnings management
Egalitarianism
Equity
Executive compensation

Expert power
Favouritism
General justice
Information power
Intemperate activism
Justice
Legal justice
Legitimate power
Machiavellian

Negotiation
Nepotism
Power
Referent power
Retributive justice
Reward power
Transparency
Unfair discrimination

Use and Misuse of Power

INTRODUCTORY CASE 8:

A QUESTIONABLE USE OF POWER IN SALOMON BROTHERS

Salomon Brothers was a Wall Street investment bank founded in 1910. It gained notoriety in the 1980s and early in the 1990s when John H. Gutfreund was the CEO of this corporation. In 1985, *Business Week* named Gutfreund the King of Wall Street.

In 1982, Gutfreund made a controversial decision. Salomon Brothers was acquired by the commodity trading firm then known as Phibro Corporation, and the new company was named Phibro-Salomon. Soon, the commodity operations were sold, and it later became Salomon Inc., which, since 1998, has been part of Citigroup. Gutfreund made $32 million on that sale, and Billy Salomon, the main shareholder, received almost $10 million.

In the 1980s, Gutfreund and the head of Salomon Brothers Government Bond Desk, Paul W. Mozer, were capturing large allocations of bonds during the auction process, which brought many to fear a monopoly in the government bond market. This was because the US Treasury had given a privilege to a handful of government bond dealers, whom it designated as 'primary dealers'. Instead of selling its new bond issues at auction in the open market, the Treasury was selling the great bulk of them to these primary dealers who, in turn, resold them to the rest of the market – with the consequent negative outcome for the US Treasury. This system made it easier for Salomon to make enormous profits for years, which could have been justified by law, if it had not been for the fact that Salomon Brothers had signed bond orders in its customers' names without their knowledge or consent. That was fraud.

In early 1990, Gutfreund made a secret deal with one of the bank's most profitable fiefdoms – risk arbitrage – to let them retain 15 per cent of the group's profits that year. As a result, at the end of the year top traders were paid tremendous bonuses.

The greatest scandal came in 1991. It was committed by two senior Salomon traders in connection with bidding in Treasury bond auctions in the USA. These traders violated Treasury rules by bidding for more bonds than allowed. Thus, the corporation could sell the bond inventory controlled by it at a higher price than if the firm had restricted itself to a bid for 35 per cent of each issue, the maximum percentage allowed. Following this procedure, a $1 billion bid was made at the end of 1990 auction, and a second of $3.15 billion in the February 1991 auction. Additionally, there had been more potentially unauthorized bids in the April 1991 auction. Later they were caught, accused of fraudulently submitting false bids to the US Treasury in an attempt to purchase more Treasury bonds than permitted to one buyer, and suspended from dealing in auctions. Salomon was fined $290 million, the largest fine ever levied on an investment bank at the time. This scandal almost brought about the end for the firm. After it, Gutfreund, being 71 years old, disappeared from the scene for a decade.

The former head of Salomon Inc.'s government securities trading was sentenced to four months in a minimum security prison for his role in the Treasury auction scandal. The US District Judge also fined Paul Mozer $30,000. He had faced a maximum of 10 years in prison and a $500,000 fine.

After the scandal of 1991, the *New York Times* started publishing articles that were sharply critical of the bank's aggressiveness, characterizing Salomon as a company governed by 'a culture of greed, contempt for government regulations, and a sneering attitude toward ethics or any other impediment to earning a buck'.[2]

Gutfreund's style was based on selecting ambitious and aggressive young people who, at Salomon, could count on giant bonuses and a success they would probably have never achieved at other firms. He forced his employees to produce profits immediately. In compensation, Salomon paid extremely high bonuses, in one case reaching $2.5 million a year. Gutfreund's secret deals and unethical behaviour were tolerated and hidden. He promoted those who were most like him – lacking any commitment to ethical principles – and his vague policies confused employees and let them make their own decisions about how to 'win' the internal Salomon competition.

Questions:

1. How was Gutfreund able to influence people around him?
2. What features seem to define Gutfreund's style?
3. In what other ways could Gutfreund have used his managerial power?

Sources: 'Private Sector; From King of Wall Street to Sultan of Supplements', *New York Times*, 12 August (2001); R. Sims, and J. Brinkmann, 'Leaders as Moral Role Models: The Case of John Gutfreund at Salomon Brothers', *Journal of Business Ethics*, 35, 4 (2002): 327–39; M.N. Rothbard, *Making Economic Sense* (Auburn, AL: Ludwig von Mises Institute, 1995): ch. 47: *The Salomon Brothers Scandal*; L. Malkin, 'Salomon Admits Traders Tried to Corner U.S. Bond Markets', *International Herald Tribune*, 10 August (2001); D. Dukcevich, 'Faces in The News, *Forbes*, 15 November (2001); 'Ex-Salomon Trader Gets 4 Months', *New York Times*, 15 December (1993); M. Lewis, *Liar's Poker. Two Cities, True Greed* (London: Hodder and Stoughton, 1999).

POWER IN CORPORATIONS

Power means 'to be able': to possess the ability to make choices or influence outcomes. Power can be held by one person or by a group.

Business and those who govern or manage business have power – sometimes, enormous power. A well-known phrase from Lord Acton (1834–1902), a British historian, affirms, 'Power tends to corrupt, and absolute power corrupts absolutely.'[3] Actually, corruption is not inevitable. Apart from social mechanisms to prevent it, it depends on the sense of justice of the powerful. This chapter deals with misuse of power, but also with good practices for a just use of power by those who run or control the firm, including corporate governance and management.

To start with, we consider that there are several types of power:

- *Formal or legitimate power*, which derives from a position within an organization or community. It comes from formal authority delegated to the holder of a position (for example, the chief executive officer (CEO)). Frequently, this is the type of power referred to, also termed *political power*.

- *Referent power*, related to those who have the ability to attract others and build loyalty because of their personal qualities

- *Expert power*, derived from a person's credibility due to his or her knowledge, skills or expertise in a certain field

- *Information power*, which belongs to those who have the reputation of being well informed or up-to-date

- *Reward power*, which refers to the ability to give others a reward – such as increasing remuneration, recognition, a promotion, greater responsibilities or other benefits

- *Coercive power*, which entails the application of negative influences; for example, demoting an employee or withholding rewards. While reward power tends to create a positive motivation, coercive power tends to generate fear. However, coercive power can be necessary and useful. All these forms of power permit influence over others.

In corporations, legitimate power is exercised through shareholders, the board of directors and managers, each of whom exerts corporate power to various degrees. This separation of powers and control runs in a cascade from shareholder to management, and contributes to avoiding a concentration of power and risk of abuse due to lack of control.

Shareholders have the power inherent in *property rights*. Effective shareholder power depends on the amount of capital owned and other features of the company. In small companies with few shareholders, effective shareholder power can be high, while minority shareholders in a large company usually have little effective power.

Nowadays, many shareholders are institutional investors – such as mutual funds, insurance companies, retirement funds, hedge funds, or banks. These institutional investors – as well as other controlling shareholders, including families, corporations and private funds – can have a significant influence on corporate behaviour.

The *board of directors* has power for governing and leading the company under the control of a *general meeting of shareholders*, who control the board of directors. Shareholders also appoint the board of directors and the auditors, satisfying themselves that an appropriate governance structure is in place.

The board achieves corporate governance by establishing and putting into effect the strategic direction and policy framework within which the corporation operates. In addition, the board supervises the management of the business and reports to shareholders on its stewardship. Special power is held by the chairperson of the board, who presides over meetings, coordinates its members' disparate points of view and tries to produce consensus.

The CEO, managers and corporate officials have their own power and responsibilities in accordance with their respective positions.[4] These include managing people, raw materials, financial funds and technological resources, through functions related to operations, marketing, finances, and information technology.

In the social context, business has power, and frequently large business corporations have huge power. We will return to this point later, dealing with the responsibility of business in society.[5] Here, we will consider power within the corporation.

POWER, RESPONSIBILITY AND JUSTICE

There is a vast bibliography discussing how power originates, or how to maintain the power associated with a position, or how to achieve more power. But power also has important ethical connotations.

At this point, it is worth mentioning Niccolò Machiavelli, an Italian political philosopher who lived during the fifteenth and sixteenth centuries. In his book, *The Prince*, he prescribes how a prince should retain control of his realm. In a certain sense, we can understand 'prince' as equivalent to a director or a manager. Machiavelli suggested that kind words and rewards can be used if they favour power, but that it is also acceptable to lie, break promises or even to use brute strength where necessary to maintain power. In a Machiavellian view, maintaining power is therefore an end that would justify questionable means, although not any means at all.[6]

Machiavelli's approach was restricted to those who rule and who act in order to maintain their power, but soon the term *Machiavellian* was coined and is still employed today to describe one who deceives and manipulates others for gain. Those who practise a Machiavellian use of power can easily rationalize their attitude as 'realism' or 'pragmatism' but, in fact, deceiving or manipulating others to retain power is a well-known form of injustice.

If someone has power, he or she should be prepared to answer for how this power has been used. In other words, power entails responsibility. One can misuse power by:

- *Exercising power unfairly.* This happens when power is used without justice. This entails not respecting other people's rights or damaging the community. For instance, a manager who dismisses an employee not for fair and proportional reasons, or indulging in unnecessary expense.

- *Exercising power inappropriately.* This includes, for instance, using managerial power to satisfy managerial ego (vanity), instead of using power to serve the company. Another inappropriate way of using power is an excessive restriction of freedom in the initiative and activity of subordinates.

- *Negligent non-exercise of power.* This occurs when those who have power do not give sufficient consideration to the obligations inherent in such power for doing the right thing. A case of negligence would be a CEO who does not act with due diligence in investigating the capabilities of a newly hired manager.

- *Cowardly non-exercise of power.* This is the case of those who know the steps they should take to act properly, but do not do so from lack of courage. For instance, an independent director of a corporate board who does not use his voice or vote to avoid damage to the corporation because he knows that his advice is contrary to the chairperson's view.

Justice

Justice provides a key guideline for a proper use of power. The German philosopher Robert Spaemann argues: 'Justice is the virtue of those in positions of power, the virtue of the strong.'[7] He adds that injustice comes about when an *asymmetric correlation of powers* exists. If, in a particular relationship, one party has more power than the other, there is the risk that the more powerful party will abuse his or her position to the other's detriment. In business, this has an immediate application to negotiations and, sometimes, to dealings with employees. The latter can be strongly affected by *abuses of power* in issues such as hiring, promotion, dismissal, remuneration, or transfer from one work location to another.

Legitimate or political power is necessary to rule communities, and what justifies power is the obligation to serve the community fairly; that is, with justice. This is also true for corporations. Actually, justice is widely recognized as an essential component of a good society. Plato, through Socrates, refers to justice as both a personal virtue and a principle for a proper order in the city-state. Similarly, the American philosopher John Rawls contends: 'Justice is the first virtue of social institutions.'[8]

Justice is a crucial human value, related to the good of friendship, but also a cardinal virtue, as noted (pp. 87–8). The celebrated Roman jurist Ulpian gave a definition of justice that has become classic: 'Justice is the perpetual and constant will to render to each one his right.'[9] This definition, although presented as a personal disposition and, therefore, as a virtue, also includes justice as a principle for social life.

There are currently many theories of justice, supported by different philosophical approaches[10] and interconnected with economics and law.[11] Frequently, justice is understood as fair distribution of things and equity, and of positions of power and influence.[12] However, the Ulpian definition suggests a broader meaning, which concerns not only ordering things and persons properly within society, but also giving to each his or her right. In line with this, three main forms or aspects of justice can be distinguished: distributive justice, commutative justice and general justice.

- *Distributive justice* refers to the distribution of burdens, honours, responsibilities and recompense (wealth, power, rewards and so on) among different people within a community. Problems of distributive justice appear, for example, in the apportioning of the tax burden within society, or in distributing economic compensations or positions within a business firm.

  In distributive justice, equity is crucial. Thus, fair distribution should consider criteria, such as contributions, merits, capacities and, in some cases, needs. In practice, justice in distributions requires establishing equitable criteria, determined with impartiality and practical wisdom, and applying them to members of the whole. Within an organization, a criterion for distributing compensation could be the contribution to wealth creation. When things are to be divided based on some property, each individual should receive a quantity proportional to his or her possession of that property (as with those who contribute capital in a business firm). In a community such as a family, the distributive criteria might be related to the needs of each member of the family.

  Strict equality in distribution, without considering merits or other significant criteria, is contrary to distributive justice. Distributive justice also precludes acting with favouritism or in an arbitrary fashion.

- *Commutative justice* basically refers to exchanges, contracts and payment of goods. In voluntary exchanges, this justice ensures that both parties end up with an equal share.

  Commutative justice takes place in the equality of value of the things addressed by a contract.[13] In contracting, when real freedom exists, equality of value is that upon which the parties agree. It requires safeguarding property rights, paying debts and fulfilling legitimate obligations to which one had freely agreed.

  Retributive justice is a form of justice related to commutative justice. It seeks to balance an injustice by rectifying the situation or responding appropriately to wrongdoing, or by restoring the equality that the injustice had removed.

- *General justice* is a third form of justice that refers to the common good, since justice is not limited to individual benefits but extends to community welfare. Underlying general justice is the conviction that every member of a community should contribute to its common good, and acting in accordance with the common good is precisely the obligation of general justice.

    Justice is therefore incomplete if two individuals fulfil an agreement that damages the community and do nothing to compensate for that damage: for instance, if they buy land to build a factory that produces noise and foul odours in an urban area. Justice is not served by their merely paying the owner for the property.

    One expects a good community to enact laws that will govern its members in ways beneficial to everyone; that is, in accordance with the common good. This is why general justice is also called 'legal justice'.

DILIGENCE AND JUSTICE IN MANAGERIAL WORK

'Management', wrote Drucker, 'is about human beings. Its task is to make people capable of joint performance, to make their strengths effective and their weaknesses irrelevant. This is what the organization is about, and it is the reason that management is a critical, determinant factor.'[14] Since management is 'about human beings', questions of justice will be inherent to all managerial work.

Managerial work includes planning activities; arranging them through rules, procedures and directions; leading the behaviours of those in an organization to accomplish a designated mission; coordinating (that is, making different people or things work together for the purpose of the organization) and controlling the results to verify whether the desirable objective has been achieved; checking possible errors and taking the required corrective actions.

Justice posits a number of issues regarding the organization of work and commercial organization, which will be dealt with later.[15] Here, we will only consider generic aspects related to justice in managerial work, which entails a sense of stewardship.

- *Dealing with due respect.* Justice in management requires dealing with people with due respect. It also excludes acting in such a way that people's development, including the manager's, is eroded. An extreme case would be pressuring collaborators into misbehaviour.

- *Promoting efficient work.* A basic obligation of justice is that managers and everybody within the organization try to work with efficiency. However, efficiency cannot be achieved at the cost of disrespecting people or committing any kind of injustice (remember that a good end does not justify a bad means).[16]

Efficiency benefits returns for shareholders, favours better wages or economic compensations for managers and employees, makes possible lower prices for clients and benefits other stakeholders.

- *Acting with diligence.* This requires an earnest and persistent application to any managerial undertaking; steady effort, assiduity, zeal and care. Budgeting one's time; monitoring one's own activities to guard against laziness, and putting forth full concentration in one's work are expressions of diligence.

  Managers can fail in their duties to justice through omissions of what was due and possible.[17] The omission might be fully deliberate but much more frequently is due to negligence or recklessness. At this point, we should remember that someone is only morally responsible for a duty when he or she fails to perform it and it is clearly identified and possible. Managerial duties are not always stated explicitly.

  Often, one must first know these duties and then situate them within one's individual circumstances and limitations. Therefore, the first responsibility of a manager is to know what *can* be done and what must be done in every circumstance. Responsibility by omission is often limited by the manager's real power, since no one can do the impossible.

  A manager's responsibility for omission can take many forms, depending on his or her power and position within the firm. A manager can bear responsibility for failing in adequately monitoring the business or the implementation of an option; for not paying sufficient attention to the tendencies of the environment; for a lack of initiative in proposing appropriate steps to keep the company competitive; for a lack of concern for developing new products, markets or processes as needed; and so on.

  Some omissions can render managers guilty for cooperating with or failing to avoid wrongdoing by others.[18] This would be the case in failing to seek to prevent wrongdoing by correction, when possible, and when there is a reasonable chance of effectiveness; failing to prevent someone from committing an illicit act when possible; failing to report harmful behaviour or crimes to the proper person when justice requires it; covering up an immoral action if doing so effectively helps to carry out that action; and protecting those who commit immoral acts so that they can continue to do so.

- *Avoiding intemperate activism.* Some omissions also involve intemperate activism; for example, running excessive risks without serious study or suitable advice. More severe are omissions that place personnel safety or personal development in jeopardy, when action would be necessary and possible. A manager who is responsible for such action not having been taken is guilty of omission.

- *Acting as role model.* Not only should managers act with justice in their own decisions, actions and omissions – their direct responsibility; they also bear responsibility for the influence they exert on other people's conduct.

Managers can influence subordinates or collaborators by persuading them to do something, giving advice, praising or criticizing behaviours. Managers, to some extent, can become role models for those around them, for good or for ill. In fact, role modelling is often considered the principal vehicle for acquiring virtues, even in organizations.[19]

- *Designing appropriate management systems.* Managers can also influence the behaviour of employees and other managers through so-called management systems. These include incentive systems, which establish rewards for the actions of employees and executives, training systems for employees, and design of professional careers and evaluation systems, which establish goals and methods.

Among the latter, the *performance appraisal*, or regular review of employee performance within organizations, which is generally carried out by the manager or supervisor of each employee under certain criteria defined by top management, is particularly significant. In the performance appraisal, often annual, the manager or supervisor usually gives feedback on employee performance; identifies training needs; forms a basis for personnel decisions such as salary increases, promotions, and disciplinary actions; provides the opportunity for organizational diagnosis and development; facilitates communication between employees and administrators and so on. Performance appraisal requires fairness but also a sense of responsibility, being aware that feedback received – and even the manner in which one deals with the employee – can motivate good behaviour and better performance.

EQUITY IN MANAGING PEOPLE

Distributive justice (p. 182) requires *equity*; that is, treating people without unfair discrimination, acting with impartiality in distribution in accordance with objective and fair criteria; being free from self-interest, prejudice or favouritism.

Egalitarianism

Equity does not mean *egalitarianism*, that is, giving an equal treatment to everybody in everything regardless of his or her personal contribution, merits or needs.

Equity entails treating differently those who are different in their personal circumstances (illness, family duties, etc.), but considering that any other in the same circumstance deserves the same treatment. Due to personal problems, some people, at a particular moment, will need more attention than others. Going this different attention is also a matter of distributive justice.

Favouritism

As noted (p. 182) acts of *favouritism* therefore run against distributive justice. Managers indulge in favouritism by hiring or granting positions within the company not because of requisite qualifications, but only to favour someone.

Obviously, there are positions in which it is necessary to feel personal confidence in someone in addition to their possessing the required skills. However, a just use of managerial power requires a sincere and upright evaluation, since favouritism can infringe on the rights of deserving candidates.

Nepotism

One particular form of favouritism is *nepotism*, which refers to the favouring of relatives, usually in employment or promotion, based upon that relationship. It is an unjust use of power, for instance, to hire a relative for a job instead of someone who might be better qualified and more willing to perform that job.

In a family business, nepotism can present specific characteristics. Nepotism might exist as it does in any other company, but there might also be a legitimate interest in hiring a member of the owning family, perhaps with the purpose of training him or her to become a manager of the firm or to introduce him or her into the family business. Being a member of the owning family might be an acceptable criterion for hiring or promoting people, especially if this criterion has been well defined and properly approved. However, it could be an injustice for the whole company if this family member is incompetent or a much worse professional than others who are not related.

MISUSE OF CORPORATE RESOURCES

One aspect of good use of managerial power is the right assignment of resources, avoiding waste. Using power for personal enrichment or the benefit of some but against the legitimate interests or rights of the company or of others, is a blatant injustice.

Embezzlement and fraud

These ethical issues, analysed previously,[20] including direct actions or covering up others' actions, are especially serious when committed by managers because they entail abuse of the confidence placed in one to manage the company. Frequently, embezzlement accompanies accounting misrepresentations or financial irregularities. Charging personal expenses to the company, using corporate goods for personal ends or withdrawing loans from the firm without proper permission are other forms of misappropriation of corporate goods for personal enrichment.

Earnings management

Earnings management is a euphemistic term used to refer to systematic misrepresentation of the true incomes and assets of a corporation. Sometimes, earnings management is termed 'creative accounting' because it is related to accounting practices that might follow the letter of standard accounting practices, but deviate from the spirit of the rules. The ethical problem of *earnings management* rests on whether the financial statements are intended to mislead people, and this is often the effect.[21]

Inappropriate or superfluous investments

Certain other forms of misuse of corporate goods are not for personal enrichment but because of lack of diligence or vanity (see p. 181). One of these is investing excessively in public relations to make those who run a company look attractive rather than for the sake of improving business profitability. Although sometimes it is difficult to establish the right amount necessary for improving the firm's image or increasing its profitability, it is relatively easy for sector insiders to identify occasions of corporate spending as exercises in personal vanity.

Luxurious offices and considerable expenses to present an appealing personal or corporate image can, again, be a form of misappropriation of corporate goods for vanity, although reasonable expenses for this purpose are certainly necessary. Prudential judgement must determine what is fitting in each case.

Another related issue involves investments of doubtful profitability to expand the firm. It is well known that a manager is frequently judged by the size and extension of the business he or she runs. A decision to expand the firm might be made in good faith, or its real aim might be to satisfy the managerial ego. In the latter case, the expenses incurred should be considered a misappropriation of corporate funds. Misleading decisions, based on vanity, would be difficult to prove in a court of law, but they do entail moral responsibility.

Conflict of interests

A risk of injustice, which can easily become a misuse of resources and a real injustice, is being in a *conflict of interests*.[22] Managers and their closest relatives might have conflicts of interest between different companies in which they are involved. If such conflicts cannot be avoided, upper management – or, in some cases, the board of directors – must be notified.

Some blatant conflicts of interest, such as any economic or commercial relationship between the manager and the company, or holding positions in competitors of the company or its group, should be avoided in every case.

It constitutes a clear lack of loyalty to use confidential company information for personal purposes, taking advantage of business opportunities of which managers might become aware by virtue of their positions. On the contrary, managers must keep secret any confidential data or information received in the course of their duties, and must not use them for their own benefit; neither should they provide them to third parties, except to fulfil legitimate duties of disclosure and transparency.

Insight 8:

Abuse of power in executive compensation?

'Executive compensation' is generally understood as the total reward provided by the firm to top-level executives in a corporation (chief executive officer, chief operations officer, chief financial officer and so on). For large corporations in the United States, executive compensation can run to many millions of dollars per year. There is a wide gap between executive pay and that of shop floor workers, and also between top American executives and comparable executives of non-US firms. The financial recompense of the average worker rose from $14,000 in 1980 to $15,900 in 2004 (a total increase of 7 per cent, or 0.3 per cent per year), while CEO compensation rose from $625,000 in 1980 to $4,500,000 in 2004 (a total increase of 614 per cent, or 8.5 per cent per year).[23]

Prof. Steven N. Kaplan defended CEO compensation in the Committee on Financial Services of the US House of Representatives considering the 15-year period from 1992 to 2007. Basically, he argued that the US economy had not done well, CEOs are not alone in the compensation explosion (he mentioned athletes, entertainment personalities and movie stars) and higher compensation was tied to higher returns. Bogle, founder and former CEO of Vanguard group, disagreed. After discussing the three groups one by one, he concluded: 'CEO compensation is seriously out of line, and too often has provided excessive and unreliable lottery-type rewards based on evanescent stock prices rather than durable intrinsic corporate value'.[24]

The real value of total CEO compensation in the US was relatively stable until the 1970s, but since then it has risen at an increasingly disparate rate. The level of executive pay did not keep pace with the dramatic growth in size of firms during the 1950s and 1960s. In those days, pay was more strongly correlated to the size of the firm than it has been in recent decades (up to 2005). Several factors might have contributed to the change. One is the extensive use in recent decades of stock options, which have become the most substantial component of executive compensation.[25]

Before the 1970s, top managers in large corporations had great power and easily avoided shareholder control. They determined their own remuneration, and could run up expenses of doubtful utility (luxury offices, public relations expenses and so on). The situation changed when investment and pension funds acquired great numbers of shares and gained corresponding power on the board of directors. Those who managed such funds understood that managers' interests should be aligned with the interests of the shareholders. The stock option was the solution.

Executives (or any other employees), by receiving stock options from their firm, acquire the right to buy shares (stock) after a certain period of time (perhaps three or four years) at a fixed price, regardless of the market price of the share at the time. Thus, if the market price of shares is higher, those who possess stock options can sell them and gain the difference between the fixed

Insight 8: (cont'd)

price (generally the price at which executives receive stock options) and the market price.

Stock options were designed to align manager and shareholder interests, and to avoid opportunist managerial behaviours against the good of shareholders, but they have brought about other kinds of opportunistic behaviour different from the kind they were supposed to discourage. Some top executives spend a limited number of years in the same company, and might try to maximize their compensation in stock options in a relatively short period. Thus, they make decisions that can influence the rise of the share price when the stock option can be executed. This can result in damage for the firm and its stakeholders, including shareholders, in the long term. This is the case, for instance, of a massive lay-off of doubtful long-term profitability, although the share price might rise when the lay-off is initially announced. Similar short-term benefits might be gained by failing to make necessary investment in research and development, employee training, or by selling useful assets unnecessarily.

Thus, stock options can be an incentive not for justice but, rather, for injustice. A practical solution would require a balanced system to prevent opportunistic behaviours and to incentivize managers to work for the good of the firm. This leads us to consider the necessity of responsible managers with a strong sense of justice.

TRUTHFULNESS IN MANAGERIAL COMMUNICATIONS

Mintzberg, after studying the real work of managers, concluded that they play 10 key roles, which can be grouped in three categories:[26]

- *Interpersonal roles*, which involve managers dealing with subordinates and peers as figureheads, leaders and/or liaisons
- *Informational roles*, which involve serving as a clearinghouse of information by being a nerve centre, disseminator or spokesperson
- *Decisional roles*, which involve working as an entrepreneur, disturbance handler, resource allocator and/or negotiator. Several roles are related to communication, particularly those of disseminator and/or spokesperson. Communication is also relevant for certain other roles, such as leader, liaison, or the one in charge of dealing with subordinates and peers, or working as negotiator.

Managers communicate information, thoughts, ideas, purposes and so on. The end of communication is to create a shared understanding, often with the intention of achieving adherence, collaboration or cooperation. The means might vary (speaking, writing, audiovisuals, sign language, gestures, and certain facts that can be interpreted as a message to a person, group or organization). However, any means requires a common language that all parties can understand.

The importance of communication skills is well recognized in the business world and in many other spheres. Such skills include listening, observing, speaking, questioning, analysing and evaluating, apart from skills in ordering one's own ideas and processing information or feedback. Communication skills are the 'technical' side of communications, whereas the moral side is telling the truth in the right way, to the right person and at the right time. This adherence to the truth is *truthfulness*.

Lies and deceptions

Truthfulness in communication requires, first, avoiding telling lies and deceiving people directly and intentionally. Otherwise, communication becomes manipulation of people, which is opposed to the requirements of the Personalist Principle. Without truthfulness, the communication of information and thoughts would not be a proper shared understanding, and trust between parties would be destroyed when lies or deception come to light.

Managers sometimes talk about themselves, and truthfulness here requires *sincerity* in speaking honestly about one's feelings, thoughts and desires. It is not compulsory to reveal any intimate sentiments but, when one speaks about oneself, it should be without duplicity, dissimulation or hypocrisy. Speaking openly and frankly is advisable in some circumstances, though not in others. Practical wisdom helps to determine what might be opportune to say in each situation.

Disclosure of information and transparency

Truthfulness is much more than not telling lies or deceiving: it requires disclosing information to those who have a right to it. This aspect of truthfulness leads to the concept of *corporate transparency*, meaning to report or provide easy access to corporate information when it is of public interest, and to be accountable to those who are involved in corporate activity.

Keeping secrets and legitimate concealment of the truth

The duty of telling the truth, and consequently the obligation of not telling lies, might on occasion be in conflict with the duty of maintaining confidentiality; for instance, with a trade secret. What should be done, for instance, when a manager or employee is asked about a matter that is a trade secret? This dilemma can often be resolved by remaining silent, or by giving a vague or ambiguous response. But what if the enquiry is relentless, perhaps including intimidation, about something secret, and where silence or an equivocal response could be easily interpreted correctly and the trade secret revealed?

An extreme case is a situation that occurred during the Second World War. A Dutchman was at home in the process of hiring a Jewish man when the Gestapo arrived. They were searching for this Jewish man, with the intention of detaining him and sending him to an extermination camp. As many would intuitively guess, the Dutchman could licitly say that he had not seen or hired such a person. Following the approach presented in this book, the reason is not that the lie is justified, since a good end does not justify a bad means[27] (the lie being a bad means). The real reason involves considering what is really the object of this action. Making a false statement is an empirical fact, not necessarily a lie. It could be a lie, if the agent speaks a falsehood with the intention of deceiving, but it could be simply an error, if the agent believes the statement to be true. In certain cases (quite uncommon ones, by the way), a false statement can be morally qualified as an act of legitimate defence when facing an unjust aggressor. The latter is precisely the object of the action of the Dutchman here. Fortunately, in business, situations of such extremity do not usually arise, but the case of unjust aggressors, inquiring about issues about which they have no right at all to know, is not so far-fetched. They might also apply pressure to obtain knowledge of a secret. If no other alternative is possible, it is acceptable to make a false statement in legitimate defence, without this being considered a lie.

An obligation sometimes exists, then, not to disclose certain facts. This is not only because they are secret, but also either because it is a private matter that one does not desire to make public, or because of the unnecessary damage that could be caused if they became known by some people. The latter can occur, for example, with a failure of an employee that can be corrected without publicity and is a matter of no public importance.

Although these are situations that justify a legitimate concealment of the truth, this does not mean that secrets must be kept indefinitely. Very exceptional cases can arise in which keeping a secret is bound to cause grave harm, which can be avoided only by divulging the truth; for instance, a dangerous product or activity considered as a trade secret. This point is related to whistle-blowing, an issue considered previously.[28]

Truthfulness in negotiation

Avoiding lies and telling the truth in negotiation often presents dilemmas. It is unacceptable to tell lies even if it would lead to a favourable result in negotiation or in any other human activity. However, in negotiations both parties generally use a language quite different from the one they would employ in other contexts. Generally, both parties begin by presenting conditions that will be reduced during the negotiation process. Both sides know this. It would be naïve if one began from the point at which one were prepared to concede. There is neither any obligation to reveal this point nor to express one's own thoughts until the negotiation makes significant progress.

In negotiation processes, one can and should act with caution, but without telling lies. If one perceives that the counterparty is lying or acting in bad faith as a part of a negotiation strategy, it is not right to sink to the same level. However, this behaviour allows one, to a greater extent than in other situations, to conceal the truth. In certain circumstances, the counterparty, maliciously negotiating, can even be considered an unjust aggressor. In this case, as noted above (p. 191), a false statement can be morally qualified as an act of legitimate defence.

GOOD ETHICAL PRACTICES OF CORPORATE GOVERNANCE

Use and misuse of corporate power affects not only managers, but also corporate governance. There is a set of practices, many with substantial ethical content, that are commonly accepted as an element of good corporate governance. The economic impact of such practices is widely recognized. They are generally included in codes of corporate governance, which include processes, policies, systems and rules. Having codes of good practice is compulsory for listed companies in many countries.

The Cadbury Report[29] pioneered the idea of presenting recommendations for good corporate governance. Later, many other countries issued their own reports.[30] The Organization for Economic Cooperation and Development (OECD) launched its *Principles of Corporate Governance* in 1999 and revised them in 2004.[31] This set of principles is one of the most influential guidelines for good corporate governance practices throughout the world (see Table 8.1).

Table 8.1   OECD Principles of Corporate Governance

OECD Principles of Corporate Governance promote:	
I. *Ensuring the basis for an effective corporate governance framework*	The corporate governance framework should promote transparent and efficient markets, be consistent with the rule of law and clearly articulate the division of responsibilities among different supervisory, regulatory and enforcement authorities.
II. *The rights of shareholders and key ownership functions*	The corporate governance framework should protect and facilitate the exercise of shareholders' rights.
III. *The equitable treatment of shareholders*	The corporate governance framework should ensure the equitable treatment of all shareholders, including minority and foreign shareholders. All shareholders should have the opportunity to obtain effective redress for violation of their rights.
IV. *The role of stakeholders in corporate governance*	The corporate governance framework should recognize the rights of stakeholders established by law or through mutual agreements and encourage active cooperation between corporations and stakeholders in creating wealth, jobs, and the sustainability of financially sound enterprises.
V. *Disclosure and transparency*	The corporate governance framework should ensure that timely and accurate disclosure is made on all material matters regarding the corporation, including the financial situation, performance, ownership, and governance of the company.
VI. *The responsibilities of the board*	The corporate governance framework should ensure the strategic guidance of the company, the effective monitoring of management by the board, and the board's accountability to the company and the shareholders.

Source: www.oecd.org/dataoecd/32/18/31557724.pdf

They were promoted through discussions involving government representatives, a large number of practitioners from the private sector, and representatives from international organizations and civil society.

The OECD considers that corporate governance affects market confidence as well as company performance. Good corporate governance is essential for companies that want access to capital and for countries that want to stimulate private sector investment. By contrast, poor corporate governance weakens a company's potential, and can even pave the way for financial difficulties and fraud. Thus, the OECD Principles state: 'the corporate governance framework should be developed with a view to its impact on overall economic performance, market integrity and incentives it creates for market promotion and transparent and efficient markets'.

Good corporate practices embrace both technical and ethical issues. Among the former are common oversight of the preparation of the entity's financial statements, internal controls and the independence of the entity's auditors, review of the compensation arrangements for the CEO and other senior executives, the way in which individuals are nominated for positions on the board, the resources made available to directors for carrying out their duties, oversight and management of risk, and dividend policy. Ethical issues relate to directors of the board largely regarding the following aspects:

Ethical behaviour

Rules of good corporate governance principles are generally based on human values such as honesty and trustworthiness, loyalty, responsibility and commitment to the organization. These rules seek to promote ethical and responsible behaviours through sound decision-making. However, rules are hardly sufficient. Also needed is training and – above all – moral qualities in directors. This requires a *careful selection of directors*, based not only on their skills and experience, but also on their virtues and commitment to fulfil their responsibilities. This duty applies to all types of directors, including those appointed as representatives of shareholders, ranging from management to independent directors.

Loyalty demands, among other things, preventing conflicts of interest. Some issues regarding conflicts of interest in directors are similar to those in the case of managers (see p. 187), while others are more specific. Codes of good governance practices usually detail these issues for directors.

Trustworthiness requires an appropriate disclosure and transparency in corporate information, as is detailed in the following. This is also necessary for the existence of an efficient capital market, especially where public companies are listed.

Diligence in governance

Boards of directors and other organs of corporate government should act in the best interests of the whole company, working diligently for the common good of the firm, and indirectly for the common good of society. This orientation requires directors with not only appropriate skills and experience, but with diligence, in terms of steady application to addressing the problems and needs of the firm, attentiveness and dedication in obtaining information, and participation in corporate decision-making.

Respecting the rights of all shareholders

This entails concern for minority and foreign shareholders, for facilitating the exercise of shareholders' rights, including effective communication of information in an understandable and accessible way, and encouraging shareholders to participate in general meetings. This is a requirement of justice to curtail abuse of the board's power and the possibility of acting to the detriment of shareholders with less power or influence.

Concern for the legitimate interests of relevant stakeholders

The law generally protects some stakeholder interest. In addition to these safeguards, corporate governance should be sensitive to any legitimate interest of stakeholders. This can involve formalizing mutual agreements and establishing mechanisms of cooperation – even some type of participation of relevant stakeholders in the corporate process, suitable to the company's size and other conditions. A well-known example of the latter is the control of the corporation in Germany, which is divided into two boards, with a 'supervisory board' that elects a 'managing board'. Half of the supervisory board consists of representatives of the employees.

Disclosure and transparency

A corporation's current and potential investors have a right to relevant information regarding the corporation, and the roles and responsibilities of the board of directors and top management. Consequently, the board needs to be accountable to investors through an appropriate disclosure of substantial matters concerning the organization. This should be timely and balanced, to ensure that all investors have access to clear, factual information. In addition, good corporate practices establish that the board should implement procedures that independently verify and safeguard the integrity of the company's financial reporting.

Business ethics in practice 8:

Sir Adrian Cadbury and the Cadbury Report

Sir Adrian Cadbury is from a British family that is well known for its family business. Cadbury was a chocolate-specialized conglomerate established in 1824. In 1969, Cadbury merged with Schweppes, whose heritage started back in 1783, when the Schweppes family perfected the process for manufacturing

Business ethics in practice 8: (cont'd)

carbonated mineral water in Switzerland. In 2008, Cadbury Schweppes was a major global beverage and confectionery company, employing over 70,000 people. It included such brands as Cadbury, Schweppes, Halls, Trident, Dr Pepper, Snapple, Dentyne and 7 Up.

Following the traditions of both companies, Cadbury Schweppes has core business principles and five pillars of corporate social responsibility: (1) human rights and employment standards; (2) ethical sourcing and procurement; (3) marketing, food and consumer issues; (4) environment, health and safety; and (5) community.

Sir Adrian Cadbury stressed that eliminating ethical considerations from business decisions would simplify the management task.[32] In fact, ethical concerns have been present in the Cadbury family company for many years. In the mid-1980s, Sir Adrian Cadbury won a prize for Ethics in Business. On receiving this prize, he said that ethical concerns within the company had not changed for years, but the new issue was the interest the public takes in business decisions and the pressure it applies, which often makes managers sidestep hard decisions. He claimed that managers must be open to the role of ethics in decision-making, knowing one's place, weighing all the competing interests carefully and getting on with doing business.

Early in the 1990s, Sir Adrian Cadbury was appointed as chair of a Committee to study 'Financial Aspects of Corporate Governance'. The sponsors of this Committee were the London Stock Exchange, the leading UK accountancy firms and the Financial Reporting Council. They wanted to raise public confidence in financial reporting and the ability of auditors to provide the safeguards sought and expected by users of company reports. This Commission published a report in 1992 known as the 'Cadbury Report',[33] which was a pioneer on good practices on corporate governance. Among many other recommendations, the Cadbury Report suggests the following:

- There should be a clearly accepted division of responsibilities at the head of a company to ensure a balance of power and authority. If the chairman is also the CEO, it is essential that the external directors provide a strong and independent counterweight.
- The calibre and number of external directors on the board should be such that their views carry significant weight in the board's decisions. They should bring an independent judgement to bear on company strategy, performance, resources, key appointments and standards of conduct. In addition, external directors should be appointed through a formal selection process so that their independence is not eroded by patronage of any kind.
- The board should establish an audit committee with a majority of independent outside directors.

Questions:

1. What do you think about Sir Adrian Cadbury's ideas?

2. How could the Cadbury Report be successfully implemented, and what problems would have to be overcome to do so?

Sources: A. Cadbury, 'Ethical Managers Make their own Rules', *Harvard Business Review*, 65 (5) (1987): 69–73; Cadbury Schweppes website: http://www.cadburyschweppes.com; M. Ysmny, 'HR as the Guardian of Corporate Values at Cadbury Schweppes', *Strategic HR Review*, 5(2) (2006) 10–11 Cadbury Committee, *Report of the Committee on the Financial Aspects of Corporate Governance* (London: GEE, 1992).

Dilemma 8

Jorge Muro was the General Manager of Trameto, a Latin American company whose main activity was the manipulation of iron laminates. Jorge had been contracted in the hope of overcoming the current situation of the company, which had been operating with losses in the two preceding years. Trameto had 500 workers and about 300 clients. In the previous year, sales had reached $100 million. Carlos Salinas and his sister Vanessa were the only shareholders of the company. Carlos, Chairman of the Board of Directors, thought that Jorge was the right person to turn the company round.

Jorge was also convinced that the company was viable and could reach a profit situation within a couple of years. This would require improving productivity and gaining new clients. However, after a few days Jorge found other problems, including numerous irregular practices and irregular accounting payments. One of these was invoicing about 3 per cent of sales without taxes on products. Around 30 clients accepted it and, sometimes, they even demanded to pay with 'undeclared income' and, consequently, without taxes. In the last fiscal year Trameto management used $3 million of undeclared income to remunerate shareholders ($1 million), to pay commissions to heads of purchases of clients ($130,000), to reward management of principal clients who paid with undeclared money ($170,000), to give incentives and complements to Trameto managers ($200,000) and to return money to some clients ($1.5 million) who had presented false invoices, an amount superior to the real figures. This latter practice permitted clients to increase costs in their own accounting and to pay fewer taxes, all while they generated undeclared income.

When Jorge joined the company, he knew that they had a small amount of undeclared income. This also happened in others companies he knew. What he did not appreciate was that it was such a great proportion of the trading figures. Neither was he aware of other frequent 'accounting' practices in Trameto, including what, in his opinion, was a clear overvaluation of some assets on the balance sheet.

Questions:

1. What do you think about the irregular practices described in this case?
2. How do you evaluate Jorge's decision to accept the post at Trameto?
3. What would you do if you were Jorge?

Summary

Power is necessary to rule communities and organizations, but power has to be practised with justice. Justice includes three basic forms: (1) 'distributive justice', regarding equity in distributions; (2) 'commutative justice', which refers to equality in exchanges; and (3) 'general justice', also called 'legal justice', which refers to acting in accordance with the common good.

Directors and managers have been appointed not to serve their own interests by taking advantage of the power they hold, but to fulfil the duties inherent in their position.

Directors and managers should act with a sense of stewardship, without negligence or recklessness, and should seek to be role models for other corporate managers and employees. Managerial good practices include being diligent and promoting efficiency within the organization, making good use of resources, avoiding conflicts of interest, favouritism and nepotism.

In some cases, executive compensation might amount to an abuse of power and, consequently, an injustice. In addition, it could have negative long-term consequences for people involved in the firm.

Good practices for corporate governance suggested by many national and international codes include, among others, respecting the rights and legitimate interests of shareholders and granting equitable treatment to all of them, as well as disclosure, transparency, and other aspects of ethical behaviour.

Truthfulness is the essential ethical condition for communication, including personal and corporate communication. In addition, truthfulness brings about credibility and good reputation.

Truthfulness requires, first, avoiding both telling lies and direct, intentional deceit. In addition, truthfulness also includes the positive duty to disclose information to those who have the right to it, and to be sincere when one prudently decides to communicate one's own feelings, thoughts or desires.

Corporate transparency consists of the disclosure of corporate information of public interest. Providing corporate transparency is both a duty and a condition for appropriate interaction between the company and its stakeholders.

There are situations in which concealment of the truth is legitimate. This occurs when it is necessary to keep secrets, safeguard privacy or avoid great damage.

In negotiating, one should act with caution, but without telling lies.

The greatest leaders forget themselves and attend to the development of others.[1]

Lao Tzu (circa 600 BC)
Chinese sage

Chapter Aims

This chapter will allow you to:

- consider various aspects of managers' work, including leadership
- distinguish between power and authority, and how this has practical consequences for understanding managerial work
- gain familiarity with the ethical aspects of several approaches to leadership and their description of the influence of moral character on leadership of organizations
- obtain insight into the importance of serving others in leadership
- know how to develop practical wisdom and discuss its significance for managers
- gain an understanding of integrity in its genuine sense of wholeness of virtue
- recognize the importance of humility and magnanimity in leadership, as well as others' virtues such as honesty, a sense of responsibility, loyalty, kindness, courage and self control, apart from justice, already considered in the previous chapter.

Key terms:

Authenticity	Kindness	Self-discipline
Authority	Leadership	Servant leadership
Being positive	Level 5 of leadership	Transactional leadership
Forgiveness	Loyalty	Transformational leadership
Gratitude	Magnanimity	Wisdom
Honesty	Moral leader	
Humility	Optimism	
Integrity	Patience	

Human Virtues in Leadership of Organizations

INTRODUCTORY CASE 9:

TYCO – LEADERSHIP IN THE AFTERMATH OF SCANDAL

For years, Tyco International was the world's largest manufacturer of fire-protection and security systems. Asides from these services, it also included electronics, healthcare, and engineering products and services. In the 1990s, Tyco had a strategy of acquiring profitable companies and operating them at continually increasing profitability for the benefit of its shareholders.

In 1992, Dennis Kozlowski became the chairman and CEO of Tyco when it was a $3 billion company. Five years later, Tyco changed its charter to be incorporated in Bermuda to avoid paying US taxes. Over the next 3 years, it achieved 20 per cent annual growth rates by acquiring 700 companies. Kozlowski hand-picked board members and dominated the work of the board.

In June 2002, Kozlowski was charged with evading money in taxes on artwork he had purchased. The Board of Directors launched an internal investigation, under the direction of an independent external counsel, to review past use of company funds by Tyco's CEO.

Kozlowski's lifestyle was quite outrageous, and other possible charges against him were found. Kozlowski used company funds to buy the artwork. In 1999, Tyco excused him $25 million in loans to pay for antiques, art and other furnishing for his New York apartment. According to the *New York Times*, the company even paid $30 million for the apartment itself, which Kozlowski considered to be the company's apartment.

These charges included those that Kozlowski had used company funds to pay for a $20,000 background check on the fiancé of a Merrill Lynch analyst, and to finance half of a $2.1 million trip for his wife's birthday in Sardinia, which included a performance by singer Jimmy Buffett.

From 1997 to 2002, Kozlowski improperly borrowed $242 million from the 'Key Employee Loan Program' and did not disclose its improper use to the board of directors. Chief Financial Officer (CFO), Mark Swartz, also improperly borrowed $72 million from that programme to fund his personal investments, business ventures, real estate holdings and trusts. Kozlowski excused repayment of $57.9 million, and relocation loans of $29.1 million to Swartz without board knowledge. Finally, he even gave interest – free loans to other employees, including $10 million to Tyco's chief legal counsel, who purchased a ski chalet in Utah. Continuing those practices, Kozlowski sold his New Hampshire estate to Tyco for $4.5 million, which was three times its fair market value. The company also significantly overpaid Swartz for some of his real estate holdings. In addition, Kozlowski spent company money on luxurious personal expenses.

In addition, in 1998 Kozlowski bought a 15,000 square foot, Mediterranean style, waterfront mansion in Florida with a pool, fountain and tennis court, using a $19 million, no interest loan from Tyco, which later was treated as a 'special bonus'. Swartz received a $350,000 cash bonus, 74,000 shares of Tyco stock, and $8 million in loan write-offs. Without ever informing the board about these transactions, other executives received smaller bonuses as well. Finally, Kozlowski improperly accelerated the vending of Tyco common stock, resulting in personal gains of $8 million; he also did the same for Swartz for half that amount. Both of them also committed fraudulent stock sales, secretly selling hundreds of millions of dollars worth of Tyco stock to company subsidiaries.

Kozlowski resigned and was replaced by Edward D. Breen, up to then former president of Motorola, who was known for his high moral standards and for his efficient management. On 25 July 2002, when this information became public, Tyco's share prices increased by 10 per cent and Motorola share prices decreased by 45 per cent. In August 2002, Tyco's CFO, Mark Swartz, was also replaced. In the course of 2002, Tyco's shares fell almost 80 per cent.

Three years later, Dennis Kozlowski and Mark Swartz were convicted for theft and fraudulent gains of more than $650 million. They were both found guilty of 22 counts of grand larceny, conspiracy, securities fraud and falsifying business records.

They were sentenced to eight to 25 years in prison for stealing $150 million. They were also fined $240 million in penalties and restitution. The New York State Judge ordered them to repay $134 million for the unauthorized bonuses and compensation between 1999 and 2001 ($97 million from Kozlowski and $37 million from Swartz).

On Breen's first day at work, almost 20 per cent of Tyco's investor base showed up in the office, wanting to know his plans for the company. Immediately after his appointment, Mr Breen took the reins of the company to help save it and to stabilize shareholder confidence. He immediately undertook the battle to recover the company's name and to rebuild investor confidence. It was his chief priority to implement the highest standards of corporate governance and ethical behaviour.

Mr Breen worked on three steps: thinking long term, focusing on steady growth from market share and product development, and cleaning up the house. In his first six months, he replaced practically all members of Tyco's board of directors and fired the entire top corporate team, along with 290 out of 300 of Tyco's managers. Then, he hired 80 executives to fill their places. In addition, he focused on cost saving integration throughout Tyco's 2,000 businesses, adopted a new delegation of authority policy to strengthen control over cash disbursements, and restructured the company's debt from $24 billion to $11 billion.

To integrate high ethical standards, Mr Breen established processes and practices that promoted and ensured integrity, compliance and accountability. The company adopted new Board Governance Principles and a new employee Guide to Ethical Conduct. The four principles that grounded the newly managed company were: integrity, excellence, teamwork and accountability. Tyco also provided a framework for its employees to understand what was expected of them with regard to their conduct and decision-making. It also established a Human Resources Department to which an employee could report ethical concerns and violations. Additionally, it made use of the international, toll free ConcernLINE, a corporate law department and an independent Office of the Ombudsman.

It took three long years before Tyco's stock value was back on track and for them to win back the confidence of the shareholders. Tyco's shares did not increase until the last quarter of 2004. In 2005, Tyco shares dropped once more after the end of the Kozlowski trial but began to catch up again in mid-2005 until 2007. Tyco's ratings by Governance Metrics International (GMI), the world's leading global corporate governance ratings agency, was 1.5 out of 10 in 2002. By 2004 and 2005, its rating had dramatically increased to 9 out of 10.

Questions:

1. Analyse Mr Kozlowski's behaviour from an ethical perspective.

2. What do you think about Mr Breen's decisions to improve corporate integrity?

3. Do you think that there is a cause–effect relationship between Tyco's financial performance and its reputation of integrity?

Sources: E. Evans, 'Tyco Focuses on Integrity to Rebuild Finance Team', *Corporate Finance*, February Issue 218 (2003); B. McGraw, 'Tyco International', in R. Kolb (ed.) *Encyclopaedia of Business Ethics and Society* (Thousand Oaks, CA: Sage, 2007): 2127; 'Can This Man Save Tyco', *Time*, 9 February (2004); Verschoor, 'Tyco: An Ethical Metamorphosis', *Strategic Finance*, April, 87, 10, (2006): 15–16; Tyco's Officer Defends Kozlowski´s Spending', *New York Times*, 26 February (2004); 'Kozlowski, Tyco Face More Questions', *CNN*, 7 August (2002); Tyco Official Website: http://www.tyco.com; *Financial Times* news data from 2002–07.

LEADING ORGANIZATIONS: AUTHORITY, NOT ONLY POWER

Directors and managers lead people within the organization to achieve common goals. Thus, in some sense, they should not only manage, in a strategic or organizational meaning of the word, but they should also be leaders. For many years, management was not distinguished from leadership, and the latter was understood as the mere exercise of power and force. In this context, what defined leaders, as well as managers, was the possession of power or extraordinary analytical skills. Character was irrelevant, except perhaps as providing energy for the giving of orders. This vision was very narrow indeed.

Identifying leadership with power means ignoring that, in practice, not only a formal organization exists; there is also a certain informal organization through which some people with no formal power nevertheless influence others. Besides, it is now well known that people have a variety of motivations, not only economic ones, to collaborate in common goals. Leading solely through a 'carrot and stick' approach is not only inhuman, but also frequently ineffective.

In the early 1960s, the view of leadership associated with power changed. Prentice suggested that a true leader has the ability to understand the complex dynamism of workers' motivations.[2] He contended that effective leaders take a personal interest in the long-term development of their employees and use tact and other social skills to encourage them to do their best; they understand people's motivations and enlist employee participation in a way that marries individual needs and interests to the group's purpose.

Later on, an influential article by Prof. Abraham Zaleznik of the *Harvard Business School*, proposed the question: 'Are managers and leaders actually different?' He argued for the need to overcome a technical vision of management, quite common at the time. He criticized this vision as incomplete, since it lost sight of 'inspiration, vision, and the full spectrum of human drives and desires'. He argued that managers and leaders are two very different types of people, although managers can, of course, also be leaders.[3] Along these lines, Kotter proposed that management and leadership are complementary, especially in a changing world. Managers would deal with planning and budgeting, organizing staff, developing and applying procedures and performance, solving problems and supervising people. By contrast, leaders would be those who motivate people and align them with the firm's goals, providing a vision and a new direction to orient future activities.[4]

A different perspective was presented by Mintzberg, who, based on empirical research, pointed out not two types of people running corporations, but managers acting in different roles.[5] He found that managers have a complex, intertwined combination of roles to play. Similarly, Pérez-López suggested that managers perform activities as strategists (related to the definition of some purpose), executives or organizers (for the structuring of such purposes through production and distribution systems) and leaders (for motivating the people who carry out the purpose).[6]

The latter view seems more realistic than that of two types of individuals running organizations (managers and leaders). A manager does, to different degrees, play the roles of strategist, organizer and leader, although some managers might participate in more activities of one type than another. All of these roles are important, but leadership seems critical to becoming a good manager. Leadership can be studied separately from managerial skills and analytical techniques but, in practice, leadership is an inseparable aspect of the manager's job: managers should lead people.

A distinction coming from Roman times can help us to understand leadership. Roman Law distinguished between *potestas* and *auctoritas*.[7] *Potestas* (power over) has an institutional dimension. It derives from one's position within an institution or organization. It refers principally to the capacity to rule over others and give orders. Contrastingly, *auctoritas* (authority) has a personal dimension. It derives from the recognition of the personal qualities of an individual. Leadership is basically *auctoritas*.

In modern times, Max Weber has dealt with power and authority extensively. According to Weber, power is the ability to impose one's will on another, regardless of the other's wishes. Contrastingly, authority is a quality that enhances power, rather than being itself a form of power. Authority means that the individual's power is 'authorized' by the group, and thus legitimized.[8]

Hunter suggested that power is capacity, while authority is an art.[9] Power is a capacity by which someone is forced to do what the individual with power wants. Authority is the art by which people voluntarily do what the individual with authority wants, due to his or her personal influence. In other words, while under power, people do what they are required to do without internal approval; under authority, people want to do what they do – that is, with internal approval. Thus, leadership is an art based on the voluntary decisions of followers.

The notion of *leadership*, although there is no consensus on its definition, is generally understood as the ability of someone (the leader) to influence people (followers) towards the achievement of certain goals. In organizational contexts, leadership refers to the influence upon organization members that fosters their willingness to contribute to organizational or common goals.

Thus many definitions of leadership include two major elements:

- The capacity of a leader to inspire others to follow
- The capacity to move others to achieve a common goal.[10]

Some analysts have laid more emphasis on the first, stressing the charismatic leader whom people wish to follow. Others, however, have focused on the common goal shared by both leader and followers. In this second view, the leader is just another individual, but has some quality that inspires trust, and others become followers.

Although there is no absolute consensus, many agree that ordinary people can become leaders. This requires the ability to influence people towards a common goal, which could be perceived as a common good. In this sense, Hunter defines leadership 'as a skill of influencing people to work enthusiastically toward goals identified as being for the common good'.[11]

MORAL CHARACTER IN LEADERSHIP

Leadership is a complex matter that depends on a multiplicity of factors, including competencies.[12] These include strategic abilities and technical skills, such as a vision of business, an orientation towards the client, business networking, persuasion and negotiation abilities, communication skills, organization, a capacity for problem-solving, good sense in allocating resources, innovativeness and entrepreneurship, and the ability to manage crises. Other competencies are crucial for the moral character of a leader.[13]

Many have pointed out that leadership requires moral character, or have stressed the importance of being a 'moral leader'.[14] 'It is character through which leadership is exercised', stated Drucker.[15] Other scholars note that ethics is at the core of leadership, and virtues are the leader's moral capital.[16] It is not our aim to discuss existing theories of leadership but it is worth mentioning some of them.

Ethics, explicitly or implicitly, is present in several theories and approaches to leadership.[17] Historically, the first theories on leadership, which emerged in the first three decades of the twentieth century, sought to find universal personality traits specific to people generally viewed as leaders, or at least some traits they showed more strongly than others. The correlations found were modest, although these studies provided an initial analysis.

Northouse suggests that recent studies emphasize five essential traits of a leader: (1) *determination*; (2) *integrity* (which Northouse connects with honesty and trustworthiness); (3) *intelligence* (to deal effectively with the situation and the followers' needs); (4) *self-confidence* (that is, confidence in oneself or one's own abilities, but not beyond them); and (5) *sociability* (that is, the quality of being sociable and the ability to create cooperative relationships).[18]

Kirkpatrick and Locke mention honesty and integrity, self-confidence (associated with emotional stability) and the desire to lead but not to seek power as an end in itself, which can be related to unselfishness and magnanimity. Apart from these virtues, they also mention some abilities or skills, such as drive (a broad term that includes achievement, motivation, ambition, energy, tenacity and initiative), cognitive ability and knowledge of the business.[19] Some of these key character traits are actually moral virtues.

In research directed by James Collins and published as a book entitled *Good to Great*,[20] which subsequently became a bestseller, he found that *professional will* and *humility* are paramount leadership qualities.

Later on, other theories tried to explain leadership in terms of leaders' behaviours, which were considered critical determinants. Leaders' feelings might have some influence in motivating people to common goals, but behaviours are central in leadership; people appreciate real facts, not simply sentiments or good intentions. Behaviour is character in action, an expression of one's virtues in dealing with others. These theories on the behaviour of leaders were followed by others that focused on the role of situations for effective leadership (contingency models).[21]

Apart from these empirical theories, some normative ones have also been proposed.[22] We will encounter some of them in the next section.

SERVING AND FOSTERING A SENSE OF SERVICE IN OTHERS

In 1978, James G. Burns presented a key distinction between two kinds of normative leadership: transactional leadership and transforming (later termed 'transformational') leadership.

Transactional leadership

Transactional leadership is based on exchanges or transactions between leader and followers to obtain mutual benefits in achieving organizational goals. In business, this leadership style is found in managers who look for cooperation through economic incentives or other rewards (or in some cases punishments) that the manager offers (or threatens). Here, ethics is reduced to fairness in the means used by the leader, such as being honest, keeping promises and fulfilling contracts. This seems essential to maintaining the adherence of followers in subsequent interactions.

Transformational leadership

Transformational leadership theory is presented in contrast to the transactional leadership approach.[23] A transformational leader creates increasing motivation in followers through a positive change in their values, attitudes and willingness to cooperate. In some way, followers also influence the leader. 'Transforming leadership', in Burns' words, 'occurs when one or more persons engage with others in such a way that leaders and followers raise one another to higher levels of motivation and morality... transforming leadership ultimately becomes moral in that it raises the level of human conduct and ethical aspiration of both leader and led, and thus it has a transforming effect on both.'[24] According to this author, transforming leaders have strong values and focus on followers' intrinsic needs rather than on short-term goals. However, the morality of transformational leadership has been questioned, with some arguing that Hitler, for instance, would qualify as a transformational leader. The answer is that an 'authentic transformational leadership' (not simply 'transformational leadership') must be grounded on moral foundations, with four components: (1) idealistic influence; (2) inspirational motivation; (3) intellectual stimulation; and (4) individualized consideration.[25] This requires moral character of the leaders, as well as concern for self and others; it also requires ethical values embedded in the leaders' vision, articulation and a programme that followers can embrace or reject.

Servant leadership

A third type of leadership, which is not necessarily opposed to the transformational kind, is known as *servant leadership*. This theory defines leaders as those who want to serve others and, thus, foster in their followers a similar attitude. More generally, this theory also emphasizes the sense of *stewardship* for people and resources adopted by managers within an organization.[26] Robert Greenleaf, a former senior manger of the American telecom company AT&T, is recognized as the father of servant leadership through his book *Servant Leadership*, first published in 1977.[27] However, traditions in ancient wisdom had already presented a spirit of service and stewardship as essential for authentic leadership.[28]

Servant leaders, as do transformational leaders, elevate people. Values and virtues are essential for servant leadership. In *Servant Leadership*, Greenleaf mentions, among other qualities of a leader, the ability to withdraw and reorient oneself to self-improvement, acceptance and empathy towards others, listening and seeking to understand them, as well as foresight, awareness, perception, persuasion, healing and serving. Several other authors hold positions very similar to that of Greenleaf.[29]

Another theory based on human motivations, called *transcendental leadership*, was proposed by Cardona,[30] following Pérez-López's thinking.[31] In this theory, the concern for others' needs and a sense of service, which both require practical rationality and virtues, are also central.

Greenleaf describes servant leadership as follows: 'It begins with the natural feeling that one wants to serve, to serve *first*. Then conscious choice brings one to aspire to lead... The difference manifests itself in the care taken by the servant – first to make sure that other people's highest priority needs are being served.' He adds that the best test for servant leadership – though difficult to administer – is this: 'Do those served grow as persons? Do they, *while being served*, become healthier, wiser, freer, more autonomous, more likely themselves to become servants?'[32]

Disposition to service

The latter theories point out a trait of moral character which seems essential for leadership: disposition to service.

Serving others means working for other people, helping them to achieve worthy objectives. It requires a permanent disposition of concern for others' needs. This is very much in line with the philosophy of servant leadership.[33] Developing a sense of service can be fostered, but its achievement depends on one's followers. Since they are free beings, one cannot assure that, if the leader is serving, the followers will become servants of others.

Pérez-López suggests two types of manager's behaviours to develop the motivation to serve others. First, do not prevent one's subordinates from acting in accordance with this kind of motivation. Second, teach them to evaluate the consequences their actions will have for others, asking in what way one's own action can contribute to satisfying others' needs.[34]

The opposite of serving others is using people for one's own interests. Using people is an expression of power, not leadership. Choosing service over self-interest includes a careful and responsible management of what has been entrusted to the leader's care. Serving others can also be related to a sense of stewardship.[35]

Concern for serving others is neither sentimentalism nor an indulgent attitude towards people's desires or interests, but concern for their authentic human needs, related to human goods (see pp. 75–8). Following others' desires blindly rather than exercising good leadership would be an irresponsible way of running an organization. In this sense, Bill George, with his long experience as a business leader, has affirmed 'Those who are too responsive to the desires of others are likely to be whipsawed by competing interests, too quick to deviate from their course or unwilling to make difficult decisions for fear of offending.'[36]

Willingness to serve others must avoid two extremes: intrusiveness into personal life and paternalism. *Intrusiveness* enters into intimate, personal matters, or fails to respect privacy, encroaching without invitation, or even permission, on inappropriate occasions. *Paternalism* tends to make decisions on behalf of others, even against their wishes, although such decisions are well intentioned. Such conduct does not serve people; rather, it denotes a lack of respect for the person's privacy and autonomy.

Whoever wants to become a leader should therefore develop willingness to serve. This requires being sensitive to the authentic needs and expectations of those around one, including needs linked to their well-being, and professional and human development. Consequently, a first obstacle to serving people is a *self-centred attitude*, which easily leads to indifference or insensitivity to the needs of others.

An attitude of serving others includes being sincere, available and communicative, and – above all – a confidence that collaborators can develop their potential. The latter can be fostered by supportive delegation of responsibilities and proper coaching.

Serving people is actually beneficial to both the one who serves and the whole organization. When a person serves others unselfishly, he or she is developing one of the highest human capacities and thus flourishing as a human being. As for the organization, serving others can awaken a desire to serve in those who are served. A sincere and persistent attitude of concern for serving others usually develops trust and willingness to help, while selfishness favours the opposite. As Block has pointed out, strategies of control 'tend to be expensive, are slow to react to a marketplace, and drain passion from human beings. With the element of service at its core, stewardship creates a form of governance that offers choice and spirit in core workers so they, in turn, can offer the same to their marketplace. When governance has the texture of service, it calls for a like response from those governed.'[37]

WISDOM IN LEADING ORGANIZATIONS

Wisdom can be understood in two senses. One is wisdom in its generic sense, meaning a profound understanding of reality, beyond empirical facts. The other is action-oriented wisdom or 'practical wisdom', (also called 'prudence' in the moral sense) which is one of the cardinal virtues, mentioned earlier,[38] and is at the heart of making sound moral judgements,[39] reinforcing practical rationality and seeking the just mean between two extremes of misconduct.[40]

Wisdom in the first sense – the generic one – was greatly appreciated in ancient times. It refers to a deep understanding of causes of situations and events. Celebrated wisdom has been presented though maxims that might be useful for leadership. Although wisdom has to be acquired by each individual, by reflection and by reflective learning from one's own experience, accumulated wisdom can be inspirational for leadership.

A wise attitude in leadership entails cherishing the truth, thinking about situations, trying to discover relevant circumstances and foreseeing future events with an eye to the long-term situation. All of this is generally attractive, while a person lacking in wisdom rarely manages to sustain lasting credibility or win followers.

Wisdom can bestow resignation and even contentment in accepting frustrating situations, which sometimes appear in business (as in the rest of life). Followers who share the frustration appreciate such calm in a leader.

Practical wisdom fosters leadership by helping one to grasp authentic values and to distinguish the relevant from the peripheral, and also by strengthening a sense of anticipation and caution. Practical wisdom confers a reflective attitude, leading one to seek creative solutions and act with a sense of ethics.

Practical wisdom also includes listening to people in one's particular vicinity, asking for suitable advice, reflecting on situations from an ethical perspective; and evaluating the morality of an action and its consequences for those. All this contributes to generating trust in those who show such wisdom.

Related to practical wisdom is human maturity, which includes equanimity, attentiveness to circumstances and potential consequences, the mental ability to understand and distinguish between relations, and rectitude in judging persons and situations.

Having a sense of responsibility is another relevant human virtue related to practical wisdom. A responsible leader promptly does what is needed after considering carefully the reasons to act and the consequences of each action, in accordance with appropriate values and criteria. This quality entails being dependable, someone in whom followers can trust.

Some behaviours develop practical wisdom. Among them, the following are worthy of note:[41]

- *Exercising experience* or reminding oneself about past events to understand clearly what usually happens when a certain type of action is performed. Experience is developed by trying to retain the significance of ethically relevant elements when examining one's past experience.

- *Striving to understand* the present situation in order to perceive what is ethically relevant. This requires evaluating people appropriately (their dignity, their rights and their needs with regard to human development).

- *Seeking advice* from prudent people and experts in order to benefit from their experience and good judgement.

- *Practising sagacity* and promptness in resolving issues that one knows well enough and has the confidence to judge for oneself (otherwise, rather than sagacity, it would be a form of imprudence). By doing so, one improves one's ability to decide, without unnecessary delay, what to do in a specific situation.

- *Reflecting on significant data,* relating pieces of information to one another in a reasonable manner and listening to sensible people. The opposite of this, for example, would be to insist that one is right with little justification, shutting oneself in without delving further into the other side's arguments.

- *Trying to foresee future consequences* that will probably flow from an action, and possible events that might combine with such consequences. This will lead one to use all necessary means to achieve the desired objectives and avoid, or at least minimize, undesirable side effects.

- *Acting with caution* in the face of any obstacles that might appear. A cautious person knows when to expect difficulties and anticipates them.

- *Developing circumspection,* being alert to special circumstances that might arise in a particular situation and that are worth noting. That implies being vigilant enough to discover the relevant circumstances of each case, distinguishing them from irrelevant ones.

- *Living rightly,* a person who is just, strong-minded and moderate is in a better position to be prudent than a person in whom those virtues are poorly developed. That is because, in practising any virtue, one also practises practical wisdom: in order to live in accordance with justice one needs to know what is right in each circumstance. The same applies to fortitude and temperance. By contrast, practical wisdom is unlikely to have taken deep root in a person who does not lead an honest life. The thought of one who fails to live in accordance with his or her beliefs is likely to become twisted so as to justify the chosen way of life. Hence the saying: 'If you don't live as you think, you'll end up thinking as you live.'

On the other hand, there are behaviours that undermine practical wisdom or prevent its growth, namely:

- Practising *guile,* or the tendency to find whatever means will achieve one's interests, putting aside any honest disposition to discover what is truly good and to distinguish licit from illicit means.

- Acting with *lack of concern for the human or ethical side* of problems. Sometimes problems are caused by an excessive anxiety about technical, economic or political aspects of a problem, to the detriment of concern for the human aspects.

- Analysing problems with *superficiality,* which prevents understanding what is the right thing to do.

- Making *rush decisions* with excessive haste to reach a conclusion without adequate deliberation or judgement.

- *Developing attitudes of self-complacency,* scorning others' advice or not submitting one's own solution to the judgement of people who could give an expert or wise opinion.
- Being *inconstant* in the execution of decisions or acting with *negligence* or laxity in doing what has to be done, including carelessness and omission of responsibilities that come with one's position.

INTEGRITY AS WHOLENESS OF VIRTUE

Knowing the right thing to do is not sufficient. Moral behaviour requires a firm adherence to the human good and following sound principles with a strong will.

Integrity confers unity in making decisions coherent with a personal life project, and in integrating various relationships (family, business and so on) into one's personal life. The opposite of integrity is corruption.[42] In fact, corruption signifies impairment of integrity, virtue or moral principle[43] and, in its generic meaning, signifies a lack of wholeness – a dividedness. When a person acts without integrity, corruption follows and spreads from one person to the next. Integrity creates trust in the uprightness of a leader's actions, whereas corruption generates distrust.

In its most genuine sense, integrity not only means coherence and unity, but also completeness, wholeness. This is its etymological meaning, derived from the Latin *integritas*, the quality or condition of being whole or undivided. As Solomon has explained: 'The word integrity means "wholeness", wholeness of virtue, wholeness as a person, wholeness in the sense of being part of something larger than the person – the community, the corporation, society, humanity, the cosmos.'[44] Integrity requires being virtuous, not with discrete, random virtues but with a harmonious development of all human virtues within one's character. In fact, 'integrity is not itself a virtue so much as it is a synthesis of the virtues, working together to form a coherent whole'.[45]

Integrity as wholeness of virtue is related to the important topic of the *unity of the virtues or connection between virtues.* Aristotle pointed this out by contrasting the difference between possessing the kinds of skills that one might have without others (a good football player is not necessarily a skilled accountant) and virtues, which, in their interconnection, shape the individual moral character.[46]

Practical wisdom is that which gives unity to virtue, since every moral virtue (justice, courage, moderation) favours the development of practical wisdom, which in turn determines the 'golden mean' of each virtue (see p. 89). Thus, practical wisdom and the other moral virtues stand in mutual need of one another and, if one virtue is lacking, the others will not be fully present either.[47] However, as Aquinas has clarified, 'imperfect virtues' can have scarce connection. This is what happens in individuals with shaky virtue development. Some virtues might be greater than others, but virtues at a low degree of development can prevent good conduct. For instance, an individual can be more just than courageous, and that can prevent him or her from *acting* with justice; or a student can have a certain sense of what to do to achieve knowledge, but laziness can prevent it.

Contrasting with the situation of 'imperfect virtues', moral virtues are connected in their 'perfect state'.[48] A high degree of justice requires both great courage for doing what is right and also moderation to avoid pleasant situations that would prevent one's acting with justice. Similarly, courage is not virtuous if it is without rectitude (justice), moderation (self-control) and discretion (practical wisdom). And so it is with the other cardinal virtues.

A person of integrity strives to achieve emotional stability and direct spontaneous motivations through rationality to avoid misbehaviours. Virtues help one to keep one's innermost self intact in spite of cultural, social or environmental pressures for wrongdoing; striving to make decisions and to act in accordance with sound principles, rather than being tyrannized by fear of 'political incorrectness'. Integrity is not only strength to resist wrongdoing; above all, it has the proactive sense of acting in accordance with the human good.

Integrity can also be attributed to collectives. As Petrick and Quinn have affirmed, 'individuals and collectives with high integrity capacity are likely to exhibit a coherent unity of purpose and action in the face of moral complexity rather than succumb to bureaucratic inertia or simplistic, irresponsible decision making'.[49]

On the foundations of the disposition to service, wisdom and integrity, there are several human virtues that seem especially pertinent to managers in their leadership role. One is justice in its strict sense. Others are honesty and loyalty, which are expressions of justice, since they refer to rectitude in dealing with others. Kindness, compassion and forgiveness express a concern and care for people, which are also related to justice in a broader sense. Other virtues are related to courage: magnanimity, patience, self-discipline and being positive, apart from courage in its genuine sense. Finally, humility, along with authenticity, is related to the cardinal virtue of moderation. We will briefly consider these virtues in the following sections, beginning with the two latter.

> **Insight 9:**
>
> **Level 5 of leadership**
>
> In 2001, James C. Collins published a book entitled *Good to Great*, which became quite successful. It concerns a research project that began five years earlier. The driving question was this: Can a good company become a great company and, if so, how? 'Greatness' was defined as financial performance several multiples better than the market average over a sustained period of time. Collins, with his team, observed cumulative stock returns at or below the general stock market level for 15 years, punctuated by a transition point; cumulative returns then rose to at least three times market performance over the next 15 years. After analysing 1,435 companies that appeared on the *Fortune 500* from 1965 to 1995, they found 11 good-to-great examples. These companies had averaged cumulative stock returns 6.9 times that of the general stock market for the 15 years after the point of transition. By contrast, they also identified comparison companies, based on similarity of business, size, age, customers and performance leading up to the transition, that had failed to make that sustained shift. For each good-to-great example, they selected the best direct comparison. They then studied the contrast between the two

Insight 9: (cont'd)

groups to discover common variables that distinguished those that made and sustained a shift from those that could have but did not.

One of the drivers of good-to-great transformations was that these companies had a CEO from the transition point who presented a leadership characteristic that Collins defined as Level 5 leadership, after considering four other levels:

- Level 1: *Highly capable individual*: Makes productive contributions through talent, knowledge, skills, and good work habits

- Level 2: *Contributing team member*: Contributes individual capabilities to the achievement of group objectives and works effectively with others in a group setting

- Level 3: *Competent manager*: Organizes people and resources towards the effective and efficient pursuit of predetermined objectives

- Level 4: *Effective leader*: Catalyses commitment to and vigorous pursuit of a clear and compelling vision, stimulating higher performance standards

- Level 5: *Executive (Level 5)*: Builds enduring greatness through a paradoxical blend of personal humility and professional will.

Collins found that many of the CEOs classified as Level 5 displayed an unusual mix of intense determination, or professional will, and profound humility. Among other marks, Level 5 leaders demonstrate an unwavering resolve to do whatever must be done to produce the best long-term results, no matter how difficult. They also showed a compelling modesty, shunning public adulation; were never boastful; acted with quiet, calm determination; and relied principally on inspired standards, not inspiring charisma, as motivation.[50]

HUMILITY AND AUTHENTICITY

Humility is sometimes considered synonymous with modesty and, in fact, Collins included 'modesty' in what he terms 'humility' (see Insight 9). However, humility can be understood in a wider sense. In most classic authors, humility means to think realistically about oneself, being aware of one's weaknesses and strengths.

Jaime Balmes, a relatively unknown nineteenth-century Spanish philosopher who seems to be the first to have considered humility in business, understood this virtue as a clear knowledge of what we are, with nothing added or taken away. He pointed out that humility helps us to recognize the limits of our capabilities, to maintain a permanent disposition to ask for advice, and to see how much we still need to move ahead.[51]

Humility concerns the truth about oneself and others. It helps one to recognize one's own talents, but goes beyond this. It is neither false modesty nor lack of self-esteem. Humility provides realistic expectations of self, with the subsequent self-confidence, a frequently mentioned quality of leaders. When based on the knowledge of one's real capacities, it is a realistic and authentic self-confidence.

Otherwise, self-confidence would have a false foundation, and this is quite risky. It can lead to visible failures, and the subsequent loss of the trust of those surrounding the leader. Humility also leads one to recognize others' merits, not blame others for one's own failures. It involves the practice of self-criticism and the willingness to change when errors or failure are detected.

The opposite of humility is arrogance, pride, conceit or an excessive sense of personal worth. Arrogant managers deem themselves irreplaceable. They do not recognize their errors and rarely rectify their wrong behaviours; neither do they acknowledge their own failures, but constantly lay the blame for them on others. They do not listen to others in order to learn; neither can they imagine that others might be right. They do not weigh the talents and achievements of their colleagues with equanimity, and resist praising collaborators for the sake of their own image to avoid the possibility of their fellows overshadowing them. Arrogance creates barriers and distrust between managers and collaborators, and this undermines their leadership. Humility has the opposite effect.

Humility is closely related to serving others. Pride can make it particularly difficult to be sensitive to people's needs. But humility can be a great help in serving people, since humility, in recognizing the truth about oneself and others, fosters the recognition of people's authentic needs.

Authenticity, or 'being oneself', is closely related to humility. Leaders with humility base their behaviour on what they actually are, not on some questionable self-image. Authenticity is emphasized by Bill George,[52] who was CEO of Medtronic.[53] For him, leadership is authenticity, not style. 'Leaders are all very different people... The only essential quality a leader must have is to be your own person, authentic in every regard'.[54] Being oneself is not, however, acquiescence to one's own shortcomings. The knowledge of weaknesses and shortcomings is, for the leader, a stimulus to strive to overcome them.

Humility contributes to the development of gratitude and favours asking for pardon for one's failures and forgiving whenever necessary: two virtues that we will consider later.

It is worth noting that humility has nothing to do with being pusillanimous. On the contrary, in a leader, humility has to go hand in hand with magnanimity, which we will consider next.

MAGNANIMITY

Being magnanimous has been defined as 'loftiness of spirit enabling one to bear trouble calmly, to disdain meanness and pettiness, and to display a noble generosity'.[55] Derived from the Latin *magnanimitas*, in its root, *magnus*, means great. Magnanimity is understood by Havard as 'striving towards great things' and, as a consequence, magnanimous leaders are 'high-minded and conscious of their potential for greatness'.[56] Those who are magnanimous set themselves great goals, and 'what is truly great in the universe is the person'.[57] These goals are not chosen exclusively out of personal interest but to favour people; they are in the best interests of the organization or community.

Magnanimity can be related to eagerness for valuable achievements, often mentioned among the traits of the leader's character. It can be recognized as a personal quality in leaders, such as Abraham Lincoln[58] or Schuman, Monet, Adenauer and Gasperi, founders of the European Union.[59]

Magnanimity can also be found in many entrepreneurs who might have resigned themselves to managing a small business but were not content to do so. On the contrary, they displayed courage and resolution, developing new initiatives that created jobs and made new and useful products available to many people. This was the case of Heinrich Emanuel Merck, who took over the family pharmacy and 11 years later established a chemical-pharmaceutical factory in Darmstadt, Germany, which became the origin of a large company. David Hilbert, founder of HP, started his business in a garage; and Earl Bakken, co-founder of Medtronic, today one of the world's largest medical technology companies, began with a modest repair company, fixing and servicing medical equipment in local hospitals.

Magnanimity is not only a virtue for 'VIPs'. Magnanimity is also present in 'little leadership', in those who seek to better themselves, striving for noble causes.

JUSTICE, HONESTY AND LOYALTY

Justice

Justice requires acting with rectitude, giving to each his or her right. As justice has been treated in chapter 8, stressing that justice gives a guideline to power.[60] People who wield power within an organization can also gain authority by a responsible use of this power through an effective service to the common good of the organization.[61] By contrast, authority can be eroded and even lost due to abuse or misuse of power.[62] Pérez-López affirmed that authority is eroded by an unjust use of power, by the non-use of power whenever it is necessary, and employing power to no purpose.[63] By contrast, using power with justice is a way to achieve authority and, therefore, leadership.

Honesty

Honesty refers to truthfulness in speech and in deeds. In plain terms, it means telling the truth; that is, conforming to facts or reality, or at least with one's own thought. In a broader sense, honesty is also an inner impulse to seek truth, preserve truth and act in accordance with truth.

According to Solomon, honesty is the first virtue of business life[64] and, without doubt, it is a pillar of leadership. Honesty is greatly appreciated as a means of creating trust. Long ago, Aquinas wrote: 'people could not live with one another if there were not mutual confidence that they were being truthful to one another'.[65]

Telling lies, creating false expectations, distorting reality, acting with hypocrisy, offering a false image of oneself, practising flattery by praising someone's fine qualities to obtain favours or giving misleading feedback are some examples of a lack of honesty. If a leader is not honest, his or her authority will be eroded. Telling the truth or deceiving in accordance with one's interests of the moment cause those that it concerns never to know what to believe or doubt. It can be readily understood that a dishonest person will not have long-term followers.

Loyalty

Loyalty is a virtue that denotes faithfulness or firmness in keeping legitimate promises and maintaining fair agreements. Loyalty can be due to a person or a group of people, a cause or an institution. As with honesty, loyalty is an aspect of justice, but one with a special identity. Loyalty as a virtue differs from an interested or emotional adhesion to something.[66] Loyalty leads, rather, to fulfilling one's commitments and offering conscious fidelity to those to whom it is due with a steadfast and devoted attachment. Loyalty as a virtue refers to moral objects and so excludes any unjust commitment or adherence to any cause that is morally wrong. In addition, as with any other moral virtue, loyalty is regulated by practical wisdom, which helps to resolve any conflicts between one loyalty and another.

Loyalty does not refer only to formal commitments: informal commitments can also be present when behaviours show that the leader is actually committed to a certain cause or goal, or even if people realize that he or she is providing continual support to a group that shares common goals.

Loyalty contributes to the smooth and efficient functioning of organizations. It generates trust, which is crucial to organizational development.[67] Loyalty must have a similar effect in promoting trust in leadership. Followers appreciate the loyalty of the leader to their common goals. By contrast, lack of loyalty or a lukewarm allegiance break trust, and the authority of leadership is eroded.

KINDNESS, COMPASSION, GRATITUDE AND FORGIVENESS

Justice, honesty and loyalty can be cold and impersonal if not accompanied by the kindness that people appreciate in dealing with each other or in life in common.

Kindness

Kindness is neither a severe manner nor excessively mild or soft behaviour. These are not external forms or simply good manners in dealing with people. Far from conventionalism, pleasant manners are expressions of humility, respect and the desire to be of service to others.

Kindness, in a sense, includes virtues such as meekness, gentleness, affability and good manners, being approachable, easy and pleasant to speak to. Kindness also entails being considerate and adopting a friendly, generous and warm-hearted attitude. Kindness can also include a moderate and opportune sense of humour and fun.

Compassion

Compassion gives one the capacity to be aware of others' distress together with a desire to relieve it. Compassion is much more than empathy to recognize or understand another's state of mind or emotion. Compassion is related to the Golden Rule and is included as a great virtue in most religious traditions.[68] Compassionate managers can deal with 'toxic emotions', including *indignation, frustration* and *dissatisfaction in corporate life*.[69]

Some empirical research based on narratives identified manners in which compassion is demonstrated and facilitated in organizations, and its effects in human and organizational behaviours. Employees reward companies that treat them humanely.[70]

Understanding people's failure is also an important aspect of compassion, but compassion is not sentimentalism. Thus, compassion, along with a sense of justice and service, prevents passivity or looking the other way when one is aware of some wrongdoing on the part of a collaborator or subordinate. They should be warned or corrected whenever necessary (but without humiliating them) with tact, in positive terms, and by providing guidelines and support.

Gratitude

Gratitude – understood as being appreciative of benefits received – is also a significant virtue in leadership and in organizational life. Although gratitude is not frequently mentioned among the leader's traits, common experience shows that people appreciate attitudes of recognition and gratitude when there are reasonable motives, and reject the contrary.

Forgiveness

Regarding *forgiveness*, feelings of *resentment, indignation* or *anger* might be present in organizations. They can be due to a perceived offence, humiliation or mistakes that make others' work more difficult. These feelings can lead to a non-collaborative attitude and, if a leader has these feelings, he or she can become distant from the followers. In contrast, those who are able to forgive are in a good position to obtain an effective reconciliation. Thus, it is not surprising that some scholars stress the important role that forgiveness has in the leadership of effective organizations.[71]

COURAGE, PATIENCE, SELF-DISCIPLINE AND BEING POSITIVE

Offering practical service to others entails overcoming certain common fears. This entails courage and several related virtues, such as patience, self-discipline and the striving to be positive.

Courage

Courage masters unease due to risks, the possibility of failure, uncertainty or other difficulties or obstacles. Thus, leaders need to be fearless enough to undertake the proper actions and to strive with others to achieve common goals. Practical wisdom helps one to understand risks, and humility fosters awareness of the capabilities one has to confront them but courage is also necessary. Courage produces daring to overcome obstacles and provides the willingness and strength to take on reasonable risks.

Daft has mentioned several aspects of courage and its meaning in leadership.[72] Courage, he contends, means accepting responsibility; an attitude of nonconformity, going against the grain, breaking traditions, disregarding boundaries, initiating change; pushing beyond the comfort zone to do the right thing; asking for what you want, saying what you think and fighting for what you believe.

Patience

Patience is a virtue that bestows the capacity to endure hardship, difficulty or inconvenience without complaint. Patience is necessary for leaders, since leadership is about people, and people have many quirks, which, without patience, could result in leaders losing their temper.

Leaders need patience for persevering in the face of delay or provocation without becoming annoyed or upset. Patience is also necessary to learn, to give followers serenity and to achieve goals. Patience helps one to act under strain, and to face difficulties, especially when they are longer-term difficulties.

Self-discipline

Self-discipline is another necessary human virtue. It can be understood as any personal effort for personal improvement, which promotes self-control and restraint. Self-discipline brings about consistent willingness, striving for valuable goals and competitiveness.

Trust in the leader and achieving common goals requires much more than good intentions. *Laziness, idleness, indolence* and, in general, lack of *personal struggle* to achieve valuable goals can jeopardize leadership. Thus, self-discipline can be considered a pillar of leadership. According to George, 'Self-discipline is an essential quality of an authentic leader. Without it, you cannot gain the respect of your followers.'[73]

A leader needs to struggle to fulfil commitments at the proper time, with industriousness, attentiveness and a sense of responsibility. All of this requires order, determination and perseverance in doing due tasks, even when the initial enthusiasm has disappeared.

Self-discipline helps to partake with *sobriety* in eating and drinking, controlling sexual impulses and, in general, practising moderation in pleasure and avoiding addictions.

Self-discipline leads to control of one's emotions, desires or actions without being driven by temper or acting in a fit of rage. Thus, self-discipline helps to maintain *emotional stability* and control even in situations that can be propitious to nervous tension or stress. In using and allocating resources, self-discipline lends itself to a sense of *austerity*, using them whenever necessary but avoiding wasteful, fanciful and luxurious expenses of doubtful profitability.

Being positive

Being positive and *optimistic* is also appreciated. Managers have to be realistic, and this is incompatible with invariably presenting the most favourable interpretation of actions and events, or always anticipating the best possible outcome. However, optimistic views have to be presented without deception or creating false expectations.

In this context, being positive is not a spontaneous attitude that some people have, but a virtue – a habit of character – that should be acquired with personal effort to overcome pessimistic views or attitudes to see only the negative side of any issue.

Business ethics in practice 9:

Leadership of Franco Bernabè at ENI, Italy

At the beginning of the 1990s, Italy suffered major political changes. The government wanted ENI, the large Italian business corporation owned by the Italian state, to be privatized. At that time, ENI was a conglomerate of 335 consolidated companies operating in 84 countries and with 135,000 employees. Its main activity was related to oil and energy.

In 1992, Franco Bernabè, only 42 years old, was unexpectedly appointed by the Italian government to head the company's privatization process. Until then, the Bernabè career with this company had been behind the scenes, where he worked as a planner and financial controller. But, from those positions, Bernabè developed effective strategic plans and gained a reputation of being a competent and honest manager.

After being appointed as CEO, Bernabè announced that ENI would be rapidly transformed from a political quagmire into a clean, market-driven business ready for its first public stock offering. Changing the current situation was his top priority. Resistance to change was quick and intense, including some members of the boards of directors and even the mass media. For years, ENI had been seen as a very special enterprise, which assured Italian access to petroleum and provided jobs, including an unhealthy share of politically appointed managers and executives. Many believed ENI was so thoroughly entrenched in politics that any attempt to change the system was a waste of time. But Bernabè had a different vision. In addition, he had the confidence that at least 85 per cent of the people in the company wanted to do good work and achieve personal excellence. His uncommon tirelessness in this advocacy for change impressed many people.

Shortly after Bernabè was appointed CEO of ENI, and the large operation termed *Mani Pulite* (*Clean Hands*) was launched by Italian authorities facing the public awareness of many corruption scandals, including embezzlement, bribery and kickbacks. A major investigation on ENI top executives was launched and 20 of them were arrested and jailed on corruption charges, including the former chairman, who committed suicide in prison.

Business ethics in practice 9: (cont'd)

Bernabè started replacing hundreds of managers with men and women with excellent technical expertise and personal qualities from lower levels within the company. Bernabè thought it was a sad but necessary decision. In the *Mani Pulite* context, he was falsely accused of taking a huge bribe. This gave him extra stress, but he pushed ahead.

Most people in the company admired Bernabè as a hero, and definitively followed him. Many also admired his strong sense of compassion for less fortunate people and an attitude to learn as a teenager.

In the first five years of Bernabè's leadership, ENI cut debt, reduced capital spending, went from a one million dollars loss to an annual profit of $3 billion and became a publicly traded company free of direct government control and interference.

Under the leadership of Bernabè, ENI Group became one of the world's most profitable oil companies. In 1998, Bernabè was appointed Chief Executive Officer of Telecom Italia. He is also an independent non-executive director of several companies.

Questions:

1. What virtues and other qualities can you identify in Franco Bernabè?

2. What would you recommend to Franco Bernabè to continue developing a culture of respecting talent, effort and good?

Sources: L. Hill and S. Wetlaufer, 'Leadership When There is No One to Ask: An Interview with ENI's Franco Bernabè', *Harvard Business Review*, 76 (1998): 80–94; Telecom Italy, Franco Bernabè, Amministratore Delegato (Porfilo): http://www.telecomitalia.it/TIPortale/docs/gruppo/Bernabe.pdf

---

Dilemma 9

The top management of a hotel chain in a Mediterranean country is aware that a market based on sun and beach, which has flourished for many years, is slowing down. Facing this situation, a future delocalization of this business to a Caribbean area is foreseeable, although not immediately. In accordance with the law, lay-offs can be carried out without other limitation than justifying them and paying an economic compensation, which in this case would not be too high. Linda, the general manager of this hotel chain, has a reputation for being a considerate person and a good leader. She believes that compliance with the law would not be sufficient and that they have to go further. However, the board of directors and the top management probably disagree on this point. She is wondering how she can convince them and what measures the company should take to minimize the negative consequences for its employees of the closing of hotels.

Questions:

1. What alternatives can you generate to solve this problem and what would be your analysis of each?

2. What specific recommendations would you suggest to Linda?

Summary

Leadership is a dimension of the management profession concerning the ability to influence people for the achievement of certain goals common to leaders and followers.

Leadership is associated not with power, but with authority: the recognition or acceptance of the leader by the followers and the willingness of these to follow the leader in pursuit of a common goal.

Ethics are to be found, implicitly or explicitly, in several leadership theories, especially in those involving virtues that shape the leader's moral character.

A transformational leader creates an increasing motivation in followers through change in their values, attitudes and enthusiasm.

Serving and fostering a sense of service in others can be associated with moral leadership. Along these lines, servant leadership theory defines leaders as those who wish to serve others and thus foster in their followers a similar attitude.

Wisdom, in a generic sense, refers to a deep understanding of reality. Accumulated wisdom in the form of maxims and behaviours could be inspirational for leadership. Practical wisdom is crucial in managers as a moral driver of their actions. Sense of responsibility for consequences is closely related to practical wisdom.

Integrity means coherence and unity, but also completeness, wholeness of virtue. This latter is its more genuine sense. Thus, a person of integrity is actually a truly virtuous person. The ability to withdraw and reorient in order to improve oneself, displaying acceptance and empathy for others, listening and seeking to understand them, as well as foresight, awareness, perception, persuasion, healing and serving.

Humility is a key virtue for leadership, along with authenticity. It is neither false modesty nor lack of self-esteem. Humility provides realistic expectations of self, with the subsequent self-confidence in the leader. Humility can accompany magnanimity, a virtue that leads one to strive for great things.

Justice, honesty and loyalty are relevant human virtues in leadership. An honest leader speaks and acts in accordance with the truth and, being loyal, the leader faithfully keeps his or her legitimate promises and fair agreements.

(cont'd)

Kindness, compassion and forgiveness contribute to followers appreciating their leader. These virtues are neither a severe manner nor soft behaviour. The following virtues can be related to kindness: meekness, gentleness, affability and good manners; being approachable, easy and pleasant to speak to.

Certain other virtues – such as having courage, self-discipline, patience and being positive – can also exert a great influence in leadership.

Part IV
Organizational Ethics

If ethics are poor at the top, that behavior is copied down through the organization.

Robert Noyce (1927–90)
Founder of Fairchild Semiconductor and Intel

Chapter Aims

This chapter will allow you to:

- gain an understanding of corporate values and guiding principles
- become more familiar with business codes of conduct and to consider several factors that can contribute to its effectiveness
- distinguish between (ideal) corporate culture and (real) organizational culture, and to consider the importance of the gap between them
- gain familiarity with the concept of organizational culture and organizational climate
- gain an understanding of ethical organizational cultures and how they influence ethical decision-making and behaviours of individuals within the organization
- discuss which factors contribute to shaping ethical organizational cultures
- discuss whether organizational structures can influence individual behaviours and how some poorly designed structural factors can foster misbehaviours
- be familiar with certain ethical principles or criteria for the designing of appropriate organizational structures and jobs
- encounter the ethical dimension of information technology and its influence on organizational structure and culture.

Key terms:

Codes of business conduct	Ethical training programmes	Participation
Corporate credo	Evaluation process	Performance
Corporate culture	Information age	Principle of Participation
Corporate guiding principles	Information technology	Principle of Subsidiarity
Corporate values	Job design	Surveillance of employees
Culture gap	Organizational culture	
Decision-making rights	Organizational structure	

Ethics in Organizational Cultures and Structures

INTRODUCTORY CASE 10:

BOEING – DOES THE PERSONAL CONDUCT OF THE CEO REALLY MATTER?

Boeing is the number one aerospace company in world and the largest manufacturer of commercial jetliners and military aircraft, which are sold on all continents. This corporation employs 155,000 people in 70 countries. However, this American icon was hit by several scandals, which raised questions about how ethical its corporate culture was. Boeing was under press surveillance for over a decade because of suspicions about unethical behaviour in handling its business.

In 2002, a senior Air Force official was illegally recruited by Boeing while she was still handling contracts for billion of dollars in which Boeing was involved. In 2003, Boeing was banned from bidding on Air Force rocket launcher contracts and, afterwards, the firm was alleged to have stolen secrets from competitor Lockheed Martin. In the same year, another alarm was the mysterious resignation of Boeing's chairman, Phil Condit.

At the end of 2003, Harry Stonecipher became Chief Executive Officer of Boeing. He received the mandate to repair the company's image, and relations with customers in the Pentagon and in the airline industry. Stonecipher, aged 68, managed to recover the reputation of the company and to restore its stock price.

Stonecipher introduced the new code of conduct, which states that 'employees will not engage in conduct or activity that may raise questions as to the company's honesty, impartiality, reputation or otherwise cause embarrassment to the company'. Harry encouraged everybody to be very strict with even the most minor unethical behaviour of Boeing employees.

Progress was going well, but an unexpected episode brought about a new scandal, although one quite different from the previous cases. Stonecipher, a married man, had an affair with Debra Peabody, 48 years old, who was vice-president of Boeing. Matters came to a head in March 2005 when, for the biannual meeting of the board of Boeing directors, which took place in Washington, Stonecipher used company funds and a company jet for Ms Peabody.

Such a scandal would not help in the repairing of the corporation's image. Directors were aware that the company was still under intense ethical scrutiny, and made an effort to show the world the ethical face of Boeing.

Shortly after, the American press published a series of articles saying that Boeing had failed to send a clear signal about its ethical behaviour because of the CEO's moral relativism. The media concentrated not so much on Stonecipher's use of company funds for the unjustifiable expenses of his girlfriend but, rather, on the fact that he had betrayed his wife and children.

One of the Boeing workers in Fullerton, quoted by the *Seattle Times*, questioned how a CEO could ask his employees to show loyalty to the cause when he was unable to demonstrate loyalty to his own wife and family. It was also argued that, as executives' personal conduct was important during the Watergate affair and in the Enron climate, the same applied here.

Lewis Platt, the board chairman, openly stated that Stonecipher was to be punished for putting the reputation of the company in doubt. Furthermore, he said that a CEO must set a standard for both professional and personal behaviour.

Debra compensated Boeing for unjustifiable benefits received from Stonecipher and resigned from the corporation, where she had worked for over 20 years. Stonecipher was fired by the board of directors but, before leaving, he received a bonus of $2.1 million for 2004.

Questions:

1. What do you think about the decision of the Boeing Board of Directors to fire Mr Stonecipher, and the arguments they provided?

2. Do you think that this decision might have an influence on the organizational culture of Boeing?

3. Do you think that a serious effort in promoting ethics in Boeing might have an influence on the ethical behaviour of the whole aerospace industry, where Boeing is still an unquestionable leader?

Sources: Boeing official website: www.boeing.com; S. Holt, 'Personal Lives of Executives under Scrutiny', *Seattle Times*, 3 March 2005; C. E. Johnson, *Ethics in the Workplace. Tools and Tactics for Organizational Transformation* (Thousand Oaks: Sage Publications, 2007): 243; F. Norris, 'Moving from Scandal to Scandal, Boeing Finds its Road to Redemption Paved with Affairs Great and Small', *New York Times*, 3 August 2005; L. Wayne, 'Ousted Chief of Boeing gets $2.1 Million Bonus for 2004', *New York Times*, 11 March 2005 and 'Executive Involved with Chief has Resigned', *New York Times*, 19 March 2005; D. Westneat, 'Boeing's Message Puzzling', *Seattle Times*, 9 March 2005.

CORPORATE VALUES AND GUIDING PRINCIPLES

Corporate values are the essential and permanent motives for acting within an organization. Corporate core values, along with corporate mission and vision, express to a great extent the business philosophy of each company. They are basic to establishing business strategy and designing the organizational structure, which determines the modes in which the organization is to operate and perform. Organizational structure can leave its mark on individual behaviour within the organization, as we will see.

Including ethics in corporate values, mission and vision is an important step towards making ethics present in the entire organization. As we will discuss, certain guiding principles and a code of business conduct can also contribute to this purpose if properly applied. However, these corporate statements are only desires for the organization. In practice, there is always an organizational culture that reflects the real beliefs, values and virtues of people involved in the organization. These can be similar to or glaringly different from the corporate statements.

Corporate values prescribe what should drive corporate governance, management and organizational activity. Corporate values are found explicitly in value statements ('corporate values') or as part of a corporate code of conduct or 'credo'. The latter present formulations based on a structure such as: 'We believe ... [values or action principles]'. A typical credo is that of Johnson & Johnson.[1] Core values can be explicit ethical values or can express concern for people in various ways. They also include values related to efficiency.

Values have to do with mission. The mission itself, as with the vision, can include some values, at least implicitly. Corporate values provide guidelines about how the mission is to be achieved.

As with the mission, corporate values can be neglected in practice: Enron is a paradigmatic example. However, many companies do take their corporate values seriously. This is the case of AES, a company operating in the energy industry. In June 1991, in the prospectus prepared for AES's initial public offering, the following statement appeared:

> An important element of AES is its commitment to four major 'shared' values: to act with integrity, to be fair, to have fun and to be socially responsible ... AES believes that earning a fair profit is an important result of providing a quality product to its customers. However, if the Company perceives a conflict between these values and profits, the Company will try to adhere to its values – even though doing so might result in diminished profits or foregone opportunities. Moreover, the Company seeks to adhere to these values not as a means to achieve economic success, but because it is a worthwhile goal in and of itself.[2]

Usually, corporate values are expressed as a set of meaningful words or short, easy-to-understand sentences, perhaps accompanied by a brief explanation, as in the case of AES. Similarly, other companies, in their respective corporate websites, espouse core values. For Procter & Gamble these are: integrity, leadership, ownership (acting as owners), a passion for winning and trust. Toyota, the famous Japanese car manufacturer, defined its values as an ideal that has already been achieved: 'We're hard-working. We're active in our community. We're committed to the environment. We celebrate our diversity. We're creating jobs. We're making history. We're building cleaner, greener cars.'

Corporate core values vary significantly from company to company, depending on industries, national cultures and the specific features of each organization.[3] In practice, however, there are a few values that can be found in many corporate values statements. This is shown, for instance, in a global survey carried out by Booz Allen Hamilton/Aspen Institute[4] among top managers of corporations from 30 different countries in five regions of the world (Table 10.1). Many common values are listed, although the rating of each value varies from one region to another, probably due to different cultural traditions and sensibilities. Thus, according to this study, ethical behaviour is more common in North American companies than in European and Asian/Pacific ones. The reverse is true, however, regarding corporate responsibility and environmental responsibility. It is noteworthy that values such as ethical behaviour/integrity, honesty and openness have a high rating in all regions, as do commitment to employees, customers and shareholders.

Table 10.1   Worldwide survey on values in corporate value statements (as a percentage)

	North America	Europe	Asia/Pacific	Global
Ethical behaviour/ integrity	95	84	85	90
Honesty/ openness	77	64	56	69
Commitment to customers	87	90	86	88
Commitment to employees	81	77	69	78
Teamwork and trust	79	64	83	76
Commitment to shareholders	67	74	68	69
Accountability	67	74	62	68
Social responsibility/ corporate citizenship	58	69	74	65
Environmental responsibility	34	55	56	46
Commitment to diversity	50	41	23	41

Source: Adapted from Lee *et al.* (2005).

Similarly, an extensive study[5] on multinational companies' business codes found that transparency, honesty/trust, fairness/impartiality, trust and empathy/respect/diversity were frequently mentioned for dealing with stakeholders. While core values of or within organizations were mentioned first, a set of related concepts with similar meaning were also included: teamwork, mutual support, interdependence, cooperation and team spirit (43 per cent). Next came responsibility/conscientiousness (33 per cent), open communication, innovation, creativity, pioneering (29 per cent), custom oriented action (19 per cent), and professionalism and entrepreneurship (14 per cent).

Guiding principles develop mission, vision and core values, describing specific patterns for their achievement. They are standards of business conduct for people involved in the organization. Procter & Gamble have as their guiding principles: 'We show respect for all individuals, the interests of the company and the individuals are inseparable, focused in our work, innovation is the cornerstone of our success, we are externally focused, we seek the best, we value personal mastery, and mutual interdependence is a way of life.'[6] Some companies present values in such a way that they include guiding principles. This is, for example, the case of Lufthansa Airways, which presents as core values: customer benefits; accent on core skills; system integration sets the pace; attractive working environment; long-term profitability; and social responsibility.[7]

CODES OF BUSINESS CONDUCT

A *code of business conduct*, sometimes called a code of ethics, is a corporate document that develops the core values and the guiding principles of a firm. It specifies criteria and rules for the correct handling of business dilemmas, issues or situations in which it is considered particularly important that managers and staff follow certain procedures approved by the firm's management. A great number of companies, particularly the largest ones, have implemented codes of conduct. In some countries and industries, codes of conduct are legally mandated for listed companies.

The immediate goal of these codes is to articulate the institutionalization of certain rules of conduct within the firm and to facilitate their internalization by managers and staff. A corporate code of conduct is not, therefore, a compendium of ethical norms; it only expresses what top management considers should be done for the good of the company and reflects what a company expects from its employees. The content of business codes can vary in accordance with the specific needs of each organization. Usually, they include ethical issues,[8] employee duties and rights,[9] and accountability with stakeholders. Although a code of conduct is not a panacea for improving ethics within organizations, a code can bring with it several benefits for the firm (see Insight 10).

A possible objection to a code of conduct is that it might conflict with the personal values of the organization's members. However, if the personal values of those members are weak, the company itself might have problems with crimes or misbehaviour. That is why a company might want to implement a code of

Insight 10:

The benefits of a code of business conduct

A written code of business conduct is not a panacea for creating ethical behaviours and, in fact, not every firm needs one. A small firm in which employees can be easily aware of what conduct is expected from them might not need such a code. However, generally speaking, having and implementing a code of ethics correctly can bring about several benefits, among them, the following:

- *Helping to express and articulate values and criteria.* This is especially relevant during the process of writing the code of conduct. It strengthens the commonality of goals and interests among the firm's areas, and opens a process of reflection on whether these values can be manifest in concrete aspects and situations; that is, whether they are really operational.

- *Sending an ethical message to the organization.* The serious implementation of a code of conduct sends a message to the organization about the behaviour that is expected. A code is a clear statement that ethics is a priority issue within the firm. While accepting that financial targets and the income statement are important, it is a warning that not all means are licit for achieving these goals.

- *Providing guidelines for decision-making and dilemmas.* Codes facilitate professional and managerial decision-making in accordance with ethical criteria for anyone who is part of the firm. Codes also provide guidance when faced with dilemmas. In this sense, the codes can help provide a framework for the employees' ethical judgement when exceptional situations arise.

- *Preventing abuses within the firm.* Codes provide employees with a tool that limits their supervisors' or managers' power and which they can use to affirm that certain conduct is not permitted.

- *Fostering corporate identity.* A code can be a tool to strengthen corporate identity and to create an ethical culture (see pp. 233–6), insofar as all actions and factors converge towards a clearly specified goal. This is particularly beneficial for large or multinational firms, and during merger or takeover processes, where cultural clashes can arise.

- *Favouring corporate reputation.* A code gives a public image of commitment and responsibility, which favours corporate reputation. This is an intangible asset that is increasingly valued. It is particularly important for large firms that are faced with high societal expectations.

- *Helping to avoid litigation against the firm.* Codes provide means that help avoid costly litigations against the firm due to employee wrongdoing.

conduct that would reinforce certain minimum ethical standards for its people. In practice, this objection is not generally of great concern if the code has been drawn from universal ethical values, good practices of the best companies, and recommendations of people and institutions of acknowledged moral reputation. A wide-ranging dialogue in drawing up the code also facilitates understanding and acceptance of the code's contents.

Regarding the application of a code in countries with different cultures, it might be possible to draw up a code that is firm on certain minimum ethical standards that must be upheld at all times (respect for human dignity, human rights and other basic ethical norms for business) but could be flexible on lesser points. This allows a degree of elasticity in interpretation without losing sight of the basic values on which the code is founded.

Basing the code on universal ethical values also offers the advantage of making it easier to achieve consensus and to be more certain of doing what is right. Indeed, most multinational companies are interested in developing a code of conduct: it enables them to integrate all their subsidiaries more securely into the company's philosophy. To manage cultural diversity within the firm, it is not enough merely to acknowledge and respect it: it is also necessary to standardize the criteria for action to ensure that the firm retains credibility and offers consistently good service everywhere.

A frequent question is whether codes are effective for improving ethical behaviour or, at least, for preventing misbehaviour.[10] Having a code of conduct in place is no guarantee that everyone will act ethically at all times. However, it cannot be proclaimed that codes do not dissuade people from unethical conduct. Perhaps the key is using these codes along with others means of improving ethical behaviours,[11] within the context of a real corporate ethical philosophy applied to the whole organization.

IMPLEMENTING A CODE OF CONDUCT

In practice, there are several factors that can contribute to the effectiveness of a code of conduct or, on the contrary, can make it completely ineffective or even produce a negative impact. If a code is implemented, it must be followed; otherwise, it sends negative messages both within and outside of the firm.[12] Among these factors are the following:

- *The purpose of a code should be clear, achievable and realistic.* It must be devised in terms of what we want the organization to be, but must also take into account the social, moral and cultural conditions of the organization and the society in which it operates.

- *A strong senior management commitment should exist.* Otherwise, it is very improbable that a code will succeed. This commitment to the code should be present throughout its development and during its implementation and roll-out throughout the organization. Codes can be ineffective, and even counterproductive, if used as a mere window-dressing operation or to provide an extenuating circumstance when faced with the possibility of a fine.

- *The code should arise from a real need and a strong motivation.* As it is a lengthy and costly process without any immediate economic return, it runs the risk of being abandoned if it is not backed up by a strong motivation, at least at the highest levels of management.
- *The code should form part of a broader ethical outlook.* The role of the code is more that of a back-up than a motor for change. Furthermore, it is important to be aware that change within the firm must be a gradual process.
- *The code should be well written and well implemented.* The code should not be too long and should be written in plain, easy-to-understand language, avoiding overly technical formulations and abstruse explanations. The implementation is also crucial.

For an appropriate implementation of such a code, several practices are usually applied:

- *Making explicit a top management's expression of commitment.* The common method is a letter from the CEO, introducing the code. Additional means are also employed: a special event organized for the presentation of the code, a video from the CEO showing a firm commitment, as well as frequent messages from top management to the organization stressing the code's validity.
- *Implementing a broad and effective process of communication and dissemination.* This can be achieved, for instance, by presentation workshops and seminars, videos, posters, a corporate website or an annual mailing to all employees with confirmation of receipt.
- *Creating the position of ethical affairs officer or 'head of compliance'.* This is a specific position or senior manager with the mission of monitoring and implementing the code, including all matters related to communication, training and the application of the code.
- *Providing a direct line.* This could be a telephone number or e-mail address for questions and remarks to the ethics officer, or even to report misbehaviours or violations of the code. In the latter use, anonymity or confidentiality should be guaranteed.
- *Training.* For a code to be effective, not only information but also training is required. This training should be part of an ethical training programme (see pp. 236–7).
- *Monitoring and auditing.* This includes several means for monitoring and reporting how the code is applied and auditing misbehaviours, inside or outside of the company.

ORGANIZATIONAL CULTURE AND ITS ETHICAL DIMENSION

Organizational culture is a part of business reality, not a statement of ideals such as a corporate mission or values. Organizational culture is a complex concept related to styles of behaviour adopted by people within an organization that have become rooted among them. It has been described, in very simple but intuitive words, as 'the way we do things around here',[13] and also as an 'amalgam of beliefs, ideology, language, ritual and myth'.[14]

The notion of organizational culture was introduced early in the 1980s,[15] when researchers were asking why US corporations had lower performance than their counterparts in Japan although productivity methods, technology and other factors were quite similar. The response was that culture, both national and organizational, could explain such differences.[16] Today, there is increasing evidence that organizational culture is a determinant of performance through employee behaviour and decision patterns, especially when the culture is strong.[17]

The notion of culture among anthropologists is older. They usually understand culture as patterns, explicit and implicit, of human activity and behaviour shared by all or most members of a group of people; something that older members of the group usually try to pass on to the young.

Edgar H. Schein, an outstanding author in this field, believes that organizational culture is the most difficult organizational attribute to change.[18] He distinguishes three levels of organizational culture. The first is beliefs, understood as assumptions or convictions about human beings, the firm and its purpose in society, and even a vision of the world in general. The second level is values. Both beliefs and values are hidden, but constitute the core of the organizational culture. The third is a set of visible artefacts such as practices, rites, symbols, norms, organizational climate and other observable artefacts, including how people interact, how technology is used, the physical layout of work spaces and so on (Figure 10.1).

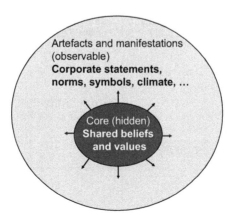

Figure 10.1   Observable and hidden constituents of a corporate culture

Among the observable aspects of culture is the 'organizational climate', which many employ as a first empirical approach to the organizational culture.[19] It refers to perceptions of an organization's members with an eye to the atmosphere of the place. One way to measure organizational climate is through questionnaires that typically include eight dimensions:[20] (1) autonomy in work; (2) cohesion (perception of togetherness or sharing within the organizational setting); (3) trust; (4) resources (perception of time demands with respect to task competition and performance standards); (5) support received from superiors; (6) recognition of members' contributions to the organization: (7) fairness (perception of justice in organizational polices); and (8) innovation (encouragement of creativity and risk-taking).

Organizational culture is different from corporate culture (see Figure 10.2). The former is the real culture, while the latter is the ideal desired by a corporation, expressed through corporate statements, including mission, vision, values, guiding principles and codes of conduct.

Organizational cultures can be easily perceived when dealing with people in an organization, especially when that organization has a long history. There are many kinds of organizational cultures; practically every company has its own, be it strong or weak, which influences its performance. There might also be subcultures within the same organization depending on countries, areas, leadership and so on. The degree to which values and beliefs are shared determines the 'culture strength'. Only if a widespread consensus exists on these values and beliefs is the culture strong and cohesive.[21]

In practice, there is generally a certain gap between corporate culture and organizational culture: between espoused values and values actually shared by a company's members. The 'culture gap' expresses the difference between desired and actual beliefs, values and practices within an organization.

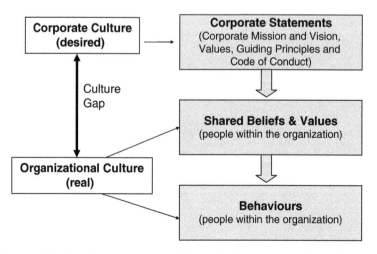

Figure 10.2   Corporate culture (desired) and organizational culture (real)

These beliefs, values and practices have an ethical dimension, since they entail shared ethical values and virtues of people within the organization. Knowledge that expresses such elements is relevant for business ethics, since it shows to what degree business ethics has actually been internalized by those who form the organization.

Another aspect has been studied by some researchers: how the ethical behaviour of an organization's members is influenced by the corresponding organizational culture. This is especially clear with misconduct, although organizational cultures can also have a positive influence.[22]

Cultures that foster ethical behaviour can be called ethical organizational cultures. A culture that specifically recognizes and respects human dignity and rights, and fosters personal flourishing might be called 'Organizational Humanizing Culture'.[23]

The question that arises is: How to develop ethical organizational cultures? This, in turn, leads to a more generic question: Which factors have an influence in shaping organizational cultures? We will consider this topic in the next section.

SHAPING ETHICAL ORGANIZATIONAL CULTURES

These cultures are built up by people interacting within an organization, but many experts see leadership as a crucial factor. Some institutionalized procedures, events or practices can also contribute to shaping organizational cultures. Expert proposals and top managers' common experience suggest the following factors for shaping an ethical organizational culture:[24]

- *Leaders' moral behaviour.* Leaders communicate beliefs and values but – above all – they are role models, for better or for worse. Setting a good example – especially, but not only, in top management – is probably the most important factor in creating an ethical culture. Leaders contribute to creating such a culture by showing consistency in what is said and what is done, by exhibiting a sincere concern for people in the way they treat them, by coaching collaborators and so on. Subordinates also observe that what they pay attention to, measure and control, and how they react to critical incidents and situations of crisis are all also significant.

- *Corporate mission, vision and values.* Well-defined mission, vision and value statements constitute a clear message to the organization when accompanied by a serious commitment to implement such statements. Reaffirming existing values in different ways and applying them to everyone throughout the organization is a good way to build up organizational culture. If corporate values are ethical, and the mission and vision are ethically correct, these corporate statements will contribute to creating an ethical organizational culture.

- *Ethical criteria for recruiting, selection and promotion.* If culture depends on people, and chiefly on managers and supervisors, it is relevant to consider ethical criteria and virtues in recruiting, selecting and promoting people in an organization.

- *Applying ethical values to decision-making.* Organizational culture is shaped by a consistent incorporation of corporate ethical values into strategic decision-making, and into the corresponding goals, policies and pro-grammes. These values must also come into play in decision-making at all levels of the company. Otherwise values remain ineffective and people understand that corporate values are only a matter of rhetoric.

- *Ethics in both the formal and the informal organization.* Integrating ethical criteria into intra-organization procedures and structures – and particularly personnel policies and practices – is another way to bring ethical values into everyday routine. We will consider the influence of the formal organization on individual behaviour later.

  The practical, everyday life of an organization is also relevant. It includes the personal styles, behaviour and interactions of people working within the organization. This is an important part of the 'informal organization', which can contribute to shaping an ethical organizational culture if such styles, behaviour and interactions are embedded within ethical values.

- *Ethical criteria in customer relations.* Focus on customer treatment, service provided to clients, reactions to customer complaints and the competitive practices employed all shape ethical organizational culture, if customer rela-tions are permeated with ethical values and the corresponding criteria.

- *Symbols and events.* Language used (for example, 'human resources' as opposed to 'people' or 'collaborators'), stories about founders of the company, great leaders, exemplary behaviours, symbols, special events and celebrations, 'ritu-als', awards, and so on can also influence the shaping of an organizational culture, and therefore an ethical organizational culture.

ETHICAL TRAINING PROGRAMMES

Many firms have introduced ethical training programmes into their organiza-tions by using seminars, discussion groups, workshops and online training. Role play and case studies based on real situations in the organization are very com-mon, along with anecdotes or histories as examples of how people should decide or act in the workplace.

The goal of these programmes is principally to communicate and explain the company's policy on business ethics, to train people to implement the code of conduct, to communicate to employees the importance senior management places on ethical behaviour in the workplace and to enhance employees' aware-ness of ethical challenges they might face at work.[25]

The training programmes are given either by people from within the firm or by outside experts. There is no agreement about which is better, since each has its benefits. Probably the best option is training by people from within the company, perhaps with some external support, since those within are more knowledgeable about the company's specific culture, its routine operations and so on.

Two main orientations can be distinguished for ethical training programmes: compliance-based and integrity-based (oriented to values).[26] Compliance refers to reinforcing a focus on the law and overemphasizing the threat of detection and punishment in order to channel behaviour in lawful directions. Underlying this model is a vision of people whose behaviour responds exclusively to self-interest and who are responsive to the personal costs and benefits of their choices, yet indifferent to the moral legitimacy of those choices. Values orientation is based on the concept of self-governance in accordance with a set of guiding principles. It includes obeying laws and rules, not as an external imposition but as a positive aspect of organizational life. The compliance approach, rooted in avoidance of legal sanctions, is generally insufficient to prevent wrongdoing.

According to some findings,[27] ethical training programmes are effective under certain conditions for reducing unethical and illegal behaviour, and increasing awareness of ethical issues. Moreover, they bring about more ethical seeking of advice within the firm, greater willingness to deliver bad news or report ethical/ legal violations to management, better decision-making because of the ethics/ compliance programme, and increased employee commitment. However, the effectiveness can be decreased if employees believe that it exists only to protect top management and the employer's self-interest. On the contrary, the effectiveness increases when there is a real leader's commitment to ethics, fair treatment of employees, rewards for ethical conduct, concern for external stakeholders and consistency between policies and actions.

REINFORCING ETHICAL ACTIONS THROUGH ORGANIZATIONAL STRUCTURES

Informal organization, which in great measure shapes organizational culture, is important in order to foster both ethical and unethical behaviour. But *formal organization* expressed through the *organizational structure* also has its role.

An organizational structure includes hierarchical dependencies, formal networks, assignment of responsibilities, processes, systems and reporting relationships established within an organization. This includes formal procedures in welcoming new employees and their initial and subsequent socialization, manners and contents of internal communication, training, criteria for allocation of rewards and status, policies and practices in dealing with senior members of staff and retirement, a process and definite criteria for dismissal, as well as performance appraisals, including individual and team performance.

Organizational structure focuses on facilitating working relationships within the firm in order to achieve business goals efficiently. But, beyond efficiency, every organizational structure also has an ethical dimension that emanates from the people who work within that structure. An organizational structure is not ethical if it fosters wrongdoing or disrespect for human beings, their rationality and freedom, their intrinsic dignity and innate rights. On the contrary, an organizational structure is ethical if it favours good behaviour and provides opportunities for the personal growth of those involved.

There is abundant empirical evidence that indicates that organizational structures encourage ethical behaviours or foster misbehaviours.[28] Three aspects of formal organizations can be especially influential in ethical (or unethical) behaviour: (1) the organizational rewards system; (2) the performance and evaluation processes, along with control and monitoring; and (3) the system of allocating decision-making rights and responsibilities.[29]

Organizational rewards system

This refers to all kinds of monetary rewards, promotions, prizes, awards and other forms of public recognition. Organizational structure contains rewards systems, mainly monetary, as incentives to foster certain behaviours, and this is often a powerful means. Rarely does the compensation system reward ethical behaviours. In practice, the noblest ethical actions, such as helping peers or acting with a real sense of service, are neither public nor economically motivated.

A problem arises when, in practice, financial or other compensations reward misbehaviours; for instance, paying kickbacks or even issuing fraudulent financial reports.[30] This occurs when organizational compensation practices are not carefully planned. Sometimes, the origin of misconduct is a lack of awareness about what a certain reward can actually incentivize. In practice, numerous rewards systems unintentionally incentivize actions that their designers had no intention of rewarding.[31]

Performance appraisal, evaluation processes and monitoring

The performance evaluation, monitoring and control processes for individuals and business units are also ethically significant – especially the performance appraisal, or the method by which the performance of a manager or employee is evaluated. Performance appraisal usually makes its assessment in terms of quality, quantity, cost and time, and values expected. The latter might be evaluated only indirectly. The evaluation process can reinforce the idea that ethical behaviours are expected while unethical ones are rejected or, at least, not rewarded.

The performance appraisal and evaluation process can fail to monitor managers and workers adequately, and permit imprudent actions or performance inconsistent with what would be ethically desirable or harmonious with corporate ethical values.

Two well-known cases in the financial sector illustrate failure in proper monitoring and control in a crucial facet of management. One is the collapse of Barings Bank in 1995, a British bank founded in 1762.[32] Its fall was the work of Nick Leeson, a young and brilliant securities trader in the Singapore branch office. Leeson had produced extraordinary profits, but his lack of prudence led him to take excessive risks – speculating chiefly on futures contracts – that eventually led to the bank's folding. Corporate executives failed to monitor him sufficiently closely and, by the time they learned of the true nature of Leeson's activities, they had suffered losses totalling £827 million ($1.4 billion). The other scandal that apparently involved a similar lack of adequate monitoring took place in the *Société Générale*, one of the oldest banks in France. In January 2008, the bank announced that a single futures trader had fraudulently cost the bank €4.9 billion, the largest such loss in history. A relatively junior futures trader allegedly orchestrated a series of bogus transactions that spiralled out of control amid turbulent markets in 2007 and early 2008.[33]

Incentive systems (rewards) and organizational pressures for results, accompanied by weak encouragement and monitoring of ethical standards, can foster wrongdoing.

The case of Sears Auto Centers in 1992 is often mentioned to illustrate this point. The company had established a plan to incentivize productivity consisting of paying service representatives a commission based on total sales. The plan also increased minimum work quotas for particular products and services in the auto repair centres in California and in other states. Workers were subjected to heavy pressure. Failure to meet quotas would result in a reduction in work hours and even loss of employment. Top management never encouraged unethical behaviour, but neither did they mention avoiding unnecessary service or monitoring questionable practices and poor work through regular evaluations of worker performance. After a conspicuous rise in consumer complaints, the licenses of all Sears Auto Centers in California were revoked. The charges alleged that the company had been systematically misleading customers and charging them for unnecessary repairs. Sears denied that any fraud had occurred, but finally agreed to pay $8 million to resolve the matter, and the director of automotive operations was fired.[34]

Decision-making rights and responsibilities

Members of an organization are empowered to make particular decisions. In some organizations, decision-making is centralized; in others, it is not. In any case, people have rights and responsibilities for making decisions. The influence of the decision-making structure can be reflected in the ethical or unethical behaviour of all members. This seems clear if one considers certain research findings that show that managers behave unethically when they perceive themselves as having little power and control over decisions or conduct, although they realize that some of their decisions are not ethically correct.[35] Moreover, lack of specific moral guidance from the organization, together with ambiguity of expectations, can create moral stress in decision-makers.[36] This suggests the necessity of giving power to employees with the capacity to make sound decisions on both business and ethical matters, and providing clear ethical guidelines, perhaps through an appropriate code of conduct.

Sometimes, all these factors merge to cause misconduct or corruption. Thus, several organizational factors that contribute to deceptive financial reporting have been identified. These include emphasis on results, pressures to meet unrealistic performance targets, upper and lower cut-offs or bonus plans, non-existent internal control systems, environmental changes that render existing control ineffective, and high levels of divisional autonomy.[37]

ETHICS IN THE DESIGN OF ORGANIZATIONAL STRUCTURES

Designing structural organizations that do not foster misconduct is a first condition for their ethical evaluation, but ethics presents other requirements for both structure and job design. This design should respect the human condition and foster personal growth of employees, as noted previously.

Until the 1970s, the predominant organizational form was characterized by clear boundaries between company and supplier, customers and competitors;

people were grouped into functions or departments with a hierarchical system of authority; and the system to ensure coordination and integration was both horizontal and vertical. From the 1980s onwards, changes ensued that led to change in organizational forms. The information processing capacity of organizations improved dramatically and, as a consequence, internal boundaries were deemed an impediment to business performance.

Since the mid-1990s, organizations have been faced with rapid improvement in communication (the Internet, cell phones) and emerging economies (China, India) are full of people able to provide low-cost manufacturing and software development. This has given rise to new organizational structures. A number of processes are labelled 'core business' or 'main activity', and mechanisms are put into place for *outsourcing* 'non-core business processes' by subcontracting a given aspect (product design, manufacturing and so on) to a third party. There are currently many theories generically known as 'new organizational forms'.[38] These can foster greater autonomy, cooperation and initiative. An ongoing ethical challenge is to design organizational structures that would humanize work and business organizations.

Two ethical principles are relevant to the design of organizational structures: (1) the *principle of participation*, and (2) the *principle of subsidiarity*.

Principle of participation

Organizational structures should consider the human condition and, more specifically, those requirements derived from human rationality, understood in a broad sense, and freedom. Acting with freedom, and the corresponding responsibility, is crucial to personal growth. This requires both accepting initiatives and promoting participation in the organization.

Participation finds its support in the social nature of human beings and the existence of differentiated goals of free beings that can be integrated through participation.[39]

Within business organizations, participation exists when employees have some sort of share in the businesses that hire them, especially in the decision-making process when it touches on topics that affect them. They should participate in the process in different degrees and manners, depending on particular situations, types of decisions, personal background, training and experience. There are different forms of participation.[40] The most elemental is asking for suggestions or help in defining problems and possible improvements. Many companies have, in fact, established a suggestion system for all employees or for a select group of them. Another way to augment participation is by creating groups of experts to make reports or even to make decisions on some aspects of the organization or organizational life.

A specific way of promoting participation is 'quality circles', groups of employees who meet regularly to discuss workplace improvements in matters such as product quality, occupational health and safety, the manufacturing process and product design. Another way of increasing participation is to authorize employees to make decisions on a great numbers of issues without permission from a supervisor or manager. Employees can also participate to some extent in hiring co-workers, designing work tasks, assessing new technologies, formulating budgets and measuring performance.[41]

Applying participation in ways appropriate to each company and culture, and adopting a participatory management is ethically praiseworthy because it means respecting human rationality and freedom, as well as contributing to the enrichment of the work of employees. In addition, participation generally motivates employees and gives the company a superior social performance.[42] A different way to increase participation, perhaps a more controversial one, is placing employees who are not top managers on the board of directors or on a supervisory board (this is the case with some large German corporations). In this manner, employees' representatives can influence decisions on corporate governance. However, this can lead to undue interference from unions, and can be a hindrance to making tough decisions in which employees' interests might be affected. Or it can slow down decisions because representatives can ask for extensive consultation among employees before agreeing on certain issues.

Principle of subsidiarity

This principle holds that a larger and higher-ranking body should not exercise functions that could be efficiently carried out by a smaller and lesser body; rather, the former should support the latter by aiding it in the coordination of its activities with those of the larger community, always under the guidance of the common good. For an organization, this means: Do not allow a large organization take over what can be done by smaller groups or organizations, or even by individuals; instead, give the smaller units support for developing their potential.[43]

A consequence of this principle for organizational structures is that the personal autonomy of employees should be respected and harmonized with the achievement of the organization's more general goals. Employees should enjoy the freedom to organize their work as much as possible, taking initiatives and making decisions within the scope of their responsibility.

The principle of subsidiarity respects and fosters human freedom in the achievement of common goals, and makes possible the contributions of diversity, without submitting everybody to a grey uniformity. At the same time, this principle favours developing one's own talents and avoids people feeling like passive elements of the whole. All of this is consistent with the common good.[44]

ETHICS IN JOB DESIGN

Ethics form part of the organizational structures in *job designs*, which refer to the planning of specific tasks and methods that a worker carries out within an organization. In its origins, job design was strongly focused on specialization, in order to enhance efficiency. The contribution of specialization to efficiency is well known, at least since Adam Smith (1723–90) emphasized this correlation in his book *The Wealth of Nations*. He provides a convincing example to illustrate the power of specialization: making pins from wire. The work in a pin factory was organized by dividing the activity into five tasks (drawing the wire, straightening the wire, cutting it, grinding the point, and attaching the head), with one worker assigned to each task. This specialization allowed a production of 48,000 pins per day. Before specialization, when a single worker did all five tasks, the production was only 200 pins per day.

At the beginning of the twentieth century, under scientific management, specialization came about as the result of a rationalized process. Efficiency increased, and so did gains for both employees and employers. However, the work was highly mechanized and the job-satisfaction level very low. This specialization brought about boredom and discontent by mandating the same job over and over. This increased absenteeism, lack of interest and a limited effort at work performance. From an ethical perspective, the treatment given to the workers was scarcely an acknowledgement of their talents and potential for personal development.

Later, innovations in the organization of work were introduced to avoid boredom. Thus appeared 'job rotation' (a systematic shifting of employees from one job to another) and 'job enlargement' (increasing the number of tasks). Even more humanistic was the 'job enrichment', which gave employees the opportunity to use a greater range of their abilities.

Another step was the 'Human Relations School', a stream of thought that emphasized psychological and emotional factors related to motivation; this exerted a significant influence on productivity. From this perspective, work design included developing good human relations, better communication (including consultation with employees on matters affecting them), less authoritarianism and motivation through psychological rewards. This was a step up towards a more human vision of work, but work design only took into account the psychological perspective in order obtain increased worker satisfaction and, ultimately, an increase in productivity. Ethics was limited to the manager's personal values, but was not integrated into work design.

In recent years, some progress has been made in work design, and several theories have been proposed, although they are not completely satisfactory for explaining the design of work in new work environments,[45] neither do they integrate work design with sound ethical ideas. The challenge remains, therefore, to develop models and practices that contribute to more meaningful work and foster personal development as part of one's job.

INFORMATION TECHNOLOGY IN THE ORGANIZATIONAL CONTEXT

Information technology (IT) refers to the development, installation and implementation of computer systems and applications. In the organizational context, IT entails the use of electronic computers and computer software, which includes computer programs, procedures and documentation that perform some functions of a computer system. IT allows one to store, protect, process and transmit information, as well as convert, protect and securely retrieve it. Sometimes, the process of communicating information is emphasized and IT is termed Information and Communications Technology, a nearly equivalent concept.

Information technology, along with telecommunications, has had a great impact not only on the corporate world, but also on society as a whole. Thus, many contend that we have moved from the 'Industrial Age' to the 'Information Age'.

Regarding its relevance to organizations, IT is closely related to structural culture and organizational culture.[46] Computers have transformed manufacturing processes, from design to production and quality verification; marketing, including advertising and sales through e-commerce; financial operations; management communications and control. IT not only provided the capability to improve performance and acquire greater knowledge, but also brought about a greater interconnection and the possibility of conversation among people within and outside of the organization. Several forms of widely utilized IT make all this possible. They include e-mail, which makes possible the rapid transmission of information and also online discussions, as well as web pages and blogs, which provide easily accessible stored information and material for conversation. Groupware is also available. The latter is especially significant in organizations, since its specifically designed software provides support for carrying out specific tasks and for decision-making.

There are a number of specific ethical problems connected with IT, which we will briefly review later, but, first, it is worth remarking on the impact of IT on organization members or those affected by them, including clients and suppliers.[47]

Computers, and IT in general, condition human work and human relations to such an extent that some question whether human beings will come to be despised while computers and computer-driven devices are looked to as being all-powerful, or whether human thought can be replaced by artificial intelligence or sophisticated algorithms. IT is a great help, and computers and other machines are, in some respects, more powerful than human beings, but they are nonetheless mere mechanical artefacts without feelings and spirituality. Furthermore, moral judgements require practical wisdom, which is a specifically human feature.

Along with many positive features, these technologies can affect employee privacy and subject people to constant surveillance. Through IT, a business can collect a huge amount of information about its employees and customers. If this information were disseminated, or even sold without permission, it would be a flagrant violation of privacy. Personal data should be obtained only with informed consent, and confidentiality is required. Moreover, since stored information can contain errors, the individuals in question have the right to access their personal data and modify it. Harm caused by negligence regarding this data is the responsibility of the employer.

The *surveillance of employees* by their employer is now easier with the help of computers, but there is a tension between evaluative surveillance and privacy, considering the current capacities of information technology. Surveillance can be legitimate or abusive.[48] In any case, human dignity and the personalist principle require that the kind of surveillance used by the company should be communicated to employees. Most countries have legal requirements regarding data protection and even electronic surveillance but, as usual, not every situation is covered by the law.[49]

Other ethical issues regarding IT have to do with how employees use these technologies. A frequent complaint concerns employees wasting time 'surfing the web', using other IT for reasons totally unrelated to the job, and using corporate software for personal reasons without permission. IT can make it easier to disseminate trade secrets and send inconvenient messages to many people with very little effort.

A third group of ethical issues refers to e-commerce, which poses ethical questions related to truthfulness, fraud, respect for privacy, and security in data processing, among others.[50] In fact, many of these are common ethical issues but, when they appear in the context of e-commerce, they have different manifestations and scope.[51]

Business ethics in practice 10:

TDIndustries – A culture of trust and servant leadership

At the turn of the twenty-first century, TDIndustries (TDI), a Texan company involved in heating, air conditioning, electricity and construction maintenance, had about 1,400 employees ('partners' in the company argot) and its economic results were clearly ahead of its competitors. For many years, it had been in *Fortune Magazine's* top 10 companies to work for.

The company was founded by Jack Lowe Sr in 1946 as an installation and service company for heating and air conditioning systems. The business grew rapidly to offer mechanical, plumbing and electrical services in Texas and in other states of the USA.

In 1952, when the concept of employee ownership was established, TDI became one of the pioneer companies in applying this concept. Three years later, Jack Lowe Sr fell very ill with tuberculosis. It was then that he reflected deeply on the Bible and other books. This inner experience led him to reinforce his management style to become one that was more strongly people-oriented.

In 1970, Jack was taken by the essay *The Servant as Leader* published by Robert Greenleaf after 40 years of working with AT&T. After reading it, he ordered hundreds of copies to be mailed to the offices of TDI. Jack became enthusiastic about this book, adopted 'Servant Leadership' as TDI's corporate philosophy and arranged regular seminars to teach it to all of the TDI employees.

The servant leadership philosophy defends the idea that genuine leadership does not depend on one's title. In fact, everyone could become a leader by, first, serving and then, through conscious choice, leading. Currently, most workers with TDI participate in seminars on servant leadership in which these points are developed.

Jack Lowe Sr passed away in 1980. After his death, his son, Jack Lowe Jr, succeeded him as CEO. The servant leadership style continued to be the core of the company philosophy, and Jack Lowe believes that this philosophy, along with a strong sense of trust, have been the basis for the company's development and an important element in overcoming several crises. Actually, this philosophy had its acid test in 1988 during a severe financial crisis in the company. Jack Lowe Jr spoke with many 'partners' (workers) and they agreed to loan money to save the company. In the 1990s, in which TDI made a significant

---

Business ethics in practice 10: (cont'd)

effort to win what they called the 'battle of quality', the culture of trust and servant leadership also played a significant role in quality implementation.

The TDI mission, which has a high degree of implementation within the company, is:

> We are committed to providing outstanding
> Career opportunities by exceeding
> Our Customers' Expectations through
> Continuous Aggressive Improvement.

According to Jack Lowe Jr, this mission is solidly embedded in TDI:

> Our organization – he said – is committed to the accomplishment of this vision over the long term. We do not believe in seizing short-term benefits to the detriment of our long-term vision. We believe in continuous, intense 'people-development' efforts, including substantial training budgets. We believe in investing in tools, equipment and facilities that enable us to better accomplish our vision.

Jack Lowe Jr states, 'When the motives for practicing servant leadership are pure, the result is not only increased profit but employee trust.'[52] He believes that the servant leadership is not a 'soft philosophy' but, rather, a practical way of seeking distinction with the resources available.

Jack was convinced that a total commitment to this philosophy had built a community where partners (workers) trusted management and listened to their thoughts and ideas; and management trusted the judgement of the partners.

Questions:

1. What do you think about the vision of Jack Lowe Jr and the TDI mission statement?

2. How would you recommend that Jack Lowe Jr continue the DTI culture in years to come?

Sources: This is an abridged version of the case study *TDIndustries: Developing a Corporate Culture*, D. Melé (Barcelona: IESE Publishing, 2002). Published with permission.

Dilemma 10

In January 1996, a US television programme, broadcast later in other countries, showed a Motorola labelled semiconductor chip in a Chinese-made mine that had been found in Cambodia. Motorola was accused of indirect cooperation in the atrocities produced by anti-personnel land mines by selling electronic components to mine manufacturers.

Dilemma 10 (cont'd)

At this time, there was a fierce campaign against anti-personnel land mines, particularly in the USA. Anti-personnel mines are explosive devices laid usually just below the surface of the ground. They are designed to kill or injure enemy combatants as opposed to destroying vehicles. However, once they are placed, these mines can also kill or seriously injure civilians. In the campaign, it was stated that land mines killed or maimed 26,000 people a year. Most of these people were civilians, up to 40 per cent of them children, living in countries trying to rebuild their society after the horrors of war. Images on TV programmes with people who had lost limbs caused great public consternation.

Motorola has clear values and a detailed code of business conduct, which include a strong permanent commitment to an 'uncompromising integrity' and to a 'constant respect for people'. This latter point means, the company explains, 'we treat everyone with dignity, as we would like to be treated ourselves. Constant respect applies to every individual we interact with around the world.' In addition, Motorola assumes corporate responsibility, meaning 'harnessing the power of our global business to benefit people. It also means doing the right thing in all aspects of our business, including how we treat the environment, our employees, our customers, our partners and our communities.' Thus, the allegations against Motorola were very striking.

Immediately, Motorola initiated an internal investigation into its export practices. Investigation went further and Motorola was in contact with two NGOs concerned with land mines (Human Rights Watch and the Vietnam Veterans of America Foundation) to find out more about the issue. In May 1996, Human Rights Watch informed Motorola that they had evidence that Motorola components were in US Volcano and Gator anti-personnel mines. Certainly, the Motorola chip was in the mines, but Motorola had never sold components to the suspected manufacturer, China North Industries.

Actually, it is very difficult to control the flow of low-cost products in an open market and to know the ultimate destination or use of these products. However, Motorola management wondered if they should do something else to avoid any possible involvement in such applications.

Questions:

1. Do you see any responsibility of Motorola management in selling components that have been used for anti-personnel land mines?

2. In your opinion, how should Motorola react to deal with these accusations in accordance with its corporate values and general ethical principles?

3. What would you recommend, if you were asked by Motorola management with regard to doing something else to avoid any possible involvement in applications such as anti-personnel land mines?

Summary

Ethics can be present in key corporate statements, such as missions, visions, core values and guiding principles. This has great importance for instilling an ethical sense in an organization, since these statements should drive the corporation's whole activity.

Corporate values, presented explicitly as 'corporate values' or 'creeds', prescribe what company leaders desire to drive corporate governance, management and organizational activity. They include ethical values or values related to improving efficiency.

A code of business conduct can bring about several benefits to organizations; it will encourage good behaviour in managers and employees if the code is a part of a real corporate ethical philosophy.

A successful code of business conduct also requires a strong senior management commitment, the existence of a real need, powerful motivation, and appropriate elaboration and implementation.

Organizational culture, which has an important ethical dimension, expresses shared beliefs and values, artefacts, styles of behaviour and practices adopted by people within an organization.

Corporate statements can be quite different from organizational culture and climate. It is a managerial challenge to overcome the 'culture gap' that usually exists between desired values and actual values within the organization.

Several factors can contribute to shaping an ethical organizational culture: leaders' moral behaviours (probably the most crucial factor); establishing and reaffirming the corporate mission, vision and values (including ethical values); ethical criteria for the recruiting, selection and promotion of managers and employees; considering ethical values in decision-making and in customer relationships; and symbols and events.

Ethical training programmes have been introduced by many firms. They can be effective under certain conditions for reducing unethical or illegal behaviour in the organization and for increasing awareness of ethical issues.

Organizational structures can reinforce ethical behaviours of individuals, mainly through rewards systems (both monetary and non-monetary), performance and evaluation processes along with appropriate control and monitoring, as well as a system for allocation of decision-making rights and responsibilities.

Organizational structures and job design should contribute to the personal growth of workers within the organization. This requires respecting initiatives and establishing appropriate participation. One should design structures in accordance with the principle of subsidiarity, which establishes that a larger and higher-ranking body should not exercise functions that could be efficiently carried out by a smaller and lesser body.

Information technology is closely related to structural culture and organizational culture. A number of ethical issues related to new forms of technology can affect employee privacy and bring about abuses in their surveillance. In e-commerce, many ethical issues are basically the same as common ethical issues in other contexts, but they have different manifestations and scope.

11

We must emphasize and give prominence to the primacy of man in the production process, the primacy of man over things.[1]

John Paul II
Pope of the Roman Catholic Church (1978–2005)

Chapter Aims

This chapter will allow you to:

- gain an understanding of the dignity of human work and how respect for human rights has a specific application in organizations
- become more familiar with the nature of the labour contract and some of its ethical requirements
- discuss some exploitative forms of labour contracts and working conditions
- consider the right of the employee to receive fair remuneration and to understand the concept of a 'living wage'
- become more familiar with certain requirements regarding working conditions, the personal rights of workers, and labour rights such as freedom of association, the right to collective bargaining and, under certain conditions, the right to strike
- gain an understanding of several forms of discrimination in employment and occupation
- introduce yourself to responsibility for the conditions in the supply chain.

Key terms:

Affirmative action	Fair remuneration	Occupational health
Age discrimination	Family discrimination	Occupational safety
Child labour	Forced labour	Racial discrimination
Collective bargaining	Freedom of association	Sexual harassment
Discrimination	Gender discrimination	Striking
Ethnic discrimination	Labour contract	Supply chain
Exploitation	Living wage	Sweatshops
Fair procedure	Mobbing	Unions

Work and Workers' Rights within the Organization

INTRODUCTORY CASE 11:

GAP – COMBATING CHILD LABOUR

Gap Inc. is one of the largest retailers in the world. It had revenues of $15.8 billion for the fiscal year 2007, employing 150,000 people. Its story started in 1969, when Doris and Don Fisher opened the first Gap shop in San Francisco. Today, they own 3,191 shops all over the world. However, Gap history is not only one big success. It has also received accusations about using child labour and sweatshops, where people work in inhumane conditions at far below minimum wages.

The first scandal hit the company in 2003, when the British newspaper *The Guardian* published a text on Gap's use of sweatshops in Asia, especially in Saipan in the western Pacific Ocean. That meant that thousands of people learned that Gap was using subcontractors who violated children's rights and forced children to do dangerous work for little money. According to Gap itself, the number of factories that violated the current code of conduct of the company regarding child labour was 136 at that time.

This culminated in Gap, along with 21 other companies, facing a class action lawsuit in Saipan. During the case, workers were said to work in unsafe conditions, and reported unpaid hours and forced abortion policies. Although Gap did not admit liability, the case resulted in a $20 million settlement.[2] Gap took a good lesson from it, and started to fight child labour, decreasing the number of sweatshops subcontractors used.

Seeking to recover its image, Gap took a number of steps to improve labour practices, set up a clear vendor code of conduct, and strict monitoring and reporting policies. Moreover, in 2004, Gap became a member of the Business Leaders Initiative on Human Rights (BLIHR), a group of 14 members working to address human rights issues.[3]

A spokesperson from Gap affirmed that the company will not tolerate child labour, and will treat this as one of the most serious violations of their code of vendor conduct.[4] In fact, Gap ceased business with 23 factories due to code violations in 2006. Furthermore, the company hired 90 people, who are located around the world, to ensure the compliance of subcontractors with Gap's code of vendor conduct.

In spite of these measures, in October 2007, a second scandal hit the company and the press headlines. After the British newspaper *The Observer* revealed that one of Gap's subcontractors in India was using child labour, the campaign against Gap started anew. In response, the company took a series of even stricter measures, terminated the relationship with its Indian partner, and announced a grant of $200,000 to improve working conditions in other factories. Gap president, Marka Hansen, said that Gap has a history of addressing challenges such as this head on. Don Hankle, a Gap spokesperson, assured media and consumers that they are acting correctly. 'Acting in an ethical way is not only the right thing to do,' he said, 'it also unlocks new ways for us to do business better.' In accordance with those words, the company published the list of actions that it has undertaken in order to fight against child labour. The document was issued on the company's website and delivered to NGOs and all interested parties in June 2008.

Questions:

1. How do you evaluate child labour as an ethical issue? Might it be justifiable in certain conditions?

2. Is Gap responsible for the poor working conditions in the subcontractors' factories or does this responsibility only fall on the Indian government or the direct employer?

3. How do you evaluate decisions taken by Gap regarding child labour, as they are described in this case?

Sources: CBS News, 'Gap Falls into Child Labor Controversy': http://www.cbsnews.com/stories/2007/10/29/business/main3422618.shtml; CNN, 'Reporting of Kid's Sweatshops "Deeply Disturbing"': http://edition.cnn.com/2007/WORLD/asiapcf/10/29/gap.labor/index.html; Gap website: www.gapinc.com; A. Gentleman, 'Gap Campaigns against Child Labor', *New York Times*, 16 November 2007; D. McDougall, 'Child Sweatshop Shame Threatens Gap's Ethical Image', *The Observer*, 28 October 2007; Save Childhood Movement website: http://www.bba.org.in/gap/index.php; Wikipedia (Gap).

DIGNITY OF HUMAN WORK AND WORKERS' RIGHTS

Human work, from an economic perspective, is both a productive factor and a cost (the 'labour cost'). In economy textbooks, work is studied in terms of supply and demand, as is any other commodity. This is convenient for the analysis of certain aspects of human work, but obviously falls short as a complete view of reality.

Similarly, in sociology, politics and, often, in management, it is quite common to refer to workers as a *workforce* – a term originating in mechanics, and another incomplete abstraction when applied to human beings. There is clearly a risk of seeing work and worker in such reductionistic terms and, consequently, dealing with workers in a very inconsiderate manner.

This is indeed what happened during the Industrial Revolution, one of the main reasons for the labour movements that brought about class strife and violence.[5] Considering human work as a mere commodity or as a mechanical force is not merely an historical oddity. This approach, even today, can be found in various countries, sometimes in the same raw form as in the times of the Industrial Revolution; sometimes an attenuated version with a few psychological modifications to improve productivity. We will consider this point later in the context of exploitative work and sweatshops.

A cursory glance at reality shows us a substantial difference between human work and mechanical work produced by a machine. The latter simply requires energy as input, while the former comes from acts of the human will and requires willingness and motivation. Even from an economic point of view, much human work is substantially more than a simple expense. Human work can be a genuine resource for the generation of income if workers are motivated and adopt a positive attitude to learning, innovating and working hard. Fostering good relations among workers, and between workers and their leaders, is a well-known business ideal.

From an ethical perspective, the most relevant observation is that human work has dignity because it is the immediate activity of a person, a being with dignity. In any production process, there is a person who is working. Ethics considers work as a human activity and emphasizes the respect that this deserves, as well as its capacity to contribute to the self-realization of workers.

In the production process, the worker not only produces things but also, in a sense, transforms him- or herself, acquiring experience, skill and habits as a consequence of the work. While making a product, the worker improves as a human being or, depending on the type of work, might be eroding his or her humanity. Thus, justice, honesty, loyalty, a sense of service and any other human value intentionally associated with work bring about the flourishing of the humanity of the worker, the subject of work.

Within this context, an interesting insight is the distinction between the objective and the subjective meaning of human work.[6] The objective meaning refers to whatever is involved in the means of production, including technology, machinery and any other instrument used to transform raw materials or to create a service, and the product itself. The subjective meaning of work refers to the subject of work; that is, the person who intentionally conducts the process, the one who works.

Independently of the economic value or social relevance of work in its objective meaning, the subjective meaning remains the same: it is a person, with intrinsic dignity. This is so, even in jobs that are very mechanical and repetitive. In this kind of work, the subject is also a conscious, free being: a person. Therefore, this labour also has dignity.

The dignity of human work entails a set of ethical requirements for the way in which it is to be organized. An elemental requirement is to respect human rights in labour, a demand strongly supported by the vast majority of international conventions.

The International Labour Organization (ILO) and other national and supranational organizations are taking on an important task in favour of labour rights and, in more general terms, human rights in the labour context. The ILO Declaration of Fundamental Principles and Rights at Work is specifically devoted to this topic. The UN Global Compact devotes four out of ten principles to labour rights and two more to human rights in business.[7]

LABOUR CONTRACTS AND WORK EXPLOITATION

The dignity of human work has an immediate application to how labour contracts should be understood. A *labour contract* is the hiring of a person to work in exchange for compensation. As with other contracts, the parties agree to an exchange. However, in the labour contract what is exchanged is human work for money or some other recompense. This gives such a contract some very particular characteristics.

When one buys a car, one exchanges a thing (money) for another thing (a car), but in a labour contract one agrees to give personal activity, devoting a substantial part of his or her life to working for a firm. If human work has dignity, and not only a price, a labour contract should be considered as the personal provision of a service, not a commodity.

The free agreement between employer and employee brings about fair contracts if both parties have similar negotiating power or a strong sense of justice. But if one party is powerful and the other is in need, there is a risk of abuse. Many countries now have laws to prevent abuse in labour contracts. However, laws can fall short of preventing some abuses, and unscrupulous employers can impose contracts very much lacking in justice.

A labour contract introduces duties of justice and special responsibilities on the part of the employer towards the employees. In accordance with the personalist principle,[8] the employer should respect workers' rights and grant them respectful treatment. Furthermore, it is desirable that the employer provide working conditions which can contribute to the employees' personal growth. The labour contract involves duties for employees as well. Employees should work according to the employer's requirements and guidelines, and serve the firm's legitimate interests with loyalty.

Labour contracts regarding the real conditions of real work within an organization can lead to an *exploitation* of workers. This occurs when a person or institution uses persons as mere productive resources for selfish purposes. Indeed, this is the leading offence against the dignity of human work.

Not only the labour contract but also the whole organization of work, with all its processes, should reflect human dignity. It would be reprehensible to choose a business process in which efficiency added economic value to raw materials, while the people involved were mistreated or suffered degradation in their humanity as a consequence.

The UN Global Compact mentions two great abuses of workers' human dignity and refers to them in two principles:

- *Principle 4:* the elimination of all forms of forced and compulsory labour
- *Principle 5:* the effective abolition of child labour.

Forced labour

Forced and compulsory labour is any employment against the employee's will, using the compulsion of violence or other threats. Forced labour, including slavery and other forms of non-free work, is clearly contrary to the personalist principle in its negative formulation.[9] Although in many countries, forced labour has fortunately been abolished by law, in practice it still remains in some places. This is why the ILO and other international organizations are pressing for effective national laws and stronger enforcement mechanisms, such as legal sanctions and vigorous prosecution against those who exploit forced labour.

Some forms of disrespect for the personal freedom of the employee can also be considered forced labour. This is the case of 'debt bondage' or 'bonded labour', which entails paying off loans directly with labour instead of currency or goods. It is a form of 'indenture labour' in which the employee is obliged to work for a specific period of time, for which he or she is paid only with accommodation and sustenance, or these essentials in addition to limited benefits (for instance, cancellation of a debt, or transportation to a country that interests the employee). This practice might be accompanied by retention of identity cards or travel documents. Although less serious, compulsory overtime is also a form of forced labour.

Child labour

Child labour refers to work done by a child, excluding household chores in their own home or schoolwork. Although in many countries it is forbidden to hire a child below a certain age (generally 14 to 17), in some developing countries one can begin full-time employment at 7 years old, or even younger. Child labour can cover a great variety of activities, most of them in the informal sector, mainly working in agriculture, as a street vendor, or performing domestic tasks in the home of a third party.

According to UNICEF there are an estimated 218 million children aged 5–17 engaged in child labour, excluding child domestic labour. Some 126 million of these children are believed to be working under hazardous conditions: in mines, with chemicals and pesticides in agriculture, or with dangerous machinery. They are everywhere, but invisible, toiling as domestic servants in homes, labouring behind the walls of workshops, hidden from view in plantations.[10]

Child labour, in general, should be considered inappropriate or exploitative. Childhood is a time to be educated, and working during this period might not only impede attendance at school, but also submit children to inappropriate influences and risks to their proper development. This is why a vast majority of countries have become signatories of the Convention on the Rights of the Child, in which it is established:

> States which are party [to the convention] recognize the right of the child to be protected from economic exploitation and from performing any work that is likely to be hazardous or to interfere with the child's education, or to be harmful to the child's health or physical, mental, spiritual, moral or social development.[11]

However, some argue in favour of child labour, contending that its absence is a luxury that many poor states and families cannot yet afford. They add, moreover, that the school alternative is not always available: it is even pointed out that, if child labour were prohibited by law, many children could fall into prostitution. The challenge is to move beyond the dilemma of choosing between child labour and child prostitution.

The solution would require imaginative solutions compatible with an absence of child labour. Perhaps in some extreme situations, light work might be compatible with the child's dignity and development. But this cannot be a general rule.

Others argue that developed countries also had child labour at the beginning of the Industrial Revolution. It is true that child labour was used only in some places, but voices of morality protested against child labour during the Industrial Revolution. In this connection, in 1891, Pope Leo XIII wrote:

> in regard to children, great care should be taken not to place them in workshops and factories until their bodies and minds are sufficiently developed. For, just as very rough weather destroys the buds of spring, so does too early an experience of life's hard toil blight the young promise of a child's faculties, and render any true education impossible.[12]

The ethical answer is that economic development cannot be achieved at the cost of children's development, by exploiting them as a mere resource. A solution would require international cooperation, and multinational companies should play their part.

Businesses should make certain that they are not complicit in human rights abuses (Principle 2 of the UN Global Compact). One way of being complicit in forced and compulsory labour and child labour is through the supply chain (see Insight 11).

Sweatshops

Another form of abuse of human dignity is working in manufacturing facilities where conditions are extremely deficient. These facilities are pejoratively referred to as 'sweatshops'. There, employees work long hours and are paid little. The right to unionize and other recognized labour rights are not often respected, regardless of any law to the contrary. Workers are sometimes placed in hazardous situations or extreme temperatures, and perhaps even subject to harassment from supervisors or other abuses from employers.

Sweatshops are often associated with poor labour regulations or scarce or ineffective inspection or means of law enforcement. These types of facilities are now mainly located in developing countries, but they have also existed in countries that are now developed. This has led some to believe that sweatshops are a step on the path to economic development and, in fact, low wages do attract investment and stimulate job creation in countries whose competitive advantage is precisely their cheap labour. However, this economic reality does not justify the working conditions in sweatshops, since this is not only an economic issue, but also a social and ethical matter.

Apart from this, some defend the existence of sweatshops by arguing that employees voluntarily accept the working conditions associated with their job. They are not forced to work but do so as the result of a free agreement. Besides, they claim, workers can choose other alternatives but believe working in a sweatshop to be better than any available alternatives. However, these arguments are flawed.[13] Workers' consent to their labour is not fully voluntary. People resign themselves to working in sweatshops because they need a livelihood. Employers have great power and can easily impose harsh working conditions and low wages. Sweatshop conditions harm workers and violate elemental human rights. Although working in a sweatshop might be preferable to other options, this is actually an exploitative practice. Respect for human dignity requires at least adhering to local labour laws, refraining from coercion, meeting minimum health and safety standards, and paying workers a living wage.[14]

FAIR REMUNERATION AND THE 'LIVING WAGE'

Employee remuneration includes wages and other economic compensations or benefits, such as health insurance, social security, personal or family grants, or profit sharing. Obtaining appropriate remuneration is linked to the right to life and to acquiring what is necessary for one's own sustenance and to bring up children. Actually, for the great majority of people, their livelihood depends on their wage, and this brings about serious ethical obligations.

The right of the employee to receive fair remuneration is a primordial labour right. Although problems on just remuneration can be found in both developed and developing countries, in the latter they can have more dramatic consequences. Basically, companies go to developing countries because of their low labour costs. This has positive effects, since they provide jobs and create wealth, part of which remains in the host country, but the risk of abuse, especially in wages, is high. This is one of the problems of sweatshops, as suggested above (p. 255). In developed countries, the problem of a just wage can be found mainly in the case of under-qualified employees and in the informal economy.

Determining a fair wage for each situation is no easy task. However, it can be argued that a person working full time should receive remuneration enough to live and support an ordinary family in conditions at least above the poverty line in each country or region, and should be furnished with the means to cultivate worthily his or her own material, social, cultural and spiritual life. Although there is the case of talented and skilled employees whose remuneration is far higher than this, fair remuneration is often a problem in sectors where employees can be easily replaced. For such situations, the concept of the *living wage* makes sense. This refers to the amount of money a full-time employee needs to either afford the basic necessities of life or rise above the poverty threshold.[15]

In practice, many countries have introduced a *minimum wage*, which is generally quite low but ensures some minimum income for one's livelihood. This view overlooks the fact that work involves not only production, but also human relations and personal activity, apart from ethical and social concerns. However, the minimum wage is questionable from a strictly economic viewpoint, since, in accordance with the law of supply and demand, it can produce high wages, and this has consequences for unemployment, preventing inflation and creating wealth. In practice, balanced solutions have to be found to make a practical living wage possible, preferably for every employee.

Beyond the issue of a minimum wage, a fair remuneration should consider the responsibilities and contribution of the employee, in accordance with distributive justice criteria. Practical wisdom helps to shape a salary policy in accordance with the economic situation of the firm and the country, as well as the competitive environment of the industry.

Insight 11:

Has a company responsibility for the working conditions in the supply chain?

Every business is involved in a supply chain, stretching from the first suppliers who provide raw materials to the last consumer. Each business has its own logistic network, or supply chain, which includes a more or less sophisticated system of organizations, people, technology, activities, information and resources to supply whatever a business needs to produce and/or deliver to the customer. Think, for instance, of an automobile manufacturer. Its supply chain includes many companies that provide car components. These assemble other components, which are purchased by other companies and so on.

Since there is risk in each link of the chain, every company seeks only its own interests and not the final user's. However, one must integrate key business processes from the original suppliers to the final user. Thus, supply chain management has emerged, with the mission of following the supply chain and facilitating exchange of information regarding market fluctuations, production capabilities and other data of common interest.

Each stage or link in the supply chain adds economic value to the product. This means seeking the lowest possible price when buying and otherwise cutting costs as much as possible. At the end of the chain, one can find companies

Insight 11: (cont'd)

that sell at low prices due to stiff competition, and which seek to decrease production costs as much as possible to increase profits. This can create pressure to lower labour costs and thus result in poor working conditions and even sweatshops.

But to what extent is a company responsible for behaviours of its supply chain firms, particularly those that are producing merchandise without respecting human rights? In accordance with the theory of responsibility,[16] the answer to this question is related to causal proximity between the client-firm and the supply-firm in which these abusive conditions occur, and the capacity of the client-firm to avoid or reduce such practices. The case of a large company is not the same as that of a small one. If the client-firm could avoid misbehaviours of the supply-firm but does nothing, then the former incurs responsibility.

A practical procedure is to require a reliable auditing of the labour conditions in the supply chain. This is one of the possibilities of auditing and certification standards carried out by independent and trustworthy institutions.[17]

OCCUPATIONAL HEALTH AND SAFETY

The right to life and physical, mental and moral integrity requires occupational safety and health. A comprehensive definition of this concept has been given by the ILO and the World Health Organization (WHO):

> Occupational health should aim at: the promotion and maintenance of the highest degree of physical, mental and social well-being of workers in all occupations; the prevention amongst workers of departures from health caused by their working conditions; the protection of workers in their employment from risks resulting from factors adverse to health; the placing and maintenance of the worker in an occupational environment adapted to his physiological and psychological capabilities; and, to summarize, the adaptation of work to man and of each man to his job.[18]

Health hazards cause illnesses and other conditions that develop over a lifetime of exposure to hazardous substances, such as asbestos, cotton dust, heavy metals, gases, solvents and certain classes of chemicals.[19] Safety hazards involve electrical shocks, cuts, burns and impairment of sight or hearing. These can originate from coming into contact with machinery parts or electrical lines, chemical explosions, fires, falls from great heights and so on. Pregnant women and disabled employees can be especially vulnerable to some risks.

Some defend employers against the charge of violating the rights of workers involved in accidents, claiming that the workers voluntarily assumed the risk. They claim that company practices were not the direct cause of the injury or death. Indeed, there are jobs, such as coal mining or construction work, that are commonly known to have high accident rates; and those who choose to do these jobs might do so freely, even though safer employment is available. However, the argument that exposing themselves to risk is a choice workers make is flawed, since such choice is often strongly conditioned by an employee's necessity.

In accordance with responsibility theory,[20] insofar as the safety risk is foreseeable there is responsibility on the part of those who can take steps to avoid it. Companies should therefore establish reasonable measures to avoid accidents and hazards for any person involved in business activity, including prevention plans to prevent accidents, and putting procedures in place that comply with the specific industry's characteristics. Information on hazards and the company's health and safety standards should be available to everybody in an accessible language. Workers and managers should be advised of the risks and dangers of their work, and be trained for all tasks for which they will be responsible prior to beginning a new assignment. This should be complemented by regular health and safety training to avoid accident risks and to respond to workplace emergencies. In some cases, workers and managers should undertake medical checks to measure and prevent instances of occupational illness.

REASONABLE DAILY WORKING HOURS AND REST

One issue related to worker health and safety involves daily working hours and one or two days to rest, as well as a time for annual vacations. A reasonable schedule in this regard is an ethical requirement based on respect for human health (avoiding stress and exhaustion), and also allowing enough time for a worker's personal life, and family and religious duties.

The problem of limiting working hours came from the time of the Industrial Revolution in Britain, where people working in large factories were submitted to long hours, sometimes 14 hours a day, and abysmal working conditions. In the face of this situation, in the nineteenth century a movement emerged asking for eight-hour working days with the slogan 'Eight hours labour, Eight hours recreation, Eight hours rest.' This demand succeeded and was accepted by an international convention, after many years of effort. Nowadays, most countries have legislation limiting hours of work, which generally includes a limit on hours worked each day, week and year, overtime work limits and payments. A weekly rest and annual vacations are also included in the legislation of most countries.

However, there is increasing pressure for working at weekends, including the 'Sabbath day' (generically, a weekday considered holy by many religions). A day or two of leisure time every week is necessary for everybody. When people lack a weekly holiday, it is difficult for employees to achieve an acceptable balance between work and personal life, paying sufficient attention to their family and the fulfilment of their religious duties. A weekly holiday provides a necessary time for worship, spiritual life, rest and leisure, and to facilitate family life. Some activities, such as public services and restaurants, are necessities, but business should organize work in such a way that people have sufficient time for leisure at the weekend. Exclusive focus on the profit motive can systematically work against weekly holidays and make human fulfilment more difficult.

FREEDOM OF ASSOCIATION, COLLECTIVE BARGAINING AND STRIKING

The UN Global Compact states in its Fourth Principle: 'Businesses should uphold the freedom of association and the effective recognition of the right to collective bargaining.' Freedom of association is, in fact, a well-recognized human right, when such gatherings pursue legitimate aims. Freedom of association is a consequence of human freedom and sociability. In business, both employees and employers should be free to create organizations, including unions. The ILO *Declaration on Fundamental Principles and Rights at Work* (1998) covers, 'the right of workers and employers to form and join organizations of their choice is an integral part of a free and open society. It is a basic civil liberty that serves as a building block for social and economic progress.'[21]

Consequently, the right to create and join unions has to be respected, and companies should permit workers to unionize and should recognize the elected workers' representatives. In the few countries where a legal prohibition of unions exists, companies should seek alternative measures for an open dialogue with employees' representatives elected to defend their legitimate interests.

In order to reinforce the negotiating power of the employees, traditionally unions have looked to collective bargaining, a positive labour right related to freedom of association and legally recognized in many countries and by international conventions. Collective bargaining is a process of negotiation between the representative of employees (frequently unions) and management or a representative of the employers' organization. The usual topics of collective bargaining are wages, grievance procedures, work hours, rest periods and breaks, and other work conditions. From the ethical perspective, the right at stake is fair treatment in negotiating employment conditions. Collective bargaining can facilitate this aim, but individual negotiation can also be fair.

Going on *strike*, or deliberate absence from work, is a means employed at times by trade unions. Striking is ethically acceptable under certain circumstances as an extreme measure to defend legitimate interests. Most countries recognize going on strike as a legitimate right but place certain limitations upon it (minimum services for public interest and so on).

However, strikes can be disproportionate and seriously affect third-party rights (think, for instance, of health care services and public transportation). That is why the law usually introduces some restrictions, and even gives employers a genuine defence against secondary boycotts promoted by unions in their demands.

Unions, which are sometimes very powerful, bear responsibility both for defending the legitimate interests of workers and for the means they use. Going on strike is a point on which labour unions should be particularly conscientious, because it causes great harm.

NON-DISCRIMINATION IN EMPLOYMENT AND OCCUPATION

Discrimination, in its etymological sense, means the action and effect of making a distinction, or differentiating one person or thing from another. Discrimination in this sense is not morally wrong. When a company selects personnel, discrimination occurs in accordance with the profile required for the job, and this is not unethical in itself. However, the word 'discrimination' as commonly used has a negative connotation, and means 'invidious discrimination': a judgement based on unacceptable ethical or legal motives.

In the UN Global Compact, discrimination in employment and occupation is defined as 'any distinction, exclusion or preference that has the effect of nullifying or impairing equality of opportunity or treatment in employment or occupation'. The document adds: 'Distinctions based strictly on the inherent requirements of the job are not discrimination', in the pejorative sense.

The Universal Declaration of Human Rights (art. 2) states: 'Everyone is entitled to all the rights and freedoms set forth in this Declaration, without distinction of any kind, such as race, colour, sex, language, religion, political or other opinion, national or social origin, property, birth or other status.' In this line, and specifically applied to business, the UN Global Compact presents in its Principle 6: 'Businesses should uphold the elimination of discrimination in respect of employment and occupation.'

The International Labour Organization stresses that 'hundreds of millions of people suffer from discrimination in the world of work' and emphasized the importance of avoiding this practice, since discrimination 'not only violates a most basic human right, but has wider social and economic consequences. Discrimination stifles opportunities, wasting the human talent needed for economic progress and accentuating social tensions and inequalities.'[22]

Problems of discrimination can arise in hiring; firing; promotional, advancement and training opportunities, among other areas. Non-discrimination in these areas means selecting employees exclusively on the basis of their ability to do the job.

In many countries, direct discrimination is banned by law, but indirect discrimination is quite frequent. It slips in through informal attitudes and practices in organizations, frequently under the appearance of non-discrimination. There are several common forms of discrimination in business.

Ethnic and racial discrimination

Although the terms 'ethnic discrimination' and 'racial discrimination' are often used interchangeably, there is a difference between them. The first signifies the less favourable treatment of persons belonging to a certain ethnic group or nationality; for instance, Koreans in Japan, or Turks in Germany. Frequently, ethnic discrimination is directed at immigrants from certain countries. Racial discrimination refers exclusively to discriminatory behaviour against certain races; for example, whites in China, or Asians in certain parts of Russia.

Gender discrimination

Men and women have equal dignity and human rights, and consequently should be treated with identical respect and consideration. Thus, any discrimination exclusively based on gender is unfair. However, such non-discrimination does not eradicate physiological and psychological differences between women and men, and sometimes even differences in needs (for instance, those related to motherhood), which should be valued and protected. In other words, equal recognition of human rights of men and women is necessary, and so is the harmonization of this with the specificity of being male and female.

Family discrimination

This takes place when employees are not equally treated with regard to their family responsibilities towards children, especially young children, disabled family members, or elderly parents. All of these family responsibilities can conflict with rigid business requirements. However, nearly everybody has some type of family bond and subsequent duties, which can sometimes become acute (illnesses and school schedules of young children, special needs of the elderly and disabled family members and so on). Business has to make some effort to help resolve conflicts between work and family responsibilities,[23] and to facilitate an appropriate conciliation between work and family life.

Religious discrimination

Religious discrimination comes into play when one person is treated less favourably than another is, has been, or would be treated in a comparable situation on religious grounds.

Some particular issues regarding religious discrimination refer to the workplace– hiring, promotion, dismissal and work conditions, and, most often, respecting the right for observing religious feasts, worship and prayers. Forbidding discreet religious symbols can be understood as religious discrimination, unless other employees or customers might reasonably feel annoyed or offended by certain symbols.[24]

Age discrimination

Age discrimination occurs when a person is treated less favourably than others because of his or her age. It most commonly takes place when older workers seek new jobs, try to sustain current employment, or compete with younger employees for a promotion.

In practice, there could be tensions between age and performance – not specifically age and youth – but this is not always so and, in any case, a sound solution requires wisdom. The legislation of many countries includes articles designed to prevent age discrimination and to protect older employees. However, it would be legitimate in some cases for a company to prefer a younger employee based on reasons other than the mere fact of age.

Political and social discrimination

This occurs when a certain group is treated less favourably than others because of membership in a social or cultural group. Discrimination on the basis of political opinions is also possible.

Affirmative action

Some, confronting discrimination, propose 'affirmative action' or 'positive discrimination'. This refers to favourable treatment, using *quotas* (a fixed number of a group), when hiring and promoting members of certain groups. Its origins go back to 1965, when the USA introduced laws encouraging corporations to hire and promote members of groups that have been the target of discrimination; for example, women and minority ethnic groups. Affirmative action aims to ensure more equitable opportunities to such persons, and to combat prejudice, favouritism, racism and sexism.

The question that arises is whether affirmative action can be justified in terms of justice, since it means discrimination against other groups, those who have not historically been targeted for discrimination. Criticism has often centred on the use of quotas, of people that is or has been discriminated against that must be admitted, promoted, or hired – even regardless of job qualifications or lack thereof. Affirmative action policies are justified only if they are necessary to overcome discriminatory effects that could not be eliminated in some other way.[25]

VIOLENCE IN THE WORKPLACE: SEXUAL HARASSMENT AND MOBBING

Workplace violence is an extreme form of disrespect for people and is recognized as a specific category of violent crime that calls for distinct responses from employers, law and communities.

The major risk factors for workplace violence include dealing with the public, the exchange of money and the delivery of goods or services. In most cases, such violence refers to simple assaults, and employees are more and more aware of their rights. Employers can provide assistance through a set of supportive actions: individual consultations, group debriefings, family assistance, workplace re-entry and follow-up services.[26]

However, violence is not limited to physical actions. In fact, most reported incidents are related to psychological violence. In employee–manager relationships, there are forms of violence such as threats and harassment, including all types of sexual harassment, mobbing and other emotional abuses.

Sexual harassment

Sexual harassment in the workplace environment entails unwelcome sexual advances that cause discomfort to one or more employees, and requests for sexual favours where refusal meets with threats and acquiescence with rewards. The range of sexual harassment can stretch from mild transgressions and annoyances to serious sexual abuses, including coerced sexual activity. Most sexual harassment, widespread and underreported, is directed against women.[27]

One form of sexual harassment is fostering hostile workplace environments. This occurs when an employee is regularly subjected to undesired touches or other physical conduct of a sexual nature, lascivious comments, sexual jokes, offensive sexual speech or gestures, displays of provocative materials and anything else that would create an intimidating, hostile, or offensive work environment. The harasser might be a co-worker, a client or somebody at a different level in the organizational hierarchy. This behaviour not only can interfere with an individual's work performance, but also is reprehensible in itself because of its disrespect for the person.

Another form of sexual harassment is perpetrated by someone in a position of power, such as a supervisor or manager. In this case, the harasser tries to obtain sexual favours in exchange for benefits, such as obtaining or keeping a job, favourable grades, promotion, a desirable occupation and so on – or else the perpetrator threatens employees who resist sexual advances. This form of sexual harassment explicitly or implicitly affects an individual's employment by an abuse of power. It is a serious injustice against the victim, or even third parties (for instance, when it leads to unfair promotions).

Prevention is the best tool for eliminating sexual harassment from the workplace. Employers are encouraged to take the steps necessary to prevent it. They should clearly communicate to employees that sexual harassment will not be tolerated. They can do so by providing sexual harassment training to their employees and by establishing an effective complaint or grievance process and then taking immediate and appropriate action when an employee complains.

Mobbing

Rights such as retaining a good reputation and enjoying an environment favourable to human growth and personal integrity clash with several forms of harassment or even violence that can occur in the workplace. One of these is *mobbing.*

Mobbing is a concept taken from zoology to describe the behaviour that some animals use to scare away one of their group. In the workplace, mobbing can be defined as the intentional and repeated infliction of physical or psychological harm by superiors on subordinates within an organization. Mobbing includes acts (performed by an individual or group) that degrade the job conditions, health, dignity and professionalism of an employee.[28]

Mobbing can consist, for example, in a systematic and persistent expressed disdain for someone or in continuous humiliation; constant and trivial nit-picking criticism; by a systematic refusal to value and acknowledge what the victim is accomplishing; by damaging his or her reputation, honour and even physical or moral integrity. While all of these are offences against human dignity, we only refer to them as mobbing when they are frequent and systematically repeated over time. In some countries, the law protects employees against mobbing and specifies in great detail exactly what it constitutes.

OTHER WORKERS' RIGHTS

Some other workers' rights are relevant in the context of a business organization: one is fairness in procedures within the organization; another is employee privacy and protection of personal data.

Fairness in procedures within the organization

The human *right to due process* is applicable to performance appraisal and other evaluations and procedures. In addition, a fair process favours the satisfaction of both employer and employee. In fact, one of the biggest factors contributing to hostility in the workplace is inequity and selective discipline. This does not refer solely to ethnic/racial, age and family discrimination: employees frequently cite favouritism and unfairness as their reasons for discomfort and intimidation at work, which can also be the basis for proving a pattern of discrimination in the workplace.

One area in which fairness is critical is that of dismissals and lay-offs. Here, the point is not whether the decision of dismissal or lay-off is ethical. In practice, both can entail stark dilemmas. When a dismissal or lay-off is unavoidable, one has to deliberate upon how to be just in the selection of who is to leave.

The right to due process includes a clear dismissals procedure, one that is known to employees. An unfair dismissal occurs, for instance, when there is no just cause for dismissal, or when it is not carried out according to a fair and established procedure.

Finally, there are *grievance procedures*. A grievance is a complaint by an employee regarding an actual or supposed circumstance regarded as just cause. Through a grievance, employees can bring workplace concerns to upper levels of management on matters relevant to their employment or conditions of service where the customary channel of discussion with a direct supervisor has proven ineffective. This process is more formal than mediation and requires that rules be strictly followed. Workers must have a right to submit grievances about the workplace without the threat of losing their job or suffering other adverse action. The company should then establish the procedures and representatives that will enable employees to make the complaints. These might be anonymous, and range from dissatisfaction with work hours to abuse, and the company should systematically and objectively review any complaint. Furthermore, each complaint should result in the notification of the company's findings on the issue.

A good practice is allowing employees the opportunity to express any disagreement regarding the notification of findings, and to have recourse to independent arbitrage. Moreover, grievance procedures are needed to provide individuals with a course of action, should they have to provide points of contact, and to try to resolve matters without recourse to an employment tribunal.

Employee privacy and protection of personal data

Recent technological advances make it possible to invade personal privacy as never before. Employers can monitor almost every aspect of their employees' jobs, especially when they are using the Internet, telephone or voice mail, and can thus listen in or read most workplace communications. Tension exists between evaluative surveillance and employee privacy, and not every type of surveillance is ethically acceptable.[29] In general terms, it is unjust for employers to use electronic surveillance to monitor employees without their knowledge or consent.

One of the crucial problems concerning protection of personal data is the disclosure of an employee's medical records and unauthorized acquisition of medical information. It should be mandatory to obtain the written consent of the job applicant or employee before disclosing the information to the employer. Regulation for employee and customer privacy protection is increasing. However, in many countries employee privacy rights are insufficiently acknowledged.

Business ethics in practice 11:

Surgikos – from *maquiladora* system to a participative work

The word *maquiladora* comes from the Spanish-Mexican word *maquilar*, which means *to assemble*. It is associated with Mexico, where the *maquiladora* programme was established in 1965 in order to create jobs for Mexican workers. Basically, a *maquiladora* is a manufacturing plant, in most cases along the border between Mexico and the USA, that receives imported materials duty free, assembles the product, and then exports the product back to the originating country (generally the United States) with very low or no tariffs. They can be up to 100 per cent foreign-owned. Instead of paying tariffs, the operators of the *maquiladoras* must provide Mexican customs with guarantees that the components and raw materials will be re-exported out of Mexico within six months. Furthermore, after finishing operations in Mexico, machinery and fixed assets must return to the USA. All workers doing piecework must be Mexicans. Thus, the Mexican factory carries out most of the manual labour part of the production. The resulting product is sent back to minor USA plants, where the process is finished, most often by packaging.

By 2001, Mexico's *maquiladora* exports represented almost half of Mexico's exports, and *maquiladora* employment had increased to employ 3 per cent of the total workforce in the country. Under Mexican law, *maquiladoras* were allowed to produce a wide range of goods, with the exception of oil and petrochemical products, and articles containing radioactive elements.

However, soon after that, between 2001 and 2002, 420 *maquiladora* plants closed, and almost 300,000 jobs were eliminated. Even so, the *maquiladora* system still exists, its competition being the cheaper labour in factories in Latin America, China and South Asia.

The positive aspects of *maquiladoras* are job creation in poor regions, and the increase in consumer welfare, due to the low costs of production and prices. Negative aspects of the system are the working conditions and low wages.[30] Moreover, the *maquiladoras* became a synonym of abuse and sexual harassment of women, although this might not have occurred in all *maquiladora* factories[31]

Surgikos was a *maquiladora* company that initially acted as did many others. Their workers' rate of pay was less than $1 per hour, and work conditions were as difficult as in any other factory of that type – monotonous and

---

Business ethics in practice 11: (cont'd)

boring. People felt as if they were merely cogs in the machine. The history of Surgikos, S.A. de C.V. goes back to 1970, when the company was set up in Juarez, Mexico. It was manufacturing disposable sheets and surgical gowns. A twin plant was set up in the US city of El Paso, Texas. Very soon the number of Surgikos plants grew to four. In October 1988, Cruz Huerta was appointed a general manager in one of the four plants of Surgikos in Juarez. At this time in Juarez, there were 22 different *maquiladoras* employing over 3,100 people.[32]

In 1990, Cruz was commissioned to open the fifth Surgikos factory, which would cover the growing demand of the US and European markets. The product stayed the same – surgical products such as gowns, shoe covers, caps, surgery sheets, coats, trousers, masks and latex gloves. The main customers were wholesale hospital suppliers and hospitals themselves.

In July of that year, Cruz Huerta opened the fifth plant of Surgikos; however, this time, the location of the plant and the manufacturing culture were to be different. The plant was opened in the Mexican city of Guadalupe and was built in cooperation with the Mexican company Productos Médicos de Monterrey. Cruz was aware that this was an opportunity to change the productive philosophy and to improve working conditions. He hired 216 people and trained them in a culture of associates. The target of the new plant was to produce 28,000 surgical gowns per day in two shifts, which was double the standard rate of production in Juarez. In this new factory, 75 per cent of workers were women, and their average age was 25. Only 5 per cent had a technical degree, and 95 per cent had an average secondary education. Cruz adopted the so-called Cellular Manufacturing system, which replaced the previously used traditional assembly line. The Cellular Manufacturing System makes the gowns to be passed from hand to hand, and workers work together as a team.

Such teamwork in a factory requires certain responsibilities and functions that could be accomplished only in a team. The new culture of work was called a 'Sociotechnical System' by Productos Médicos de Monterrey. Eight employees form a participative team in which each actively contributes to improvements on both human and technical levels. The important fact is that the supervision in such a system was reduced to minimum, and self-management took place of the supervision. Each team of eight people had one coordinator, who was supposed to pay attention to the needs of the team, and deliver a daily report on the production, quality and wastage.

The new manufacturing culture also incorporated such systems as *kanban* (a signalling system to trigger action) and *just-in-time* for reducing in-process inventory. The first was to reduce wastage, and the second was to reduce production time.

The participative work system gave employees a feeling of belonging in their team. Furthermore, they felt involved in all stages of the production

---

Business ethics in practice 11: (cont'd)

process, which stimulated their self-discipline. Moreover, the quality, maintenance and engineering departments gave every team their technical support. The human resources, training and medical departments gave every team human support, such as advice on wages, personal development and safety measures. Every two weeks, the teams presented their achievements, goals and new ideas to the management group. A record was achieved of zero accidents with loss of production time.

The results of the new participative system of work appeared very soon. Employees were very satisfied and costs were cut, self-managing helped to reduce the inspections by 65 per cent in the sewing area, and by 80 per cent in the sealing area. The waste was kept below 2 per cent, thanks to the reporting of wastage, which was prepared by each team. Downtime due to mechanical faults was reduced by 60 per cent, and reworking costs were reduced from $68,500 in 1991 to $24,000 in 1992. Two years later, Cruz Huerta said that his goal of developing a model plant had been achieved. The company provided employees with a social security system, developed primarily for women employees. In addition, it contributed to the community where the employees belonged with significant contributions to retirement homes and orphanages.

Questions:

1. What is your judgement about the *maquiladora* system from both an economic and ethical perspective?

2. Do you think that the work organization of the fifth Surgikos plant is ethically better than the other four? Why?

Source: This case is an abridged version (published with permission) of the case study M. A. Llano Irusta, 'Surgikos, S.A. de C.V.', published by IPADE Business School, Mexico, extended by the author with some complementary information.

Dilemma 11

Charles Daniels, aged 45, was an employee of Lockheed Martin, the world's largest military contractor. He worked in this company as an aviation electrician and he was among the highest skilled and best paid electricians on the job.

Daniels started to have problems with his co-workers in 1999, during a stint in Jacksonville, Florida. Daniels was the only African-American in a small unit of workers. One day, a white co-worker from South Carolina said he was disgruntled because protesters had forced the state to remove the Confederate battle flag from the state capitol. He said the country would have been

Dilemma 11 (cont'd)

better off had the South won the Civil War. A second co-worker responded that African-Americans should have been exterminated, the way Adolf Hitler dealt with Jews.

Later on, Charles and his co-workers moved to another job site in the state of Washington. The co-workers threatened him after learning that he had complained about their behaviour. Daniels explained: 'They told me they knew some people in the Aryan Brotherhood and they could make me disappear.' Some time later the unit where he worked moved to Hawaii. There, Daniels was again the target of persistent verbal abuse by co-workers and a supervisor through racial slurs and offensive language while repairing military aircraft. Finally, Daniels left the company in 2001 and filed a legal suit that same year. He pleaded he had been subjected to racial epithets and threatened with bodily harm at the workplace.

A human resources director of Lockheed Martin said that she investigated Daniels' complaints and confirmed that racial comments were made. But she dismissed such comments, saying, 'Boys will be boys.' In addition, some weak remedial actions were taken based on the facts presented during the court case.

At the beginning of 2008, the Equal Employment Opportunity Commission (EEOC) announced a major settlement of a race discrimination and retaliation lawsuit against Lockheed Martin for $2.5 million. This was the largest ever settlement for an individual racial discrimination case. EEOC said in a statement: 'Daniels was also subjected to multiple physical threats, such as lynching and other death threats after he reported the harassment.' Now, the settlement must be approved by the US District Court in Hawaii. In addition to compensating Daniels, the settlement will cover attorneys' fees and other costs.

The EEOC said Lockheed 'failed to discipline the harassers and instead allowed the discrimination against Daniels to continue unabated during his two-year tenure even though the company was aware of the unlawful conduct'.

Lockheed strongly disagreed with the EEOC's characterization of the case. 'We regret that the EEOC, for whatever reason, has chosen to distort the factual record in this matter', said a company spokesman. In fact, Lockheed Martin had a code of conduct that purports to explain 'how to prevent, recognize, and address various harassment issues in the workplace'. In addition, the company applauds diversity and has ethics programmes, including business conduct compliance training. The company blamed the incident on 'a small number of first-line employees in a small, single operating unit of the company'.

The Vice President of Ethics and Business Conduct at Lockheed Martin was wondering what else she should do to prevent similar situations. She reported to the Executive Officer and to the Ethics and Corporate Responsibility Committee of the Board of Directors.

Questions:

1. What might you have done if you had been the human resource manager in charge of this case?

2. What might explain why the corporate code and ethical programmes of Lockheed Martin were not effective in preventing harassment issues in the workplace?

3. What would you recommend to the Vice President of Ethics and Business Conduct of Lockheed Martin?

Sources: Lockheed Martin website; *The U.S. Equal Employment Opportunity Commission*, 2 January 2008: http://www.eeoc.gov/press/1-2-08.html and Darryl Fears, 'Lockheed to Pay $2.5 Million In Racial Discrimination Case', *Washington Post*, Staff Writer, Thursday 3 January 2008: p. A02.

Summary

Human work has dignity because it is an immediate activity of persons. Thus, it cannot be considered a mere economic factor, a human resource or an anonymous production force.

The dignity of human work entails a set of ethical requirements in its organization. The first is to respect human rights in labour, a point strongly supported by the vast majority of international conventions.

In consistency with human dignity, labour contracts should be classified as a personal service rather than a commodity.

Exploitation of workers is the main offence against the dignity of human work. Forced and compulsory labour, child labour and facilities with poor working conditions and disrespect for workers' rights are shameless forms of worker exploitation.

Fair working conditions include just remuneration, a safe and healthy environment, reasonable daily working hours, reasonable weekly time off, annual vacation time, freedom of association, freedom to engage in collective bargaining and the right to strike.

An important issue in work organization is the need to avoid unfair discrimination based on membership in an ethnic, racial, social, cultural or political group, or based on family situations, or for reasons of sex, age or religious beliefs. Affirmative action or reverse discrimination can be legitimate in certain limited situations.

Workplace violence refers to assaults and, more commonly, to sexual harassment and mobbing.

Other issues regarding workers' rights are justice in procedures – especially those concerning dismissals and lay-offs – respecting privacy and protecting personnel databases.

Business should require working conditions suitable to human dignity and human rights in its supply chain. The responsibility for preventing exploitation in the supply chain is greater when a company has the capacity to control and influence suppliers in its chain by changing misbehaviours regarding labour (or other issues).

Marketers must embrace, communicate and practice the fundamental ethical values that will improve consumer confidence in the integrity of the marketing exchange system.[1]

American Marketing Association

Chapter Aims

This chapter will allow you to:
- gain an understanding of consumer rights and to know of what they consist
- discuss the role of marketing in promoting responsible consumption
- discuss the concepts of 'consumer sovereignty' and 'consumer paternalism' and common criticisms of them
- distinguish between two philosophies regarding the seller's responsibility to give the buyer all relevant information
- consider how to introduce ethical values into consumer marketing research and market research
- acquire information on ethical issues regarding products
- discuss the concept of fair price and abuses in pricing
- become familiar with a set of ethical criteria for sound advertising
- gain insights into ethics in distribution and sales.

Key terms:

Advertising ethics	Distribution channel	Obsolescence
Advertising testimonials	Dumping	Offensive advertising
Caveat emptor	Endorsements	Packaging
Caveat venditor	Fair price	Predatory pricing
Consumer advocacy	Genuine service	Price collusion
Consumer paternalism	Informed consent	Price discrimination
Coactive monopoly	Intrusiveness	Price gouging
Consumer rights	Labelling	Price-fixing
Consumer sovereignty	Market research	Puffery
Consumerism	Marketing	Sale abuses
Deceptive advertising	Marketing research	Warranty
Demonstrations	Mock-ups	

Ethics in the Organizing of Marketing

INTRODUCTORY CASE 12:

MATTEL – MASSIVE RECALL OF TOYS

Mattel Inc., which is now a large corporation with about 26,000 employees around the world, was born in 1960 in Southern California in a small garage workshop, set up by Ruth and Eliot Handler and Harold 'Matt' Matson. The first Mattel products were picture frames and dollhouse furniture. Mattel had great success in the toy market, with the Barbie doll being the most famous Mattel product. It was first made in 1959, and inspired by Ruth's daughter, Barbara. Today, the Barbie line is responsible for 80 per cent of Mattel's profits. Fisher-Price, American-Girl and Hot-Wheels are currently brands of Mattel.

For years Mattel has been involved in corporate philanthropy. In 1978, it established the Mattel Children's Foundation, which focuses on charities related to children's health, and mainly on the Mattel's Children's Hospital at UCLA. The Foundation provides, among others, funds for disaster relief and for care for HIV-AIDS afflicted children. In 2006, $4.8 million in cash was given to 500 non-profit organizations in the USA and 48 charitable organizations worldwide. In that year, the Foundation's programmes benefited over 5 million children.

In 1997, Mattel created and implemented a set of guidelines called *Global Manufacturing Principles*, which are some of the most detailed and comprehensive in the consumer products industry. A third-party audited real adherence to such principles and Mattel posted the results for public viewing on its corporate website.

In 2000, Mattel formally adopted a *Vision and Values Statement* as a moral compass for the company. Mattel emphasizes that its employees are responsible for acting with integrity, treating others with dignity and respect, being honest and fair in all transactions and consistently striving to 'do the right thing'. In addition, Mattel states: 'Our values include a commitment to obey the law of the countries and communities in which we do business. As a company conducting business around the world, Mattel's operations are subject to the laws of many governments. We must comply with all applicable laws, rules and regulations wherever Mattel does business.'

In January 2003, Mattel formally rolled out its *Code of Conduct to Employees*, to provide a common point of reference for Mattel employees worldwide. Procedures established for business operations were to be consistent with the code of conduct. Annually, an independent committee evaluated compliance with the code.

The code of conduct includes the following article on product quality and safety:

> Mattel's reputation for product quality and safety is among its most valuable assets, and our commitment to product quality and safety is essential. Children's health, safety and well-being are our primary concern. We could damage our consumers' trust if we sell products that do not meet our standards. Commitment to product quality and safety is an integral part of the design, manufacturing, testing and distribution processes. We will meet or exceed legal requirements and industry standards for product quality and safety. We strive to meet or exceed the expectations of our customers and consumers. Any compromise to product safety or quality must be immediately reported to Worldwide Quality Assurance.[2]

Previous to the promulgation of the code, Mattel had had some toy safety problems, especially with those made in China, which were the vast majority of its range. In 2001, the Consumer Product Safety Commission fined Mattel $1.1 million for not notifying the agency about a line of toys that was defective and, as a result, six children were injured playing with them. The company withdrew the products.

In 2004, Mattel faced problems again and voluntarily recalled 314,000 units of Batmobile plastic cars, after reporting that over a dozen children were injured. In November 2006, the company recalled over 2 million Polly Pocket toys due to several injuries caused by the toys' loose parts that had been reported. The US government said that at least one American child died and 19 others needed surgery after swallowing magnets used in toys. Mattel also recalled toys such as the Cars' character Sarge, Barbie, Tanner Playsets, Doggie Daycare, Shonen Jump's One Piece and Batman Manga.

Mattel's third toy recall included 675,000 units of various Barbie accessory toys sold from October 2006 until August 2007, 8,900 units of Big Big World 6-in-1 Bongo Band toys, and 90,000 units of Geo Trax Locomotive Toys.

In August 2007, the most massive toy recall in Mattel's history took place. Almost 18 million toys made in China posed dangers, such as toys including magnets that could be swallowed or toys that included lead paint.

The massive recall of toys made in China caused both political and public reaction. Some Western politicians took advantage of this fact to defend forms of economic protectionism and a higher degree of monitoring. Journalists reported that, since government regulations controlling industry were weak in China, many Western companies moved their manufacturing operations there to save money.[3] Despite the negative publicity, investors did not pummel the stock. Shares of Mattel fell 57 cents, or 2.4 per cent, to $23. As with the events of five years before, Mattel reports do not clearly show the quarterly losses because of that recall. However, its annual report on the official Mattel website openly says that the recalls and product liability claims could harm its reputation and sales, and increase costs.

It was in fact the consumer reaction that was decisive. The international community divided into those who were going to boycott and those who were going to continue buying toys from China, since 80 per cent of toys made worldwide were being produced there.

The Mattel CEO, Bob Eckert, claimed that his company had the most rigorous testing in the world. He explained: 'We make toys in several markets around the world. And the fact is that since most of the toys are made in China, most of the problems with manufacturing, the recalls, come from Chinese toys. When we've made toys in other markets over the years, we've had recalls from those markets'.[4]

With all of the allegations thrown at China by the international community, the Chinese government had to react. Li Changjiang, director of the Department of Quality, Inspection and Quarantine of China, said that: 'The products exported by China have high quality standards, but some control organizations (foreign) have applied incorrect data and came up with wrong solutions.' Li also said that, in the case of Mattel, they returned 19 million parts of which 85 per cent of the returned product were designed by the company itself and were produced in accordance with the instructions of the importer.

After this statement was made, Mattel Inc. took the blame again and even officially apologized to China and Li Changjiang. In September 2007, Mattel's top executive admitted that the recalls, signifying tainted toys, were not always the Chinese nation's fault, and that 'Mattel takes the full responsibility for those recalls, and apologizes to Li, and to all consumers'.[5]

The 2007 full-year report states that Mattel's operating income was $730.1 million, up $1.3 million and included charges of approximately $110 million, related to the company's product recalls.[6]

In 2008, in the letter to the editor section of the *Harvard Business Review*, Marla Flecher, a lecturer on public policy at John F. Kennedy School of Government, University of Harvard, questioned Mattel's social responsibility. She said: 'Mattel's CEO, Robert Eckert, has defended his company's practices of disclosing safety problems on its own timetable, not regulators'.' In answering her, David Vogel, professor of business ethics at the University of California at Berkeley, said that although he agreed that compliance with labour standards had been uneven, he considered Mattel to be a socially responsible company in 'its willingness to establish an independent monitoring council with full access to the 13 factories Mattel own and operate in China – and allow the council to make the results of its auditing public. Few other Western firms have accepted such extensive auditing requirements and made their labour practices so transparent.'[7]

Questions:

1. Did Mattel change its attitude about unsafe toys from 2001 to 2007?

2. Did Mattel exhibit responsible behaviour in the massive toy recall in 2007?

3. What would you recommend that Mattel's management do to avoid these types of problems in the future?

Sources: CNN: http://www.money.cnn.com/2004/04/14/news/fortune500/mattel_batmobile/index.htm; 'Mattel Shares Tumble on Another Global Recall of Toys made in China', Financial Times, 15 August 2007; 'Beijing Blames Mattel for Toys Recall', Financial Times, 24 August 2007; 'Mattel Issues New Massive China Toy Recall', MSNBC, 14 August 2007, http://www.msnbc.msn.com/id/20254745/; K. Marshall and R. Kelley, 'Mattel Announces Third Toy Recall', CNN Money, 5 September 2007, http://www.money.cnn.com/2007/09/05/news/companies/mattel_recall/index.htm; 'Mattel CEO: 'Rigorous Standards after Massive Toys Recall', CNN, 15 November 2007, http://www.edition.cnn.com/2007/US/08/14/recall/index.html; 'Good Morning America' with Chris Cuomo, 'Mattel CEO Defends China Operations', ABC News, 14 August 2007, CNN videos: www.cnn.com/SPECIALS/2007/news/toy.recall/; 'Mattel Defends Itself on Safety of Toys', USA Today, 14 August 2007; Mattel Corporate website: www.mattel.com; Wikipedia (Mattel).

MARKETING, CONSUMER RIGHTS AND CONSUMERISM

Marketing focuses on discerning the needs and wants of clients and customers in order to produce, promote, distribute and sell appropriate ideas, products and services.

The organizing of marketing includes planning and executing activities to achieve this goal. This, in essence, is the role of marketing, which is crucial within a business organization. It requires the elaboration and implementation of a marketing strategy. First, one needs to select and analyse a target market, a group of people to whom a product or service will be introduced. Second, one creates a 'marketing mix', which includes a combination of decisions regarding the product or service, its sale price, the means of promotion and the placement of the product for distribution. These four 'Ps' (product, price, promotion, and placement) are the hinge on which marketing practices turn; consequently, the ethics of marketing must focus primarily on them.[8]

Satisfying the needs and wants of a particular target market, and sometimes stimulating new wants, is therefore the final end of marketing. The marketing mix is the means to this end. Ethics, as in other fields, concerns both ends and means.

Consumer rights are crucial to the ethics of marketing. People, in their role as consumers, have human rights derived from being persons endowed with dignity; they also have rights derived from the contract of sale. Most of these are recognized by governments of numerous countries seeking to protect consumers. Governmental regulations for consumer protection provide additional rights, with the corresponding access to legal recourse. In addition, in many countries there is a strong *consumer advocacy*[9] movement that seeks to protect and inform consumers by requiring such practices as truth in packaging and advertising, product guarantees and improved safety standards.

In 1962, in response to growing demands from consumer movements for legal rights for consumers, the US president, John F. Kennedy, announced he would work to protect and promote four basic consumer rights: (1) the right to safety; (2) the right to be informed; (3) the right to choose; and (4) the right to be heard. Later, in 1985, the United Nations proposed Guidelines for Consumer Protection, which was expanded in 1999.[10] These entail obligations for sellers and for governmental agencies.

The UN Guidelines include a number of general principles that lay the groundwork for protecting and promoting consumer rights. They contain the following basic rights:[11]

- *Right to safety.* The consumer has a right to be protected from dangerous products that are hazardous to life or property.
- *The right to full value.* The consumer has a right to receive a product that meets the expectations created through advertising and promotion so that the consumer obtains full value for the money spent.
- *The right to be informed.* The consumer has a right to be informed about the quality, quantity, potency, purity and price of goods and services so as to be able to make an informed choice. This offers protection against dishonest or misleading advertising and labelling.
- *Right to choose.* The consumer has a right to be able to select products from a variety of goods and services at competitive prices. This right is violated by unregulated monopolies or when products of satisfactory quality at a fair price cannot be assured.
- *The right to education.* Consumers must have access to educational programmes or other appropriate means to acquire knowledge and skills needed to make informed, confident choices about goods and services, while being aware of basic consumer rights and responsibilities and how to act on them.
- *Right to be heard.* The consumer has a right to present legitimate complaints to an appropriate person or institution and to receive an adequate response in the case of abuse in commerce.
- *Right to recourse and redress.* The consumer has a right to receive a fair settlement of just claims, including compensation for damage suffered as a result of misrepresentation, shoddy goods or unsatisfactory services.
- *The right to representation and participation.* Consumers' interests should receive due consideration in appropriate forums and be represented in policy-making institutions that regulate the development and control of products and services.
- *The right to a healthy environment.* Consumers have a right and a duty to act within patterns that promote sustainable consumption. All human beings, not only as consumers, have a right to live and work in an environment that does not threaten the well-being of present and future generations.

Marketing favours sales and economic activity, and consequently the creation and maintenance of new jobs. However, marketing can also bring about consumerism,[12] by encouraging people to purchase and consume goods in excess of their basic needs, even to the point of causing themselves physical or moral damage. Often, buying completely superfluous goods is mere conspicuous or invidious consumption, perhaps an expression of the confusion of possessions with human excellence.

One can argue that consumerism is not a marketing issue but a personal decision of the consumer. Certainly, the consumer bears personal responsibility for purchasing decisions, but marketing motivates such decisions. Responsibility for consequences[13] can be seen here. Such responsibility is particularly relevant when marketing – or advertising, as a crucial part of marketing – aims to persuade people to consume dangerous products (for example, alcohol) or is addressed to vulnerable segments of the population, such as children or teenagers. We will return to this point later in our consideration of advertising (pp. 286–7).

Apart from personal effects, a progressively greater consumption of goods has long-term consequences for a sustainable development:[14] the planet's capacity for providing natural resources and absorbing waste is not infinite. In this connection, many voices have warned about the continued deterioration of the global environment due to rampant consumerism, mostly in industrialized countries. They demand more sustainable patterns of production and consumption.

The phenomenon of consumerism, as noted, is primarily a question of lifestyle and personal choice, but external influences can help to promote more responsible consumption and persuade people to adopt simpler ways of life. Education about responsible consumption, mass media and an appropriate cultural environment can make a sensible contribution to moderating consumerism. They can also contribute to overcoming the rampant confusion between what a person is and what he or she possesses, or the error of considering possession an end in itself.

To sum up marketing has a role in consumerism and in creating responsible consumption balanced by a reasonable level of economic activity. Developing efficient marketing, with favourable financial and ethical results, is often a real challenge, requiring the courage and imagination to serve people while making a satisfactory profit.

CONSUMER SOVEREIGNTY, PATERNALISM AND GENUINE SERVICE

Three different philosophies can be applied in dealing with clients; what is known as 'consumer sovereignty', 'paternalism' and finally what we can call a 'genuine service'.

Consumer sovereignty

Consumer sovereignty argues that clients and consumers are solely responsible for their own decisions and that the marketer has no responsibility whatsoever for their purchases. This approach leads managers to organize marketing with consumer desire – and, of course, profitability – as the only criteria. This approach stresses respect for the freedom and autonomy of consumers, which is a consumer right. However, it falls short on several counts.[15] First, the buyer's wants and preferences are not amoral; on the contrary, they are subject to ethical evaluation, and selling is a way of cooperating in such an action. To cite an extreme case, by selling weapons to a terrorist group, the seller is cooperating with terrorism. Analogously, by selling hazardous products of any kind, one cooperates with any harm caused.

Second, given the real conditions of many markets, consumers might not have accurate or sufficient information to form rational preferences and make a choice. Many products are highly sophisticated, and often those who manufacture or sell them have far more information about the product and its use than many clients can possibly obtain. With additional information provided by the seller, clients might change their preferences and make different purchase decisions. Third, stakeholders other than consumers can also have preferences, and even rights, that might conflict with consumer preferences (for example, shopping on Sunday). Although, in general, business should attend to the wishes of clients and customers, this could be problematic in some cases.

Consumer sovereignty is restrained by legal requirements. Fortunately, the law prohibits some possible abuses, but it is hardly likely that laws alone would be sufficient to ensure ethical marketing throughout the world. The landscape is even wider if one considers Internet commerce (e-commerce).

Paternalism

At the opposite extreme of consumer sovereignty is the position of paternalism: the idea that the manufacturer and seller are the only ones with sufficient information to make the right decisions. Paternalism is a well-intentioned attitude but does not show sufficient respect for consumer autonomy or maturity in decision-making. It fails to take into account that customers can have different perspectives and gather additional information.

Paternalistic attitudes can prevent consumers from enjoying a selection of alternatives or discussing other options before making a choice, or it might seek to prevent them from taking even the slightest risk. When consumers acquire a product or service, they should consider price, quality and the associated level of risk. Customers – not sellers – should decide for themselves whether they prefer a lower price at the cost of a greater risk, once they have obtained sufficient information. Respecting customer decisions is a way of honouring human freedom. However, this respect should be accompanied by a genuine sense of service, which is a fourth marketing philosophy.

Genuine service

Unlike both consumer sovereignty and paternalism, a genuine attitude of service or 'due care' encourages the understanding and serving of the customer's real needs and legitimate wants, neither supplying hazardous goods nor disregarding consumer autonomy.

First, genuine service requires giving customers accurate information that will allow them to make a rational decision, adopting a *caveat venditor* attitude ('Let the seller beware') instead of the *caveat emptor* ('Let the buyer beware') (see Insight 12).

Genuine service requires avoidance of causing damage. Thus, according to this approach, it is illicit to sell products that violate human dignity (for example, prostitution, pornography and weapons for terrorists), and products that can reasonably be deemed intrinsically harmful, because they can only be used to cause physical or moral damage to consumers (for example, the uncontrolled sale of narcotic drugs).

Genuine service also includes not persuading potential consumers, through advertising or other means, to use carelessly those products that are harmful when improperly or immoderately consumed (for instance, wine, liquor and perhaps tobacco, although nowadays tobacco is generally considered an intrinsically harmful product). This is particularly important in the case of vulnerable population segments, including children and youth, who might be convinced to buy or consume products of this nature.

A genuine sense of service requires values and a sense of stewardship. The American Marketing Association, one of the largest professional associations for marketers with about 40,000 members worldwide, states in its ethical code for marketers:[16] 'marketing practitioners must recognize that they not only serve their enterprises but also act as stewards of society in creating, facilitating and executing the efficient and effective transactions that are part of the greater economy'. This ethical statement is based on six key values (see Table 12.1), each of which includes a set of practical norms.

Integrity, fairness, trust, respect and empathy are especially relevant for marketing in a multicultural and multinational context, but virtues are also indispensable. Virtues seem especially relevant in so-called 'relationship marketing', which emphasizes customer retention and continual satisfaction rather than individual transactions and per case customer resolution.[17]

Table 12.1   Values adopted by the American Marketing Association

Values	Contents
Honesty	To be truthful and forthright in our dealings with customers and stakeholders.
Responsibility	To accept the consequences of our marketing decisions and strategies.
Fairness	To try to balance justly the needs of the buyer with the interests of the seller.
Respect	To acknowledge the basic human dignity of all stakeholders.
Openness	To create transparency in our marketing operations.
Citizenship	To fulfil the economic, legal, philanthropic and societal responsibilities that serve stakeholders in a strategic manner.

Insight 12:

Caveat emptor versus *caveat venditor*

Consumer sovereignty often shares the view of the classic Latin aphorism, *caveat emptor*: 'Let the buyer beware'. This motto has been used in commerce to claim that a buyer should not expect compensation for defects in a purchase that is unfit for its ordinary purpose. There is no warranty; the buyer takes the risk.[18] In accordance with the *caveat emptor* principle, the seller should only warn of substantial latent defects in the product, but not of anything else that might discourage a purchase decision.

Today, considering the asymmetry in information between the seller and the customer with many products, an attitude of *caveat emptor* ('Let the buyer beware') seems insufficient. The alternative is *caveat venditor*; that is, 'Let the seller beware'. – underlining the need for the seller to be held accountable and to take responsibility for the product beyond what is evident or can easily be discovered by the buyer. This requires selling products of a reasonable quality and giving ample information so as to facilitate an informed decision. It is not necessary to include obvious facts in this information, or to reveal, say, that the competitor down the block sells the same product at a lower price. Special sensitivity is necessary when a product is sold to vulnerable customers who might be easily misled.

ETHICAL VALUES IN MARKETING RESEARCH AND IN MARKET RESEARCH

Companies use consumer *marketing research* to obtain information about particular aspects of the market, generally related to consumer behaviours, whims and preferences. This requires systematically gathering, recording and analysing data, often employing statistical methods. Marketing research can be done to determine what product might be marketable or what innovations a product might require in the near future, to analyse the effects of marketing campaigns and, in general, to obtain data for decision-making in marketing issues.

Related to marketing research is *market research*, which has a broad focus on the market. It includes analysing market structure, competitors, barriers to entry and exit of a specific market, legislation applicable, technological advances, tendencies in the industry, and any other factors that might be significant for making strategic decisions about products, new markets or distribution innovations.

Marketing and market research involve ethical issues related to the means of obtaining information.[19] These issues are generally found in professional codes of marketing researchers. Following are some of the main concerns:

Informed consent

Participants in a survey should be aware of the purpose of research and agree to participate in such research. Informed consent is a right related to the personalist principle. This consent includes at least tacit permission to have their answers recorded.

Researchers can be tempted to neglect informed consent when gaining access to difficult settings to obtain critical information, or when seeking simply to avoid trouble. Often interviewers begin by presenting vague explanations of the purpose of the survey and ask irrelevant questions to create a relaxing atmosphere, before moving on to more sensitive matters. Some participants, such as children, the elderly, immigrants and the uneducated might be less aware of their rights and be particularly vulnerable to such manipulation.

Privacy and confidentiality

Apart from informed consent, participants should maintain their privacy. This means that an individual has not only the right to choose or refuse to participate in a survey, but also the right to avoid answering certain questions if he or she considers them inappropriate or simply prefers not to opine. In addition, the interviewer has to maintain respect for individuals and their positions.

Data from participants should be kept confidential and used only for the purpose of the survey. Shopping online presents particular problems on this point; special care is required to ensure responsible research. Customer education on shopping online can help users to be aware of which information the seller is recording, and to maintain their privacy and sensitive personal data under their own control.

Deception and harm

Honesty requires telling the truth when conducting surveys or using other methodology. Respondents' cooperation must not be based on misleading information about the general purpose and nature of the project when their agreement to participate is being obtained. All such statements must be honoured.

Objectivity in reports

Marketing research should be done with objectivity and rigour, without manipulating or exaggerating the results. Since professionals in this field often work for companies or institutions, they should avoid any bias towards the outcomes their sponsors hope to find.

ETHICAL ISSUES REGARDING THE PRODUCT

A product, generically, is anything a seller exchanges in the contract of sale, including material products, services or even ideas. The buyer expects both tangible and intangible attributes to be adequate for the product's ordinary use, and this is part of the implicit contract.

From a marketing perspective, there are three important features of the product: (1) brand, which distinguishes a seller's product from competitors'; (2) packaging; and (3) labelling. Brand, the reputation of which is built over time, is based on quality, safe use, durability and the manufacturing warranty of products included in it. Attentiveness to these aspects is also important on ethical grounds, since they contribute to human well-being. On this point, as with many others, focus on short-term profits without sufficient attention to the elements that build brand reputation can jeopardize that reputation and, thereby, long-term profits as well. However, the pressures to produce short-term profits to which the seller is sometimes subjected can lead to the temptation to sell without a sufficient sense of responsibility.

In order to avoid abuses and protect consumer rights, a strict product liability has been established in the legislation of most countries. Some liability regulations are fully consistent with ethical issues concerning the product.

Among such issues, the following are especially pertinent:

Type of product and obsolescence

As pointed out earlier, some products are harmful in themselves or dangerous depending on the use made of them. Among the latter are firearms, alcoholic beverages, tobacco and gambling.[20] Their distribution is generally regulated and tolerated only in limited circumstances.

Another ethical issue is selling counterfeit products, including unauthorized copies of patented inventions, trademarks and copyrighted material.[21] This type of sale is unacceptable because it violates propriety rights and this, in most countries, is also illegal. In addition, counterfeit products can be sold at a substantially lower price, which can be considered a form of unfair competition – but they can also be passed off as genuine and sold at the same price as the authentic product when it is difficult to spot the difference, which is a deception.

Durability and obsolescence of a product can be ethically problematic. Products cease to be usable if they have a limited durability, or because they are no longer competitive (if other, technologically superior products have made them obsolete – a fairly common fate in the high-tech industry) or out of fashion, or because spare parts are no longer available. Another possibility is that the design includes a planned obsolescence with the purpose of greater profits (some batteries, for example). These issues have to be analysed case by case, taking into account the honesty and uprightness with which the selling is (or is not) carried out, and also the buyer's consent to accept the product's limitations.

Quality, usage and safety

The *quality of products*, and especially the quality/price ratio, is both a competitive advantage for business and a way to serve people's needs. Reasonable safety is a requirement for every product. Quality might vary, but products must be safe for the use for which they have been designed. However, how much safety is necessary depends on the specific application of each product. For instance, a high-end car might be made with more resistant and expensive materials than those of a more modest vehicle. However, all cars need to meet minimum safety standards, and these are often legal requirements. Similarly, in every product, economizing cannot be an excuse to design or manufacture something that might injure or harm consumers.

Another aspect of concern for safety is the information provided for the correct use of the product. Sometimes, what is unsafe is not the product itself but its misuse. Since manufacturers have fuller knowledge about what they produce, they are obliged to provide appropriate instructions so that the consumer can use it correctly.

Regulation of the legal liability of manufacturers – especially of food, pharmaceuticals and other consumer products – is extensive in most countries.

Packaging

Packaging usually helps to differentiate a product, to give it an undertone of quality and to render it more attractive. But packaging can be excessive, which entails an unwarranted consumption of resources as well as higher prices. Often packaging is so unnecessarily bulky that it is difficult to deal with. A balanced solution is necessary. Moreover, as packaging sooner or later becomes waste, it is also an environmental problem. An ethical improvement in this area would be to use the least possible packaging compatible with the necessary benefits of an appealing presentation, and to employ biodegradable materials or help recycle packaging waste.

Labelling

The words on the label and packaging are usually the customer's main source of information for making an educated purchase decision. The customer's right to be informed implies the business's responsibility to provide clear, accurate and sufficient information about the product. Ambiguity and misleading claims on labels are unacceptable when the information concerns a product's essential features. Some labels, attractive for marketing reasons, can mislead consumers, even without an explicit lie. An example of this might be a bottle of cooking oil with a label that proclaims 'cholesterol-free!' when the product actually contains saturated vegetable fats and hydrogenated oils, which the human metabolism converts into cholesterol.

Warranties

Products should be sold without concealed defects in essential parts. The seller also offers a warranty, which guarantees the quality and safety of the product, and expresses the seller's specific obligations concerning its performance. The warranty is often implicit, or there are legal requirements of a generic warranty for a certain period of time, assuming an ordinary use of the product. There are also 'express warranties' explicitly communicated to the customers that can include specific statements. Both types of warranties are promises that should be honoured.

Recalls

In spite of the efforts of many companies to offer safe products, it might happen that a dangerous product is detected after it reaches the marketplace. A responsible reaction in such cases is to recall the product, although this might involve a costly operation. Otherwise, the company would bear responsibility, due to its omission,[22] for harm or damages suffered by consumers. Moreover, in many cases, the financial cost associated with liability for the product and the reputation lost could be even higher than the cost of recalling the product.

FAIR PRICE AND ABUSES IN PRICING

Pricing products is a crucial point in marketing. If the price is too high, fewer people will buy, and the profit might be small, but if the price is too low, the profit might also be modest. Beyond profit, however, pricing involves a question of justice.[23]

The issue of a *just or fair price* was treated in the Middle Ages by Aquinas as a significant case of commutative justice; that is, justice associated with exchanges, and was addressed again in the sixteenth and seventeenth centuries in the School of Salamanca, Spain.[24] A progressively deeper knowledge of open markets led to the understanding that a fair price is a complex issue shaped by many factors, including production and distribution costs (of which the cost of capital is an element), the relative scarcity of the product, the subjective value based on personal needs or wants, risks that the buyer incurs, replacement costs, and the price of close substitutes. Just price is not the result of a mathematical formula, but of a rational and unbiased estimation.

There is no doubt that what economists term an 'equilibrium price' in perfect competition is a fair price. Under these conditions, neither producer nor consumer has the market power to influence prices. This price, which corresponds to 'market equilibrium', is established through competition in that the amount of goods or services sought by buyers is equal to the amount of goods or services produced by sellers. Competition prevents abuse of power and leads to fair prices.

However, business people seek a higher price than the one obtained in perfect competition. For this purpose, they offer 'product differentiation' to try to attract buyers willing to pay more because the product or service is distinct from the conventional one. The buyer judges that this difference is worth a higher price. Innovative products can also be offered relatively expensively if a product is well received, at least in the stage of the product cycle growth when competition is not yet too fierce. These prices are also fair if buyers freely accept them. In particular, the higher price of a new product, in some ways, compensates for its lower price when the market is later glutted with rivals, or for decline in the demand for a product because another more advanced item has appeared on the scene.

There are several ethical issues regarding pricing, including the following:

Price gouging

An extreme example of unfair pricing occurs when sellers take advantage of civil emergencies by hoarding provisions of food or other basic goods and then selling them at much higher prices than normal. This is referred to as *price gouging*. Frequently, this term is also used for any commercial practice inconsistent with a competitive free market, or when completely unexpected revenues appear (*windfall profits*).

Monopolies and monopsonies

In Chapter 2 (p. 31), we considered the problem of monopolies and monopsonies in a market economy. They are situations of asymmetry of power, in which injustice can occur unless sound regulation prevents it. A particularly serious situation is that of a monopoly, which brings about unfair prices in products regarding a basic buyer need, such as food or pharmaceuticals. A high price is more acceptable when the monopoly involves luxury or unnecessary goods (for instance, jewellery, works of art or luxury cars).

A *coactive monopoly* is a business concern that prohibits competitors from entering the field (for example, electricity supply from a company imposed by the government). In such cases, it is impossible to compete through prices, after sales service, innovation, technology and so on. Competition tends to lead to fair prices but, in a coactive monopoly, prices are not the result of competitive forces and are likely to be higher than would commonly be called fair.

Sometimes a company or brand enjoys a monopoly, or a vast market share, in a certain region. This is not a coactive monopoly, though, because other sellers can compete, and the price offered is probably fair. This would be the case, for instance, of a brand of beer that had exclusive control in a country. If the price were too high, consumers could choose another brand or a substitute drink.

Price fixing and collusion

Price fixing refers to an agreement between business rivals to sell a certain product or service at the same price, carried out through collusion between two or more sellers. The goal is to avoid free competition, generally to push the price as high as possible for the mutual benefit of sellers at the expense of buyers, although sometimes it is also to fix, peg, discount or stabilize prices. Price fixing is sometimes termed *price collusion* to emphasize the agreement, usually secretive, to avoid fair competition.

Small companies can follow the price established by a large firm. This is not price fixing as such because there is no explicit agreement to act illegally.

Apart from this form of price fixing between competitors, which can be termed 'horizontal', there is another 'vertical' type that occurs between manufacturer and wholesaler, wholesaler and distributor, or distributor and retailer.

Price fixing is generally unethical, since it distances businesses from fair competition. It is also frequently forbidden by law. However, it might sometimes be morally justifiable as a legitimate defence of producers facing monopsonies or collusion among buyers. This might be the case with some raw material production, mainly in developing countries.

Predatory pricing and dumping

Predatory pricing is a pricing policy based on selling a product at a very low price, even below the production costs, with the intention of driving competitors out of the market or to avoid potential new competitors from entering it. Short-term profits fall, but if the goal is achieved, the firm will have fewer competitors or can even become a monopoly. Restricting competition permits the raising of prices above the level the market would otherwise bear, and brings about more overall profits.

Predatory pricing, also known as destroyer pricing, is not ethically acceptable because its direct intent is not to compete fairly but to destroy rivals. It is an anti-competitive practice, prohibited in many countries, although it might be difficult to prove that such a practice really exists in a particular case.

The origin of predatory pricing might be in a price war, in which rival firms undertake a series of price reductions. If one firm reduces prices, the others reduce their own even more. In a price war, all firms lose profits and, in the end, the firm with less capacity to survive will be obliged to abandon the market. In this case, the resulting low prices can be acceptable if they are only a defence against the aggressive tactics of competitors.

Dumping is a term used for depredatory pricing in international trade. It occurs when a manufacturer in one country exports a product to another at a price that is either below the price the second country charges in its home market or below its costs of production. The moral status of dumping might seem to be identical to the judgement on domestic predatory prices if the purpose is to do away with the import country's own products. However, free trade between economies at different stages of development is a complex matter. Actually, dumping involves a number of ethical and legal issues,[25] and a more accurate judgement would have to take into account all the relevant circumstances of each situation.

Discriminatory practices in pricing

A final issue involves *price discrimination*, which occurs when the seller charges different customers different prices for the same product without genuine justification. Price discrimination can also involve charging two buyers the same price when it costs more to supply one than another. In some cases, the price charged can change through a transparent process to incentivize early purchase or purchase during a certain period (as with many airplane tickets). But all clients can benefit equally from this measure. There is no price discrimination by client here.

In some countries (the United States, for instance), it is illegal to discriminate between different distributors on price without a suitable justification. Some common price discrimination practices cannot be considered unethical, however. There is discrimination by age group and student status (which is quite common in theatres, movies, museums and tourist attractions), employee discounts, incentives to increase market share or revenues at the retail level (coupons, rebates, bulk and quantity pricing, seasonal discounts, and frequent buyer discounts) and incentives for industrial buyers.

Another discriminatory practice is *price skimming*. This consists of charging a relatively high price for a product or service at first, then reducing it over time. As noted above, this seems ethically acceptable if there is no abuse of the customer's quest to satisfy basic needs.

Charging those who have more purchasing power higher prices than others is another form of pricing discrimination that is not necessarily wrong. There are several examples of this. One is 'premium pricing' as opposed to 'economic pricing' (for instance, business class in airplanes, or premium coffee in some coffee chains). The latter can be beyond the marginal cost of production, whereas with the former, a similar or slightly superior product can be sold at a very high price. There are financial reasons for doing this, as losses from the economy product are more than compensated for profits from the premium product. Another example is selling medicine to developing countries at a lower price than in developed countries, although here one should avoid a scenario in which these same medicines are resold to developed countries through unofficial, unauthorized and unintended distribution channels (the grey market). From an ethical perspective, the example of selling medicine more cheaply is not only licit but also laudable as a form of distributive justice and solidarity.

Besides these practices, there are some much more ethically doubtful cases of charging lower prices for some consumers and higher prices for others.[26] Another more than questionable practice is to charge higher prices for products sold in poor areas to exploit the population's inability to travel to more affluent regions to purchase goods or obtain information about more competitive prices.

ETHICS IN ADVERTISING

We mentioned promotion as one of the key elements of the 'marketing mix'. Promotion includes advertising, publicity, public relations, personal selling and sales promotion. For reasons of space, we will focus only on advertising.[27] Advertising is a paid, non-personal message communicated to a certain audience through mass media, generally to promote the consumption of products or services or to improve the company's or brand's reputation. Publicity has similar goals but is carried out by offering a news story to the mass media at no charge.

Advertising can be designed to convey information, but generally it tries to persuade potential consumers to buy products and services, or advises them how to obtain and use them. Advertising can be focused on creating and reinforcing a brand image or brand loyalty. It can also be oriented towards generating or increasing habits to capture consumers. There are a number of ethical issues in advertising that we need to examine, but the primary question concerns the legitimacy of the persuasion itself – the essence of advertising – and how far advertising should be permitted to go with that persuasion.

Respect for the consumer's responsible and free choice

Persuasive advertising has been criticized on the grounds that, in certain common types, it overrides the autonomy of consumers by provoking desires in such a way that a necessary condition of autonomy – the possibility of decision – is removed. This might suggest that nearly any persuasive advertising is ethically wrong,[28] but this position seems exaggerated. Much persuasive advertising cannot be judged so manipulative as to eliminate the consumer's autonomy or ability to make a responsible and free choice. Of course, there is persuasive advertising that can be manipulative, but there is also another kind that is both persuasive and respectful. One might be influenced by advertising or motivated by it, but this does not mean manipulation is necessarily present; one can reflect and then freely decide for or against what an advertisement proposes.

An example of a lack of respect for consumer autonomy is *subliminal advertising*, a manipulative technique which introduces an image (for example, advertising a soft drink) for one twenty-fifth of a second during a movie. The audience cannot see such an image, but it is retained in their minds and then, under certain conditions, can, in some people, produce a desire for what is pictured – at least, in those who already enjoy the product. Apart from any ethical reservations about this technique, its efficacy is being questioned today.[29]

Advertising directed at children is problematic,[30] for they are not capable of resisting or understanding marketing tactics before a certain age. However, children influence their family and, after a certain age, can even spend their own money on snacks and unhealthy food, fashionable clothes, entertainment goods and so on, especially during pre-adolescence and the teen years. Another vulnerable audience can be found in developing countries, where some people might not be sufficiently familiar with skilled marketing ploys and how powerful their tactics are. In developed countries, too, the less educated, the emotionally immature or the weak-willed can also be vulnerable to certain techniques.

Apart from respecting the consumer's autonomy in decision-making, ethics in advertising requires other conditions that we will address in the following. Marketing managers and advertising professionals, in adhering to these conditions, need not only an ethical sense and courage, but also the imagination and creativity to resist the often powerful pressure to achieve results at any cost.

Truthfulness

Truthfulness is the ethical condition of any human communication, as noted before.[31] In advertising, many ethics problems centre on dishonesty. A clear transgression of truthfulness is presenting false statements which deceive and persuade people to engage in transactions they would otherwise avoid; for instance, to assert: 'This is the best-selling car of the year' when it is not, or claiming for any product qualities it does not possess:

- *Deceptive advertising.* Some advertisements, although not based on false statements, can nevertheless be deceptive, considering the audience to which the message is addressed. Examples of deception in advertising could be, for example, presenting a blown-up photograph of a small car in an advertisement that targets children, which might lead them to think that they would be able to drive it; or presenting images that suggest a non-existent cause–effect relation (say, presenting a fragrance as a means to attract girls, or promising a guarantee of happiness to those who drink a certain soda).

- *Testimonials and endorsements.* Sometimes advertising messages are given by people – generally ordinary customers – who recommend a product based on their favourable experience. These testimonials can have a certain persuasive effect.

Endorsements are usually provided by celebrities or experts (professionals, outstanding sports figures, movie stars and so on). They are designed to lead consumers to believe that an advertising message reflects opinions, beliefs, findings or experiences of a party other than the one sponsoring the advertisement.

Many consumers might not take testimonials and endorsements seriously, but others might believe what such 'fellow customers', celebrities or experts, say or, at least, be influenced by them.

- *Demonstrations.* In advertising, practical demonstrations seek to show, through a practical application, that a product of a certain brand – say, a detergent – is superior to all its rivals. In fact, this might be true, or it might not. It might also be that the product used in the demonstration is not the one being advertised.

- *Mock-ups.* These refer to life-sized or even larger representations. They are used in advertising for a visual presentation of a product, such as an ice cream or a succulent cut of meat, through appealing photography. Mock-ups used in advertisements might include not only a full-sized photograph, but also a representation of other products or the genuine product enhanced in some way (for example, a vegetable soup with many more pieces of vegetables than the real one contains). Mock-ups can easily involve deception and, consequently, are subject to regulation in many countries, as are many other advertising practices.

- *Puffery.* This refers to subjective, superlative expressions that praise a product or service, or to vague and general statements with no specific facts.[32] Puffery is not properly false advertising or deception, as everybody can understand that it is an exaggeration or embellishment of the product's qualities. However, puffery might be an expression bordering on untruthfulness that could deceive some. Puffery actually functions as a deception when people cannot readily identify the exaggeration involved and are misled. Discernment is required to determine whether a particular piece of puffery is ethically acceptable. It is also true that puffery can be a step onto the slippery slope of deception and fraud.

Respect for people's dignity and rights

Respect for people's dignity and human rights is a basic requirement, in advertising as in life. A lack of respect for people is manifest when images degrading to women (or men) are used as advertising. This is so when they are presented as mere sexual objects to attract the attention of an advertisement's audience.

Respect for human dignity also requires avoiding advertising messages with scenes of cruelty or violence. Advertising should also respect the privacy of the individual and the right to one's own image and reputation. A similar attitude should be maintained with regard to private and public institutions.

Non-offensive advertising and good taste

Advertising can be described as offensive when its form or message disgusts people – and not necessarily the vast majority. Messages that offend ethnic groups, religious beliefs and so on are not responsible advertising.

Lack of respect for people, advertising products that some find offensive ('socially sensitive products') and bad taste can all cause consumers to become irritated and respond negatively. Both personal and social factors converge on this point.[33]

No excessive intrusiveness

Advertising is usually presented to people without their permission. It enters the home, by means of the Internet, television, newspapers, magazines or phone calls, or one involuntarily encounters it when driving or walking down the street, reading a newspaper or magazine, or perhaps at the cinema. Sometimes, it is even excessively intrusive and annoying. A sense of responsibility aids in self-regulation but, besides this, in many countries there is also strict regulation to avoid excessive invasiveness. This applies to advertising along roads and by megaphones or billboards; it also places limitations on interruptions of television programmes, telemarketing invading home privacy and so on.

Fair competition

Advertising can be contrary to fair competition if it uses false or unverified information when comparing a firm's own products with those of competitors, or if it discredits or denigrates a competitor. In some countries, it is even forbidden to mention competitors by name when comparing products, and advertisers are reduced to badmouthing 'Brand X'.

Also, contrary to fair competition is introducing confusion between the advertised product and another well-known brand, plagiarizing the advertisements of other companies.

Responsibility for social impact

Advertising of products which are dangerous or can be misused is tightly regulated or even forbidden in many countries. Among them those already mentioned (p. 281), such as firearms, alcoholic beverages, tobacco, gambling, and other controversial products or services. These measures are ethically justifiable to avoid undesirable consequences.

Advertising can reflect social values but, in some ways, it also actively promotes those values. In this regard, advertisers and businesses have a duty to express and foster an authentic vision of human development in their material, cultural and spiritual dimensions.[34]

ETHICS IN DISTRIBUTION AND SALES

Distribution and sales are arranged in different ways. In some cases, producers can deliver their products directly to individual consumers, but they often have only an indirect relationship with consumers, and product distribution is carried out through intermediaries, including agents, wholesalers and retailers. Industrial products can be delivered directly to industrial users or indirectly through middlemen.

Along the chain of an organization, from the producer to the final user – the marketing or distribution channel – the price of the product is incrementally increased. On this point, apart from the price problems discussed above, one can find a typical justice issue derived from abuse of power at some link of the distribution chain. One of the intermediaries might have enormous negotiation power over the next. This is the case, for instance, of huge stores and small suppliers. The latter might sell a great volume of commodities to a single client. On the one hand, this facilitates the sale, but on the other, the huge store can exploit its negotiation power by imposing on the small producer prices that are so low that it becomes an exploitative relationship.

Another ethical issue within the *distribution channel* is 'gift-giving' to people who make decisions that can favour sales or commercial transactions in some way – which can sometimes be a manner of covering up bribery or even be a brazen bribe itself.[35] Clear guidelines within a company or for an entire industry can help to avoid extortion and questionable practices.

In sales, there are many ethical issues that include certain techniques of persuasion and inducements. In some cases, these can include misrepresentation or some other sort of manipulation.

Many *ethical issues in sales* concern individual behaviours of salespersons and representatives, who might often feel a tension between the loyalty to the seller they represent and the buyers that they are supposed to be serving. Honesty requires telling the truth about the product's features and avoiding unfair or inaccurate comparisons about a rival product.

Certain external conditions can push people towards misbehaviours in personal selling. For instance, salespersons are more prone to act wrongly when there is great intensity of competition or revenue pressures on sellers from their organization (especially in hard times) to promote a product, when compensation systems are based mostly on commissions, when gifting or bribes are common in a certain industry, when sales training (including ethical aspects) is non-existent or abbreviated, and when a sales representative has limited selling experience.[36] Sales managers bear responsibility for preventing abusive sale practices.

A final issue is that clients' privacy has to be respected and their personal data and purchase behaviour kept confidential, as should that of employees.[37]

Business ethics in practice 12:

Imaginarium SA – Giving a real service

Imaginarium SA is a Spanish retail chain of educational toy stores, targeting children from birth to nine years old. It was founded in Zaragoza, Spain by Mr Félix Tena in 1992. Imaginarium has been growing constantly since. It reached 330 shops in 29 countries in the first 15 years. Now, this company is a multi-channel, multi-product and multinational company oriented toward families and children.

Imaginarium has an integrated business model, in which the firm controls and decides what products will be manufactured and in what quantities. The same executive team controls the whole business process from the design of the toys to their sale. The majority of toys cannot be found in any other competitive store. Price is not the main basis for competition with other toy stores. The company is driven by a clearly defined mission and a set of values. Its corporate mission is 'to make a positive, joyful and creative contribution to the human development of children, worldwide'.

The toys are carefully selected through a number of criteria. They should encourage children to play actively with their toys and stimulate their imagination, but they should not be sexist, racist or violent. Imaginarium toys try to stimulate the cognitive, sensorial, psychomotor development of children. Under the slogan 'turn off TV and turn on imagination', parents are informed about the necessity to develop the child's creativity. Values such as solidarity, diversity, respect for the environment, respect for one's own body, a sporting and healthy life are also associated with Imaginarium toys. The development of social responsibility is fostered by letting children play at different professions, such as pretending to be doctors or teachers.

One of the most important features of Imaginarium is the highly educated staff. They are helpful in giving advice on the product and in explaining the educative purpose of the toys. Retail and store attendants are toy and children's game specialists, and many of them are college trained in psychology or pedagogy. Parents appreciate the expert advice that has the reputation of being sincere, even at the cost of not selling a product. Staff turnover is significantly lower than the industry average.

Moreover, the emotions of children – such as pride, joy, peace and amusement – seem to be an important factor, which builds an excellent Imaginarium–customer relationship.

The company operates in a relational context with families, keeping track of their active participation in Imaginarium activities through Club Imaginarium. At the end of 2007, there were over one million families registered. A loyalty card was launched in October 2004 to allow the company to record the annual purchase volumes of club members. The company uses limited media advertising, usually relying on mail order catalogues.

Imaginarium management was initially reluctant to sell their products online, since selling through the Internet could be perceived as having an adverse effect on the retail stores and on the company's image. After all, the customers purchasing online cannot touch and feel the product, and there is a higher possibility of delays and errors. There is the added disadvantage that parents cannot seek the advice of the company's toy specialists. However, in the end, the company decided to do it. The latest strategic change has been in

---

Business ethics in practice 12: (cont'd)

widening its scope from a retail chain of educational toys to a brand supplying products and services to families with young children, but with the same criteria in choosing toys and children's games.

Questions:

1. Which values and ethical aspects can you find in the Imaginarium philosophy and culture?
2. Could you provide an example of any business you know in which commercial service simultaneously provides the real service and satisfaction of clients and employees, and also business success?

Sources: Abridged version of case study M-1173-E 'Imaginarium', authored by L. Berasategui, F. Parés and L. G. Renart (Barcelona: IESE Publishing, 2003). Published with permission. It includes some updated information provided by Professor Renart.

Dilemma 12

Aadhaar was very excited with his new job after obtaining his degree in business administration on the East Coast in the USA. He was the son of Indians who had immigrated to America 30 years ago. Now, he was in San Francisco working with his uncle Narayan in a second-hand car business owned by his uncle and Ashoush, his uncle's partner. Both had started up this business 25 years before, initially exporting cars to their home country. They continued with import–export operations of cars but now their main business was the domestic market for second-hand cars.

Narayan, who was 60 years old, had no children, thus, Aadhaar thought he would succeed his uncle when he retired five years later. He has been told that, and even that he would inherit his uncle's estate when he passed away. Narayan was now well off after years of working hard.

Actually, Aadhaar already knew his uncle's business a little, since he had spent two summers working in the administration and accounting department. Narayan wanted Aadhaar to know everything about the industry, including selling, car import–export operations, and contacts with people in the industry. Aadhaar started with sales. One of the veteran employees would be his mentor and explain details on how to sell second-hand cars.

The first client to come up was a young married couple. After seeing several cars, they showed a great interest in one of them, which Aadhaar had driven some days before. He knew that the gas consumption of this car was

Dilemma 12 (cont'd)

extremely high. The employee gave the clients all kinds of explanation praising the excellence of the car, but not a single word about gas consumption. Aadhaar said nothing, trying to learn. Eventually, the young couple bought the car for a significant amount of money. Afterwards, Aadhaar asked the employee about his silence on the subject of gas consumption. He told Aadhaar, 'Mentioning this point could make the sale fail.' If they do not ask, say nothing. If they ask you can answer something ambiguous: 'Not too much' or 'like any car of its kind'. If they insist, you can decrease the consumption rate. This is not a formal warranty.

Aadhaar learned that employees frequently lie in response to client questions and, sometimes, they even manipulate the odometer to decrease the apparent number of miles travelled by the vehicle. In the workshop, some flawed mechanical elements are substituted for other old elements and some repairs only serve for a short time. When Aadhaar asked questions about the ethical dimensions, the answer was along the lines of: 'This is common in our business. If you do not work like this you will never be rich.'

In dealing with suppliers, Aadhaar learned a number of practices that he could not have imagined, such as inviting them to seedy clubs before closing a deal and using bribes whenever necessary without further considerations. Aadhaar discovered that these and practices of deceit were greatly extended within the company, although his uncle had never mentioned this dark side of his business.

He did not feel comfortable with these practices and, after six months, he thought that he had to make a decision about his professional career. Perhaps it would be best to speak with his uncle, expressing his disagreement and presenting the challenge to improve the 'culture' of the company. Another option could be to do nothing and to try to change the situation when he had taken over the company. He could leave the company and search for a different career but, if he chose this option, what would be his uncle's reaction? What he did not consider was to adapt his moral convictions to that business climate and to try to acquire the 'skills' apparently required in the second-hand car business, although he was not completely sure about this.

Questions:

1. What is your evaluation of the practices described and the reason given by the veteran employee?
2. What would you recommend to Aadhaar to make a sound decision?

Summary

Ethics of marketing refers to the ethical dimension of planning and executing what to sell, including ideas, products and services, and how to promote, distribute and sell them appropriately.

Consumer rights include the right to safety, the right to full value, the right to be informed, the right to choose, the right to education, the right to be heard, the right to recourse and redress, the right to representation and participation, and the right to a healthy environment.

In the face of both 'consumer sovereignty' and 'consumer paternalism', marketing driven by a 'genuine sense of service' should adopt as a motto *caveat venditor* ('Let the seller beware'), instead of *caveat emptor* ('Let the buyer beware').

Both marketing research and market research should be carried out with honesty, respect for privacy and due consent. Objectivity in reports is also required, avoiding any manipulation or exaggeration of the findings.

There are several ethical issues regarding the product: (1) type of product and obsolescence; (2) quality; (3) usage and safety; (4) packaging; (5) labelling; (6) warranties; and (7) recalls.

Pricing policies and practices include a question of justice. Perfect competition tends to avoid price gouging or any other abuse in pricing. What might be questionable are prices associated with certain monopolies or monopsonies, price fixing and collusion, predatory pricing and dumping, and some practices in price discrimination.

Advertising commonly seeks to persuade people. This is not intrinsically wrong but can, under certain circumstances, be manipulative, especially when targeting vulnerable audiences (children and the unlettered or immature, among others).

Ethics in advertising requires: (1) respect for the consumer's autonomy and responsible choice; (2) truthfulness (although some hyperbolic expressions in praise of a product can be accepted if the audience can easily see through them); (3) respect for human dignity and rights; (4) being inoffensive and in good taste; (5) avoiding excessive intrusiveness; (6) practising fair competition; and (7) taking responsibility for the advertising's social impact.

In the distribution channel, injustices can occur. A typical situation is the abuse of a weaker party by a more powerful one who imposes draconian conditions of sale.

In sales, there are several unfair techniques of persuasion and sales inducements that are often, though not always, illegal.

Part V
Societal Business Ethics

13

The famous Statue of Liberty on the US East coast should be complemented with a Statue of Responsibility on the West coast.[1]

Viktor Frankl (1905–1997)
Austrian neurologist and psychiatrist

Chapter Aims

This chapter will allow you to:

- obtain a general view about the historical evolution of the concept of corporate social responsibility
- discuss in what sense corporations bear responsibility
- distinguish between implicit and explicit corporate social responsibility
- discuss three objections to corporate policies and activities for social interests and whether business can alleviate poverty
- discuss how corporations respond to social demands and the path to corporate responsibility
- be introduced to the four main theories of responsibility of business in society: Corporate Social Performance, Corporate Stakeholder Responsibility, Strategic Corporate Social Responsibility and Corporate Citizenship
- learn the origin of the notion of sustainability and its current meaning
- become familiar with the concept of the Triple Bottom Line
- discuss why corporate accountability is so important
- become more familiar with auditing and reporting on corporate social responsibility and sustainability.

Key terms:

AA1000	Explicit responsibilities	Strategic corporate social
Base of the pyramid	Global reporting initiative	responsibility
Corporate accountability	(GRI)	Sustainability
Corporate citizenship	Implicit responsibilities	Triple bottom line
Corporate social performance	Microcredit	
Corporate stakeholder	SA 8000	
responsibility		

The Social Responsibility and Accountability of Business

INTRODUCTORY CASE 13:

NIKE – A TRUE SOCIAL REPORT OR MISLEADING ADVERTISING?

Nike was founded in 1968 by Philip Knight. For more than three decades, this company had been a corporate success story and the largest athletic shoe company in the world. In the early 1990s, it first contracted the manufacturing of shoes in Japan, then in Taiwan and Korea. Finally, practically all Nike subcontracted production was moved to Indonesia, Vietnam, China and Thailand, where the labour costs are much lower than in the United States. Apparently both sides benefited. Thanks to investments of such pioneers as Nike, which entered into risky contexts of political uncertainty, the local economies and infrastructures developed.

Nike endeavoured to build high quality products at affordable prices and part of the core marketing strategy has always been to sell products that are good value for money. However, the company was subject to negative press, lawsuits and demonstrations after 1996, when a columnist of the *New York Times* vehemently criticized Nike working conditions. The allegations stated that Nike had built its wealth and products with the 'slave' labour of young Asian women. Joel Joseph from the USA Foundation, for instance, accused Nike of paying underage Indonesian workers 14 cents an hour to make the company's line of Air Jordan Shoes.

Nike reacted to critics by explaining that its manufacturers were Asian companies that it merely contracted. The hiring party has no legal obligation to control the practices of contracting and no responsibility for their behaviour. A second argument was that, although not required by local law, Nike improved working conditions. Although Vietnamese child labour legislation allowed for the employment of workers at age 16, Nike imposed a minimum age of 18 so that employees could complete high school education. In the face of the economic crisis in Asia in the late 1990s, Nike's intervention meant that food supplements for employees were increased.

Nike was not the only company on the receiving end of strong reaction from public opinion. Other companies in the apparel industry were also severely criticized for the working conditions in Asia and Latin America. In 1996, the US President, Bill Clinton, gathered together a group of presidents of the sector for a meeting. President Clinton challenged them to take steps to improve working conditions around the world and to provide the public with information it could use to make informed purchasing decisions. As a consequence, the Fair Labor Association (FLA) was born and incorporated in May 1999. The FLA requires affiliated companies to abide by a workplace code of conduct and monitors requirements. In addition, it established an accreditation programme to determine whether company obligations were met, and instituted a public reporting mechanism to inform consumers about company participation and compliance. Nike joined the FLA from its inception.

In early 1997, Nike hired Andrew Young, an opponent of child labour, to tour and audit factories in Asia. Nike also used such means as letters to editors, articles, campus visits and made a statement of corporate responsibility, establishing a code of conduct with six new standards: (1) factory monitoring; (2) minimum age requirements; (3) environmental security; (4) employee education programmes; (5) expansion of its micro-loan programme; and (6) transparency of corporate responsibility practices. Some NGO representatives admitted that Nike was targeted not so much due to its practices being appreciably different from those of others but, instead, due to its market share leadership. However, one Ernst & Young audit of a particular Vietnamese facility showed that there was no drinking water and there were toxic chemical concentrations up to 177 times the permitted limits. With regard to the labourers, 48 of the 50 worked longer hours than those permitted, workers were punished for taking time off to attend weddings and funerals, and 80 per cent had never read the code of conduct.

Another problem appeared in January 2001, when Jonah H. Peretti, a customer and a graduate student of MIT, asked that his sneakers be personalized with the addition of the word 'sweatshop', a request that the company rejected. Then he ordered shoes bearing a colour photograph of a Vietnamese child making shoes. Nike again refused to comply, and the story appeared in the *Wall Street Journal* and on television. Nike protested that it reserves the right to cancel any order up to 24 hours after receiving it before delivery and insisted that it did not hire children. At this time, Nike's subcontractors in Asia operated 150 factories employing more than 450,000 workers.

In October 2001, Nike released its first Corporate Social Responsibility Report, compiled by both internal and external monitors, which stated that the firm should improve in such areas as working conditions. Critics considered this as a means of advertising. They said that this was not fair since advertising, which tolerates a certain degree of persuasion, is quite different from CSR reporting, which has more stringent requirements in terms of objectivity.

In April 1998, Marc Kasky sued Nike, claiming that it made statements to Californians that were false and misleading about its labour practices and about working conditions in factories that made its products. In 2002, the California Supreme Court held that Nike's responses to public criticism constituted commercial speech. According to the court, the company's comments on its 'corporate responsibility' policies were 'advertising'. Nike appealed to the US Supreme Court, which did not condemn Nike. However, the justices recognized that this is a complex issue, stating that Nike's speech represents a blending of commercial speech, non-commercial speech and public debate. Although *Kasky v. Nike* has been resolved, an important debate was opened regarding the credibility of corporate social reports and their real value.

Questions:

1. What was the cause of the public reaction against Nike?
2. Can the decisions taken by Nike after the public reaction in the 1990s be considered social responsibility?
3. What do you think about the lawsuits and the corresponding judgements in both the California Supreme Court and in the US Supreme Court?
4. In what way do you think that corporate social reports can gain credibility and become a useful tool for stakeholder information and for corporate reputation?

Sources: B. Dennis, 'Nike Inc., Case 16', *University of Georgia*; D. L. Spar and Jennifer L. Burns, 'Hitting the Wall: Nike and International Labor Practices', *Harvard Business School*, 15 September (2000); L. R. Kahle, D. M. Boush and M. Phelps, 'Good Morning, Vietnam: An Ethical Analysis of Nike Activities in Southeast Asia', University of Oregon, *Sport Marketing Quarterly*, 9, 1 (2000); K. Bell De Tienne and L. W. Lewis, 'The Pragmatic and Ethical Barriers to Corporate Social Responsibility. Disclosure: The Nike Case', *Journal of Business Ethics* (2005); 'Much at Risk in Nike Case', *Advertising Age*, 73, 42 (2002); 'Nike "Free Speech Appeal" Rejected', *BBC* (26 June 2003); *In the Supreme Court of California*, http://www.bulk.resource.org/courts.gov/states/Cal/S087859. PDF, *CFIF.ORG*, http://www.cfif.org/htdocs/legal_issues/archive/to_sort/nike_case.htm

---

SOCIAL RESPONSIBILITY OF BUSINESS: AN HISTORICAL OVERVIEW

Corporate responsibility is related to the fact that business has power and freedom. Large business corporations can often wield enormous power – economic, technological, political, socio-cultural and environmental. Economic power of business comes from corporate control over finances and resources. Technological power is due to business influence on new technological development and its implementation. Corporations sometimes exercise political power by trying to influence public policy, laws and regulations. They also exercise socio-cultural power through business activities, such as advertising and marketing. These, along with their products and services, influence individuals and social groups in terms of attitudes, expectations and consumerism. Finally, corporations have environmental power, because of their capacity, either to safeguard the natural environment or to ignore pressure to do so. In corporations, as in individuals, power implies responsibility.

The concept of corporate social responsibility (CSR) emerged against the opinion that business has only economic duties. Sometimes, too, it arose as a reaction to some particularly abusive behaviour, especially monopolistic practices at the end of the nineteenth century. The idea of corporate responsibility was reinforced when, in the early decades of the twentieth century, the size and power of business corporations increased dramatically. The idea that 'power requires responsibility' grew in popularity.

Keith Davis, a well-known scholar in the field of business and society, wrote in the middle of the 1960s, '*social responsibility arises from social power*. Modern business has immense social power in such areas as minority employment and environmental pollution. If business has power, then a just relationship demands that business also bear responsibility for these actions in these areas' (author's emphasis). He added that 'business shall operate as a two-way open system, with open receipt of input from society and open disclosure of its operation to the public'.[2]

Management scholars especially turned their attention to the social responsibility of business people after Bowen, who in 1953 wrote *Social Responsibilities of the Businessman*.[3] The literature expanded during the 1960s, stressing that social responsibility theories presume that the corporation not only has economic and legal obligations, but also certain duties to society.[4]

The concept of CSR was not, however, accepted peacefully. On the contrary, in the 1960s and 1970s, an intense debate took place and continues to this day.[5] Facing those who defended CSR, Milton Friedman, a well-known fellow of the Chicago School of Economics, along with some others, adopted a position clearly contrary to any social responsibility of business besides creating wealth for its owners. Milton Friedman, with his wife Rose, wrote:

> In such an economy [free market], there is one and only one social responsibility of business – to use resources and engage in activities designed to increase its profits so long as it stays within the rules of the game, which is to say, engages in open and free competitions, without deception or fraud.[6]

Later, in a famous *New York Times Magazine* article, he reconfirmed this approach by contending: 'the only one responsibility of business towards society is the maximization of profits to the shareholders, within the legal framework and the ethical custom of the country'.[7]

Despite ups and downs over the years, the movement in favour of corporate social responsibility won numerous supporters among both academics and practitioners, and an extensive literature on this topic has grown up. Many have argued that, besides their economic responsibility towards their shareholders, companies also have social responsibilities towards their employees and other social groups with a stake in the company's activities (stakeholders). Some added that business has to respond to social expectations to obtain social legitimacy, or a 'licence to operate' from society.[8]

Another argument propounded by Peter Drucker has also played an important role in the success of CSR implementation: 'The proper "social responsibility"', he wrote, 'is to tame the dragon, that is, to turn a social problem into economic opportunity and economic benefit, into productive capacity, into human competence, into well paid jobs and into wealth'.[9]

At the turn of the twenty-first century, a renewed interest in CSR emerged in several countries due to several drivers. Among them, *market drivers* for CSR, such as consumers with a preference for socially responsible products and services; *social drivers*, including NGOs, activists and mass media; *governmental drivers* from governments who in various ways encourage CSR; and *investor drivers*, who search for socially responsible investments.[10]

In Europe, a new impulse for CSR took place in 2001 when the European Union published a Green Paper on 'Promoting a European framework for corporate social responsibility'. In its introduction, the Green Paper states:

> although the prime responsibility of a company is generating profits, companies can at the same time contribute to social and environmental objectives, through integrating corporate social responsibility as a strategic investment into their core business strategy, their management instruments and their operations.[11]

There are many different definitions of corporate social responsibility,[12] most definitions describe it as a notion whereby companies consider their social and environmental impact and integrate these concerns into their business operations. CSR is assumed on a voluntary basis; that is, beyond the legal obligations imposed on the company.

One of these definitions of CSR – one that explicitly includes the idea of ethical behaviour as a key component of CSR – can be found in a report entitled *Corporate Social Responsibility: Making Good Business Sense*. This report was given by a working group created by the World Business Council for Sustainable Development (WBCSD), an association of CEOs of more than 200 large multinational companies. The definition is as follows:

> Corporate social responsibility is the continuing commitment by business to behave ethically and contribute to economic development while improving the quality of life of the workforce and their families as well as of the community and society at large.[13]

In the report, the priority CSR elements were identified as:

- Human rights
- Employee rights
- Environmental protection
- Supplier relations
- Community involvement
- Stakeholder rights
- CSR performance monitoring and assessment.[14]

Similar elements can be found in other relevant international proposals.

DOES THE CORPORATION REALLY BEAR RESPONSIBILITIES?

In the business world, it is quite common to talk about 'corporate responsibility' ascribing responsibility to business firms or large corporations as a whole. But is it the corporation, as such, or their managers who bear responsibilities? Or perhaps, do both individuals and corporations bear responsibilities, but of different types? Arguments have been offered for and against the existence of 'corporate moral responsibility' throughout the course of a long debate that began in the late 1940s and has not yet altogether ended. These arguments are closely related to the view of the firm that one chooses to assume.[15]

Corporate moral agency

Peter French is a well-known representative of those who think that corporate organizations can be held morally responsible.[16] He argued that corporations perform actions with an intention, which can be attributed only to the organization and not to any of its members. He also points out that corporations have organizational or responsibility flow charts that delineate stations and levels within the corporate power structure, and it is possible to recognize corporate decision rules or 'corporation policies'. These elements make up what he calls a 'corporate internal decision' (CID) structure, which incorporates the acts of real (biological) persons. Thus, whatever 'power' the firm already has or might be able to generate is harnessed towards the accomplishment of its aims; the intentions and acts of various biological persons can be subordinated and synthesized – 'incorporated' – into the firm's own. French concludes that organizations can be held morally responsible for their acts.

This approach has been the target of criticism. One objection is that his picture of the corporation is oversimplified on at least two important counts. First, French assumes that the organizational chart invariably represents the real corporate decision hierarchy, which is somewhat questionable. Second, his account of the CID structure is a very narrow perspective from which to discern how corporate decisions are actually made.[17]

Individual moral responsibility

There is a second view held by those who believe it impossible to view corporations as moral agents bearing responsibility for anything. They understand that when we attribute moral judgements to a company, such judgements can be transferred to directors or managers who made the decision in question, or who are responsible for a given omission. Those who promote this view usually also hold that a corporation is no more than an aggregate of individuals – that, in itself, it is nothing, only a name (a fictitious entity).[18]

According to this outlook, official corporate goal statements might not reflect the true nature of the organization's operations; neither can we necessarily infer true goals by looking at actual operations, since we cannot isolate the organization's intent from its behaviour. The goals that determine the functions to be performed by the members are not those of an organism as a whole. Rather, they are the particular, possibly overlapping goals of those members and other individuals. Thus, one can claim that organizations have no intentions or goals at all.

Velasquez, a proponent of this second view, suggests that corporate acts do not originate in the corporations but in their members; that intention cannot be attributed to the corporations when the acts are carried out by those members. Moreover, he points out that blame and punishment are only imputable to individuals, and for this reason only individuals can be identified as moral agents.[19]

Corporations as quasi-moral agents

There is an intermediate position, which holds that there is a risk that corporate moral agency theory leaves culpable individuals unidentified and unpunished, and a doctrine of corporate moral responsibility in which blame cannot be ascribed to any individuals is indefensible.[20] But this view also agrees that the idea of corporate responsibility is both intelligible and useful.[21] In fact, common language in many ways treats corporations as single units, or agents, and not only with respect to responsibilities; for instance, 'corporate social responsibility', 'corporate values', 'corporate mission' and 'corporate identity'. In addition, many corporations survive longer than their individual members. At least, in some corporations, there are shared values and intersubjective agreements for making decisions, and it is both meaningful and useful to ascribe to organizations the capacity for conscious and intentional behaviour.[22]

Thus, there are good reasons to ascribe a certain moral responsibility to corporations. However, common sense suggests that, no matter how many arguments can be given in favour of considering a corporation as a moral agent, there are notable differences between a physical person and a corporation. Strictly speaking, only persons have rationality, self-determination and conscience, and therefore only they are moral agents and bear responsibility. The corporation can be, at most, a 'quasi-moral agent'. Considering a corporation a 'quasi-moral agent' entails accepting that there is such a thing as 'corporate intention', although not as autonomous and independent as individual intentions. 'Corporate intention' can be morally evaluated, although it is the result of actions performed by individuals and the cooperative work carried out by the firm's members.

Actions carried out by corporate members working together can be ethically evaluated as 'collective action'. However, this does not preclude also considering the responsibilities of the individual decision-makers involved in this collective action, or any other decisions on the running of the firm. Indeed, corporate responsibility falls upon the members of the board of directors, the managers and the employees, who to various degrees participate in the pursuit of corporate goals and share 'corporate responsibility'.

In other words, discussing and dealing conceptually with corporate responsibilities does not entail eliminating personal responsibility in favour of the corporate variety. On the contrary, it is a challenge to assume personal responsibilities for the whole, which otherwise might be exempt from any responsibility.

CORPORATE RESPONSES TO SOCIAL DEMANDS

Corporations face social demands related to labour relations, product safety, consumer information, pollution, environmentally friendly products, global warming or any other social issue that can arise not only from media and non-governmental organizations (NGOs), but also from stakeholders or from any informal social sensibility.[23]

Non-governmental organizations

Some NGOs are now particularly active and can adopt a collaborative or a hostile attitude towards corporations. It is worth recalling that NGOs are voluntary, non-profit organizations whose goals are delivering services to those in need of relief, developmental and humanitarian aid and so on, or advocating certain social or public policies (ecology, human rights, the defence of human life, animal welfare and such). Sometimes, both goals can be integrated in one organization. NGOs are increasingly important in many societies. They are an expression of the freedom and vitality of society, and often render it a great service. However, sometimes, NGOs can behave questionably and create trouble for business. There is also a risk that they might depend on external funding agencies, a situation that can cast doubt upon their fidelity to meeting the needs of the people they purport to serve.[24]

NGOs devoted to public service generally seek to establish relationships with business firms willing to collaborate in their activities, arguing that they will be an effective channel for the corporation to act with social responsibility or corporate citizenship.[25] By contrast, NGOs whose goal is to serve as an advocate of public policies exclude such collaboration and often incite companies or governments to change their practices or introduce legislation to avoid abuses. However, there are also NGOs that show willingness to participate in dialogue and promote collaboration between companies and NGOs to achieve social goals.

Strategies of business response

A business can even perceive social issues in its environment that are not yet specific social demands, but which could develop into social demands at a future time.

Facing social demands and social issues, a business firm can adopt several strategies. In 1973, Ackerman described four basic strategies of business response that are still valid:

- *No response*: When the social environment presents specific social demands to the firm and the firm's response is to do nothing. This inactivity can exasperate those affected and the company runs the risk that social groups might undertake actions against it.
- *Reactive*: The firm defends itself, gives arguments for its performance and resists changing. If the pressure increases, the company might give in to change after a certain amount of resistance. This strategy can erode the reputation of the firm if management tries to justify the barely justifiable, or if it accepts the change and eventually has to go back and rectify the prior position. However, it might

Table 13.1   Stages in the path to corporate responsibility

Stage	Action
Defensive	The corporation denies practices, outcomes, or responsibilities.
Compliance	The corporation adopts a policy-based compliance approach as the cost of doing business.
Managerial	Corporations embed the societal issue in their core management processes.
Strategic	Corporations integrate the societal issue into their core business strategies.
Civil	Corporations promote broad industry participation in corporate responsibility.

Source: Adapted from Zadek (2004).

be the right strategy if the firm can give a convincing response to pseudo-ethical protests or demands that cannot be met for some important reason.

- *Interactive*: The firm accepts responsibility and presents a change of attitude in order to meet social demands. When the company's behaviour has been wrong, this appears to be a good strategy.

- *Proactive*: In this strategy, a business faces social issues before social demands arise. This is consistent with human excellence and a good business strategy, if you consider that it can take a long time from the moment when a company detects a social issue until the point at which it is capable of giving an effective response. Companies that do not take social issues seriously are likely to come up with a solution only when it is already too late, and will then have to face the consequences.

En route to assuming corporate social responsibilities expressed by stable policies and practices, most companies have to follow a number of stages similar to the strategies regarding individual issues. Zadek discovered that the path a corporation follows to become more socially responsible comprises five stages[26] (see Table 13.1). They range from a defensive attitude to the integration of social responsibility to a strategy to lead the action of a whole industry.

CRITICISM AND ANSWERS TO CORPORATE SOCIAL RESPONSIBILITY

Some particular corporate responsibilities can become mandatory through specific law. In practice, one can find corporate responsibilities that are required by law or by consolidated customs in some countries. In other countries, these responsibilities are strictly voluntary in the absence of any legal compulsion. In this way, one can distinguish between implicit and explicit social responsibilities:[27]

- *Implicit social responsibilities* consist of values, norms and rules assumed by corporations that are derived from the mandatory or customary requirements of their respective stakeholders.

- *Explicit social responsibilities* are proclaimed as policies and activities that a company assumes and articulates for particular social interests. They generally include corporate philanthropy, corporate community involvement and other social actions performed for or on behalf of the corporation.

Generally, there is no point regarding implicit responsibilities; however, some question whether companies should assume explicit responsibilities, and even deny that corporations might have legitimacy to act in social matters. Three main arguments are presented against CSR:

- Some argue that social problems are the exclusive responsibility of the state, and companies are not charitable institutions
- Explicit social responsibilities generate a cost that goes against shareholders' rights or could undermine the efficiency of the company in its specific activity and mission
- Critics add that social problems are too varied and complex to be tackled and managed by companies.[28]

These objections, although adequate from certain perspectives, fall short in some areas.

Social problems are, first, problems for society

Regarding the first objection, one can argue that some social problems have their origin in business activity as a secondary effect (for instance, pollution and industrial diseases). In this case, it is hard to accept that business has no responsibility for these problems, even though avoidance of them is not mandatory by law. Explicit responsibilities go further than this, and their rationale is that social problems are generated within society and that the whole of society has a responsibility to solve these problems, either by initiatives from individuals or social groups or by the state. It is not clear why social problems should be the exclusive responsibility of the state.

Certainly, in many countries the state puts considerable effort into solving social problems and providing social welfare funded by taxes. However, the welfare state has its limits and, in some countries, is in crisis; its efficiency is questioned because heavier taxes and greater bureaucracy is entailed. Apart from this, government intervention to solve social problems is detrimental to the freedom of initiative and lacks the human warmth and effectiveness of direct action by those closest to the problem. Thus, some advocate for less state intervention and more civil society action. In this sense, the state should encourage, and even subsidize, social initiatives by citizens or private institutions, including corporations.

Business, although obviously not a charitable institution, cannot blithely ignore what is going on in society and its position as a *social actor* within society. This is why, in some way, corporations should contribute, along with other social institutions and individuals, to improving social well-being to the best of their ability.

Explicit social responsibilities can be profitable

Regarding the generation of a cost that goes against shareholders' rights and interests, a number of social activities promoted by a corporation are probably profitable if chosen wisely, because of the good reputation generated by such activities. Many see CSR not a cost but, rather, as a profitable investment, and the findings of several empirical researches suggest that corporate virtue in the form of social responsibility and, to a lesser extent, environmental responsibility is likely to pay off.[29]

But, beyond the economic argument, which is often inconclusive, a company should contribute to the solution of social problems out of a sense of responsibility, and not only because of any resultant profitability.

Business contribution to social purposes does not mean the expenditure of an enormous amount of corporate resources in order to help society, not losing efficiency In most cases, a modest allocation of corporate resources to social activities neither moves the company away from its specific mission, nor decreases business efficiency. A prosperous retail chain will not go bankrupt if it devotes 1 per cent of its Christmas sales profits to providing food for countries with starving populations, especially if we consider that doing so might persuade a great number of people to make their purchases in its stores.

Actually, the debate about whether it is in an organization's best financial interests to engage in CSR has not closed.[30] This long-running dispute has now been complicated by new viewpoints. On the one hand, some suggest linking social responsibility to core business objectives in order to obtain strategic advantages. In this way, Porter and Kramer argue that corporate growth and social welfare do not necessarily constitute a zero-sum game.[31] On the contrary, they contend that if corporations were to analyse their opportunities for social responsibility using the same frameworks that guide their core business choices, they would discover that CSR can be very different from a cost, a constraint, or a charitable deed – it can be a potent source of innovation, competitive advantage and a social value.[32]

Companies often do not directly manage social problems

Regarding the third objection, companies rarely tackle social problems directly. In many cases, they do not have the required specific capabilities. In general, it is not the point that business should become involved in managing social problems. In the previous example, it does not make sense for the retail chain to organize the distribution of the 1 per cent of sales profits to needy countries. However, in some cases, corporations have both the resources and the people with appropriate skills for solving specific problems.[33]

Regarding the fact that social problems are indeed highly varied and complex, there is no objection to businesses not becoming involved. However, this does not mean that companies should ignore these problems. The best thing would be to pick out a few situations to which to contribute effort and leave the remainder for others to deal with. Companies will need to seek good advice and act on the basis of objective criteria, avoiding arbitrariness. The direction to be taken should not be determined by the tastes or interests of the chief executive but, rather, using criteria such as the company's capabilities, how close the problem is in relation to the company's activities, the benefits to the company in the long run, the amount of attention the problem receives from other institutions, and the urgency of a specific social need that the company is in a position to resolve.

CORPORATE RESPONSIBILITY: MAINSTREAM THEORIES

The role of business in society is complex, with many competing and overlapping theories and approaches.[34] We will summarize the particularly relevant ones: corporate social performance, corporate stakeholder responsibility, strategic corporate social responsibility and corporate citizenship.[35]

Corporate social performance

The origin of the concept of corporate social performance (CSP) goes back to the 1970s, and even earlier. Starting in the 1960s, a wave of protests against big business made it clear that a new approach to the responsibility of business in society was needed: the old one was proving too abstract and vague. This period was marked by loud outcries against abuses in product information and safety, protests against racial discrimination, demands for protection of workers' health, angry public reactions against certain business practices and the use of bribery in foreign countries, and dramatic industrial accidents[36] that many people thought could have been avoided. There was also a fair amount of criticism of capitalism as a whole, and of corporate executives in particular.

Companies were pressured to respond to the specific social problems of the day. Accordingly, Ackerman and others suggested that the notion of 'corporate social responsibility' should be replaced with 'corporate social responsiveness', which was intended to convey the idea of a rapid corporate response to specific societal demands.[37] For example, if a company received a few complaints about the safety of a particular product, it would have to respond by immediately investigating the matter, finding out what could be done to make the product safer, and determining how to prevent any further complaints of the same nature. Companies would therefore need to have an organized process for responding to complaints and social pressure. They would also have to be proactive and try to anticipate complaints so that measures could be taken to prevent them.

The screening of social issues related to business and the corresponding corporate responsiveness was incorporated into business practices, not as a substitute for CSR, which offers general principles, but as a complement to this concept. Thus, the notion of corporate social performance appeared as a synthesis of three elements[38] defined by Wood as follows:[39]

- *Principles of social responsibility.* These are expressed on the institutional, organizational and individual levels through three principles. (1) The 'institutional principle' is also called 'the principle of legitimacy' because it concerns the legitimacy of business. (2) The 'organizational principle' refers to how the involvement of the firm in its social environment is to be carried out. (3) The 'individual principle' considers managerial discretion within every domain of CSR.

- *Processes of corporate social responsiveness.* These are the processes in which social issues are analysed, the environment is screened and assessed, and guidelines for stakeholder management are provided.

- *Outcomes of corporate behaviour.* These are relevant in terms of evaluating social impact, and formulating and implementing social policies and programmes.

In Wood's model, these principles are based on social expectations and demands, and even on orientations suggested by public policy. This is problematic for a number of reasons. First, in a pluralistic society one finds different expectations of business, some of which might be contradictory. Second, in a global context, social expectations change from country to country or region to region. Third, although society demands influence on business, business also, up to a point, has a certain capacity to change its environment; this is precisely why society cherishes certain expectations of business. Fourth, in some countries, social expectations and demands fall short of commonly accepted ethical standards (safe working conditions, pollution, corruption, female equality, work and family balance, minority rights and so on). To overcome such failings, these principles of corporate social responsibility should be built upon a foundation of ethics. We will return to this point in the next chapter (pp. 325–7).

Corporate stakeholder responsibility

Some advocates of the stakeholder view of the firm[40] prefer to consider 'corporate stakeholder responsibilities' rather than CSR. This concept stresses that corporate responsibilities are not generically due to 'society' but, rather, to stakeholders: firms are therefore to create economic, social and ecological value for all the firm's constituencies.

This approach posits the problem of conflicting responsibilities among stakeholders. To solve this problem, one must apply justifiable moral principles and not an arbitrary balance of stakeholder demands.[41]

This approach avoids the conceptual abstraction of CSR by addressing specific interests and practices, and by visualizing responsibilities to each group of people affected by business activity.[42] In practice, such a view of the responsibility of business in society is accepted in many companies.[43]

Stakeholder engagement refers to practices that the organization undertakes to involve stakeholders in its activities in a positive manner. Although such practices might have different aims, they generally involve the responsibility of the firm towards its constituencies (employees, shareholders, customers and so on). This occurs when stakeholder engagement respects the legitimate interests of stakeholders in accordance with moral principles.[44]

Although corporate stakeholder responsibility has some strong points, some complain that the concept of stakeholders does not adequately expresses the complex social, economic and organizational realities managers face.[45] Another criticism is more philosophical, and concerns the purpose of business in society, as we have discussed in a previous chapter.[46]

Besides, the stakeholder responsibility approach has been accused of being a risk for managerial opportunism. As managers enjoy wide discretion on how to serve stakeholder interests, an unscrupulous manager can appeal to such interests while actually seeking selfish advantage.[47] However, managerial opportunism is doubtless a problem, but not one that appears exclusively when the stakeholder approach is employed. Besides, it could happen that stakeholder groups, under certain conditions, will help maintain managerial accountability.[48]

Strategic corporate social responsibility

Those who are in line with Friedman's view,[49] that business firms have no other social responsibility beyond their function to generate wealth, often recognize that there exist today increasing internal and external pressures on business organizations to fulfil broader social goals.[50] Ignoring them can be risky for profits, while considering them can, to a certain degree, bring about bolstering the organization's public image, being in alignment with industry or community expectations, providing a source of motivation for employees, or even achieving marketing advantage or other direct economic impacts.[51]

Considering that a positive correlation between CSR and financial performance might exist, those in line with Friedman's position accept corporate social responsibility if, and only if, it contributes to the bottom line (even if only in the long term). Along these lines, the concept of *strategic corporate social responsibility* (SCSR) has been introduced. This is defined as 'policies, programmes and processes that yield substantial business-related benefits to the firm, in particular by supporting core business activities and thus contributing to the firm's effectiveness in accomplishing its mission'.[52]

Following the model, CSR can be considered through a supply-and-demand lens that permits the determination of an 'ideal' level of CSR in each situation by cost–benefit analysis, with equilibrium between CSR costs and the financial performance obtained. This level depends on several factors, such as the size, amount of diversification, research and development, advertising, government, sales, consumer income, labour market conditions and the stage in the industry lifecycle.[53]

This approach overcomes a narrow view of business excluding any social goal; however, it reduces CSR to a simple business instrument. Apart from this, it might in practice prove quite unreliable for evaluating the correlation between long-term profits and the ideal level of CSR.

Corporate citizenship

The term *corporate citizenship* (CC) was introduced in the 1980s, or even earlier, mainly through practitioners, to indicate philanthropic corporate practices and the concern of business for the community in which it operated. In the 1990s, this concept attracted positive business attention and grew more and more popular. This was due, at least in part, to certain factors that have transformed the relationship between business and society, such as globalization, the crisis of the welfare state and the power of large multinational companies.

Currently, the notion of CC, although it is often taken to be synonymous with CSR, has taken on a wider scope. It refers to the corporation's role in society and its impact on its stakeholders. Some authors point out that corporate citizenship involves building good relationships with stakeholders, and that such citizenship is the very same thing as doing business well.[54] Others emphasize that CC entails respect for and promotion of universal human rights.[55]

Facing globalization challenges, 34 CEOs of the world's largest multinational corporations signed a document during the 2002 World Economic Forum in New York: 'Global Corporate Citizenship – the Leadership Challenge for CEOs and Boards'. They gave the following definition, which is still used by the World Economic Forum: 'Corporate citizenship is about the contribution a company makes to society through its core business activities, its social investment and philanthropy programs, and its engagement in public policy.'[56]

This definition highlights this broader scope not only by including 'engagement in public policy', but also by adding 'the manner in which a company manages its economic, social and environmental relationships, as well as those with different stakeholders, in particular shareholders, employees, customers, business partners, governments and communities determines its impact'.[57]

Corporate citizenship is a notion that, at least in a certain interpretation, is consistent with the approach followed in earlier chapters regarding the business firm and its purpose in society. We will consider this concept again in the next chapter.

SUSTAINABLE DEVELOPMENT AND THE TRIPLE BOTTOM LINE

Moving beyond theories to practice, an increasing number of companies are taking note of a concept that has been broadly disseminated during the past two decades: *sustainability* and *sustainable development*. This notion initially arose from a growing concern about pollution, the accelerating deterioration of natural resources and other threats to the planet. With this concern in mind, together with its consequences for economic and social development, the United Nations created the World Commission on Environment and Development (WCED) in 1983. One of its documents (the Brundtland Commission Report)[58] contended that a sustainable development is one that 'meets the needs of the present without compromising the ability of future generations to meet their own needs'.

Sustainable development later acquired a wider meaning, including aspects regarding people and the social environment, looking to future generations. Thus, the concept of sustainability provides a new perspective, since its focus is on the consequences of human actions, including business actions, for the human and natural environments, now and in the future. This idea was applied to business corporations. A sustainable corporation integrates economic, environmental and social criteria into its strategy and management. While it recognizes that corporate growth and profitability are important, it also requires the corporation to pursue societal goals, specifically those related to sustainable development – environmental protection, social justice and equity, and economic development. Corporate sustainability includes strategies and practices seeking to protect, support and enhance both human and natural resources, balancing both current and future needs.

Related to sustainability, the notion of a 'triple bottom line' (TBL) was introduced by Elkington. According to this author,[59] there are three aspects that are actually relevant to evaluate a company's performance: (1) the economic; (2) the environmental; and (3) the social – or, as some prefer, a complete business performance appraisal has to include what are succinctly described as the triple 'P' of 'People, Planet and Profits'. In practice, the TBL refers to 'economic prosperity', 'environmental quality' and 'social justice':

- *Economic prosperity.* Generally speaking, this is understood as meaning profits for shareholders. Economic prosperity means profits for the entire host society and therefore includes the economic impact of a business activity on its environment. This comprises the employees' learning in terms of skills, experience and knowledge acquired through working for a firm.

- *Environmental quality.* Refers to the use of raw materials, renewable and non-renewable resources, ecologically destructive practices, conservation and the use of energy, pollution in all its forms caused by business activity, waste produced and its eventual disposal, along with other issues related to environmental sustainability.

- *Social justice.* This is related to people affected by business activity. Social justice concerns employees' needs and rights, including health, safety and opportunities for training and development within the company, participation of employees in business activities and the fostering of an entrepreneurial culture. Social justice also includes community involvement of a business and any business activity in favour of its social environment.

The notion of the triple bottom line is becoming increasingly popular, especially for large companies, but also for others whose activity is subject to strict social scrutiny. One way to make the implementation of this concept practical is through accountability reports that consider people, planet and profits, particularly the Global Reporting Initiative (GRI) (see p. 315), which is closely connected with the TBL. However, the TBL has also been criticized on grounds such as an alleged lack of theoretical rigour and effective audit assurance.[60] In spite of its limitations, the TBL has been achieving positive results, such as 'bringing into the public domain certain corporate information that, for the most part, might otherwise remain private. The apparent success of TBL so far strongly indicates that this enhanced flow of corporate information is in the public demand'.[61]

Insight 13:

Can business alleviate poverty?

Nearly 4 billion people live on less than US$2 a day, out of which 1.1 billion people exist on less than US$1 a day. These people, mostly living in developing countries, represent about 60 per cent of the world's population. They are the poorest socio-economic group in the world, so they constitute what is called the 'Base of the Pyramid' (BoP). Most of them encounter serious barriers to entry into business organizations and their incomes do not permit access to products that are common in developed countries and even basic to satisfying certain human needs. Causes of this problem are complex and the solution needs the convergence of several social actors. But, the question that arises is whether these people are irremediably condemned to live in such situations of poverty, without a minimum standard of living and well-being. Another question is what business can do to alleviate poverty.

There are a number of initiatives undertaken in recent years with positive results. Probably the best known is the *microcredit*, started by Muhammad Yunus, who was awarded the Nobel Peace Prize in 2006 for introducing the concept, and his Grameen Bank.[62] The poorer population, who were previously bypassed by the mainstream financial services providers, can now have access to microcredits to develop small but profitable businesses. In its early stages, the microcredit was provided by NGOs but, more recently, for-profit financial institutions are also offering microfinance products.[63]

Providing products for the BoP with sustainable profits is a challenge in many industries. Some authors believe that companies can have a potential market at the BoP while simultaneously helping to eradicate poverty.[64] Others are not optimistic about the profitability of the BoP for multinationals. Instead, they suggest that the private sector can play a key role in poverty alleviation by seeing the poor as producers rather than consumers, and buying from them.[65]

An example of the first view is an alternative very cheap home PC developed in India, where conventional PCs are too expensive. The Nova NetPC, created by Indian firm Novatium, has only very basic hardware. It includes a keyboard, a monitor and four USB ports, and uses a central network server to run software applications and store data. The Nova NetPC user package is available for US$50, while US$75 extra has to be paid for the monitor, although a TV monitor can also be used. Its monthly subscription has been priced at US$10, including 30 hours Internet access.[66] This case, and many others, makes clear the opinion that India is a source of innovation, precisely for focusing on the BoP.[67]

Other alternatives have been proposed. One is joining the efforts of non-profit institutions and business. Another is creating partnerships between companies and income-poor communities in developing countries to co-create business and markets that mutually benefit the companies and the communities. Thus, in 2006, Solae, a subsidiary of Dupont, launched 'The Base of Pyramid Protocol' in India to address the issue of malnutrition and food security. They sold fresh food, prepared using locally sourced ingredients and cooked by an 'outreach team' skilled in culinary arts and nutrition.[68]

CORPORATE ACCOUNTABILITY

Accountability refers to giving explanations and justifications for one's activity to those who have expectations or rights related to it.[69] More accurately, the Institute of Social and Ethical Accountability elucidates: 'to account for something is to explain or justify the acts, omissions and risks and dependencies for which one is responsible to people with a legitimate interest'.[70]

The oldest understanding of corporate accountability is that a company must render an account of its activities to its shareholders by means of an annual financial report. This includes three key financial statements (the balance sheet, the income statement and the statement of cash flow), which are audited by certified public accountants. However, such a document has important limitations as an accountability mechanism. One of these is the lack of certain economic information (concerning, for example, intangible assets, intellectual capital and forward-looking information). Another shortcoming has to do not merely with the economic, but also with the human, social and environmental aspects of the company's performance. It might previously have been assumed that shareholders are only interested in financial results, but an increasing number of investors want to know how those results were attained. In other words, they would like to know more about corporate conduct in terms of ethical, social and environmental responsibilities.

Apart from shareholders, other stakeholders – namely, employees, customers, suppliers and the local community – also have expectations, and even a legitimate interest in knowing about corporate activities that affect them, in some cases in the most crucial aspects of their lives. Thus, corporate accountability should be wider, extending beyond shareholders. Considering this increasingly common perspective, corporate accountability can be defined as 'the continuous, systematic, and public communication of information and reasons designed to justify an organization's decisions, actions, and outputs to various stakeholders'.[71]

In the context of sustainable development, the idea was introduced that corporations must be held accountable not only for financial results, but also for social and environmental matters. This was articulated under the aforementioned (p. 312) 'triple bottom line' accounting, which requires presenting financial, social and environmental reports.

Many companies issue annual sustainability reports. These were initially focused exclusively on the environment, but many companies are now enlarging their reports to include social issues. This is a significant expression of what is known as corporate accountability.

Corporate accountability reports can help to build a reputation, as can the existence of certification of responsible and ethical corporate behaviours, and reputation generates trust.[72]

We will now briefly review three significant proposals on corporate reporting and certification. Corporate reputation is considered a spontaneous and efficient mechanism of social control, pushing companies to act in accordance with public requirements. Corporate reputation can facilitate entry into a new market, cooperation among firms and with public and private institutions, and can confer competitive advantages.

AUDITING AND REPORTING ON CSR AND SUSTAINABILITY

Social accounting, auditing and reporting are closely related to corporate accountability regarding CSR and sustainability. Organizations undergo an audit, sometimes to obtain a certification of being socially responsible or sustainable, or to write a report. In this way, corporations make themselves accountable to their stakeholders and usually commit themselves to following the audit's recommendations.

SA 8000 certification

This was launched by the Council on Economic Priorities with the goal of improving working conditions. Based on the principles of the thirteenth International Human Rights Convention, it is used to audit companies and contractors alike in multiple industries and countries. It is available to any organization of any size, in any industry, anywhere in the world. The auditing of factory compliance is carried out by an independent verification system. This certification offers companies the opportunity to demonstrate to stakeholders that working conditions within the company itself, or the firms included in the supply chain, meet the standards included in SA 8000. These standards focus on child labour, forced labour, health and safety, freedom of association and the right to collective bargaining, discrimination, disciplinary practices, working hours and compensation, and management systems.

Global Reporting Initiative (GRI)

The Global Reporting Initiative (GRI) is probably the most popular method for accountability reporting worldwide. It is not limited to large corporations. In fact, it is applicable to small companies, large multinationals, public sector firms, NGOs and other types of organizations. The first version of GRI was launched in 2000 by the Coalition for Environmentally Responsible Economies (CERES) and the Tellus Institute, with the support of the United Nations Environment Programme. Since then, other revisions have been published.

The GRI includes a conceptual framework composed of principles for the development of reports, characteristics and indicators for the disclosure of the economic, environmental and social performance of a company. These three aspects constitute its sustainability performance. This is why the GRI is essentially a sustainability report.

The principles of transparency and stakeholder inclusiveness are the starting point for the preparation of a sustainability report and provide the context within which all its other principles belong. Other principles define the report's content and quality, and give guidance on how to set its boundaries. One of the strengths of GRI is that it provides comparability and timeliness. This constitutes, to some extent, an improvement on corporate reports on social and environmental accountability in which only favourable items are described, and which make comparisons with other companies in the industry more problematic.

The AA1000 standard

AccountAbility 1000 is a framework and guide aimed principally at improving accountability, auditing, and ethical and social reporting. It is a standard of processes, not a substantive performance standard. It specifies those processes that an organization should follow by means of stakeholder engagement and dialogue. It proposes indicators, goals and communication systems, as well as ways of linking social and ethical issues with companies' strategic and operational management. AA1000 was first presented in 1999 by the Institute for Social and Ethical Accountability (ISEA), based in the United Kingdom, and has been adopted by companies in and outside of Europe. Its main strength is a broad engagement with stakeholders, which can create an image of concern for them. One weakness of AA1000 might be its lack of substantive ethical standards. Another is its implementation, which can be complicated and costly.

Business ethics in practice 13:

United Laboratories – From *Bayanihan* culture to CSR

United Laboratories (Unilab) is one of the Philippines' flagship companies. It employs over 3,000 people, providing them and their families with different kinds of benefits, such as hospitalization fees, training, educational benefits, material compensation and different kinds of family assistance. Furthermore, it enjoys a leading presence in Asia and many of its products have become top brands in Indonesia, Thailand, Malaysia, Singapore, Hong Kong, Vietnam and Myanmar.

United Laboratories had its beginnings in a small corner shop in downtown Manila. It was founded by José Y. Campos, shortly after the Second World War and before the USA granted independence to the Philippines. After the Japanese occupation, the supply of drugs was very limited. Penicillin and sulfonamides (sulfas) to treat infections were brought by American soldiers and then sold on the black market. On one hand, this made the medicines available for people; on the other hand, the prices were so high that not many could afford to buy the medicines. Thus, the delivery of good quality medicines to the Philippine poor was, from the very beginning, one of the main purposes of Unilab. Campos met an American soldier, Robert Horowitz, who had had a pharmacy before the war. Shortly afterwards, they jointly set up 'United Drug', where Horowitz was in charge of the production and Campos handled the marketing and distribution.

Campos stamped the company with a strong business philosophy inspired in indigenous Philippine values, mainly by the concept of *Bayanihan*, enriched with the Christian-Catholic Faith by Unilab's founder. *Bayanihan* means *heroic cooperation* and can be interpreted as *working together towards*

Business ethics in practice 13: (cont'd)

the common goal, in terms of fullest economical, social, cultural and spiritual development.

Bayanihan leads to hard work, and every individual is aware that he or she is carrying his or her own share of the whole burden and, if one fails, it results in a proportionate increase in the weight upon others. *Bayanihan* also emphasizes individual development, and requires providing the conditions for people to express their talents.

Unilab's credo, which includes the *Bayanihan* concept in its first point, was formulated as follows:

We believe that we are UNITED IN THOUGHT AND ACTION, and from this
we derive our strength and our spirit of *Bayanihan.*

We believe in the NOBILITY OF OUR PURPOSE – In the service of medicine,
for the welfare of our people.

We believe that INTEGRITY IS LIFE TO US, and to preserve it we must maintain ethical standards of the highest order.

We believe that TRUTH IS OUR CHALLENGE, and our search for truth is our
contribution to the advancement of medical science.

We believe in EQUALITY AND JUSTICE FOR ALL; that our greatest asset is our
human asset, whose endeavors must be given meaning and dignity.

We believe in the DIVINE PROVIDENCE, whose love has sustained us, whose
blessing give fulfillment to our lives.

The company took an early decision to serve the country's poor and young population and be aware of its corporate social responsibilities. After the Second World War, when the Philippines was experiencing very bad economic conditions, social pricing policy forced Unilab to sell most of their products at 20–60 per cent below their competitors' prices.

Unilab management policy regards its employees as the first managerial obligation. This follows the founding ideas of Campos, who used to say: 'take care of your people and the people will take care of the customer'. The company also understands that it should serve the entire Philippine society, addressing the therapeutic and nutritional needs of the country's poor population, and giving good service to the medical profession; for example, by sponsoring medical education for medical professionals. Apart from this, Unilab has been helpful to the victims of several floods and typhoons in the Philippines.

Unilab has received various international and national awards, such as Best Employers in Asia from Hewitt Associates and Dow Jones on two occasions, and Marketing Company of the Year by the Philippines Marketing Association, or Most Outstanding Employer of the Year by the Personnel Management Association of the Philippines. In May 2006, José Campos was honoured by the Philippine Medical Association as the 'Father of the Philippine Pharmaceutical Industry'.

Questions:

1. What strengths and weaknesses can you see in the Unilab corporate philosophy?

2. How is it possible to make medicine 'accessible to the poor', selling at a price 20–60 per cent below their competitors' prices and still be profitable?

3. According to the information provided here, can Unilab be considered a responsible company?

Sources: R. G. Ibanez, 'Bayanihan: The Many Great Lessons of United Laboratories, Inc.' (Anvil Publishing: Pasig, Filipinos, 2002); S. G. Quito, More Profiles of Generics Manufacturers, Manila Times: http://www.manilatimes.net/national/2008/feb/04/yehey/top_stories/20080204top6.html; United Laboratories website: http://www.unilab.com.ph/about/bayanihan_symbol_of_ul.asp; V. T. Villegas, 'The Cultural Basis of the Good Company, Corporate Social Responsibility from a Filipino Christian Perspective', http://www.stthomas.edu/cathstudies/cst/conferences/thegoodcompany/Finalpapers/Villegas%20Final%20paper.pdf

Dilemma 13

A multinational company based in Europe planned an important investment to build a shipyard in a developing country in Africa, where wages were significantly lower than in Europe. In the chosen town, they found a plot that was not excessively large but was still sufficient for the purpose of the company. Around the site they chose was a densely populated town. In this town, as well as the rest of the country, there was a high degree of underemployment. So, the tentative announcement to build a new shipyard was very well received.

The local government would facilitate the supply of all licences and a majority of the population welcomed this new business. However, a significant portion of the people, especially the neighbourhood close to the land where the shipyard would be built, expressed great concern. They were concerned about the noise, traffic congestion and other environmental inconveniences. There were no legal prohibitions regarding the project and it does not seem too easy to find another site with the required technical and economic conditions.

Questions:

1. What stakeholders are relevant in this project? What would be its positive and negative impact on each of them?

2. How do you evaluate this project in terms of the social responsibility of business?

3. What would you recommend to those who have responsibility for making a decision about this project?

Summary

In the past few decades, a great debate has raged about whether or not business has responsibility for its social impact, beyond its creation of wealth. While some contend that the only social responsibly of business is to create value for shareholders, others maintain that business has a responsibility for its social and environmental impact.

Many companies adopted CSR through several stages, from a reactive position to understanding that CSR is strategic and even to promoting corporate responsibility in the industry.

Corporate responsibility can be understood in an analogical manner, although this does not entail eliminating individual moral responsibility, which always has a person as its subject.

Today, many agree that businesses should incorporate aspects of social responsibility, which more than likely have a positive influence on the long-term profitability of business.

Implicit social responsibilities consist of values, norms and rules assumed by a corporation, derived from mandatory or customary duties towards their respective stakeholders, while *explicit social responsibilities* are proclaimed as policies and activities that a company assumes and articulates for the sake of certain social interests. The latter generally include corporate philanthropy, corporate community involvement and other social actions performed for or on behalf of the corporation.

Objections to corporate social responsibility can be refuted by pointing to business as a social reality, part of society and not an isolated economic institution.

Several theories on the social responsibility of business have emerged. The following are particularly relevant: (1) corporate social performance; (2) corporate stakeholder responsibility; (3) strategic corporate social responsibility; and (4) corporate citizenship.

Several companies have found manners to alleviate poverty through business actions.

Sustainable development is an increasingly popular concept that aims to meet society's present needs without compromising the ability of future generations to meet their own. Appling this to business means that corporations need to be held accountable not only for financial results, but also for social and environmental ones.

The triple bottom line gives three criteria for corporate accountability: (1) financial; (2) environmental; and (3) social (profits, planet and people). The global reporting initiative (GRI) is the most popular method for accountability reporting worldwide.

Corporate accountability, which is related to corporate reputation, provides continuous, systematic and public communication of information of business activity to society and, in particular, to the various stakeholders.

Business, labour and civil society organizations have distinct skills and resources that are vital in helping to build a more robust global community.[1]

Kofi A. Annan (1938–)
Seventh Secretary-General of the United Nations, Nobel Prize in 2001.

Chapter Aims

This chapter will allow you to:

- become more familiar with the current meaning and conceptual foundations of 'corporate citizenship'
- know how to order corporate social responsibilities
- discuss ethical principles for responsibilities in corporate citizenship
- distinguish between primary, secondary and tertiary responsibilities of business in society and to gain an understanding about them
- consider corporation–government relationships and some related ethical issues
- reflect on how a corporate citizen deals with closing plant and outsourcing
- gain an understanding of leading with a sense of corporate citizenship.

Key terms:

Civic rights	External responsibilities	Political rights
Closing plants	Globalization	Primary responsibilities
Concentric circles of respon-	Lobbying	Secondary responsibilities
sibilities	Outsourcing	Social rights
Corporate citizenship	Political contributions	Tertiary responsibilities

Corporate Citizenship

INTRODUCTORY CASE 14:

SHELL'S BRENT SPAR BUOY AFFAIR – WHAT LESSONS CAN WE LEARN?

Brent Spar was an oil storage and tanker-loading buoy in the Brent oilfield to the east of Scotland operated by Royal Dutch Shell. It became an issue of public concern in 1995, when, 20 years after the opening of Brent Spar, Shell decided to take it out of use and to dispose of it. This was not easy. Brent Spar had a total weight of 14,500 tonnes and measured 137 metres from top to bottom, 109 metres of which were under water. The main body had a diameter of 29 metres; the main storage area was divided into six tanks with a total storage capacity of 300,000 barrels of oil.

Different projects were examined, but finally the favoured option was that of detonating explosives and sinking Brent Spar to a depth of 2.5 km, 250 km from the west coast of Scotland. Shell UK maintained that deep-sea disposal was the cheapest option available. The company estimated that sea disposal would cost $7.4 million compared with $28 million for land disposal. The British government publicly supported Shell's disposal plans.

Soon, Greenpeace, a well-known environmentalist NGO, launched a campaign to alert public opinion to the dangers of dumping the Brent Spar, arguing that the Brent Spar still contained a considerable amount of toxic waste that could endanger deep-sea wildlife. Moreover, if the buoy were dumped at sea, it would crush some deep-sea inhabitants when it hit the bottom. Additionally, Greenpeace publicized the existence of more than 200 platforms in the North Sea that were to be decommissioned, warning of the possibility that the seabed might soon become a graveyard of obsolete oil platforms.

In short, the environmentalists' concerns addressed two distinct areas. First, there were the immediate effects of sea disposal. Sociologist Brian Wynne has called these 'first-order risks' – impacts measurable and describable by science. Then came the wider social implications, or 'second-order risks', and many questions that went beyond science, such as whether Brent Spar would set a precedent for other structures and substances, or whether or not we can we trust a case-by-case approach to prevent cumulative damage. Shell consistently maintained that its preferred option of disposal was deep-sea. With a few notable exceptions, such as the *New Scientist*, most scientists commenting since the event have agreed.

On 30 April Greenpeace activists aboard an inflatable dinghy launched anti-Brent Spar action. They doubted the figures published by the multinational. Greenpeace claimed that there were still 5,500 metric tonnes of oil on board, 100 times the amount quoted by Shell. Greenpeace won support for its views among the general public and gained followers in different European countries. Its campaign portrayed Shell, the world's largest private oil company, as being interested only in profit.

Shell, on its part, tried to bring the occupation of the activists aboard the platform to a legal end. On 18 May, it applied to the Edinburgh Court of Session for a warrant to remove approximately a dozen Greenpeace activists from the installation. However, the judge granted a warrant to remove only one man, Jonathan Castle, since warrants could only be granted against named people, and the court did not know the other activists' names.

Despite this, on 11 June Shell started towing the Brent Spar into the Atlantic Ocean to the deep-water disposal site. In response, Greenpeace started a campaign to mobilize public opinion and establish an effective boycott of Shell gasoline stations. In addition, some Shell stations fell victim to violent actions. That very same day, two Greenpeace activists landed on the Brent Spar by helicopter.

On 15 June, Shell's shares fell seven points on the London Stock Exchange. On 17 June, environmental groups picketed Shell gasoline stations in the UK. Hundreds of thousands of Europeans, especially in Central and Northern Europe, had started a boycott of Shell products. In Denmark and Germany, gasoline sales had fallen by almost half in one week and, in Sweden, some companies had cancelled their oil supply arrangements with Shell. All of these actions had economic consequences, which saw a sharp fall in sales of up to 50 per cent. In Germany alone, the company lost the equivalent of $11 million.

Political parties of all persuasions took a stand on the issue, even though the company's decision had the approval of the British government. The Social Democrats (SDP) called for an extraordinary session of the Federal Parliament (Bundestag) to debate the future of obsolete oil platforms. Meanwhile, in the UK, John Major and his Conservative Party supported the legality of the deep-sea disposal plan, and insisted that it was the best environmental solution available.

Shell reacted by taking the decision to stop the operation to sink the buoy and announcing that they would study possible options for the disposal of the platform. The Norwegian government agreed to store the buoy provisionally in the Norwegian Cove Erfjord. Another decision of Shell top management was to commission an independent audit of the Brent Spar's contents and to investigate Greenpeace's allegations. This was charged to the Norwegian foundation Det Norske Veritas (DNV).

Greenpeace admitted that it had given incorrect information, and apologized to Shell on 5 September, admitting that there had been miscalculations in the amount of oil claimed to be remaining in the Brent Spar, since their tests were only done in some and not all of the tanks. On 18 October, the DNV presented the results. Of the 5,500 metric tons of oil that Greenpeace claimed the Brent Spar contained, only 74–132 metric tonnes were actually present. There were 56 Tm of metals, and not the 100 Tm alleged by Greenpeace.

Then, Shell organized a competition for possible alternatives. About 400 proposals were submitted to dismantle the platform without sinking it. Finally, Shell consulted some 20 to 30 companies on what to do with the platform, after which it would shortlist six for a final offer. Some of the proposals proposed transforming the platform into a hotel or a floating Casino. Others suggested transforming it into an artificial reef or a marine farm. Nevertheless, the most feasible proposals were the engineering proposals for its dismantling. Although Greenpeace stood by any solution other than the sinking of the Brent Spar, the company insisted that it was the best alternative and that it was the only option approved by the British government, which would have to approve any other new proposal considered.

In March 1996, Shell set up a website to inform and to initiate a debate about the future of the Brent Spar. In October 1997, a series of sessions was conducted between the representatives of the petrol industry and environmental organizations to discuss the solution. Finally, on 29 January 1998, Shell announced its plans to convert the Brent Spar into a port for ferry vessels in Norway. A proposal was accepted by the British government and finally took effect on 10 July 1999.

Questions:

1. Do you think the decision of Shell about the deep-sea disposal of the Brent Spar buoy was correct?

2. What is your judgment about Greenpeace's behaviour?

3. Did Shell act with a sense of responsibility?

Sources: Abridged case study 'Shell's "Brent Spar" Loading Buoy (A)', authored by D. Melé and L. Jardí (Barcelona: IESE Publishing, 1997). Published with permission. It has been extended from the following sources: Shell website: www.shell.com/brentspar/ *Environment Health Perspectives:* www.ehponline. org/docs/1995/103-9/forum.html; Greenpeace: http://www.archive.greenpeace.org/odumping/hazardous/ reports/submission.html; and http://www.archive.greenpeace.org/comms/toxics/dumping/jun20.html; *Global Environmental Change,* June (1992): 111; *Multinational Monitor,* www.multinationalmonitor.org/hyper/ mm0795.03.html; *New Scientist,* www.newscientist.com/article/mg15721246.900-forum–in-deep-water—- brent-spar-may-have-found-a-home-but-the-dumping-debate-continues-says-mark-huxham.html; Wikipedia (Brent Spar/Criticism to Greenpeace).

CORPORATE CITIZENSHIP IN THE GLOBAL CONTEXT

The term *citizenship*, taken from political science, is at the core of the notion of *corporate citizenship*. The notion of citizen evokes individual duties and rights within a political community. Obviously, business firms are citizens in the same way as individuals.[2] However, the term also contains the more general idea of being part of a community.

Taking corporate citizenship as an analogy makes sense, at least within the Aristotelian tradition, in which business firms can be seen as an integral part of the society. In this tradition, the key concept of citizen is 'participation' rather than individual rights, as occurs in the current liberal state.

For Aristotle, being a citizen is basically to have 'the right to participate in the public life of the state, which was more in the line of a duty and a responsibility to look after the interest of the community'.[3] This can be applied to the consideration of business in society. This is a crucial point for societal business ethics. According to Solomon, 'the first principle of business ethics is that the corporation itself is a citizen, a member of the larger community and inconceivable without it... Corporations like individuals are part and parcel of the communities that created them, and the responsibilities they bear are not the products of argument or implicit contracts, but intrinsic to their very existence as social entities.'[4] In making this statement, Solomon contrasts this perspective with many models of CSR, which frequently implicitly concur with the Friedmanian assumption (see p. 300) that corporations are autonomous, independent entities, although they add the necessity to consider some responsibilities to the surrounding community. The notion of corporate citizenship is grounded in the business organization's community membership and in the interdependence of all community members.

Being a good corporate citizen, therefore, entails compliance with every fair mandatory or customary requirement towards their respective stakeholders. But, as should an individual good citizen, being a corporate citizen requires paying attention to social concerns and, to some degree, contributing to the solving of social problems within the capacities and mission of each firm.

Corporate citizenship has attained more and more a global sense. Now, societal relationships in business are not only international, but also global, since the world is, in certain respects, an interconnected and unified society. Business is immersed in the phenomenon of globalization, which describes the way in which our world now functions as a unified whole. A phenomenon caused by technological advances that make worldwide communication and transportation easy, along with socio-cultural, political and economic factors.

Although globalization is more complex, often this concept is only understood in economic terms. Economic globalization is made up by spreading technology around the world, world trade, foreign direct investment in any nation, capital flows from one country to another and migration. Globalization entails integration of businesses and national economies into a global economy. Thanks to globalization, now *the world is flat*,[5] in terms of commerce and competition and, ideally, all competitors have an equal opportunity.

Globalization permits business to undertake global trading, offshore out-sourcing and the use of supply chains.[6] This brings about new opportunities for developing countries and new ways of competition among business. In spite of the positive aspects, globalization posits ethical problems and brings about discontentment.[7] Even so, there is an anti-globalization movement that includes a great variety of ideologies. In general terms, globalization is accused of favour-ing the interests of the ruling classes and fostering situations in which interna-tional financial institutions and large multinational companies abuse their power and cause flagrant injustices.

Mainstream economists, some conservative thinkers and supporters of market-based economic integration have responded to the critics of globalization. Moral voices usually proclaim that economic globalization has to go along with glo-balization of ethics and solidarity. Others, such as the Nobel Laureate Josep T. Stiglitz, are seeking practical ways that can lead to better globalization that would be respectful to people and the environment. Global corporate citizenship applied with wisdom can be a good answer.[8]

ETHICAL PRINCIPLES FOR CORPORATE CITIZENSHIP RESPONSIBILITIES

Wood, as previously mentioned,[9] suggested that principles of social responsibil-ity can be expressed in institutional, organizational and individual principles. The following is a re-interpretation from an ethical perspective:

Principle of legitimacy (institutional principle)

In the person-centred approach,[10] legitimacy is determined by the principle that governs the whole social order, including business: the principle of the common good. Thus, what gives moral legitimacy to business is its orientation towards the common good. As noted, the common good includes respect for persons and their inalienable rights, an adequate level of social welfare and socio-economic development as material means for personal improvement, and peace, understood as the stability and security of a just social order.[11]

Business contributes to the common good through its multi-ends, and the responsibilities of business in society are related to these ends, which as previ-ously discussed,[12] are the following:

- Creating useful goods and services efficiently and fairly
- Supplying added economic value with justice and distributing it with equity
- Providing jobs, opportunities and organizational conditions in accordance with human dignity and human rights
- Promoting the necessary relationships between the firm and its constitutive stakeholders, fostering reciprocity, collaboration and cooperation among them
- Striving for the continuity and sustainability of the firm
- Being a good corporate citizen.

The principle of the common good can solve a controversy regarding the political role of business and its engagement in public policy in acting as a corporate citizen.[13] In practice, an effective social control is necessary to avoid abuses of corporations under the pretext to being corporate citizens (see Insight 14).

Principle of concentric responsibilities (organizational principle)

The institutional principle, despite being extremely important, is very general; it does not tell us exactly what the order of priority between the parties should be. Companies, as with individuals, could hardly attend to the interests of all people, or groups of people, with whom they interact or are interdependent. Frequently, this is physically impossible and, at other times, the interests of these groups are in conflict. The organizational principle, along with the managerial principle (which follows), helps us to determine an appropriate order in responsibilities.

The organizational principle is based on the idea that the responsibilities of businesses should follow a certain order. Carlos Llano, considering the individual, suggested that there are 'concentric circles of responsibilities', with the level of responsibility diminishing as we move further from the 'I' at the centre.[14] He suggests that the order should be established according to the nature of the role performed. Specifically, he proposed as a correct order: 'I' – family – company – industry – society. Applying these criteria, we can define concentric circles of corporate responsibilities, taking as the centre the person who has the maximum executive responsibility within the organization.

Some criteria can be given to establish priorities for ordering responsibilities. The first criterion is that responsibilities derive from the purpose of the firm of contributing to the common good in accordance with the specific mission of each firm and its inherent activities. In this sense, we can distinguish between *internal responsibilities* (responsibilities associated with the specific business mission) and *external responsibilities* (the responsibilities of a business in social concerns that are different from its core activities). In accordance with this first criterion, 'internal responsibility' has priority over 'external responsibilities'.

The second criterion is that a firm has greater responsibility to immediate interdependent groups of stakeholders than to other social groups without such interdependence. Interdependence between two individuals or groups generates the moral responsibility of collaborating with each other. It derives from the common good associated with the interdependence of two groups. This leads us to consider, as a priority, the legitimate demands and expectations of the primary stakeholders; that is, those stakeholders related more closely with the firm and necessary for its survival. Usually, primary stakeholders are employees, shareholders, customers, suppliers and the community.

The third criterion is that moral proximity determines priority. One has greater responsibility for those who are closer because of the 'quality' of the links in terms of depth and substance. Consider an individual: it does not, for example, seem logical to neglect one's own family responsibilities in order to look after a stranger. Similarly, a manager bears greater responsibility to care for his or her collaborators and employees than others that do not have a connection with the firm. The CEO's responsibility towards employees who have served the firm loyally for many years should also be greater than for those who have just arrived.

Principle of managerial responsibility (Individual principle)

Being universal in application, the two previous principles do not tell us exactly what should be done in any particular case. Managers should consider the common good and the right order in responsibilities with practical wisdom.[15] This means carrying out a careful deliberation on the circumstances of the case and considering the foreseeable outcomes, and seeking advice from those who can provide it. Then, the manager should judge the different alternatives wisely and choose the best. Finally, the manager should execute the decision at the appropriate time and in the appropriate manner.

Deliberation requires the obtaining of sound information. Thus, it is crucial to listen to stakeholders, as well as people inside or outside the company who can provide good advice. Stakeholders not only have explicit demands on the company, but also expectations and needs – and managers should know what these are.

A practical way to identify demands, expectations and needs is to establish a formal or informal *stakeholder dialogue,* and even engaging stakeholders in generating socially responsible policies or practices.

Some companies consider central stakeholder dialogue, although frequently they only see such dialogue as a process with which to respond to criticism regarding their social and environmental actions that has been levelled at them by NGOs, media and others groups. In practice, it seems that stakeholder dialogue has an impact on creating trust and in organizational learning.[16] But, beyond this reactive use of stakeholder dialogue, it can probably be an efficient way to manage corporate social responsibilities based on more accurate information. Stakeholder dialogue, apart from contributing to the better management of corporate citizenship, can be a source of innovative ideas.[17]

The managerial responsibility principle also refers to the responsibility of the manager to contribute to the common good (the legitimacy principle) by building enduring and mutually beneficial relationships with all relevant stakeholders, which brings about social capital[18] – the 'capital' generated by connections within and between social networks based on group membership, relationships, networks of influence and support.

CORPORATE RESPONSIBILITIES

Considering the institutional principle and the multi-ends of the firm,[19] six interrelated categories of responsibilities can be enumerated for the corporation. All of them are moral and social responsibilities, although they focus on different scopes (see Figure 14.1).

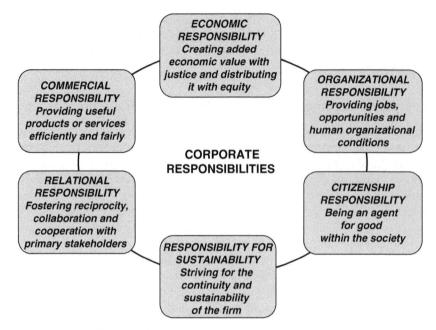

Figure 14.1   Responsibilities of the corporation

Economic responsibility

Economic responsibility is answered by creating, with justice, as much added economic value as possible, and distributing it with equity. This is the most basic corporate responsibility because, if a business fails to create sufficient economic value, the sense of other responsibilities would be lost. This responsibility requires, first, generating as much wealth as possible and sharing it fairly, with justice. The term 'as much as possible' (not maximizing) refers to the responsibility of maintaining a high level of operational efficiency and being committed, in that the firm is as profitable as possible, acting fairly and respecting the other primary responsibilities of the firm.[20] Creating wealth therefore means generating greater economic utility to make a profit now or to improve the company's capabilities so that it will make a profit in the future. Thus, creating wealth means balancing wisely, both in the short term and the long term.

Creating added economic value with justice requires acting with and promoting integrity in every business relationship. This includes respecting the human dignity and universal human rights of everybody involved in the business activity; honouring legitimate contracts and agreements; acting with honesty, fulfilling fiduciary duties towards shareholders, managing business responsibly, searching for a fair return on their investments; maintaining compliance with legality (except if it is evidently contrary to human rights or other sound ethical principles); and avoiding damage to the natural environment, including discharging effluents or waste poisonous to humans, animals or plants, and so on.

The responsibility of sharing added economic value with equity among those who have contributed to its generation, while considering the best interests of the firm as a whole, is a delicate matter of distributive justice. Sharing such wealth includes a reasonable return to shareholders, a fair remuneration to managers and employees, and a wise policy of dividends and investments. The policy concerning dividends and investments should consider future corporate requirements for the firm's continuity and for wealth creation. This is a complex matter that exceeds the limits of this book but, in any case, it requires considering all relevant factors and establishing appropriate criteria with practical wisdom.

Commercial responsibility

Commercial responsibility is shown by providing useful products or services efficiently and fairly. Efficiency leads to the production and delivery of useful and accessible products to society in accordance with the mission of the firm. This responsibility also requires the provision of products or services on fair terms with regard to quality, price and service. Products should be really useful in order to satisfy human needs and legitimate wants. Wealth creation is a consequence of providing useful products and services.

Organizational responsibility

Organizational responsibility is achieved by providing jobs, opportunities and human organizational conditions, in accordance with human dignity and human rights, which can foster the personal growth of people involved in the organization. This responsibility should be carried out in accordance with the mission of the firm and considering workers' capabilities and networks, efficient processes, innovation and consideration of each individual and his or her circumstances and professional career. Human and professional capabilities and networks shape human and social capital, making the other responsibilities possible together with efficient processes and innovation in its broader meaning. Personal growth includes both professional and human dimensions. Organizational responsibility contributes to providing better goods and services, and to the obtaining of higher profits.

Relational responsibility

Relational responsibility is demonstrated by fostering reciprocity and cooperation between the firm and its primary stakeholders (employees, shareholders, clients, customers, suppliers and community). This includes considering and trying to satisfy the legitimate interests of the constitutive stakeholders of the firm. Relationships based on collaboration and cooperation are not merely an ethical requirement; these conditions form a crucial norm for maintaining durable relationships in the future. Collaboration and cooperation with stakeholders can be a source of competitive advantage. According to Jones, 'firms that contract (through their managers) with their stakeholders on the base of mutual trust and cooperation will have a competitive advantage over firms that do not'.[21]

Citizenship responsibility

Citizenship responsibility is shown by being an agent for good within society. This responsibility includes paying taxes, complying with fair laws, avoiding negative impacts on society, and acting as a good corporate citizen in helping to solve social problems. The latter includes actions that the company undertakes, beyond the sphere of its specific activities, to improve certain aspects of its social environment (external responsibilities).

Responsibility for sustainability

This responsibility refers to the striving for the continuity of the firm, and for maintaining its sustainability. This responsibility leads to achievement in the long term in competitive conditions and in a sustainable way. It requires an appropriate strategy, good corporate governance and good management in leading the organization in such a way that the company will be able to continue to serve society in the longer term by maintaining or creating jobs where people can grow, producing more useful and more affordable products, and generating more wealth.

CONCENTRIC CIRCLES OF CORPORATE CITIZENSHIP

Applying the organizational principle previously mentioned, three circles of responsibilities can be distinguished for ordering responsibilities of a corporate citizenship: primary, secondary and tertiary (see Figure 14.2).

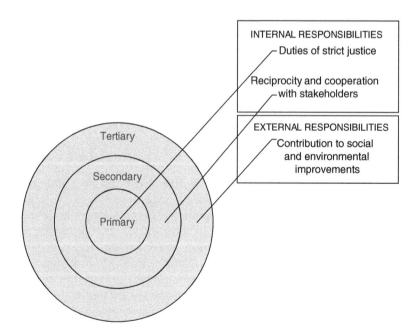

Figure 14.2   Concentric circles of corporate responsibility

Primary responsibilities

Primary responsibilities refer to the duties of strict justice towards people, including the obligation of both commutative and distributive justice. They include duties of justice related with economic, commercial organizational and citizenship responsibilities along with responsibility for sustainability. Primary responsibilities are, among many others: (1) respecting human rights; (2) honouring contracts; (3) labelling products with accurate and relevant information; (4) avoiding fraud; (5) having compliance with fair laws; (6) providing clear, honest annual reports and financial statements; (7) respecting offers that have been accepted; (8) fulfilling fiduciary duties to shareholders harmonizing with other duties; (9) not interfering unfairly in the activities of competition; and (10) avoiding damaging the local community or environment (abuse of natural resources, pollution, waste).

Secondary responsibilities

Secondary responsibilities refer to relational responsibilities of reciprocity and cooperation with the stakeholders of the firm. They are internal responsibilities, beyond contractual duties and other obligations of strict justice. They derive from existing interdependence and the intrinsic value of each group of stakeholders, and consist of improving the impact this specific activity has on the company's stakeholders beyond the bare minimum and promoting ways of cooperation with them.

Secondary responsibilities are not well specified in rules of behaviour. On the contrary, they need to be determined in each situation, taking into consideration concurrent circumstances, the legitimate stakeholder interests, social demands and the external impact of business activity. Furthermore, they require acting with creativity and being proactive.

Secondary responsibilities are, for instance: (1) giving employees the necessary training to maintain their employability; (2) keeping regular suppliers informed of developments inside the company and projects that might affect them in the future, and helping them to improve their processes; (3) responding quickly to customer complaints, inquiries, suggestions and requests; (4) maintaining an active dialogue with primary stakeholders; (5) working with competitors to improve ethics conduct in the industry; (6) helping customers to achieve a responsible consumption; and (7) contributing to the improvement of the local environment in which a company operates.

Management should try to harmonize legitimate stakeholder interests. These criteria for concentric responsibilities, accompanied by a prudent judgement, ought to be used for solving conflicting stakeholder interests.

Tertiary responsibilities

Tertiary responsibilities are a part of 'citizenship responsibility' and refer to corporate contributions to improve some aspect of society and the natural environment. They are 'external responsibilities', which, as noted, are not directly related to the company's specific activity or to its immediate stakehold-ers. (1) Hiring disabled people; (2) fostering family values; (3) promoting women's rights; (4) fighting against discrimination; (5) integrating emigrant workers and other marginalized groups; (6) supporting universities and research centres; (7) extending professional training; (8) reforestation – these are just a few of the social issues in which companies (some more so than others) can collaborate in order either to solve society's problems or to better social or environmental conditions. In doing so, they might also improve the business environment.

Companies carry out tertiary responsibilities in different ways. One is by shar-ing their accumulated experience or assigning some of their managers or employ-ees to provide advice or management expertise on social issues in which they have a special competence (new technologies, organizational methods and so on). Occasionally, companies might possess the means with which to improve the socio-cultural environment (for example, by distributing cultural products or supporting social initiatives, or even by exerting pressure to have certain laws or customs changed). Last, but not least, companies can provide economic resources to sponsor artistic, cultural and sporting events, or make donations to charity.

The borderline between tertiary responsibilities and the other two types of responsibility is not always well defined. Some activities included within tertiary responsibilities can be indirectly related to primary or secondary responsibility. For instance, hiring disabled people or giving support to a local sports club can have a positive impact on the local community and foster collaborative rela-tionships with this stakeholder (secondary responsibility). Many activities in this category can create a positive reputation for the company, providing a beneficial effect in company incomes (primary responsibilities).

CORPORATION–GOVERNMENT RELATIONSHIPS

Governments and, more specifically, the state should provide these conditions along with others such as political stability, a solid currency, efficient and fair pub-lic administration, and good public services. As noted,[22] business needs such con-ditions to operate. Business usually enjoys services from governments that favour its activity, including transportation infrastructure, police, military and juridical systems, as well as representation in international trade negotiations. In addition, education and professional training, a health care system and other services pro-vided by the state or by some social initiative can also benefit business activity.

In return, business provides tax revenues to governments and, in various ways, contributes to social stability by providing employment, and supplying products and services necessary for life. Taxes also permit the implementation of social poli-cies and a certain redistribution of wealth, which is another way of contributing to the satisfaction of basic human needs and, thus, to greater social stability.

Leaving aside the argument that many services assumed by the state could be managed more efficiently by public initiatives, with the consequent reduction in taxes, it seems clear that governments are necessary for many of the functions required by business.

Corporation–governmental relations are reciprocal – at least, in democracies. Business benefits from the political order, which sees to public needs; governments also benefit from prosperous and efficient businesses.

However, these relations can be complex, and they vary according to country or context. These relations can also present ethical challenges, especially on topics related to the regulation of business and interventions of governments in business activity.[23] Two controversial issues often treated in business ethics are business *lobbying* to influence legislators and regulators, and *business contributions to political campaigns.*

Lobbying

Business legislation and regulations are, obviously, very important for firms: regulations can constrain growth plans, limit capabilities, reduce or increase capital gain taxes, or open up new opportunities. When confronting regulators – including legislators, civil servants or politicians – businesses can exert pressure in order to defend their interests. These types of actions, termed 'lobbying', are generally carried out by organized groups of business people or representatives of an industry.[24] The phenomenon of proxy pressures by major companies has evolved and adopted different forms in different countries or supranational institutions such as the European Union.

Frequently, lobbying has a negative connotation, calling to mind corruption or abuse of power, using it to introduce amendments in regulatory proposals or to introduce new regulations favourable to business interests but contrary to the general interest of the country or the common good. However, lobbying is not necessarily unethical. There is nothing wrong with defending legitimate interests or providing information to regulators about the situation of an industry, or communicating corporate interests. Actually, each social group, including business, has better knowledge of its own interests than do others, and such knowledge might be relevant for regulators, along with the knowledge of other people's interests. Moreover, business has the same right to participate in the political process as consumers, labour unions, environmentalists and other social groups.

In practice, in many countries business lobbies are recognized and regulated by the government through certain mechanisms that provide transparency and facilitate fair play. However, specific ethical issues appear in various contexts not always covered by regulations.[25]

Political contributions

Political contributions are even more controversial than lobbying, since businesses would most probably be making financial contributions to political campaigns in order to reduce taxes or be rewarded unfairly with public contracts on the campaign's success.

Some argue that contributions to political campaigns, along with lobbying and actions of interest groups, can undermine the will of the people and even the democratic system itself.[26] In some countries, such contributions are illegal; in others, they are regulated; in yet others, they are nearly, or altogether, uncontrolled. Accountability, transparency and social control might avoid corruption in lobbying and contributions – at least, up to a certain point. Thus, the less the control, the higher the risk of corruption.

Insight 14:

Are multinational corporations supplanting the state?

Matten and Crane have suggested 'an extended view of corporate citizenship' in descriptive – non-normative – terms.[27] According to this view, corporate citizens engage in initiatives related to *social, civil* and *political rights* in situations where government ceases to administer those rights, or where governments have not yet administered them, or where the administration of citizenship rights might be beyond the reach of the nation-state government.

These authors note that there are companies, generally multinational ones, that pursue initiatives traditionally reserved to the welfare state, such as education and health care for certain populations (social rights). In some situations, other companies capacitate or constrain citizens' civil rights, which provides freedom from abuses and interferences of third parties (civic rights). A well-known case was the allegation that, in 1995, Royal Dutch Shell did nothing or even supported the Nigerian military dictatorship in its execution of the writer and environmentalist Ken Saro-Wiwa and a number of other Ogoni community members for their political organizing against Shell.[28] Some companies, on the other hand, act as conduits for the exercise of individuals' political rights. This happens, for instance, when individuals and groups pressure companies for help in facilitating their political participation in society (political rights). Thus, political action is addressed to corporations rather than governments. This might involve single-issue campaigns, anti-corporate protests, consumer boycotts and so on.

Probably this type of corporate conduct is not so common, but in playing such a role, corporations are, to some extent, supplanting functions that the liberal state had assumed. Although the state should guarantee social, civil and political rights, society as a whole, including business, is not exempt from responsibility. However, considering the clout business has, it is certainly capable of preventing the democratic participation of a population, making it impossible for them to choose appropriate political channels for the exercise of their political rights. Misunderstandings and faulty implementations of social and civic rights might ensue. In other words, if corporations are going to act according to this extended view of corporate citizenship, some means must be devised to control and hold them accountable.

Currently, some societies face the paradox that large corporations powerful enough to contribute efficiently to the solutions of significant social problems can also act against the common good. In the near future, just as governments are accountable to their citizens, and, to some degree, population controls the government through democratic mechanisms, some mechanism will need to be implemented to constrain corporations that have become engaged in public policy.

CORPORATE CITIZENSHIP FACING OUTSOURCING AND CLOSING PLANTS

A particular issue in which a good corporate citizenship is tested is outsourcing and closing plants.

Outsourcing entered into business argot in the 1980s to mean the practice of transferring production or services that could be performed by a firm – perhaps, once it had actually performed them – to an external company. In other words, outsourcing is a subcontracting process to a third party in which a product is designed or manufactured to be sold to the contracting firm.

Among the common reasons for outsourcing are cost savings, cost restructuring (by dismissing fixed costs and making variable costs more predictable), improving quality (although this is not always so), absence of the need for specific knowledge, specialization or the capacity to produce what is transferred. Outsourcing allows firms to concentrate on the core business activities they can manage more efficiently and consider more profitable.

Globalization makes offshore outsourcing possible by transferring production or services to multiple offshore locations. Typical offshore outsourcing activities include manufacturing, the manning of call centres and information technology.

Offshore outsourcing is not only a business matter, but also a public issue. Public opinion usually criticizes this practice, arguing that it damages the local labour market. Professionals become unemployed when offshore outsourcing is cheaper, other workers feel that employment is insecure, and manufacturing plants or service centres might be closed and their production moved to countries where wages are lower.

Another criticism is that offshore working conditions can be of lower standards than those at the contracting company, perhaps even sub-human. On the positive side, offshore outsourcing promotes jobs in developing countries and can lower prices and/or increase profits while creating jobs and opportunities for new investment.

Ethical problems therefore emerge regarding two groups of people: domestic and offshore workers. Regarding domestic workers, we must remember, first, that the labour market is different from other markets in that it is not only based on conditions of supply and demand. People are not a mere commodity. Second, if the firm is a community of people, and not merely an instrument for making profits, lay-offs should be carried out with criteria other than simple economics; that is, following human and ethical requirements.

Consequently, eliminating jobs or closing manufacturing plants or service centres, if necessary, should be carried out in such a way as to avoid as much suffering as possible to domestic workers and, if possible, to help the laid-off workers find new jobs. Some possible corporate actions in these circumstances might be the giving of appropriate economic compensation, facilitating outplacement, or giving a reasonable period of time before the cessation of their employment in order to give them time to find an alternative job. In any case, treatment should be appropriate to the human condition of workers, including giving relevant and true information at the proper time and equitably selecting people to be laid-off.

This can be summarized in three conditions for a just and sociable responsible termination of employee employment: (1) just cause; (2) due process; and (3) mitigation of harmful effects.[29] Similar considerations and criteria can be identified for closing plants.[30]

Workers in the offshore country are naturally entitled to respect for their human dignity and human rights. Human dignity and rights are universal and must be respected in every situation. The necessity for jobs in these countries does not permit exploitation, such as paying extremely low wages or providing sub-human work conditions.

LEADING WITH A SENSE OF CORPORATE CITIZENSHIP

As noted above, social responsibility will probably pay off. However, the debate about whether it is in an organization's best financial interest to engage in CSR is not closed.[31] This long-running dispute has now been enriched with a new viewpoint. Aguilera *et al.* have suggested that a complex set of motives can lead business firms to engage in actions of social responsibility.[32] These authors distinguish three groups of motives, which can be found at individual, organizational, national, and transnational levels:

- *Instrumental motives*: These consider the effects of social responsibility on profits, the need for fiscal control, short-term interests of shareholders and competitiveness.
- *Relational motives*: These are the need for a sense of belonging and the social cohesion derived from acting with social responsibility.
- *Moral motives*: These are related to the need for a meaningful existence, higher-order values and the intrinsic responsibility of business.

These motives are not completely independent but are, rather, interrelated. Moral motives can have an influence on relational motives, and relational motives on instrumental motives. Considered simultaneously, these three motives can explain why an increasing number of companies engage in CSR practices beyond the narrow economic, technical and legal requirements.

Traditionally, CSR has been seen as an add-on to economic activity, perhaps without any acknowledgement that business has a social dimension as well as an ethical one. When strategy and social responsibility are regarded as two disconnected activities, the social impact of the strategy will probably be neglected.

Every manager needs a clear and accurate idea of the firm's role within society and how to integrate its social role with its economic role. In line with this, two key criteria can be recommended for leading a business to act as a corporate citizen:

- *Clear vision of corporate citizenship*: This notion refers to the role of a business as a social actor participating in social concerns and contributing to the common good. This is accomplished not only through the specific activities associated with its own mission, but also through social investment and philanthropy programmes, as well as a certain amount of appropriate engagement in public policy. Thus, the concept of corporate citizenship is different from other associated concepts of corporate social responsibility, corporate philanthropy and sustainability, and is more comprehensive than any of these.

- *Full integration of corporate citizenship into the whole organization*: Corporate citizenship has to be linked to corporate values, since it has a natural connection to them. For this reason, corporate citizenship should be seen as a part of the overall strategy and corresponding structure of the organization (see Figure 14.3). It should not be the exclusive concern of a few departments charged with dealing with social issues and performing social activities. Similarly, corporate citizenship should not focus on tactics but should, instead, be a simple response to specific events, or possibly a practice tied to a particular stakeholder.

Other aspects of formal and informal organization should also be consistent with corporate citizenship. This includes leadership, and managerial systems and practices, as well as communication, motivation, stakeholder engagement and employee training. Finally, corporate citizenship should be integrated into methods of evaluation, auditing and reporting. In essence, corporate citizenship should inform the entire business organization and its corporate activity.[33]

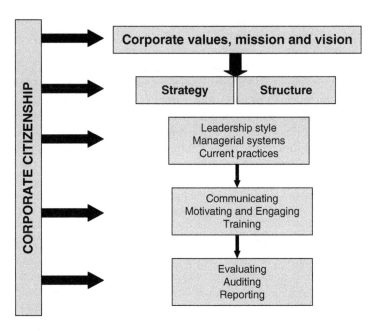

Figure 14.3   Corporate citizenship in the whole organization

---

Business ethics in practice 14:

Infosys Technologies – One of India's most admired companies

Infosys Technologies was started in 1981 by Narayana Murthy, together with six other people, with a total capital of $250. Three decades later, Infosys Technologies became a global leader in information technologies and consulting, with revenue of over $4 billion in 2008. The company is present worldwide, with offices and development centres in India, China, Australia, the Czech Republic, Poland, the United Kingdom, Canada and Japan. Infosys Technologies employs over 91,000 people.

Initially, the company had settled on a strategy of moving up the value chain by offering high-end consulting services such as system integration and technology strategy. Infosys had to compete with IBM Global Services, Accenture and the Electronic Data Systems Corporation, which were well-established companies in India. The company's founders believed that there was little opportunity to develop software for the local market, and so set their sights on the USA. However, in the 1990s Murthy decided to compete with multinationals in India as well. Later, Infosys became a strong global competitor.

Today, Infosys offers consulting services, application services, systems integration, product engineering, custom software development, maintenance and re-engineering, independent testing and validation services, IT infrastructure services and business process outsourcing. Infosys pioneered the global delivery model (GDM), which is a combination of onshore and offshore models, helpful when the job must be done quickly close to the client's base. The company then uses the resources of partners in different parts of the world.

Infosys put the power of the GDM into the consulting business, which meant that, for consulting services such as package implementation, Infosys could in future apportion some work to India, taking its blended rate to $75 to $80 an hour when multinationals were charging $125 to $130. To clarify, Infosys' hourly rate in India for its mix of services was then about $37 to $38.

In 2000 alone, the company's revenues grew by 80 per cent, with profits climbing to 115 per cent. Just a year before that, Murthy had passed his presidency title to the youngest of the founders, Nandan Nilekani, claiming that the company had taken new challenges of growth and he felt the need to share his responsibility with another person. Such change would allow him to concentrate exclusively on strategic issues in the next millennium. Nandan became the new CEO, and Murthy remained the chairman and chief mentor.

The Infosys mission is 'to achieve our objectives in an environment of fairness, honesty and courtesy towards our customers, employees, vendors, and society at large'. Core values of Infosys include 'customer delight, leadership by example, integrity and transparency, fairness and pursuit of excellence'.[34]

Murthy's concern was more for the long term rather than for the short term. He believed that there are four basic business principles for business:

Business ethics in practice 14: (cont'd)

- Predictability of revenues
- Sustainability of those predictions
- Profitability of those revenues
- The need to have a 'de-risking model', which means that Infosys should not be reliant on any customer or market.[35]

Murthy was also convinced that running the business using simple rules is the best way, as simple rules are easy to communicate, easy to practise, easy to understand and difficult to cheat anybody with. For example, one of the rules was not using corporate resources for personal benefit; thus, even while travelling with his wife, he refunded the company the difference between a single and double hotel room. He believes that the way to maintain the best credibility is always to walk the talk.

For Murthy, 'the primary goal of companies should be to seek respect from the customer and exceed their expectations. Seek respect from your colleagues and remain fair, transparent and accountable. Do not violate the law of the land in pursuit of profit and live in harmony and peace with society.'[36] He thought that the key to success was combining ethical practices and corporate governance. Employees first had to believe in the values in order for the whole system to work. As Murthy claimed, you cannot monitor every person.

In recruiting practices, Infosys gives no special treatment to family members, as is the case in most Indian companies. The only condition for job candidates is 'learnability', defined as the ability to derive generic knowledge from specific experiences and apply it in new situations. Infosys is not concerned with specific software skills, believing that the company offers the requisite training programmes. The only matter of consequence is a good performance after that point. Considering 'learnability', Infosys simply wants dependability, predictability, sustainability, consistency, reliability, uniformity and all the qualities that help a company act ethically.

Infosys hires and trains persons with disabilities and those with a below average socio-economic background. For this, in 2006 Infosys BPO received the Helen Keller award from the National Centre for Promotion of Employment for Disabled People (NCPEDP) for being the most disabled friendly company.

Furthermore, Infosys gives priority to diversity. The company emphasizes the need for giving equal rights to women at work, inviting them to forums for women leaders and establishing Infosys Women Inclusivity Network (IWIN), which promotes an appropriate work environment. Women comprise 30 per cent of their workforce.

One concern for Infosys Technologies is protection of the environment by water management. It recycles wastewater so that it can be reused for primary and secondary purposes. It also measures its utilization of energy by means of energy audits. The data collected is used to achieve the company's increasing levels of energy conservation. The company is also dedicated to waste segregation.

Business ethics in practice 14: (cont'd)

The company also contributes considerable funding for youth develop-ment, treating this as the best investment for the future of India. The Catch Them Young programme organizes summer camps for Hindu children in order to introduce them to information technologies. The Infosys Founda-tion, Education & Research Group conducts the Infosys Extension Programme (IEP), which comprises the Infosys Fellowship Programme, the Rural Reach programme, and Train the Trainer.

Apart from that, the company supports the health system in India. It con-structed the Infosys Super-specialty Hospital at the Sassoon in the city of Pune (West India). The government run hospital caters to poor patients who have no access to treatment in private hospitals. Infosys also constructed a paedi-atric department at the Capitol hospital in Bhubaneswar; a hospital for tribal persons at H.D. Kote, Mysore; a hospital to treat patients with brain fever in Bellary; and a recuperation centre at the Kidwai Cancer Institute in Bangalore. Infosys has also donated surgical equipment and ambulances to medical cen-tres and hospitals in Tamil Nadu, Karnataka and Orissa.

Among the long list of Infosys' involvement in culture and education, there is the work of the Infosys Foundation, and its financial support for the art of India. For example, Infosys is sustaining the tradition of handloom weaving in Pochampalli village (Southern India). Automation has rendered hundreds of Hindu families unemployed. Moreover, the Foundation is trying to sustain the traditional art of music, poetry and storytelling, called Gamaka, and sponsored the folk festival in Karnataka in which 100 craftsmen from 20 states in India participated. This way, the company provides direct market opportunities for rural artisans.

Since the beginning of the new millennium, Infosys has been showered with different types of acknowledgements and international awards. By 2004, the company had won a number of awards for its HR practices, with the focus on the company's learning organization and learning programme. It was ranked as the number one place to work in India by Hewatt & Associates and India's leading business magazine, *Business Today*. Moreover, the magazine *Computer World* acknowledged Infosys to be one of the 100 best places to work in the USA. Infosys was also ranked in first place in a corporate governance survey conducted by CLSA across Asia (excluding Japan).

Questions:

1. Following the description provided by this case, what characteristics can give an approach to the corporate culture at Infosys?

2. Do you think that the corporate culture at Infosys could be applied to other companies within the same industry? What about companies in other industries?

(cont'd)

Sources: Infosys Official Website: www.infosys.com; R. Velamur and J. Mitchell, 'Infosys Technologies: Powered by Intellect, Driven by Values', IESE Business School (Barcelona: IESE Publishing, 2006); M. Jayashankar and S. Prasad, 'Remaking INFY', Businessworld, 22 September (2003); Infosys Annual Report for the fiscal year ended 31 March, 2005, http://google.brand.edgar-online.com/EFX_dll/EDGARpro.dll?FetchFilingHTML1?ID=3 678820&SessionID=ISLiWqxOZWOKd47; Infosys Sustainability Report 2007–08: 3, www.infosys.com/beyond-business/infosys-sustainability-report-0708.pdf. Speech addressed to MBA students at IESE Business School, in Barcelona, Spain, 27 April 2007.

Dilemma 14

Hennes & Mauritz AB (operating as H&M) is a clothing company, known for its inexpensive and fashionable clothing for women, men, teenagers and children.

H&M has more than 1,500 stores in 28 different countries and more than 68,000 employees. The company, based in Sweden, has its own team of designers of about 100 professionals. However, the company does not own any factories. Instead, it has about 800 suppliers, mainly from Europe and Asia, supported by 20 production centres which, among other tasks, monitor compliance with a strict code of conduct and promote good working conditions. This code emerged as a reaction to certain accusations regarding child labour employed by some H&M suppliers in the 1980s and 1990s.

In addition, H&M had several social projects in developing countries, supporting and donating money and clothing to international organizations such as Oxfam, the Red Cross, UNICEF, Caritas and Mentor. This latter action is a non-profit organization that works to prevent the use and abuse of all harmful addictive substances, whether legal or illegal, among children and young people.

Frequently, H&M marketing campaigns use top models or well-known stars, including Madonna and Kylie Minogue, as well as images of characters from popular fiction and animation, such as Snoopy, for its collection of pyjamas and lingerie, and Superman for its children's clothing lines. They disseminate advertising through several channels, including newspapers, television advertisements and H&M shops. In 2005, the British model Kate Moss was contracted. She already had deals with companies such as Chanel, Burberry and Dior. However, before the campaign started the *Daily Mirror*, a popular British tabloid newspaper, showed images of Kate Moss ingesting cocaine. In the days that followed, this image was spread by other mass media. The situation disturbed H&M's management, since it seemed contradictory to give support to preventing drug addiction and, at the same time, to run an advertising campaign with someone who appeared to be a cocaine user. In addition, many of H&M's customers are teenage girls. However, the model had already been contracted for the imminent H&M advertising campaign and it could be argued that she should be given a second chance.

Questions:

1. How would you evaluate the advertising campaign with Kate Moss from an ethical and social responsibility perspective?
2. Do you think it would be ethical to break the contract in the given circumstances?
3. What would you do if you had the final say in this affair?

Summary

The notion of corporate citizenship is grounded in the business organization's community membership and in the interdependence of all community members.

Consistent with the multi-ends of the firm, the corporation bears economic, commercial, organizational, relational, sustainability and citizenship responsibilities.

Three basic ethical principles for articulating corporate responsibilities of citizenship can be defined: (1) institutional; (2) organizational; and (3) individual.

The institutional principle presents the common good of society as the moral source and justification for social responsibilities of business.

The organizational principle (or principle of concentric responsibilities) includes three types of hierarchically ordered responsibilities: (1) primary responsibilities, which refer to the company's specific activities; (2) secondary responsibilities, which consist of improving the impact this specific activity has on the company's stakeholders beyond the bare minimum; and (3) tertiary responsibilities, which relate to actions that the company undertakes, beyond the sphere of its specific activities, in order to improve certain aspects of society or the natural environment.

The individual principle establishes the necessity of manager discretion to determine the content of concentric responsibilities with practical wisdom.

Corporation–government relationships require reciprocity and cooperation. Business lobbying is acceptable as long as the interest of one party does not prevail over the common good. Business contributions to political campaigns should follow the same criteria, but, in practice, the risk of abuse is high. Many countries prohibit such contributions or require a high degree of transparency.

When it is necessary to close plants or outsource products and services, the extent to which a company accepts its role as corporate citizen becomes apparent. A socially responsible termination of employment includes just cause, due process, and mitigation of harmful effects.

To lead a company in its role as corporate citizen requires a clear vision of this concept, an understanding of corporate citizenship as an essential aspect of business, the integration of this notion into the strategy and structure of business, and, consequently, into

(cont'd)

leadership style, managerial systems and managerial practices. Communication, motivation, stakeholder engagement and employee training should also be imbued with the notion of corporate citizenship. Finally, corporate citizenship should be evaluated, audited and reported.

Human beings are at the centre of concern for sustainable development. They are entitled to a healthy and productive life in harmony with nature.

UN Rio Declaration on Environment and
Development (1992), Principle 1

Chapter Aims

This chapter will allow you to:

- learn more about environmentalism and the current philosophical debate on the environment
- gain an understanding of four environmental ethics approaches
- consider the concept of 'animal welfare' and its implications for business
- reflect on the resource depletion problem and the responsible use of natural resources
- consider the necessity of a responsible use of energy in business activities in the face of the current state of the natural sources of energy and global warming concerns
- be familiar with various aspects of pollution in air, water and soil, as well as other forms of pollution, and some ways of avoiding it
- consider business responsibility in waste production, disposal and recycling
- know how some businesses apply strategies for environmental sustainability.

Key terms:

Animal liberation
Animal welfare
Anthropocentrism
Atmospheric pollution
Biocentrism
Biodegradable
Carbon dioxide
Deep ecology
Deforestation
Dominative-anthropocentrism
Ecocentrism
Ecofeminism

Ecological conscience
Energy resources
Environmental ethics
Environmentalism
Environmentalist movement
Global warming
Integral pro-active strategy
Light pollution
Natural environment
Noise pollution
Ozone-depleting substances
Pollution

Population growth
Proactive strategy
Product stewardship
Radioactive contamination
Reactive strategy
Recycling
Resource depletion
Social ecology
Soil pollution
Stewardship
Visual pollution
Water pollution

344

Environmental Business Ethics

INTRODUCTORY CASE 15:

BHOPAL, INDIA – COULD THE WORST INDUSTRIAL DISASTER HAVE BEEN AVOIDED?

The worst industrial disaster in the history of the world took place on the night of 2 December 1984 at the Union Carbide India Ltd (UCIL) plant, a subsidiary of Union Carbide USA. It occurred in the city of Bhopal, Madhya Pradesh, a state in central India – one of the country's poorest. The direct cause of the tragedy was the leakage of 40 tons of methyl isocianate (MIC), a gas used to make pesticides. Cocktails of deadly gases began drifting in clouds through the densely populated city streets. As a consequence, 6,903 people died, many in their sleep. In the following days and months, thousands of people waited for help in the streets, in their homes and in overcrowded hospitals. Up to a total of 20,000 lost their lives during the following years. In addition, 20,000 were severely harmed and 850,000 were affected. The government of India controlled information pertaining to the accident that had occurred in order to maintain its political legitimacy.

The indirect causes of this disaster are more complex. The plant was built in the 1960s, against recommendations by experts because of its hazardous nature and its construction in densely populated Bhopal, which had a population of 900,000. Afterwards, slums around the factory were allowed – or, at least, not forbidden – which prevented the speedy evacuation of people in the event of an accident. No appropriate structure for environmental control existed.

Before the catastrophe, Union Carbide was the third largest US chemical company and the seventh largest in the world, with 99,000 employees. In the 1970s and the early 1980s, the company enjoyed a reputation for environmental concerns outside India and, in terms of complying with the Occupational Safety and Health Administration's standards, was rated in first place by the US National Council of Economic Priorities among the eight largest chemical companies.

In spite of positive reports on the company's operations outside India, an internal audit of the Bhopal plant gave different results. In 1982, it was said that human, technological and organizational factors were in need of attention. Two years later, the company reported that they had corrected several of these deficiencies, and that there were two on which work was in progress – (1) malfunction of the safety mechanisms, such as alarms; and (2) the potential for an accidental overfilling of the MIC storage tank. It was these two shortcomings that caused the catastrophe.

Apart from the technical defect of the safety mechanisms, there were some managerial problems and employees' morale was low. The Indian authorities required that operative control of the plant be kept in the hands of nationals. Appropriate training was not given, and the plant director's experience was insufficient. Management had no contingency plans in the event of emergencies.

Union Carbide had to bear extremely serious consequences for the Bhopal disaster. The production of MIC was stopped and safety improvements costing $5 million were installed at West Virginia, where MIC was also produced. Later on, Union Carbide closed different MIC plants, dismissing over 4,000 people.

Immediately after the tragedy and in the following years, the company said that, among other measures, it provided $2 million in aid to the Prime Minister's Relief Fund, sent international medical experts to help victims, gave $5 million to the Indian Red Cross and $90 million to the charitable trust for the hospital in Bhopal.

In February 1989, the Supreme Court of India directed a final settlement of all Bhopal litigation of $470 million. Union Carbide and UCIL made the full payment to the Indian government immediately. However, it seems that only a part of that sum reached the victims. Eventually, Union Carbide India was taken over by the government of India.

Hundreds of survivors and relatives of the dead, together with NGOs, are still accusing the company authorities of the death of thousands, demanding medical care, more compensation, removing the toxic waste from the facility and transporting clean water to residents in the area. Thousands of people protested against the government's negligence in this case two years after the accident. Protests continued in the following years. In spring 2008, approximately 50 victims of the disaster walked from Bhopal to Delhi and, having set up camp near government buildings, waited for the politicians' answer to their demands.

Union Carbide claims that the immediate reaction was right, and generally accepted moral responsibility for the tragedy.

The good news is that the accident was a wake-up call for India and the global chemicals industry. Since the tragic event, stringent laws have been introduced to avert such accidents and large Indian chemical companies have made significant investments to control pollution. Furthermore, the International Council of Chemical Associations (ICCA) settled the Responsible Care Initiative, which drives continuous improvement in health and safety performance in the chemical industry.

Questions:

1. What causes can you find for the Bhopal disaster?

2. Up to what point is Union Carbide responsible for the deaths of so many people?

3. What is the responsibility of the Indian government for the building of the plant?

4. What lessons can we learn from this case?

Sources: Bhopal Website: http://www.bhopal.com/irs.htm; J. Fernández-Fernández, *Bhopal*, in R. W. Kolb, 'Encyclopedia of Business Ethics and Society' (Sage Publications: Thousand Oaks, 2008): 167–8; Jackson Browning Report: www.bhopal.com/pdfs/browning.pdf; *BBC*: news.bbc.co.uk/2/hi/south_asia/4064527.stm; D. Lapierre and J. Moro, *Five Past Midnight in Bhopal: The Epic Story of the World's Deadliest Industrial Disaster* (New York: Warner Books, 2002).

ENVIRONMENTALISM AND THE PHILOSOPHICAL DEBATE ON THE ENVIRONMENT

Human beings and nature are interdependent. Humans take food, air, water and raw materials from the natural environment and deposit waste in it. Each generation receives the environment as a legacy from preceding generations and will, in turn, pass it on to their children. As noted,[1] sustainable development takes place when the responsibility towards future generations is borne in mind and people act as stewards of natural resources. Environmental business ethics deals with the ethical behaviour of businesses regarding the natural environment, sustainability and stewardship.

Advocacy for environmental protection from destruction or pollution, as well as the first demands for business to treat the natural environment with respect, arose in the 1960s. One concern was the use of certain chemicals, such as DDT and other pesticides, which brought about the death of birds and the accumulation of pesticides in the food chain.[2] Activists were also worried about rivers fouled by pollution – sometimes even by highly toxic metals, such as lead and mercury – and about oil-based waste in the oceans. They also traced radioactivity in food – radiation was then used as a means of food preservation.

As a result, a movement emerged to safeguard the natural environment, exerting pressure on corporations, to avoid pollution and depletion of natural resources, and on governments, for more stringent regulations.

Soon, a philosophical debate emerged on the root causes of environmental problems and to examine the formulation of an appropriate philosophy of the relationship between humans and nature. Lynn White initiated this debate by blaming Christianity and the Bible for environmental problems.[3] According to White, regarding humans as the apex of creation and claiming divine permission to 'subdue the earth' was the ultimate cause of the Western environmental crisis.

However, this position was vigorously criticized.[4] What the Bible states is that in the beginning humans (man and woman) were created in the image of God, and God blessed them, saying, 'Be fruitful and multiply, and fill the earth and subdue it'.[5] This text, according to the most common interpretation, reveals that men and women have an inherent dignity, being made in the image of God, and are thus superior to all other creatures on earth. But 'subduing the earth' does not mean that humans have either a divine right to despotic domination or absolute ownership of every non-human being on earth. This is made clear in other biblical texts: for instance, in Psalm 24, in which it is recognized that 'the earth is the Lord's and the fullness thereof, the world and those who dwell therein'; and in Psalm 104, which declares that 'God is just in His concern for wild species and their habitats as He is in His care for human beings'. These, and other biblical texts, lead most experts to the interpretation that humans are called to dominate the earth as *stewards* – responsibly, not as despots.

The real cause of current ecological problems is related to the economic and cultural forms of late modernity, rather than to religious influence on culture. The origin of a domineering mentality of man over nature is rather common in some Renaissance thinkers, specifically Francis Bacon (1561–1626), who saw the human–nature relationship in terms of unlimited domination for the sake of humankind, using science and technique as tools. Knowledge was seen, therefore, as simply a power for dominating nature. Capitalism, with its focus on the accumulation of wealth and its disregard for the environment came to reinforce a sense of absolute dominion.

Continuing the debate on root causes, some argued that widespread environmental destruction had as its cause the 'population explosion',[6] while others put it down to the consumption driven lifestyle of certain peoples rather than population size as such.[7] Finally, there are streams of thought – namely 'social ecology' and 'ecofeminism' – that consider that the root of our ecological crisis lies in certain social structures, or in the domination of a few over the majority. Actually, there is no consensus on the causes of environmental problems; they are complex, and many factors have probably contributed to the current situation.

After the pioneering discussions, the philosophical debate branched off into two main directions. One centred on ethical obligations regarding non-human beings and – above all – our responsibilities to future generations who might find a greatly deteriorated planet. Another view, more controversial, held that we have obligations *to* nature, not only *regarding* nature. Obligations to nature can include animals (at least, some animals) and even trees and mountains, which would be seen as the bearers of legal rights.[8]

At the same time, some have advocated the fostering of an 'ecological conscience', which would lead to a more austere lifestyle: this would involve scaling down consumption, saving energy and promoting renewable energy sources, avoiding pollution and resource depletion, recycling waste and other practices.

Changes in the lifestyles currently prevalent in developed countries would be beneficial for solving certain ecological problems and even for a less materialistic vision of life, since excessive materialism precludes human excellence. However, the extreme change in lifestyle proposed by some radical ecologists could take us back to the pre-industrial era. This would bring about disastrous consequences for poor and agrarian populations in underdeveloped countries.[9]

In this context, a line of thought on the environment called 'deep ecology'[10] defends the need for a new vision of the human–nature relationship. In deep ecology philosophy, people are seen as a mere part of nature, although with the capacity to disturb it. It also proclaims a biospheric egalitarianism, in which the living environment as a whole has the same right to live and flourish as people do. Given this idealized conception of nature, a means to self-realization would be to see oneself as existing in a thorough interconnectedness with it.

Few would question the fitness of living in harmony with nature. However, deep ecology goes beyond this, diluting humanity within nature. This radically materialistic view contrasts with a more widely accepted outlook: that humans, though part of nature, also transcend it because of their inner world, which expresses a significant spiritual dimension. These two anthropological views have important consequences for environmental ethics, as we shall see in the next section.

ENVIRONMENTAL ETHICS APPROACHES

Environmental ethics, and consequently environmental business ethics, is closely related to environmental philosophy. The starting point of environmental ethics is an inquiry into the value of the human and non-human environment (living and non-living things) – usually called the 'natural environment', or simply 'environment' – and the requirements for a proper relationship with it. Different views on human–nature relationships, such as those already mentioned, bring with them very different proposals for environmental ethics. There are at least four relevant approaches:

Dominative anthropocentrism

This approach takes the human being as not only being at the centre of the universe, but also possessing an absolute right to dominate any non-human creature on the planet. Human individuals are seen as autonomous beings endowed with knowledge and the power to dominate the earth for their own use – and the nearly unlimited right to do so. This approach has been prevalent in business for years, supported by the belief that the technological impact on nature could be easily absorbed, and by a cultural context in favour of the accumulation of wealth and an immoderate consumerism. Under the assumptions of the anthropocentric–domination approach, unchecked organizational exploitation of natural resources is seen as legitimate, and even desirable. Today, however, the idea that business's impact on nature is so easily absorbed is no longer credible. Abuses in the exploitation of natural resources, abundant pollution in all its forms and an increasing quantity of waste products are obvious for all to see.

Unrestrained domination of nature as a driver for behaviour is ethically unacceptable for two reasons:

- The natural environment is the human habitat, and it is integral to the common good to preserve it well for the sake of both current and future generations
- Human rationality requires an acknowledgement of the intrinsic nature of each being and of its place in the cosmos. Animals, for instance, have a sensitive nature, and some can live close to, and even in a 'friendly' relationship with, humans.

Biocentrism

In stark contrast to the previous view, in biocentrism human beings are not considered the centre of the world. Instead, what is central is life – any kind of life. This is what biocentrism means (from the Greek *bio*, life, and *kentron*, centre). This position holds that all life forms not only possess intrinsic value, but are also *equally* valuable; and human beings are merely one animal species co-existing with others, without any particular dignity to give them pre-eminence over other animals. In consequence, the well-being of all life must be taken into consideration.

Many would agree that all forms of life can be appreciated and are valuable in some way, but it is difficult to argue that all are equally valuable, since human beings have an interior spiritual structure (intellectual knowledge, free will, moral conscience), traditionally termed 'soul', which confers an intrinsic superiority upon humans over any other form of life on earth.

Ecocentrism

Here, the centre is not life itself but the ecosystem, or complete community of living organisms and the non-living materials of their surroundings functioning together as a unity. Humans, as with animals, are part of a complex ecosystem. While biocentrism concentrates on protecting the life of individual animals, ecocentrism focuses on the whole. From this perspective, environmental ethics consists of achieving an equilibrium of natural ecosystems. Thus, protecting a specific animal is not acceptable if this leads to serious ecological damage.

From an ethical perspective, reducing ethics in order to achieve the equilibrium of natural ecosystems is more than questionable. Objections similar to those against deep ecology can be posed, as that ideology is closely related to ecocentrist ethics.

In business management, so far, only a few authors have presented an ecocentric paradigm as an alternative to anthropocentrism understood as absolute domination.[11] Critics argue that the ecocentric proposal is rooted in a romantic conception of nature, misanthropic in its desire to remove humans from their privileged position. It is further accused of using a controversial tone and of being selective in its treatment of environmental information.[12]

Stewardship

While dominative anthropocentrism has been the target of increasing criticism, other philosophical perspectives argue in favour of anthropocentrism with a human face.[13] Along these lines, stewardship-anthropocentrism, or simply 'stewardship', is a philosophy based on the idea that humans transcend nature but should act as stewards of it. Humans, in this view, are the central fact of earth, and only they possess dignity and authentic rights.

Stewardship holds that development is not to be understood as a mere indiscriminate possession of things and unfettered consumerism. On the contrary, development should be – above all – both human and sustainable, which means employing material goods with moderation and a sense of responsibility, as a tool for human flourishing, with concern for future generations. This version of anthropocentrism is also consistent with the human-centred approach adopted in this book.

Stewardship entails respect for biodiversity.[14] In the face of the desire to use living elements for purely economic aims, a sense of stewardship demands that one take into account the nature of each living being and their mutual connections within an ordered system: the cosmos.[15]

Anthropocentrism stewardship is found in the Rio Declaration at the Earth Summit (United Nations Conference on Environment and Development), which underscores the fact that 'human beings are at the centre of concern for sustainable development'.[16] But, at the same time, it adds that a healthy and productive life has to be achieved in harmony with nature. A managerial stewardship of the environment reconciles respect for nature and the attainment of reasonable profits.[17]

ANIMAL WELFARE

One immediate consequence of the above-mentioned approaches to environmental ethics is the consideration given to animals in each. Some, in line with biocentrism, proclaim that animals have rights, or even demand 'animal liberation'.[18] This position would prevent using animals for food or clothing, or for testing new drugs or other scientific research. They argue that animals have an intrinsic value, similar or equal to that of the human person, and that using them for food, clothing or science recognizes in them only an instrumental value.

The philosophical and ethical grounds of this position are weak: that animals have an intrinsic – understood as infinite or absolute – value, and that they furthermore have rights, is difficult to prove. Animals have interests, but only human beings have rights – because only they have duties.

Aristotle argued that nature has made all things specifically for the sake of man: 'after the birth of animals, plants exist for their sake, and that the other animals exist for the sake of man, the tame for use and food, the wild, if not all at least the greater part of them, for food, and for the provision of clothing and various instruments'.[19] This idea is also in accordance with the great monotheistic religions. Contrastingly, Hindu civilization gives animals practically the same respect as humans. However, anyone who cares to scratch the surface of this belief will see that this is not for the animals' sake, but because of respect for humans, in light of the belief that ancestors return in an animal form.

Obtaining food for survival is a human right closely related to the right to life. Would it make sense to allow people to die from starvation when it was possible to feed them with meat? Many agree that there is nothing inherently wrong with using animals as resources for human purposes, though there is an obligation to ensure that they do not suffer unnecessarily; that is, to provide 'animal welfare'.[20]

Animal welfare is consistent with the recognition that animals have their own identity as individuals of certain species with life, sensitivity and certain capabilities. Moreover, many recognize in animals God's creatures, and this is another reason to show kindness towards them, and to recognize that they have a value, albeit one altogether inferior to the intrinsic value of each person endowed with dignity.

In line with animal welfare, many cultures provide rules for appropriate slaughter, and for limiting animal distress, pain and fear. The stewardship approach accepts the instrumental value of animals for humans, allowing owning, feeding and raising animals. But this should be integrated with a sympathetic attitude towards them. Similar arguments can be made for using animals for clothing. Cruelty to animals is contrary to human dignity, and those who deal improperly with them can acquire a cruel character.

All this suggests that businesses using animals should provide animal welfare in their operations – avoiding, for instance, overcrowding in poultry farms or other situations in which animals might experience distress or neglect. Scientific experimentation with animals for testing or research can be conducted for the ends of benefiting human health or saving human life, within reasonable limits, and always with the proviso of avoiding animal suffering whenever possible.

RESPONSIBLE USE OF NATURAL RESOURCES

The exploitation of natural resources is necessary for human life; in fact, throughout the history of humankind natural resources have been extracted by hunting, farming, fishing, mining, and foresting. However, resources are often exploited beyond their rate of replacement, which is contrary to sustainable use and an attitude of stewardship. Using natural resources without any criterion other than the accumulation of capital, with absolute dominion, poses a serious danger for the future. Thus, *resource depletion*, understood as the exhaustion of raw materials within a region, should be avoided.

Various issues regarding resource depletion are causing growing concern, due to non-sustainable exploitation. Among these are generally mentioned deforestation, over-fishing, and over-exploitation of land.

Immoderate logging for the timber industry brings about *deforestation*, which is of special concern in some regions, such as the Amazon and other tropical rainforest regions. This happens in the presence of clear-cutting, in which the majority of all trees in a forest sector are cut down. Deforestation can also be produced by the 'land conversion' of forests in order to obtain arable land, pasture or areas for urban use. These practices, as well as forest fires, bring about the problems of erosion and desertification. Elimination of forests disturbs the environment, since trees, along with other plants, undergo photosynthesis, which transforms carbon dioxide in the air into oxygen and carbon by absorbing solar energy. The carbon is retained by the tree or plant. In addition, the removal or destruction of huge areas of forest can reduce biodiversity and even affect climate and geography.

One crucial natural resource is *water* – essential for human life. There is a finite supply of fresh water, stored in aquifers (sometimes contaminated by soil pollutants), surface water (rivers, lakes) and the atmosphere. Oceans are also a potential water resource, but desalinization is necessary for most usages, and this requires a great deal of energy and a costly investment that not every country can afford. Considering the overall scarcity of usable water and the prevalence of water pollution, the term 'water crisis' was introduced long ago to reflect the worldwide predicament. In many countries, water is becoming scarce, and a moderate and efficient use of it is a real responsibility of business.

ENERGY RESOURCES AND THE RESPONSIBLE USE OF ENERGY

Energy sources are crucial for economic activity. Currently the most important source is fossil fuels, which account for about two thirds of world energy consumption. Basically, *fossil fuels* are coal, petroleum and natural gas. These natural, non-renewable resources are the main fuel source for domestic and industrial usages. They are efficient forms of energy but the amount available is limited. Furthermore, their combustion for the generation of energy produces carbon dioxide, which is problematic due to its effect on global warming (see Insight 15).

Insight 15:

Carbon dioxide and global warming

Global warming refers to the increase in the average temperature of the earth's near-surface air and oceans registered since the mid-twentieth century. This notion has become a popular concept, especially since 2007 when the Inter-governmental Panel on Climate Change (IPCC) presented a challenging report on the subject. This group of experts, along with former US Vice President Al Gore, received the Nobel Peace Prize in that same year. Al Gore himself presented *An Inconvenient Truth*, a film about climate change that has enjoyed worldwide distribution.

In one century (between 1905 and 2005), the average global air temperature near the earth's surface increased about 0.74°C, but the climate model projections summarized by the IPCC indicate that in 2100 the average rise will be 6.4°C in relation to the temperature in 1980–99. There is uncertainty about the effects of global warming, but it could bring about glacier retreat, ice melting from the earth's poles and rising sea levels – apart from possible changes in weather, agriculture yields and the extinction of species.

Insight 15: (cont'd)

According to 30 scientific societies and academies of science, including all the national academies of science of the major industrialized countries, the origin of global warming is the increasing production of carbon dioxide and its greenhouse effect in the atmosphere. Some scientists, though, have voiced disagreement with some findings of the IPCC regarding global warming and its anthropogenic origin.[21]

Whatever the case might be, since 1994 efforts have been under way to achieve international agreements to reduce global warming. In 1997, the United Nations Framework Convention on Climate Change (UNFCCC) signed the Kyoto Protocol, which has been in effect since 2005. Its objective was to reduce carbon dioxide and five different greenhouse gases thought to cause climate change. In 2007, the Bali Global Warming Conference achieved an agreement with which to negotiate a roadmap for future talks on eventually reducing greenhouse gas emissions. United Nations delegates hailed the agreement as an historic step in the prevention of future global warming.

Responsible corporations have accepted the challenge to redesign processes to save energy and reduce carbon dioxide emissions. In accountability reports, companies often include efforts made to reduce such emissions.

An alternative to fossil fuels is *nuclear power*, which is used to generate electricity (sometimes also for the propulsion of naval vessels) commonly through nuclear fission by means of controlled reactions. It is a clean and efficient way to obtain electric power and currently meets about 15 per cent of world energy needs. The sources of nuclear energy are practically unlimited. The increasing price of petroleum and global warming, presumably due to fossil fuels, encourage an increased use of nuclear power.

Indeed, many countries have already opted for nuclear power. However, in other countries there is a certain political resistance to constructing nuclear power plants on the grounds of safety. These fears have grown up due to a few famous nuclear accidents, among them the incident at the Chernobyl plant in the former Soviet Union in 1986. It was a traumatic collective experience that caused damage to many people, even some quite distant from the site of the plant. Another threat is the possibility of a terrorist attack on a nuclear power station. However, nowadays these can be equipped with numerous safety features. In fact, safety features in power stations are usually redundantly duplicated; the security level in the face of a potential terrorist attack seems all but guaranteed. If this is so, there are no serious objections to employing nuclear power to generate electricity.

Renewable energy sources are desirable but, currently, insufficient. The most widely used form of renewable energy is the traditional biomass, such as wood burning, which accounts for about 13 per cent of world energy consumption. This is followed by hydroelectricity, which comprises about 3 per cent.

Hydroelectric power stations use rivers or reservoirs through large (or sometimes small) hydroelectric installations. *Solar thermal energy* for heating water makes up about 1.3 per cent of the total. Other renewable sources cover less than 1 per cent of consumption, although they are increasingly relied upon in some countries. Among the latter, *wind power* and *photovoltaic cells* seem promising. Wind power is generated through wind turbines (more rarely these are also used to crush grain or pump water). Sunlight can be transformed into electric current through photovoltaic cells. Much more marginal even than these methods, are other forms of renewable energy, such as those that use rain, tides or geothermal heat.

Biofuels for transportation are increasingly common as alternatives to gasoline. These are produced using sugarcane and maize or other grains as raw materials, put through a fermentation process to produce ethanol. Biofuels made with grains are subject to ethical controversy since they have the perverse effect of driving up food prices in poor countries.

Businesses can *save energy* and contribute to its conservation by reducing consumption of energy services (for example, by avoiding unnecessary heating or air conditioning, turning the lights off when not in use, or decreasing wattage in Christmas decorations).

The *efficient use of energy* – using less of it to provide the same level of service – is achieved by replacing technical devices, processes, facilities or transportation systems with more efficient ones. Specific actions in this field are, for example: replacing incandescent lights with low-consumption lights that produce the same level of illumination, improving insulation, constructing energy-efficient buildings, redesigning industrial processes and rethinking methods of transportation.

AVOIDING POLLUTION IN ALL ITS FORMS

Pollution refers to the introduction of contaminants into an environment, usually the atmosphere (air), water or soil by the discharge of harmful substances, along with other forms of pollution such as noise, heat or light. Business can be a source of pollution through mining, factories and transportation, for example.

Atmospheric pollution

This is caused by gases, solid particles and, sometimes, by biological materials (volatile organic compounds). It can harm humans and animals, or damage the environment.

Combustion of fossil fuels to generate energy for power stations and motor vehicles produces carbon dioxide, which is not toxic but affects global warming. Such combustion can also be a source of pollutant gases with some degree of toxicity (carbon monoxide, nitrogen oxides and sulphur dioxide) and small particles.

Carbon dioxide is produced by incomplete combustion of carbon, nitrogen dioxide comes from the reaction of nitrogen from the air, and sulphur dioxide from sulphur contained in coal (much less in petroleum) with oxygen from the air. Sulphur dioxide and nitrogen oxides can react in the atmosphere to produce acids; this can result in *acid rain*, with adverse effects on forests, fresh water and soil, killing off insect and aquatic life forms as well as causing damage to buildings and even possibly impacting human health.

Another origin of atmospheric pollution is industry (cement, petrochemical, pharmacy and others, each with specific pollutants).

Finally, some products can introduce pollutants into the air when in use or when spilled during the manufacturing process. One particularly dangerous group of chemicals is chlorofluorocarbons (CFCs) or freons – more generically haloalkanes – which can be employed for a number of domestic or industrial usages including propellants, flame retardants, refrigerants, material for fire extinguishers and solvents. Haloalkanes are *ozone-depleting substances* (ODSs) since their photodissociation brings about the reduction of the ozone layer in the earth's stratosphere. The ozone layer prevents the most harmful ultraviolet light from passing through the atmosphere where it increases skin cancer, damages plants and reduces plankton populations in the oceans. An international treaty signed in 1987, known as the Montreal Protocol, banned substances that deplete the ozone layer. Fortunately, in most cases substitute products have been found and most countries, following the Montreal Protocol, ban those that cause damage.

Water pollution

Rivers, groundwater, lakes and oceans can become contaminated by human activity with subsequent harm to the aquatic organisms and plants that live there. Some toxic pollutants, such as heavy metals, can be difficult to eliminate in drinking water for humans and animals. Outfalls from factories and leaking underground tanks can be major sources of water pollution entering into a waterway, along with effluents from wastewater treatment plants. Sometimes, water pollution does not come from a specific source but, rather, from the cumulative effect of small amounts of contaminants spread over a large area.

Water pollutants include chemicals with or without toxic and pathogenic substances. Even the latter, if not properly treated, will produce diseases in both humans and animals. Waterborne diseases cause many deaths in countries where the purification system for drinking water is inadequate.

A particular problem with water pollution (and sometimes also land pollution) is the release of effluents containing nutrients for plants, basically compounds of nitrogen or phosphorus (usually in the form of phosphates, a component of detergent). The excessive growth and decay of plants due to nutrient pollution can affect the ecosystem through oxygen reduction and its consequences for water quality, fish and other animal populations.

Oil spills, generally due to accidents, can pollute waters and soil. Several serious marine oil spills have occurred in recent years, including the 'Exxon Valdez', in Alaska, USA, in 1989, 'Erika' in France in 1999 and 'Prestige' in Spain in 2002. All of these affected marine life and coastlines.

Natural water bodies can also be the recipients of thermal pollution due to emissions of hot water used as a coolant in power plants or in certain industrial processes. The corresponding rise in temperatures can alter organisms living in rivers or lakes.

Soil pollution

This type of pollution occurs when chemicals are released by particularly dangerous spills or by the rupture of underground storage tanks. It can also accompany the application of herbicides, pesticides and chlorinated hydrocarbons or be the result of direct discharge of industrial wastes into the soil.

Heavy metals are both water and soil pollutants. Among them, mercury, plutonium and lead are particularly toxic to animals and humans. Their accumulation in the body over time can cause serious illnesses. Cadmium, vanadium and tungsten are also heavy metals with certain toxicity, although they can be beneficial for particular organisms under certain conditions. Humans and other living organisms require varying amounts of 'heavy metals', such as iron, cobalt, copper, manganese, molybdenum and zinc, but excessive levels of these can be detrimental. Percolation of surface water contaminated by heavy metals, pesticides and so on to subsurface strata can contaminate water supplies.

Soil is not only deteriorated by pollution. There are a number of environmental problems related to the soil, such as overgrazing, land degradation, salinization, acidification, desertification and erosion. These are mostly related to agriculture and the farming business.

Business can cause other types of pollution, including visual pollution, noise pollution and light pollution.

Visual pollution

This includes large billboards on roadsides and streets, scarred landforms and surface mining. The latter can impact topography, vegetation and water resources. The reconstruction of vegetation is usually a requirement for strip mining and other surface mining operations.

Noise pollution

Noise pollution refers to displeasing sound that disrupts the activity or balance of human or animal life. It can damage physiological and psychological health. Noise can be a side effect of business activity that affects neighbourhoods. The origin of business noise can be found in factory machinery and other production activities, transportation systems, and occasionally in construction work.

Light pollution

This is excess or obtrusive light caused by light trespass and over-illumination – for instance, in advertising, and commercial properties.

Radioactive contamination

This is the uncontrolled distribution of radioactive gases, liquids or particles generally due to accidents in the production and use of radioactive material; for instance, in nuclear power stations, by nuclear fuel reprocessing or through radioisotopes used in nuclear medicine.

There are technical processes that do a great deal to limit atmospheric pollution in power stations and in industry. These processes are able to control particles (mechanical collectors, electrostatic precipitators, baghouses, and particulate scrubbers), and also to control pollutant gases (scrubbers, catalytic and non-catalytic reduction of nitrogen oxides, volatile organic compounds, abatement by active carbon and other methods). It is more difficult to eliminate pollutant gases from motor vehicles, although there are also methods of decreasing it. The most elemental way is by going to the cause. Thus, by eliminating lead, an additive that improves motor yield, one avoids the production of toxic lead oxide. Nowadays, the addition of lead is prohibited in many countries.

There are also technical processes that contribute to preventing water pollution, and security systems that reduce or prevent pollution due to spills and leakages, along with alternatives that play a similar role in the context of soil pollution. Thus, when pollution exists, in most cases the cause might be lack of will and economic motives rather than technical problems.

BUSINESS RESPONSIBILITY IN WASTE PRODUCTION, DISPOSAL AND RECYCLING

Production processes bring about different types of waste. Product packaging becomes waste and products themselves sooner or later suffer the same fate. Waste should be managed to reduce its negative impact on the environment and, ultimately, on society.

Business is directly responsible for waste produced in its manufacturing process and for its appropriate disposal. Indirectly, business has a responsibility for enhancing environmental conditions; for instance, by facilitating recycling or using biodegradable packaging.

The disposal of waste can be accomplished by means of landfills, incineration or combustion. Waste disposal deserves special concern when waste contains toxic substances, or if the method of waste elimination can produce a poison. The latter is the case with some plastics or solvents containing halogens that produce dioxins when incinerated. This is what happens with PVC plastic and with liquids used in the dry-cleaning industry.

Waste management deals with the production, collection, treatment and disposal of waste. It includes three main concerns: reducing, reusing and recycling waste:

- *Reducing waste*, which means attacking the cause. This can be attained by reduction of waste in the manufacturing process and in packaging, which entails improving efficiency, and might be achieved through innovative types of materials.

- *Reusing material* and repairing equipment as much as possible rather than replacing it are other ways of avoiding waste. However, on this point a dilemma can arise between economic and environmental-ethical criteria. Due to labour costs, repairing is not always the most economical alternative, and marketing strategies might focus on new products rather than on long-lasting ones.[22] We will return to this point in the next section.

- *Recycling*, a process by which waste or old products are converted into new products. Recycling not only prevents the loss of potentially useful materials, but also reduces the consumption of fresh new ones and the energy spent in their manufacture. Recyclable materials include glass, paper, metal, textiles and plastic.

When it comes to waste disposal, business can favour the environment by packaging with *biodegradable material*. After some time, these products are broken down by micro-organisms, while non-biodegradable material can long remain without decaying and being absorbed. Sometimes, the use of biodegradable material is required by law but there is always a social responsibility.

Related to these activities is the concept of *product stewardship*, which requires managing the product, taking into account its entire lifecycle, including its production, use and ultimate redundancy. Responsibility in product stewardship includes all those involved in reducing the product's impact on human health and the environment over its lifespan.

Manufacturers, retailers, consumers and government agencies are the actors typically involved in product stewardship. The responsibility of manufacturers includes appropriate planning for the recycling or disposal of the product at the end of its useful life. It also entails using packaging that minimizes waste and the corresponding environmental impact. Manufacturers can even pay to facilitate the recycling of obsolete products or for their proper disposal. Retailer and consumer responsibilities consist of ensuring proper disposal or recycling of products at the end of their useful lives. Government agencies can reinforce product stewardship by measures that incentivize or punish those involved in the product stewardship process.

A number of products with severe environmental impact have already been the object of particular attention due to their quantity or degree of harmfulness. Among these are carpets, electronic goods, fluorescent lighting, gas cylinders, medical sharps (needles, syringes and lancets), mercury products, paints, pesticides, pharmaceuticals, phone books, radioactive devices, thermostats and tyres.[23]

Product stewardship requires a specific solution in each case. For instance, electronic waste – such as obsolete computers and television sets – might be sent to developing countries. However, some electronic goods contain toxic substances – including lead, mercury, cadmium and such – that pose a threat to human health and the environment. An appropriate manner of selectively collecting electronic goods is necessary. This involves planning by the manufacturers, the collaboration of consumers and retailers, and legislation to oblige compliance.[24]

CORPORATE STRATEGIES FOR ENVIRONMENTAL SUSTAINABILITY

Traditionally, in many businesses wealth creation has been associated with raw materials and energy used, in such a way that economic growth requires a proportional amount of those resources. Usually, waste and pollution produced were also related to economic growth. However, nowadays there is an increasing awareness that non-renewable resources are not unlimited and that their price will probably continue to increase. In addition, the earth's ecosystems can no longer absorb the waste and emissions of production and consumption.

Now, the question is how a company can be environmentally responsible and simultaneously be profitable and competitive. A business facing this problem can adopt three different strategies:

A reactive strategy of pollution control

This consists of complying with current legislation governing the control of pollution in each country, or even disregarding the law if there is no effective enforcement of it. It might be argued that the costs of pollution control reduce the profit margin and, worse, introduce a competitive disadvantage if one's rivals take no measures beyond those that are strictly mandatory.

A proactive strategy of pollution prevention

This uses cleaning technologies to purify effluents beyond the requirements of current legislation whenever this might be reasonable and necessary. Apart from being the right thing to do, these measures can constitute an intelligent anticipation of future legislation, with the consequent increase in reputation. In addition, businesses with a proactive strategy can lobby public authorities to introduce appropriate legislation. This could oblige competitors with a reactive strategy to enhance their own pollution control and could, thus, avoid competition based on cutting pollution related costs.

An integral proactive strategy

This is a strategy based on changing processes or adopting designs to favour the environment and product stewardship. The goal is to redesign products to make them more durable, reusable and recyclable, using recycled materials and avoiding toxins as much as possible. As this goal is associated with manufacturing and delivery costs, an imaginative effort is necessary to create both environmental and financial value. One possible way is a three-pronged strategy:[25] (1) integration of science; (2) knowledge intensity; and (3) productivity improvement. Science permits, for instance, the creation of materials with similar features from renewable sources (corn sugar instead of petrochemicals). Greater intensity in knowledge leads to the creation of sustainable economic value by developing less material intensive means, and placing greater emphasis on technology, know-how and information systems. Great emphasis on productivity, of course, can save costs, which can make a company competitive as well as environmentally responsible.

Within the proactive strategy, Hart and Milstein have pointed out three sets of drivers by which business can contribute to the sustainability of the global environment:[26]

- Increasing resource efficiency and the prevention of pollution
- Operating in a transparent and responsible manner based on a very well-informed, active stakeholder relationship
- Developing and using technologies that can provide innovative and potent solutions to render the basis of many of today's material intensive industries obsolete.

The permanent challenge for business is to gain competitive advantage while applying the product stewardship philosophy through cost savings, revenue enhancement, liability reduction and image enhancement. There are engineering systems that help to understand the flow of materials and wastes throughout the lifecycle of a product or system, from raw materials acquisition to final disposal.[27]

Business ethics in practice 15:

Waste Concern – Cash for trash in Bangladesh

The Waste Concern Group is a non-governmental research organization, working closely with government, the private sector, international organizations and local communities to improve the environment in Dhaka, Bangladesh, and in other regions of the country. It was founded in 1995 by the architect Maqsood Sinha and the engineer Iftekar Enayetullah. Its motto is: 'Waste is a resource'. Since then, they have contributed to waste recycling, environmental improvement, renewable energy and poverty reduction through job creation and sustainable development.

The organization is 'non-profit', though it is connected to four 'for-profit' companies, two based in Bangladesh that are branches of Waste Concern (Waste Concern Consultants and Waste Concern Baraka Agro Products Ltd), and two based in the Netherlands (WWR Bio Fertilizer Bangladesh Ltd and Matuail Power Ltd) that are a joint venture of Waste Concern and World Wide Recycling BV. The latter is an international investor and operator of sustainable waste treatment facilities, and uses proven technology for recycling and energy production.

Waste Concern also works with a Dutch company using carbon dioxide emissions trading as the Clean Development Mechanism. This means that in order to use more carbon dioxide than is allowed by international law, one has to buy the rights of another party, who is willing to forfeit these in return for compensation, which is generally financial.

Business ethics in practice 15: (cont'd)

The main activity of Waste Concern focuses on Dhaka City, the capital city of Bangladesh, a country with a population of over 144 million people and one of the highest population densities in the world (1,000 people per square km). Bangladesh has a considerable waste problem. The main concern is the capital city of Dhaka, where approximately 10 million people live and produce around 3,000 tons of waste per household; over half of this is collected by Waste Concern.

Dhaka provides public land for composting purposes. Waste Concern collects solid waste house-to-house in rickshaw bicycles and takes it to processing plants where organic waste is separated from other rubbish. Then the waste is made into enriched bio-fertilizers. The Group arranges for fertilizer companies to purchase and nationally market the compost-based fertilizer. Waste Concern has five composting plants in Dhaka: one of 10–12 tons per day capacity, two of 3 tons per day capacity, and two of 1 ton per day capacity.

The principal activity of Waste Concern is composting, which gives a good alternative to conventional solid waste management options, reducing the amount of waste to be transported and dumped, and producing the valuable raw material for fertilizers. The composted product is mainly sold to fertilizer producing companies that blend this compost with additives to suit different customers. Sales of the product are made through existing agriculture services and the retail networks of these companies. Thus, the compost marketing is done by letting others do the individual marketing of the compost. Waste Concern also provides jobs to hundreds of the poor, who collect waste and help to solve the waste problem in Bangladesh. In addition, Waste Concern has had great financial success.

Currently, Waste Concern conducts research, provides consultation services, project assistance, support for institutional development, capacity building and innovation, and implementation of projects in such fields as solid waste management and resource recovery, clinical and hazardous waste management, waste water treatment, community based environmental improvement, municipal services planning, environmental impact assessment, energy and waste audit, industrial pollution control, environmental management system, climate change and a clean development mechanism, eco-friendly agriculture and organic farming.

Questions:

1. What is the key to success of Waste Concern?
2. How did Waste Concern change an environmental problem into an economic opportunity?

(cont'd)

3. What conditions would be necessary to apply similar strategies in other developing countries?

Sources: Waste Concern Website: www.wasteconcern.org; J. Mitchell and J. Mair, 'Waste Concern: Turning a Problem into a Resource' (Barcelona: IESE Publishing, 2006); C40 Large Cities Climate Summit, www. nycclimatesummit.com/casestudies/waste/waste_dhaka.pdf; C. Zurgbrugg, S. Drescher, I. Rytz, A.H.Md. Maqsood Sinha and I. Enayetullah, 'Decentralised Composting in Bagladesh, A Win-Win Situation for all Stakeholders', *Resources, Conservation, Recycling*, 43 (2005): 281–92; www.wasteconcern.org/Publication/rcr_composting_bangladesh_zurbrugg_2004.pdf

---

Dilemma 15

Two immigrants from Asia worked hard to build a business devoted to the disposal of dry-cleaning waste in the western United States. This waste product basically consisted of liquid solvent perchloroethylene (PCE), a hazardous chemical. According to the laws of the state where they operate, this liquid should be incinerated.

The owners of the business complied with environmental requirements when they started; however, their business grew so rapidly that they became overwhelmed by the volume of waste coming from 240 dry-cleaners. In addition, they realized that the cost of incineration was several hundred dollars per drum more than burying it in a landfill.

One of the partners proposed to the other that they could mislabel containers of dry-cleaning waste containing PCE and bury them in landfills instead of having them incinerated. He argued that burying containers is also a form of being environmentally responsible and that the risk of being caught was not too high.

Questions:

1. What do you think of the arguments given to avoid incineration of PCE?
2. What would you recommend to these businessmen if your opinion were sought?

Summary

Environmentalism, which includes both actions in defence of the non-human environment and philosophical debates, has an impact on governments and corporations.

Four approaches can be distinguished in environmental business ethics, which are based on four different philosophical approaches to the human-nature relationship: (1) dominative-anthropocentrism; (2) biocentrism; (3) ecocentrism; and (4) stewardship. The latter is consistent with a person-centred approach to business ethics.

(cont'd)

Animals can be used for food and clothing, but animal welfare should be provided for in business operations – for instance, avoiding overcrowding in poultry farms or other situations in which animals can experience distress or neglect. Scientific experimentation with animals can be conducted, within reasonable limits, in the interests of human health or to save human life.

Natural resources should be used responsibly, avoiding resource depletion. Deforestation is of special concern in some regions.

Fossil fuels – such as petroleum, natural gas and coal – are non-renewable energy sources that meet about two thirds of world energy consumption needs. Their combustion produces carbon dioxide, which causes global warning. The alternative is nuclear power, which involves some associated risks.

Renewable sources of energy such as hydroelectric energy, wind power, photovoltaic cells and solar heating are still marginal, but their use is increasing.

A responsible business contributes to energy conservation by reducing consumption of energy services and by an efficient use of energy.

Pollution is a major environmental issue in many business activities. There are three main types of pollution: (1) the atmosphere (through gases and solid particles); (2) water (liquid effluents); and (3) soil, along with other less frequent forms of pollution, such as noise, light and visual pollution. These forms can be prevented in most cases through the use of non-polluting alternatives, or by using technical means to avoid emissions of pollutants. Radioactive pollution deserves particular consideration.

Business can contribute to efficient waste management by taking action to reduce waste production and by favouring reuse and recycling. An appropriate disposal of waste is particularly important when it contains toxins.

Business can adopt three environmental strategies: (1) a reactive strategy of pollution control in accordance with regulations (at least enforceable ones); (2) a proactive strategy based on pollution prevention; and (3) an integral proactive strategy, based on changing processes or adopting designs to favour the environment and product stewardship.

Notes

1. THE ROLE OF ETHICS IN BUSINESS

1. Address of Sir Geoffrey Chandler to BT's 'Just Values' conference in January 2003 (referenced in Christie, 2005).
2. Quoted by B. L. Toffler, *Final Accounting: Ambition, Greed, and the Fall of Arthur Andersen* (New York: Broadway Books, 2003: 16).
3. Toffler, *op. cit.*: 118.
4. Toffler, *op. cit.*: 105.
5. Toffler, *op. cit.*: 62.
6. Toffler, *op. cit.*: 66.
7. Some studies show that the moral reasoning of many people depends on their current stage of moral development (Kohlberg 1981, 1984). Cultural environment and other factors are also influential (see, for instance, Church *et al.* 2005 and Treviño and Weaver 2006).
8. Especially on religious grounds (Melé 2006).
9. One is dated as early as 1913 (Oliverio 1989).
10. See a short history of business ethics in recent years in De George (2006).
11. For more details on the Lockheed case, see Velasquez (1982: 169–72).
12. For instance, De George (1982) and Velasquez (1982). Subsequently, many other editions of these and others works have been published.
13. See, for example, DesJardins (1984), Solomon (1992, 1999, 2004), Koehn (1995) and Hartman (1996).
14. The concept of stakeholder gained popularity with Freeman (1984).
15. We will deal with these two concepts in Chapter 12, pp. 299–316, and Chapter 14, pp. 324–37.
16. Nash (1990: 5).
17. On this point, see, for instance, Toffler (1986: 20).
18. This is, for instance, the position of Paine (2000a, 2003).
19. See Hosmer (1995).
20. Brenkert (1998) developed this point.
21. See Román (2003).
22. See Clark and Payne (2006).
23. See Hagen and Choe (1998).
24. It was carried out by Aspen Institute in collaboration with the management consulting firm Booz Allen Hamilton (Kelly *et al.*, 2004). Although the response rate was low (3.5 per cent), 350 senior executives is a significant number – at least, for a first approach.
25. Paine (2003).
26. Bhide and Stevenson (1990) provided some examples that show that ethics does not always pay off in economic terms.
27. This was already suggested by Socrates more than 2,400 years ago. Literally, he stated: 'Seeing then that there are these two evils, the doing injustice and the suffering injustice – and we affirm that to do injustice is a greater, and to suffer injustice a lesser evil.' (Plato, *Gorgias*, 8).

28. 'Corporations' is usually used in a broad sense to mean all kinds of businesses. In this book, we will use the term 'corporation' in this broad sense, unless explicitly otherwise pointed out.
29. This was especially emphasized by Davis and Blomstrom (1966).
30. See MacMillan *et al.* (2000).
31. For instance, Weaver *et al.* (1999).
32. See, for instance, Treviño and Weaver (2006).
33. This dilemma arose from a dialogue between Socrates and Euthyphro. This is why it is known as the 'Euthyphro Dilemma'. Literally, the question was formulated as follows: 'Is the pious loved by the gods because it is pious, or is it pious because it is loved by the gods?' (Plato, *Euthyphro*). This dilemma has been revived over time and is still alive today. Some people only accept ethics based exclusively on religious precepts, while others reject any ethics that have any connection with religion.
34. In this sense, 'moral theology', which considers both faith and reason, is better applied to business problems than pure 'religious ethics'.
35. Thus, the ranking of *Harris Interactive* (www.harrisinteractive.com), which is based on a wide survey on the perception of the corporate reputation among the stakeholders of each company.
36. http://www.jnj.com/connect/about-jnj/jnj-credo/
37. Phil Donahue's interview with James E. Burke, quoted by L. S. Paine, 2003: 31).

2. BUSINESS IN SOCIETY: ARE THE MARKET AND REGULATIONS SUFFICIENT?

1. Arrow (1973: 315).
2. See, for instance, Haeffner (1989), Kowalczyk (1991) and Crosby (1996).
3. See Chapter 7, pp. 157–9.
4. See Kreps (2003).
5. See a summary of this point in Argandoña (2008).
6. See Salanie (2000) and Kreps (2003).
7. On market failures see, for instance, Cowen (1992) and Salanie (2000).
8. See Chapter 13, pp. 304–5.
9. See, for example, Albert (1993) and Amable (2003).
10. See Chapter 4, pp. 79–80 and 84–6.
11. This is what, in similar words, wrote Pope John Paul II (1991, n. 42) regarding the ethical acceptability of capitalism:
    If by 'capitalism' is meant an economic system which recognizes the fundamental and positive role of business, the market, private property and the resulting responsibility for the means of production, as well as free human creativity in the economic sector, then the answer is certainly in the affirmative... But if by 'capitalism' is meant a system in which freedom in the economic sector is not circumscribed within a strong juridical framework which places it at the service of human freedom in its totality, and which sees it as a particular aspect of that freedom, the core of which is ethical and religious, then the reply is certainly negative.
12. On abuses in pricing, see Chapter 12, pp. 283–6.
13. In Chapter 6, pp. 129–46.
14. Friedman (1962, 1970).
15. Arrow (1974)
16. See Edwards (2004), on civil society.
17. We will consider the relationship between NGOs and corporations in Chapter 13, pp. 304–5.

18. See Vogel (2005).
19. An interesting discussion on the limits of the law can be found in Stone (1975).
20. We will go back to this point in Chapter 5, p. 144.
21. Llano (1997: 57).
22. http://www.regions.cummins.com/sa/pages/en/whoweare/cumminshistory.cfm
23. Cummins corporate website: www.cummins.com
24. R. Nelson (1992) 'Training on Ethics: Cummins Eng. Co.', *Journal of Management Development,* 11 (4), 21–33.
25. See the study about Cummins' ethical standards published by the Center for the Study of Ethics in the Professions from the Illinois Institute of Technology, http://www.ethics.iit.edu/codes/coe/cummins.engine.co.ethical.standards.html
26. Cummins' Code of Conduct, http://www.cumminsindia.com:8080/xsql/cumminsIndia/CIL/PDF/cummins_inc_codeconduct.pdf
27. http://www.epa.gov/Compliance/resources/decrees/civil/caa/cummins-cd.pdf
28. http://cfpub.epa.gov/compliance/cases/#571
29. 'Cummins Engine Co.', Center for the Study of Ethics in the Professions, Illinois Institute of Technology, http://www.ethics.iit.edu/codes/coe/cummins.engine.co.ethical.standards.html
30. Cummins official website, http://www.cummins.com/cmi/content.jsp?siteId=1&langId=1033&menuId=1&overviewId=2&menuIndex=1
31. See Cummins Sustainability Reports in its corporate website: www.cummins.com
32. '100 Best Corporate Citizens 2007', *Corporate Responsibility Officer,* 2 (1), 20, January/February 2007.
33. The ranking comes from *Business Ethics Magazine,* which later changed its name to *Corporate Responsibility Office.* See www.business-ethics.com

3. CULTURAL DIVERSITY, COMMON VALUES AND INTERNATIONAL STANDARDS

1. Hofstede (2003, 2004).
2. See, for instance, Thomas (1996).
3. In simple words, the Golden Rule can be stated to be: 'Put yourself in the place of others.' In Chapter 4, p. 79, we will consider this principle in greater detail.
4. For a deeper discussion of cultural relativism and universal ethics, see Bowie (1989) and Frederick (2002), along with Rachels and Rachels (1995, ch. on Cultural Relativism), and Kransz (1989).
5. We take the following story from Bowie (1989).
6. Puffer and McCarthy (1995).
7. Whitcomb *et al.* (1998).
8. De George (1996).
9. McMahon (1981).
10. Quinn and Jones (1995: 34), who follow a thoughtful study by Hausman and McPherson (1993).
11. Lewis (1987) and Moses (2001).
12. 'An Interfaith Declaration: A Code of Ethics on International Business for Christians, Muslims and Jews', www.cauxroundtable.org/AnInterfaithDeclaration.html
13. Dalla Costa (1998).
14. Kidder (1994).
15. This meeting was organized in 1992 by the Aspen Institute and carried out by the Josephson Institute of Ethics.
16. Josephson (1997), quoted by Schwartz (2005).
17. www.ilo.org

18. www.fairlabor.org
19. www.ceres.org
20. www.iccwbo.org/home/environment/charter.asp
21. www.unglobalcompact.org/AboutTheGC/index.html
22. www.un.org/Overview/rights.html
23. www.ilo.org/dyn/declaris/DECLARATIONWEB.static_jump?var_language=EN&var_pagename=DECLARATIONTEXT
24. www.unep.org/Documents.Multilingual/Default.asp?DocumentID=78&ArticleID=1163
25. http://www.unodc.org/pdf/corruption/publications_unodc_convention-e.pdf
26. www.cauxroundtable.org
27. www.oecd.org/dataoecd/56/36/1922428.pdf
28. For more details, see Melé (2006).
29. See Pava (1997, 1998).
30. For a further explanation, see Tamari (1997).
31. See Green (1997).
32. See Carver (2004).
33. Friedman (2001) has developed this point.
34. An excellent synthesis of this teaching is the *Compendium of Catholic Social Doctrine*, published by the Pontifical Council for Justice and Peace (PCJP) (2004).
35. See Eglise Orthodoxe Russe (2007).
36. See Herman (1998).
37. See Roels (1997).
38. See, among others, Rice (1999), Naugthon and Naugthon (2000), Chachedina (2001), Saeed *et al.* (2001), Cone (2003) and Haniffa and Hudaib (2007).
39. On this point, see Haniffa and Hudaib (2007).
40. See Sharma and Talwar (2004).
41. Schumacher (1999).
42. The following systesis is taken from Ip (2009).
43. See Ip (2009).
44. See Romar (2004).
45. Romar (2002).
46. Ip (2009).
47. See Maher and Wong (1994).

4. ETHICS, AT THE CORE OF HUMAN ACTION

1. Follett (1940).
2. *Fortune*, 21 May 1990: 59.
3. Principles are also understood as fundamental ideas that govern thought, but here we only consider principles regarding behaviours.
4. *Nicomachean Ethics, II*, 1.
5. Paine (1996).
6. *Nicomachean Ethics* II, 6.
7. Koehn (1995: 536).
8. Koslowski (1995: 183).
9. Polo (1996: 114).
10. MacIntyre (1993: 144).
11. See Chapter 5, pp. 115–20.

12. See Chapter 1, p. 10.

13. Term introduced by Anscombe (1958). Aristotle presented the concept of *eudaimonia* as the highest, most inclusive end of the human life. *Eudaimonia* is a Greek term popularly translated as happiness. However, this word hardly expresses what Aristotle meant, since happiness is usually understood as a state of mind related to joy and pleasure, and consequently a subjective perception of well-being. Contrastingly, for Aristotle *eudaimonia* has an objective sense. Currently, 'human flourishing' is often preferred as a translation of *eudaimonia*.

14. Aristotle discusses this point in the first chapter of the *Nicomachean Ethics*. For a philosophical discussion of the concept of human flourishing, see Frankel *et al.* (1999). See also Spaemann (2005).

15. MacIntyre (1993: 136–7).

16. Maslow (1943, 1954).

17. Maslow (1970).

18. Alderfer (1969).

19. Max-Neef (1991).

20. Other authors have proposed another list of human goods by considering what practical rationality can discover from natural human inclinations (Aquinas, 1981 [1273], I–II, q. 94, a. 3; Oderberg, 2000: 34–45) or by intuition (Finnis, 1986: chs III and IV). Although some overlap could probably be discovered with these lists, this is beyond our purpose here.

21. Truth can be defined as the agreement of one's thoughts with reality, or the conformity of the intellect to things.

22. See several formulations of the Golden Rule in http://www.tralvex.com/pub/spiritual/index. htm#GR

23. This is specially stressed by Spaemann (2006).

24. See Chapter 3, pp. 53–7.

25. See further developments in Williams (2005).

26. On this point, see Novak (1998).

27. Aquinas emphasized that a person is expressive of dignity (Williams, 2005: 155, footnote 25).

28. Kant (1993: 36).

29. See the Appendix to this chapter.

30. Wojtyla (1981 [1960]: 41). Here we prefer to use 'Personalist' rather than 'Personalistic', as this English translation does.

31. Literally, Wojtyla affirms: 'The person is the kind of good which does not admit of use and cannot be treated as an object of use and as such the means to an end.' He adds: 'A person is an entity of a sort to which the only proper and adequate way to relate is love.' (1993: 41).

32. See, for instance, Finnis (1986) and Williams (2005).

33. John Locke, a British thinker, is frequently presented as the most prominent philosopher on Human Rights Theory (or 'natural rights', as Locke preferred to say). Previously, human rights were substantially defended in Spain, mainly by Francisco de Vitoria (in the sixteenth century) on the rights of the Indians after the discovery of America (Hernández, 1984); and even by Aquinas in the thirteenth century (García-López, 1979). Within Roman Law, Ulpian held that certain universal rights exist beyond the rights of citizenship because there is a natural law that precedes positive law (*Encyclopedia Britannica*. Article on Historical Development of Human Rights, http://www.britannica.com/eb/article-10502/human-rights#742072. hook).

34. See further details in Wikipedia (History of Human Rights).

35. On this point, see Sen (1999).

36. Stanford Encyclopedia of Philosophy: Hannah Arendt: http://www.seop.leeds.ac.uk/entries/arendt/ (2006).

37. The roots of the 'common good' concept can be found in Aristotelian thought. In recent times, it has been especially stressed by Maritain (1947, 1951 and 1971) and by Catholic social tradition (see Pontifical Council for Justice and Peace, 2004: ch. 4, II and Bertone, 2007).
38. Finnis (1986: 165).
39. On 'organizational citizenship behaviour', see Werner (2006).
40. For a discussion of others' meanings of virtue, see MacIntyre (1985).
41. We will consider how practical wisdom is developed in Chapter 9, pp. 108–9.
42. This point was highlighted by Aristotle. See Koehn (1995) and Hartman (2006).
43. Many believe that animals are God's creatures, and, consequently, they refer to the Creator respecting animals in their own identity. We will consider the ethical issues of using animals for food, clothing and scientific experimentation in Chapter 15, pp. 351–2.
44. These and other virtues are presented and briefly analysed in Chapter 9, pp. 205–18, in the context of leadership.
45. On this point, see Aristotle in *Nicomachean Ethics,* II, 6.
46. See *Protagoras* 330b and *The Republic,* IV.
47. In the *Book of Wisdom* (8, 7).
48. In *The Meditations* (3, 6).
49. Regarding this latter, see Aquinas (1966 [1273]).
50. See Appendix, Chapter 3, pp. 90–4.
51. Among them Pieper (1966), Geach (1977) and Jaroszynski and Anderson (2003).
52. A similar classification can be found in Shaw (1996).
53. Kant (1993)
54. The second formulation is also quite popular. We refer to the latter in this chapter in the context of the Personalist Principle.
55. Kant (1993 [1785]: 30).
56. See, for example, De George (1999) and Velasquez (2001).
57. See Bowie (1999) and Bowie and Werhane (2005).
58. See Simmons (1992).
59. Locke 1989 [1689]).
60. This sentence is attributed to Francis Hutchenson, a British philosopher of the eighteenth century.
61. Bentham (1996 [1780]).
62. Mill (2001 [1863]).
63. For further discussion of utilitarianism see, for example, Smart and Williams (1973) and Taylor (1982). A radical criticism is provided by Finnis (1983), who questions whether utilitarianism is even an ethical theory.
64. Philosophers of this tradition are Thomas Hobbes (1588–1679), John Locke (1632–1704) and Jean-Jacques Rousseau (1712–78).
65. Rawls (1999 [1971]).
66. Donaldson and Dunfee (1994, 1999).
67. Habermas (1990, 1993).
68. See Steinmann and Löhr (1994), among others.
69. For example, Moriarty (2005).
70. Especially as a consequence of several influential scholars, including Anscombe (1958) and MacIntyre (1985).
71. Among others, Solomon (1992, 2004), Koehn (1995) and Hartman (1996).
72. On this point, see Hartman (2006).
73. On Thomistic Ethics, see MacInerny (1997).

74. Particularly in *De Legibus* and *De Re Publica*.
75. See Melé (1999).
76. See Velasquez and Brady (1997) and Velasquez (2008).
77. Gilligan (1982) and Slote (2007).
78. Actually the application of Personalism to business ethics is still in its infancy. Whetstone (2002), for instance, fits in moral leadership, and especially the view of the servant leader, with Personalism.
79. Wojtyla (1981, 1993), Mounier (2001) and Bowne (2007), among others.
80. www.michelin.com/corporate/front/templates/affich.jsp?codeRubrique=74&lang=EN
81. *Ibid.*
82. www.michelin.com/corporate/front/templates/affich.jsp?codeRubrique=76&lang=EN
83. F. Michelin, *And Why Not? Morality and Business* (Maryland: Lexington Books, 2003): 1.
84. *Ibid.*: xvi.
85. *Ibid.*: 26.
86. *Ibid.*: 9.
87. *Ibid.*: 78.
88. *Ibid.*: 20.
89. *Ibid.*: 7.
90. *Ibid.*: 80.
91. *Ibid.*

5. INDIVIDUAL RESPONSIBILITY AND MORAL JUDGEMENTS IN BUSINESS

1. Bernanos (1955).
2. Report of the Special Investigative Committee of the Board of Directors of WorldCom, http://www.sec.gov/Archives/edgar/data/723527/000093176303001862/dex991.htm#ex991902_24
3. *Ibid.*
4. C. Cooper, *Extraordinary Circumstances: The Journey of a Corporate Whistleblower* (Hoboken, NJ: Wiley 2008).
5. See a broader discussion of freedom and responsibility in Bok (1998).
6. *Nicomachean Ethics*, III, 3.
7. Legal studies, apart from this responsibility, also consider 'civil and administrative responsibility'.
8. See Wikipedia (Liability).
9. See, for instance, Crosby (1996).
10. Llano (1991: 69–146).
11. Existentialist philosophy, particularly that of Jean-Paul Sartre (2003), emphasized this responsibility to the point of giving it an absolute value. This is problematic since, in Sartre's way of thinking, the human being has no link with the transcendent, so the responsibility is only that of each individual to him- or herself. This leaves a vacuum where some idea of this type of engagement ought to be.
12. See Novak (1996).
13. See *Nicomachean Ethics*, III. Following Aristotle, Aquinas considered responsibility in the context of human acts (1981 [1273], I–II, q. 6–21).
14. In law, it is called *reckless* or *wanton negligence* when acts occur that would be classified as crimes, had they been performed with malice.
15. Milgram (1974).

16. Eichmann was a Nazi SS Lieutenant Colonel. He was charged with facilitating and managing the logistics of mass deportations of Jews to ghettos and extermination camps in Nazi occupied Eastern Europe. He has often been referred to as the 'architect of the Holocaust'.

17. This is defended by Harman (2000: 223), who argued that character traits do not exist. Doris (2002: 28) added that personality traits make no significant contributions to predicting and explaining behaviour. Others openly disagree (Solomon, 2003; Card, 2005 and Alzola, 2008).

18. See a brief description of these experiments in Alzola (2008).

19. See a deeper discussion on this point in Solomon (2003).

20. See Comer and Vega (2008).

21. Whistle-blowing is studied in Chapter 6, pp. 140–1.

22. This theory was first developed by Thomas Aquinas (1981 [1273], I–II, 6, 18). These three elements – intention, object and circumstances – have been considered in social and business contexts by Barnsley (1972), Melé (1997), Crockett (2005), and Arjoon (2006), among others.

23. See Chapter 6, pp. 144–6.

24. See Chapter 4, pp. 75–8.

25. See Chapter 4, pp. 75–85.

26. As mentioned above, some habits, once acquired, decrease the responsibility for an action, but not the responsibility for developing such habits in the first place. This is the case of laziness, which makes it difficult to fulfil a duty, a habit that might have been acquired in the distant past, even in one's youth. Similarly, controlling one's aggressive impulses or lacking courage to overcome fear can be due to lack of character.

27. See Mangan (1949). For criticisms and replies to the Principle of Double Effect, see Oderberg (2000: 96–105).

28. On the Principle of Double Effect, see also Oderberg (2000: 88–96). Mangan (1949: 43) formulated four conditions necessary for a person licitly to perform an action that he or she foresees will produce a good effect and a bad effect. They are that: (1) from its very object, the action in itself is good – or, at least, neutral; (2) the intention is to achieve the good effect, not the bad effect; (3) the good effect will not be produced by means of the bad effect; (4) there be a proportionately grave reason for permitting the bad effect. Walzer (1977: 151–9) pointed out a fifth condition: (5) the agent minimizes the foreseen harm, even if this involves accepting additional risk or forgoing some benefit.

29. This could be the case of large corporations cooperating with the wrongdoing of a contractor somewhere along their supply chain. On responsibility for supply chains, see Chapter 11, pp. 256–7.

6. FREQUENT ETHICAL ISSUES IN BUSINESS

1. Spaemann (1989: 10, 12).

2. Contracts are extensively treated in law studies. See, for instance, Vietzen (2008). For contracts and other issues of business law, although limited to the US, see Cheeseman (2000).

3. Labour contracts will be considered in Chapter 11, pp. 252–5.

4. See Chapter 4, pp. 77–8.

5. See Chapter 12, pp. 383–6.

6. For further information on this controversy, see, for example, Vachani and Smith (2004), De George (2005), Werhane and Gorman (2005), Brennan and Baines (2006), and Byrne *et al.* (2006).

7. See more details on this point in Ostas (2008). On corporate fraud, see Comer (1998, 2003).

8. From a legal perspective, a number of factors are considered to determine whether a particular piece of information can be qualified as a trade secret (Marsnik, 2008).

9. For further details, see Marsnik (2008).

10. See Brittain-Catlin (2005).

11. It can also include different types of stock-market contracts, such as contracts for the subscription, purchase or sale of securities, forward contracts, options and financial futures and index futures.

12. For instance, Fishman and Hagerty (1992).

13. Particularly, Leland (1992) and Manne (1966, 2005).

14. For a further discussion, see Werhane (1989, 1991), Moore (1990), Baker and Edelman (1999), Snoeyenbos and Smith (2000), and Engelen and Liedekerke (2007), among others.

15. This is the main argument underlying the EU legislation that prohibits insider trading (Council Directive 89/592/EEC of 13 November 1989 (No. L 334/30, Introduction)).

16. See Miceli and Near (1992).

17. See Chapter 5, pp. 109–10.

18. See Larmer (1992).

19. Loyalty can mean: 'utilitarian loyalty', 'emotional loyalty' and 'virtuous loyalty' (Melé, 2001).

20. http://www/usdoj.gov/criminal/fraud/fcpa/

21. *The Text of the Convention on Combating Bribery of Foreign Public Officials in International Business Transactions* (this is the complete name) is available in: http://www.oecd.org/document/21/0,3343,en_2649_34859_2017813_1_1_1_1,00.html#Text_of_the_Convention

22. http://www/unodc.org/pdf/crime/convention_corruption/signing/Convention-e.pdf

23. See http://www.unodc.org/unodc/en/treaties/CAC/signatories.html. Some countries, however, included a few reservations, mostly regarding the writing of some articles of this document.

24. www.transparency.org

25. See Argandoña (2001, 2003).

26. See Anand *et al.* (2005).

27. See Chapter 5, pp. 120–2.

28. I owe this insight to Argandoña (2005), in his broad discussion of the issue of facilitating payments.

29. See more details of this GM policy in Murphy (1998: 81–5.)

7. THE PURPOSE OF THE FIRM AND MISSION-DRIVEN MANAGEMENT

1. Taken from Drucker (1974: 41).

2. On this point, see Ellsworth (2002).

3. See Duska and Ragatz (2008).

4. http://www.geocities.com/TimesSquare/1848/ikea.html

5. http://www.merck.com/about/mission.html

6. Corporate website of Ben & Jerry's: http://www.benjerry.com/our_company/our_mission/

7. www.pg.com/company/who_we_are/ppv.jhtml

8. Cardona and Rey (2008).

9. *Trustees of Dartmouth* v. *Woodward*, 17 U.S. (4 Wheat.) 518, 636 (1819), quoted by Phillips (1992).

10. Although a business corporation, strictly speaking, refers only to a large firm, the term is also usually employed as a synonym of firm, regardless of size. Here, we use both concepts interchangeably.

11. This is made clear in the work of Jackall (1983).

12. Although homo oeconomicus may be a good approximation to human behaviour when individuals act in markets, many experiments show that individuals often do not act completely selfishly.

13. This is made explicit in Evans and Freeman (1988: 151) and Freeman (1997: 71), who propose this view.

14. Freeman (2000: 176).

15. This is the proposal of Keeley (1988, 1995).

16. Barnard, a pioneer in management thought showed that cooperation was a key in organisations (see Barnard 1968 [1938]). Since then, this has been a generally accepted idea.

17. p. 26. On 'civic friendship' see p. 84.

18. A set of individuals interacting for a common goal is not sufficient to build a community. This requires an enduring unity, a common action and a shared purpose. If you consider a group of people working together to help a person who has suffered an accident, they are not a community. Neither is a group of people with a common goal enough: a few individuals waiting for a bus who agree to share a taxi, for example. However, other groups of people, such as a family, a neighbourhood or a company have enduring unity, apart from some common action and a shared purpose; they are therefore communities, although the degree of unity might range from strong to weak.

19. Solomon (1994: 277).

20. For an historical analysis of the rise of shareholder value as a principle of corporate governance in the United States, see Lazonick and O'Sullivan (2000).

21. See Friedman (1962, 1970).

22. See Elegido (1995).

23. Particularly, Jensen (2001: 302).

24. This point is emphasized by Jensen (2001) and Sundaram and Inkpen (2004).

25. Simon (1997 [1959]).

26. Evans and Freeman (1988: 151).

27. Freeman (1994) has also accepted that the purpose can be defined in different manners within the stakeholder approach by applying different theories; for example, managers ought to act in the interests of stakeholders (fair contracts theory), or to maintain and care for relationships and networks of stakeholders (feminist standpoint theory).

28. Clarkson (1995).

29. Evans and Freeman (1988).

30. This is the case in Clarkson (1995).

31. Donaldson and Preston (1995).

32. Freeman (1999: 235).

33. Some researchers have questioned whether business management focused on stakeholder needs brings about a financial return superior to others that are exclusively oriented to shareholder short-term interests. We will return to this point in Chapter 15, p. 307.

34. Jensen (2001).

35. On this point, see Phillips *et al.* (2003).

36. See Chapter 4, pp. 84–6. Some authors have applied the notion of the common good as a key concept for defining the purpose of the firm. Among others, Argandoña (1998), Alford and Naugthon (2002), Melé (2002), Fontrodona and Sison (2006), Koslowski (2006) and Sison (2008).

37. A similar list has been provided by Llano (1997, ch. 8) and Melé (2002).

38. See Chapter 13, pp. 311–2 on sustainable development.

39. Chapter 14 provides a further development of the concept of corporate citizenship.

40. http://www.pg.com/company/who_we_are/ppv.jhtml

41. Koslowski (2006: 72).

42. See Chapter 2, pp. 35–6.

43. Solomon (1999: 46).

44. See Messner (1965).

45. Handy (1999: 50). On this point, see also Handy (2002).
46. Handy (1997: 28).
47. Berle and Means (1932). Previously, Berle (1927) had already referred to this topic.
48. See Jensen and Meckling (1976).
49. On this point, see Insight 8 in Chapter 8, pp. 188–9.
50. 'Self-fulfilling theories' influence people to act according to theoretical descriptions or predictions (Merton, 1957). On this topic applied to management, see Ferraro *et al.* (2005).
51. See Eisenhardt (1989).
52. George (2003: 20).

8. USE AND MISUSE OF POWER

1. In French: *La justice et le pouvoir doivent être réunis, pour que ce qui est juste puisse être puissant et ce qui est puissant peut être juste* (Pascal, 1954: 1160).
2. *New York Times* (1991): A26, mentioned by Sims and Brinkmann (2002: 334).
3. Letter to Bishop Mandell Creighton, 3 April 1887. Quoted by Oxford Concise Dictionary of Quotations (3rd edn, Oxford: Oxford University Press, 1993), 1, 5 from L. Creighton, *Life and Letters of Mandell Creighton* (1904), vol. 1, ch. 13.
4. The chief executive officer (CEO) or chief executive is in charge of overall management and has the final responsibility for decisions made within corporate activity. The CEO reports to the Board of Directors and, sometimes, directly to the stockholders. Top management can include, apart from the CEO, senior managers who are close collaborators of the CEO. Intermediate managers basically monitor activities of subordinates and generate reports for upper management. Intermediate managers also have power, although more limited than that of top managers.
5. See Chapter 13, pp. 299–300.
6. Actually, Machiavelli did not justify all types of means. For instance, he held that cruel actions should be swift, effective and short-lived.
7. Spaemann (1989: 38).
8. Rawls (1999: 3).
9. Incorporated in the Justinian's *Digest* (1,1). See Watson (1998).
10. MacIntyre (1988) provides an interesting insight on this point.
11. In particular, Scherer (1992) presents an interdisciplinary view that considers justice from perspectives of philosophy, economics, law, sociology and psychology.
12. This is common in modern theories of justice. See, for instance, Kolm (1996).
13. Money was introduced into society to gain some form of adequate measure and representation between objects and services of different value.
14. Drucker (1989: 221).
15. See Chapter 11, pp. 250–67 and Chapter 12, pp. 274–90, respectively.
16. See Chapter 5, pp. 112–13.
17. See Chapter 5, p. 108.
18. See Chapter 5, pp. 109–10.
19. This point has been developed by Moberg (2000).
20. See Chapter 6, p. 133.
21. See Gaa and Dunmore (2007).
22. See Chapter 6, pp. 134–5.
23. Bogle (2005), mentioned by Bogle (2008: 22).
24. Bogle, (2008: 25).
25. See the study by Frydman and Sacks (2007) regarding levels and structures of executive pay from 1936 to 2005.

26. Mintzberg (1973).
27. See Chapter 5, p. 112.
28. See Chapter 6, pp. 140–1.
29. Cadbury Committee (1992).
30. See links in http://www.ecgi.org/codes/all_codes.php
31. The Organization for Economic Cooperation and Development (OECD) is an international organization of developed countries, created in 1961, that accepts the principles of representative democracy and free market economy. It brings together the governments of 30 countries and shares expertise and exchanges views with more than 100 other countries and economies. Its goals include supporting sustainable economic growth, boosting employment, raising living standards, maintaining financial stability, assisting other countries' economic development and contributing to growth in world trade.
32. Cadbury (1987: 70).
33. Cadbury Committee (1992). See also in European Corporate Governance Institute,: http://www.ecgi.org/codes/documents/cadbury.pdf

9. HUMAN VIRTUES IN LEADERSHIP OF ORGANIZATIONS

1. Quoted from Warneka *et al.* (2007).
2. Prentice (1961).
3. Zaleznik (1977).
4. Kotter (1990).
5. Mintzberg (1975).
6. Pérez-López (2002: ch. 8).
7. See D'Orts (1997: 37–9).
8. See Mommsen (1992).
9. See Hunter (1998, ch. 1).
10. See Llano (2004: 52).
11. Hunter (1998: 28).
12. See, for instance, Daft (1999) and Northouse (2007).
13. See Cardona (2005).
14. Thus, Hosmer (1994), Connock and Johns (1995), Kanugo and Mendonca (1996), Ciulla (1998, 2002), Coles (2000) and Maak (2006).
15. Drucker (2005: 155).
16. Respectively, Ciulla (1998) and Sison (2003).
17. See Ciulla (1995), Daft (1999) and Northouse (2007), among others.
18. Northouse (2007).
19. Kirkpatrick and Locke (1991).
20. Collins (2001).
21. See, for example, Daft (1999: 62–120).
22. See Ciulla (1995).
23. Apart from Burns (1978), see also Bass (1990) on this point.
24. Burns (1978: 20).
25. Bass and Steidlmeier. (1999).
26. This aspect is especially emphasized by Block (1996).
27. Greenleaf (2002).
28. Wikipedia (Servant leadership).

29. Including De Pree (1990), Senge (1990), Covey (1991), and Hunter (1998).
30. Cardona (2000).
31. Pérez-López (2002: ch. 8).
32. Greenleaf (2002: 27).
33. See Spears (1995, 1998).
34. See Pérez-López (1998: 97ff.).
35. Stewardship in leadership has been especially stressed by Block (1996).
36. See George (2003: 12).
37. Block (1996: 21–2).
38. See Chapter 4, p. 87.
39. See Chapter 5, pp. 114–15.
40. See Chapter 4, p. 89.
41. See Llano (1996) and also Pieper (1966) and Ramirez (1978).
42. This point has been developed by Paladino *et al.* (2007: ch. 1).
43. Definition from the Merriam-Webster Online Dictionary: http://www.merriam-webster.com/dictionary/corruption
44. Solomon (1999: 38).
45. *Ibid.*
46. *Nicomachean Ethics* (VI, 13).
47. For a further discussion of Aristotle's position on the unity of virtues, see Hughes (2001: 109–16).
48. Aquinas (1981[1273], I–II, 65, 1).
49. Petrick and Quinn (2000: 4).
50. Excerpts from Collins (2001).
51. See Balmes (1981[1845]: 191–2). Llano (2004: xii–xiv) has rediscovered this author, adding interesting insights on humility in leadership.
52. George (2003, 2007).
53. See 'Business ethics in practice', pp. 194–6.
54. George (2003: 12).
55. This is the meaning of 'magnanimity' according to the Merriam-Webster Online Dictionary, http://www.merriam-webster.com/dictionary/magnanimity
56. Havard (2007: 3).
57. Llano (1997: 154–5).
58. See Goodwin (2006).
59. See Havard (2007).
60. See Chapter 8, p. 181.
61. The latter is the specific content of what is termed 'general justice' (see p. 183).
62. Some practical aspects of use and misuse of managerial power have been dealt with in Chapter 8.
63. Pérez-López (1998: 105–6). See also this volume (p. 181).
64. Solomon (1999: 91).
65. Aquinas (1981[1273], II–II: 109, 3, 1).
66. See Melé (2001).
67. On this point, see Rosanas and Velilla (2003).
68. See Chapter 4, p. 51.
69. Frost (2003).
70. Dutton *et al.* (2002), Kanov *et al.* (2004); Lilius *et al.* (2008).
71. Cameron and Caza (2002). On virtue of forgiveness in managing people within organization, see Kurzynski (1998).
72. See Daft (1999, pp. 380ff).
73. George (2003: 24).

10. ETHICS IN ORGANIZATIONAL CULTURES AND STRUCTURES

1. This can be seen in 'Business ethics in practice 1' p. 18.
2. Mentioned by Paine (2000b: 2).
3. See, among others, Langlois and Schlegelmilch (1990), Schlegelmilch and Robertson (1995), Scholtens and Dam (2007).
4. See Lee *et al.* (2005).
5. It was carried out by Kaptein (2004).
6. Procter & Gamble corporate website.
7. Lufthansa corporate website
8. See Chapter 7, pp. 129–46.
9. See Chapter 11, pp. 251–65.
10. Empirical research shows conflicting results. Some find satisfactory results, but others are more pessimistic According to Kaptein (2008), a recognized expert in business codes, there are reasons for the divergent findings: varying definitions of key terms, deficiencies in the empirical data, and methodologies used and a lack of theory.
11. See Somers (2001).
12. For more details, see Ethics Resource Center (1990).
13. Deal and Kennedy (1982: 4).
14. Pettigrew (1979: 572).
15. See Pettigrew (1979), Deal and Kennedy (1982), Peters and Waterman (1982) and Schein (2004 [1984]), among others.
16. See Schein (1990).
17. See Kotter and Heskett (1992) and Goffee and Jones (1996).
18. Schein (2004 [1984]).
19. See Ashkanasy *et al.* (2000) for an overview of current research, theory and practice on organizational culture and climate field.
20. See Koys and Decotiis (1991).
21. See Arogyaswamy and Byles (1987).
22. See, for instance, Sethia and Von Glinow (1985); Treviño (1990), Sims (1992, 2000), Douglas *et al.* (2001) and Sims and Brinkmann (2002), among others.
23. See Melé (2003).
24. On this topic, we follow, partially, Schein (2004 [1984]) and the PriceWaterhouse Change Integration Team (1996: 98ff). The latter, after interviewing over 200 senior level corporate executives in a variety of manufacturing and service organizations, states: 'culture change does not result from a focus on culture itself, nor does it flow from training programs, wish lists of values and beliefs, or instructing people about customers. Such initiatives don't work.' To reshape culture, they propose that managers must focus on the six important 'levels' that create and shape culture: (1) leadership actions; (2) vision, purpose and strategy; (3) performance measures; (4) structure; (5) people practices; and (6) competitive context. In our proposal, these generic suggestions on shaping organizational culture have been applied to ethical organizational cultures.
25. See Weber (2007), for more details.
26. See Paine (1994).
27. Specifically, Treviño *et al.* (1999) and Weaver and Treviño (1999).
28. See, among others, Lindsay *et al.* (1996), Harvey (2000), Schminke (2001), Brickley *et al.* (2002), and Treviño and Nelson (2004).
29. Brickley *et al.* (1997) and James (2000).
30. Metzger *et al.* (1993) and Treviño and Nelson (2004).

31. See, for example, Kerr (1975) and Jansen and Von Glinow (1985).
32. See a summary in Drennan (2004).
33. See Wikipedia (*Société Générale*) and reference provided there.
34. Paine and Santoro (1993). For a summary of this case, see Petrick and Quinn (1997: 202–3).
35. See Waters and Bird (1987, 1989) and Bird and Waters (1987).
36. See Waters and Bird (1987).
37. Merchant (1987, cited by Metzger *et al.*, 1993: note 86).
38. See Palmer *et al.* (2007).
39. For a further development of participation within organizations, see Cludts (1999).
40. See Kaler (1999).
41. See Peters (1988).
42. See Collins (1996).
43. See a further development and case study in Melé (2005).
44. See Chapter 4, pp. 84–6.
45. See Torraco (2005).
46. See Harrington (1991).
47. For an overview regarding ethical issues in IT, see De George (2002).
48. On this point, see Moore (2000).
49. On this latter point, and regarding legality in the USA, see Halpern *et al.* (2008).
50. See Maury and Kleiner (2002).
51. On this point, see Kracher and Corritore (2004).
52. 'Servant Leadership: A Model that can Pay Great Dividends', *Dallas Business Journal – Small Business Insights,* 28 August 1998.

11. WORK AND WORKERS' RIGHTS WITHIN THE ORGANIZATION

1. Pope John Paul II (1981: n.12).
2. Wikipedia: http://www.en.wikipedia.org/wiki/Gap_Inc.
3. Gap official website: http://www.gapinc.com/public/SocialResponsibility/csr_supply_chain_overview.shtml
4. Gap official website: http://www.gapinc.com/public/SocialResponsibility/sr_faq.shtml#a113
5. See, for instance, Deane (1965) and Messner (1965, 1976).
6. Pope John Paul II (1981: n.6).
7. See Chapter 3, p. 54.
8. See Chapter 4, pp. 79–82.
9. See Chapter 4, pp. 81–2.
10. http://www.unicef.org/protection
11. UN Convention on the Rights of the Child (1989), art. 32.1: http://www.unhchr.ch/html/menu3/b/k2crc.htm
12. Letter-Encyclical '*Rerum novarum*' (1891: n. 42).
13. Zwolinski (2007) has discussed it.
14. On this, see Arnold and Bowie (2003, 2007).
15. This is the definition of 'living wage' given by Collins (2008: 1300).
16. See Chapter 5, p. 117.
17. We will return to this point in Chapter 13, pp. 315–16.
18. This definition was adopted by the Joint ILO/WHO Committee on Occupational Health at its first session in 1950 and revised during its twelfth session in 1995. Quoted by Wikipedia: 'Occupational Safety and Health',

19. Boatright (1993): 354.
20. See Chapter 4, pp. 115–17.
21. Available at http://www.unhcr.org/refworld/publisher,ILO,,,425bbdf72,0.html
22. http://www.ilo.org/global/About_the_ILO/Mainpillars/Therightsatwork/lang–en/index.htm
23. See more in Scott (2007)
24. For more details, see Melé (2008a).
25. See Beauchamp (2008).
26. US Department of Labor, OSHA: http://www.osha.gov/SLTC/workplaceviolence/otherresources.html; http://www.dol.gov/ILAB/media/reports/nao/violenceworkrisk.htm#024
27. See Bell *et al.* (2002).
28. On mobbing, see Vandekerckhove and Commers (2003).
29. See Moore (2000).
30. J. M. Logsdon and P. Forsythe, 'Maquiladoras', in R. W. Kolb, *Encyclopedia of Business Ethics and Society* (Thousand Oaks: Sage Publications, 2008): 1324–5.
31. *Labor Rights*, http://www.laborrights.org/files/Mexico2006SPAN.pdf. K. Lydersen, 'The Disappeared', In *These Times*, 19 May (2003), http://www.inthesetimes.com/article/321/
32. 'La Industria maquiladora en Ciudad Juárez': http://docentes.uacj.mx/rquinter/cronicas/maquilas.htm

12. ETHICS IN THE ORGANIZING OF MARKETING

1. American Marketing Association, *Statement of Ethics*, General Norms, adopted in 2004. See http://www.marketingpower.com/AboutAMA/Pages/Statement%20of%20Ethics.aspx
2. http://www.mattel.com/about_us/Corp_Governance/ethics.asp
3. 'Good Morning America' with Chris Cuomo, 'Mattel CEO Defends China Operations', ABC News, 14 August 2007. CNN videos, http://www.cnn.com/SPECIALS/2007/news/toy.recall/
4. 'Good Morning America' with Chris Cuomo, 'Mattel CEO Defends China Operations', ABC News, 14 August 2007. CNN video interviews, http://www.cnn.com/SPECIALS/2007/news/toy.recall/
5. 'Mattel Apologizes to China over Recalls', MSNBC, 21 September (2007), http://www.msnbc.msn.com/id/20903731/
6. Mattel Reports 2007 Financial Result: http://www.shareholder.com/mattel/news/Q407/Q407Release.pdf
7. E. M. Felcher, 'Socially Responsible Lobbying' (with a response from D. Vogel), *Harvard Business Review*, 86 (2008): 135.
8. See, for example, Smith and Quelch (1993), Chonko (1995), and Murphy and Laczniak (2006). These authors provide interesting insights into marketing ethics, which are partially reflected in this chapter.
9. For an overview of 'consumer advocacy' movement, see Chapter 2, p 34.
10. See these Guidelines at http://www.un.org/esa/sustdev/publications/consumption_en.pdf.
11. We follow Buchholz (2008).
12. 'Consumerism' sometimes refers to 'consumer advocacy', (see p. 34) but here we use this term with the common meaning, which suggests a progressively greater consumption of goods, and even a certain attachment to materialistic values or possessions, to the detriment of ethical and spiritual values.
13. See Chapter 5, pp. 115–17.
14. See Chapter 15, pp. 311–12.
15. See Myers (2008).
16. http://www.marketingpower.com/content435.php
17. See Murphy (1999) and Murphy and Laczniak (2007).

18. Merriam-Webster Online Dictionary, www.merriam-webster.com/dictionary/Caveat%20emptor
19. Zikmund explains this issue in detail (2003, ch. 5).
20. See Davidson (1996).
21. See Chapter 6, pp. 132–3.
22. See Chapter 5, p. 108.
23. See Walsh and Lynch (2002) on justice in pricing.
24. See Chafuen (1986) and Elegido (2009).
25. See Delener (1998).
26. One such behaviour is retail price discrimination when buying the same volume of goods, overcharging small retailers on the real price; for example, imposing stricter financial conditions than bigger retailers.
27. Ethical aspects of other means of promotion are dealt with, for example, in Chonko (1995).
28. See Crisp (1987).
29. See Taylor (2008).
30. Beder (1998) has dealt with marketing to children, including advertising.
31. See Chapter 8, pp. 189–91.
32. On this topic, see Preston (1997).
33. On this topic, see, for example, Fritz (1979), Aaker (1985), Fam and Waller (2003) and Beard (2008).
34. See Pontifical Council for Social Communications (1997: n. 17).
35. See Chapter 6, p. 141.
36. On this point, see Laczniak (2008).
37. See Chapter 11, pp. 264–5.

13. THE SOCIAL RESPONSIBILITY AND ACCOUNTABILITY OF BUSINESS

1. Phrase attributed to Viktor E. Frankl, author of the best selling book *Man's Search for Meaning.*
2. Davis (1975: pp. 20–1)
3. For an historical overview of the CSR movement, see Carroll (2006) and Frederick (2006).
4. See Davis (1960, 1967) and McGuire (1963).
5. For current debate on CSR, see Windson (2006) and Marsden (2006).
6. Friedman and Friedman (1962: p. 133).
7. Friedman (1970).
8. On this latter point, see DiMaggio and Powell (1983).
9. Drucker (1984: p. 62).
10. On this point, see Moon (2007) and Habish *et al.* (2004). This latter refers only to Europe.
11. http://ec.europa.eu/employment_social/soc-dial/csr/greenpaper_en.pdf.
12. Some of them can be found at: http://www.ic.gc.ca/epic/site/csr-rse.nsf/en/h_rs00095e.html
13. Holme and Watts (2000: 8). These authors co-chaired the mentioned working group of WBCSD.
14. *Ibid.*
15. Discussed in Chapter 7, pp. 158–60.
16. Mainly in French (1979, 1984).
17. See Metzger and Dalton (1996, p. 530).
18. Chapter 7 discusses this view, pp. 157–9.
19. See Velasquez (1983, 2003).
20. As Garrett (1989) pointed out.
21. Thus, Goodpaster and Matthews (1982), Pruzan (2001) and Moore (1999).
22. These arguments are taken from Pruzan (2001).

23. See Chapter 2, p. 34.
24. See Kamat (2003).
25. See Chapters 13 and 14.
26. Zadek (2004)
27. Distinction introduced by Matten and Moon (2008).
28. These arguments were already presented by Friedman in his famous article of *New York Time Magazine* in 1970, mentioned on p. 300.
29. In 2001, Margolis and Walsh published a study reviewing 95 empirical studies on the relationship between financial performance and social performance of corporations from 1972. Their findings show a positive correlation between most companies involved in CSR activities and their respective financial results. Others, although minor in number, present a negative correlation. Finally, a third relatively small group of findings shows practically no correlation. These findings can be questioned for methodological reasons because economic results depend not only on ethical behaviour or social responsibility, but also on many other factors – such as products, market, technical competences, and so on. Subsequent studies using more sophisticated methodology suggest that corporate virtue in the form of social responsibility – and, to a lesser extent, environmental responsibility – is likely to pay off (Orlitzky *et al.* 2003).
30. Some arguments regarding this debate can be found in Roman *et al.* (1999), McWilliams and Siegel (2000, 2001), and Margolis and Walsh (2003).
31. Porter and Kramer (2006)
32. On implementing these ideas, see Milliman *et al.* (2008).
33. During a hurricane in 2005, one of Wal-Mart's actions was to send 1,500 truckloads of free merchandise and food for 100,000 meals to relieve the situation. Neither governments nor social institutions had the capabilities to organize such a response as this.
34. See Garriga and Melé (2004).
35. For a wider explanation of these theories, see Melé (2008b).
36. This was the case of the 'Bhopal disaster' in India (1984), in which at least 3,000 people died (see Introductory Case 15, pp. 345–7). Another was the 'Chernobyl disaster' in Russia (1986), resulting from a major release of radioactivity into the environment following a massive power explosion that destroyed the reactor.
37. See Ackerman (1973).
38. Carroll (1979) was the one who introduced this idea.
39. Wood (1991)
40. Wheeler *et al.* (2003) and Freeman and Velamuri (2006), among others. See Chapter 7, pp. 162–3, for the stakeholder view of the firm.
41. See Freeman (1994).
42. Blair (1995) and Clarkson (1995).
43. Collins and Porras (1994) and Collins (2001),
44. Greenwood (2007) discussed this point.
45. This is the position of Gioia (1999).
46. See Chapter 7, pp. 160–7.
47. See Sternberg (2000), Jensen (2001) and Marcoux (2003).
48. See Phillips *et al.* (2003).
49. See Friedman (1962, 1970)
50. Husted and Salazar (2006).
51. See Milliman *et al.* (2008), Aguilera *et al.* (2007) and Basu and Palazzo (2008).
52. This definition is given by Burke and Logsdon (1996, p. 496).
53. On this point, see McWilliams and Siegel (2001).
54. This is basically the position of Waddock and Smith (2000).
55. Wood and Logsdon (2002).

56. See   http://www.weforum.org/site/homepublic.nsf/Content/Global+Corporate+ Citizenship+Initiative
57. *Ibid.*
58. UN World Commission on Environment and Development (1987).
59. See Elkington (1998).
60. Robins (2006).
61. Robins (2006, p. 12).
62. J. Gangemi, 'What the Nobel Means for Microcredit', *Business Week Online*. 16 October 2006. http://www.businessweek.com/smallbiz/content/oct2006/sb20061016_705623.htm Accessed on 13 June 2008.
63. See Akula (2008).
64. This is the view of Prahalad (2004) and Hart (2007).
65. See Karnani (2007).
66. http://www.thehindu.com/2007/09/25/stories/2007092557791800.htm
67. Prahalad (2003). Innovation in distribution is also important to sell to the BoP. It can eliminate distribution costs and create new routes through which resources can be distributed. In this line, we find another relevant example in the initiative of the Scojo Foundation, which, in spite of being a non-profit organization has found a market solution to provide low cost reading glasses, for about US$3. According to this foundation, there are more than 700 million people living in poverty who don't have access to reading glasses. For professions such as tailors, electricians, and goldsmiths, their precarious working lives along with their families' lives depend on their ability to see up close. The vision problem can often be solved without going to an oculist. The Scojo Foundation has developed a franchise model in several countries in Africa, Asia and Latin America. They provide the tools, knowledge, products, and support for franchise partners to implement such microfranchises within their existing operations, adding both profit and social value. In the first six years, the Scojo Foundation and its partners sold over 80,000 pairs of reading glasses, and trained over 1,000 entrepreneurs to run the franchises http://(www.scojofoundation.org/2_1_mission.html).
68. http://www.johnson.cornell.edu/sge/research/bop_india.html
69. The concept of accountability was already introduced in Chapter 4, p. 102.
70. ISEA (1999, p. 18).
71. Pava (2008, p. 451).
72. See Swift (2001) and Bebbington *et al.* (2008).

14. CORPORATE CITIZENSHIP

1. 'A New Coalition for Universal Values', *International Herald Tribune*, 26 July 2000: http://www.un.org/News/ossg/sg/stories/articleFullsearch.asp?TID=31&Type=Article
2. Wood and Logsdon pointed out 'business citizenship cannot be deemed equivalent to individual citizenship – instead it derives from and is secondary to individual citizenship' (2002: 86).
3. Eriksen and Weigård (2000: 15).
4. Solomon (1992: 148).
5. This is the title of a well-known work by Friedman (2007) that relates to globalization.
6. See Chapter 11, pp. 256–7.
7. See, for instance, Green and Griffith (2002) and Stiglitz (2003).
8. Stiglitz (2006).
9. See Chapter 13, pp. 308–9.
10. See Chapter 4 pp. 74ff.
11. See Chapter 4, pp. 84–6. In Chapter 7, pp. 162–7, the common good is related to the purpose of the firm.

12. See Chapter 7, pp. 164–5.
13. On the potential role of business, see Matten and Crane (2005) and Moon *et al.* (2005).
14. Carlos Llano (1991: 76f. and endnote 4). Llano recognized that this term is inspired by ideas coming from the Spanish philosopher Ortega y Gasset via José Gaos.
15. See Chapter 4, p. 87.
16. See Burchell and Cook (2006).
17. See Ayuso *et al.* (2006)
18. On this point, see Maak (2007).
19. See Chapter 7, pp. 84–6 and a summary on p. 325.
20. In non-profit or social-interest companies, wealth creation is not a responsibility because this is beyond the scope of their mission. They can even work with losses if they are able to achieve donations to equilibrate the former.
21. Jones (1995: 422).
22. See Chapter 2, p. 27.
23. This has been mentioned in Chapter 2, pp. 30–2, although only briefly, since dealing with this matter in any depth would require much more space.
24. The term 'lobby' seems to come from the gathering of members of Parliament and peers in the hallways (lobbies) of the Houses of Parliament, in London, before and after parliamentary debates.
25. See, for example, Keffer and Hill (1997) and Barker (2008). Brooke Hamilton III and Hoch (1997) provided some practical suggestions for ethics in lobbying.
26. On the latter point, see Moss (2008).
27. Matten and Crane (2005)
28. See Wikipedia (Ken Saro-Wiwa).
29. See Garrett and Klonoski (1987: 86–7)
30. See Chapter 5, pp. 117–20, regarding the Principle of Double Effect and 'Business ethics in practice 5', on closing a plant.
31. Some arguments regarding this debate can be found in Roman *et al.* (1999), McWilliams and Siegel (2000, 2001) and Margolis and Walsh (2003).
32. Aguilera *et al.* (2007).
33. Waddock (2002) presents interesting insights on leading corporate citizens.
34. *Infosys Sustainability Report* 2007–08: 3, http://www.infosys.com/beyond-business/infosys-sustainability-report-0708.pdf
35. *Ibid.*
36. Speech to MBA students at IESE Business School, in Barcelona, Spain, 27 April 2007.

15. ENVIRONMENTAL BUSINESS ETHICS

1. In Chapter 13, pp. 311–12.
2. This fact was highlighted by Carson (1962) in her book *Silent Spring*.
3. See White (1967).
4. See Whitney (1993) and Attfield (2001).
5. This text is found in the first book of the Bible (*Genesis* 1:28).
6. Thus, Ehrlich and Brower (1968) and Meadows *et al.* (1972).
7. Commoner (1971) and Passmore (1974) advocated this view.
8. The latter position was held by Feinberg (1974) and Stone (1974), among others.
9. As Guha (1989) pointed out.
10. It was introduced by the Norwegian philosopher Arne Naess (1989) and later became popular in the United States.
11. This is the case, for instance, of Shrivastava (1995) and Purser and Park (1995).

12. For instance, Newton (2002).
13. See Ariansen (1998).
14. Biodiversity, in simple terms, refers to all the species living in a particular area or on the entire planet. Scientists usually use biodiversity in a more precise manner to designate the variety of living organisms (plants, animals and micro-organisms) within a natural unity (ecosystem) and their complex interactions, along with their interactions with the non-living aspects of their environment. About 20 million distinct biological species have been found on Earth, and each has its own role in maintaining the ecosystem.
15. See Pope John Paul II (1987: n. 34). In addition, ecosystems that suffer considerable loss of biodiversity are less likely to rebound successfully from disturbance events. This can ultimately spell trouble for current or future generations.
16. See the quotation at the head of this chapter.
17. On this point, see Manning (2004).
18. These are the positions of Regan (1983) and Singer (1990), respectively.
19. *Nichomachean Ethics*, I, 8.
20. On this point, see, for instance, Frey (1980) and Cohen (1986).
21. See specific references in Wikipedia (Global warming).
22. See Chapter 12, p. 281.
23. See, for instance, the Product Stewardship Institute, a US non-profit organization that works to reduce the environmental impact of consumer products, http://www.productstewardship.us
24. See Gable and Shireman (2001).
25. According to Holliday (2001), this is the strategy followed by DuPont.
26. Hart and Milstein (2003).
27. See Veroutis *et al.* (1996).

References

Aaker, D. A., 'Causes of Irritation in Advertising', *Journal of Marketing*, 49, 2 (1985): 47–57.

Ackerman, R. W., 'How Companies Respond to Social Demands', *Harvard Business Review*, 51, 4 (1973): 88–98.

Aguilera, R. V., D. E. Rupp, C. A. Williams and J. Ganapathi, 'Putting the S Back in Corporate Social Responsibility: A Multilevel Theory of Social Change in Organizations', *Academy of Management Review*, 32, 3 (2007): 836–63.

Akula, V., 'Business Basics at the Base of the Pyramid', *Harvard Business Review*, 86, 6 (2008): 53–7.

Albert, M., *Capitalism against Capitalism* (London: Whurr, 1993).

Alderfer, C., 'An Empirical Test of a New Theory of Human Needs', *Organizational Behavior and Human Performance*, 4, 2 (1969): 142–75.

Alford, H. and M. Naugthon, 'Beyond the Shareholder Model of the Firm: Working toward the Common Good of a Business', in S. A. Cortright and M. Naugthon (eds), *Rethinking the Purpose of Business. Interdisciplinary Essays from the Catholic Social Tradition* (Notre Dame: Notre Dame University Press, 2002): 27–47.

Alzola, M., 'Character and Environment: The Status of Virtues in Organizations', *Journal of Business Ethics*, 78, (2008): 343–57.

Amable, B., *The Diversity of Modern Capitalism* (New York: Oxford University Press, 2003).

Anand, V., B. E. Ashforth and M. Joshi, 'Business as Usual: The Acceptance and Perpetuation of Corruption in Organizations', *Academy of Management Executive*, 19, 4 (2005): 9–23.

Anscombe, E., 'Modern Moral Philosophy', *Philosophy*, 33 (1958): 1–19. Reproduced in R. Crisp and M. Slote (eds), *Virtue Ethics* (Oxford: Oxford University Press, 1997).

Aquinas, T., *Treatise on the Virtues* (Englewood Cliffs, NJ: Prentice-Hall, 1966 [1273]).

Aquinas, T., *The Summa Theologica*. Edited by Fathers of the English Dominican Province (London: Burns Oates and Washbourne, 1981[1273]).

Argandoña, A., 'The Stakeholder Theory and the Common Good', *Journal of Business Ethics*, 17 (1998): 1093–102.

Argandoña, A., 'Corruption: The Corporate Perspective', *Business Ethics: A European Review*, 10, 2 (2001): 163–75.

Argandoña, A., 'Private-to-Private Corruption', *Journal of Business Ethics*, 47, 3 (2003): 253–67.

Argandoña, A., 'Corruption and Companies: The Use of Facilitating Payments', *Journal of Business Ethics*, 60, 3 (2005): 251–64.

Argandoña, A., 'Capitalism', in K. Kolb (ed.), *Encyclopedia of Business Ethics and Society* (Los Angeles: Sage, 2008): 257–65.

Ariansen, P., 'Anthropocentrism with a Human Face', *Ecological Economics*, 24, 2/3 (1998): 153–62.

Aristotle, *Politics* (Oxford: Oxford University Press, 1948).

Aristotle, *The Nicomachean Ethics*. Translated by David Ross (Oxford/New York: Oxford University Press, 1980).

Arjoon, S., 'Ethical Decision-Making: A Case for the Triple Font Theory', *Journal of Business Ethics*, 71, 4 (2006): 395–410.

Arnold, D. G. and N. E. Bowie, 'Sweatshops and Respect for Persons', *Business Ethics Quarterly*, 13, 2 (2003): 221–42.

Arnold, D. G. and N. E. Bowie, 'Respect for Workers in Global Chains: Advancing the Debate over Sweatshops', *Business Ethics Quarterly*, 17, 1 (2007): 135–45.

Arogyaswamy, B. and C. M. Byles, 'Organizational Culture: Internal and External Fits', *Journal of Management*, 13 (1987): 647–59.

Arrow, K., 'Social Responsibility and Economic Efficiency', *Public Policy*, 21, 3 (1973): 300–17.

Arrow, K. J., *The Limit of Organizations* (New York: Norton, 1974).

Ashkanasy, N. M., C. Wilderom and M. F. Peterson, *Handbook of Organizational Culture and Climate* (Los Angeles: Sage, 2000).

Attfield, R., 'Christianity', in D. Jamieson (ed.), *A Companion to Environmental Philosophy* (Oxford: Blackwell, 2001).

Ayuso, S., M. A. Rodríguez and J. E. Ricart, 'Using Stakeholder Dialogue as a Source for New Ideas: A Dynamic Capability underlying Sustainable Innovation', *Corporate Governance: The International Journal of Effective Board Performance*, 6, 4 (2006): 475–90.

Baker, H. K. and R. B. Edelman, 'The Effect of Announcements of Corporate Misconduct and Insider Trading on Shareholder Returns', *Business & Professional Ethics Journal*, 18, 1 (1999): 47–64.

Balmes, J., *El Criterio*, 13th edn (Madrid: Espasa-Calpe, 1981 [1845]).

Barker, D., 'Ethics and Lobbying: The Case of Real Estate Brokerage', *Journal of Business Ethics*, 80, 1 (2008): 23–35.

Barnard, C., *The Functions of the Executive* (London: Oxford University Press, 1968 [1938]).

Barnsley, J., *The Social Reality of Ethics* (London: Routledge & Kegan Paul, 1972).

Bass, B. M., 'From Transactional to Transformational Leadership: Learning to Share the Vision', *Organizational Dynamics*, 18, 3 (1990): 19–31.

Bass, B. M. and P. Steidlmeier, 'Ethics, Character, and Authentic Transformational Leadership Behavior', *Leadership Quarterly*, 10, 2 (1999): 181–217.

Basu, K. and G. Palazzo, 'Corporate Social Responsibility: A Process Model of Sensemaking', *Academy of Management Review*, 33, 1 (2008): 122–36.

Beard, F. K., 'How Products and Advertising Offend Consumers', *Journal of Advertising Research*, 48, 1 (2008): 13–21.

Beauchamp, T. L., 'Affirmative Action', in R. W. Kolb (ed.), *Encyclopedia of Business Ethics and Society Thousand Oaks* (Los Angeles: Sage, 2008): 31–5.

Bebbington, J., C. Larrinaga and J. M. Moneva, 'Corporate Social Reporting and Reputation Risk Management', *Accounting, Auditing & Accountability Journal*, 21, 3 (2008): 337–61.

Beder, S., *Marketing to Children* (Wollongong, New South Wales, Australia: University of Wollongong, 1998).

Bell, M. P., M. E. McLaughlin and J. M. Sequeira, 'Discrimination, Harassment, and the Glass Ceiling: Women Executives as Change Agents', *Journal of Business Ethics*, 37, 1 (2002): 65–76.

Bentham, J., *An Introduction to the Principles of Morals and Legislation* (Oxford: Oxford University Press, 1996 [1780]).

Berle Jr, A. A., 'Management Power and Stockholders Property', *Harvard Business Review*, 5, 4 (1927): 424–32.

Berle Jr, A. A. and G. C. Means, *The Modern Corporation and the Private Property* (New York, Chicago: Commerce Clearing House). For a recent edition see Berle Jr, A.A. and G.C. Means: 1991, *The Modern Corporation and the Private Property*, with a new introduction by Murray L. Weidenbaum and Mark Jensen (New Brunswick, NJ: Transaction Publishers, 1932).

Bernanos, G., *The Last Essays of Georges Bernanos* (Why Freedom?) (Chicago, IL: Henry Regnery, 1955).

Bertone, T., *L'Etica del Bene Comune nella Dottrina Sociale della Chiesa* (Città del Vaticano: Libreria Editrice Vaticana, 2007).

Bhide, A. and H. H. Stevenson, 'Why Be Honest if Honesty Doesn't Pay?', *Harvard Business Review*, 68, 5 (1990): 121–9.

Bible, The Holy. New Revised Standard Version (Princeton, NJ: Scepter, 1966).

Bird, F. and J. A. Waters, 'The Nature of Managerial Moral Standards', *Journal of Business Ethics*, 6, 1 (1987): 1–13.

Blair, M. M., *Ownership and Control: Rethinking Corporate Governance for the Twenty-First Century* (Washington, DC: Brookings Institution, 1995).

Block, P., *Stewardship: Choosing Service over Self Interest* (San Francisco: Berrett-Koehler Publishers, 1996).

Boatright, J. R., *Ethics and the Conduct of Business*, 2nd edn (New Jersey: Prentice Hall, 1993).

Bogle, J. C., *The Battle for the Soul of Capitalism* (New Haven: Yale University Press, 2005).

Bogle, J. C., 'Reflections on CEO Compensation', *Academy of Management Perspectives*, 22, 2 (2008): 21–5.

Bok, H., *Freedom and Responsibility* (Princeton: Princeton University Press, 1998).

Bowen, H. R., *Social Responsibilities of the Businessman* (New York: Harper & Row, 1953).

Bowie, N. E., 'Business Ethics and Cultural Relativism', *Multinational Ethics* (Englewood Cliffs, NJ: Prentice Hall, 1989): 366–82.

Bowie, N. E., *Business Ethics: A Kantian Perspective* (Oxford: Blackwell, 1999).

Bowie, N. E. and P. H. Werhane, *Management Ethics* (Oxford: Blackwell, 2005).

Bowne, B. P., *Personalism* (Whitefish, Montana: Kessinger Publishing, 2007).

Brenkert, G. G., 'Trust, Morality and International Business', *Business Ethics Quarterly*, 8, 2 (1998): 293–317.

Brennan, R. and P. Baines, 'Is there a Morally Right Price for Anti-Retroviral Drugs in the Developing World?', *Business Ethics: A European Review*, 15, 1 (2006): 29–43.

Brickley, J. A., C. W. Smith Jr and J. L. Zimmerman, 'Ethics, Incentives and Organizational Design', *Journal of Applied Corporate Finances*, 7, 2 (1997): 20–39.

Brickley, J. A., C. W. Smith Jr and J. L. Zimmerman, 'Business Ethics and Organizational Architecture', *Journal of Banking & Finance*, 26, 9 (2002): 1821–35.

Brittain-Catlin, W., *Offshore: The Dark Side of the Global Economy* (New York: Farrar, Straus & Giroux, 2005).

Brooke Hamilton III, J. and D. Hoch, 'Ethical Standards for Business Lobbying: Some Practical Suggestions', *Business Ethics Quarterly*, 7, 3 (1997): 117–29.

Buchholz, R. A., 'Consumer's Bill of Rights', in R. W. Kolb (ed.), *Encyclopedia of Business Ethics and Society* (Los Angeles: Sage, 2008): 438–9.

Burchell, J. and J. Cook, 'Assessing the Impact of Stakeholder Dialogue: Changing Relationships between NGOs and Companies', *Journal of Public Affairs*, 6, 3/4 (2006): 210–27.

Burke, L. and J. M. Logsdon, 'How Corporate Social Responsibility Pays Off', *Long Range Planning*, 29, 4 (1996): 495–502.

Burns, J. G., *Leadership* (New York: Harper Torchbooks, 1978).

Byrne, S., P. Davey, K. McFarlane, J. O'Brien and C. Templeton, 'Patent Rights or Patent Wrongs? The Case of Patent Rights on AIDS Drugs', *Business Ethics: A European Review*, 15, 3 (2006): 299–305.

Cadbury, A., 'Ethical Managers make their own Rules', *Harvard Business Review*, 65, 5 (1987): 69–73.

Cadbury Committee, *Report of the Committee on the Financial Aspects of Corporate Governance* (London: GEE, 1992).

Cameron, K. and A. Caza, 'Organizational and Leadership Virtues and the Role of Forgiveness', *Journal of Leadership Studies*, 9, 1 (2002): 33–48.

Card, R. F., 'Individual Responsibility within Organizational Contexts', *Journal of Business Ethics*, 62 (2005): 397–405.

Cardona, P., 'Transcendental Leadership', *Leadership & Organization Development*, 21, 4 (2000): 201–6.

Cardona, P., *How to Develop Leadership Competencies* (Pamplona: Eunsa, 2005).

Cardona, P. and C. Rey, *Management by Missions* (New York: Palgrave Macmillan, 2008).

Carroll, A. B., 'A Three-Dimensional Conceptual Model of Corporate Performance', *Academy of Management Review*, 4, 4 (1979): 497–505.

Carroll, A. B., 'Corporate Social Responsibility: A Historical Perspective', in M. J. Epstein and K. O. Hanson (eds), *The Accountable Corporation. Corporate Social Responsibility*, 3 (2006): 1–30.

Carson, R., *Silent Spring* (Boston: Houghton Mifflin, 1962).

Carver, R. H., 'If the River Stopped: A Talmudic Perspective on Downsizing', *Journal of Business Ethics*, 50, 3 (2004): 137–47.

Chachedina, A., 'Islamic Business Ethics', in L. C. Becker and C. B. Becker (eds), *Encyclopedia of Ethics* (New York/London: Routledge, 2001): 887–9.

Chafuen, A. A., *Christians for freedom: late-scholastic economics* (San Francisco: Ignatius Press, 1986).

Cheeseman, H. R., *Contemporary Business Law*, 3rd edn (Englewood Cliffs, NJ: Prentice Hall, 2000).

Chonko, L. B., *Ethical Decision Making in Marketing* (London: Sage, 1995).

Christe, I., *What is Our Case? Back to Basic in Corporate Responsibility* (2005). Available at: http://www.isfp.co.uk/businesspathways/issue20.html

Church, B., J. C. Gaa, S. M. K. Nainar and M. M. Shehata, 'Experimental Evidence relating to the Person–Situation Interactionist Model of Ethical Decision-Making', *Business Ethics Quarterly*, 15, 3 (2005): 363–83.

Ciulla, J. B., 'Leadership Ethics: Mapping the Territory', *Business Ethics Quarterly*, 5, 1 (1995): 5–28.

Ciulla, J. B. (ed.), *Ethics, the Heart of Leadership* (New York: Praeger, 1998).

Ciulla, J. B., *The Ethics of Leadership* (Belmont, CA: Wadsworth, 2002).

Clark, M. C. and R. L. Payne, 'Character-Based Determinants of Trust in Leaders', *Risk Analysis: An International Journal*, 26, 5 (2006): 1161–73.

Clarkson, M. B. E., 'A Stakeholder Framework for Analyzing and Evaluating Corporate Social Performance', *Academy of Management Review*, 92 (1995): 105–8.

Cludts, S., 'Organisation Theory and the Ethics of Participation', *Journal of Business Ethics*, 21, 2/3 (1999): 157–71.

Cohen, C., 'The Case for the Use of Animals in Biomedical Research', *New England Journal of Medicine*, 315, 14 (1986): 865–70.

Coles, R., *Lives of Moral Leadership* (London: Random House, 2000).

Collins, D., 'How and Why Participatory Management Improves a Company's Social Performance', *Business & Society*, 35, 2 (1996): 176– 210.

Collins, D., 'Living Wage', in R. W. Kolb (ed.), *Encyclopedia of Business Ethics and Society* (Los Angeles: Sage, 2008): 1300–3.

Collins, J., *Good to Great: Why Some Companies Make the Leap, and Others Don't* (London: Random House, 2001).

Collins, J. and J. I. Porras, *Built to Last: Successful Habits of Visionary Companies* (New York: HarperCollins, 1994).

Comer, D. and G. Vega, 'Using the PET Assessment Instrument to Help Students Identify Factors that Could Impede Moral Behavior', *Journal of Business Ethics*, 77 (2008): 129–45.

Comer, M. J., *Corporate Fraud*, 3rd edn (Aldershot, UK: Grower, 1998).

Comer, M. J., *Investigating Corporate Fraud*, 3rd edn (Aldershot, UK: Grower, 2003).

Commoner, B., *The Closing Circle* (London: Cape, 1971).

Cone, M. H., 'Corporate Citizenship. The Role of Commercial Organizations in an Islamic Society', *Journal of Corporate Citizenship*, 9 (2003): 49–66.

Connock, S. and T. Johns, *Ethical Leadership* (London: IPD, 1995).

Cooper, C., *Extraordinary Circumstances: The Journey of a Corporate Whistleblower* (Hoboken, NJ: Wiley, 2008).

Covey, S., *Principle-Centered Leadership* (New York: Summit Books, 1991).

Cowen, T. (ed.), *Public Goods and Market Failures: A Critical Examination* (New Brunswick, NJ: Transaction Publishers, 1992).

Creighton, L., *Life and Letters of Mandell Creighton* (London: Longmans, 1904): vol. 1, ch. 13.

Crisp, R., 'Persuasive Advertising, Autonomy, and the Creation of Desire', *Journal of Business Ethics*, 6 (1987): 413–18.

Crockett, C., 'The Cultural Paradigm of Virtue', *Journal of Business Ethics*, 62, 2 (2005): 191–208.

Crosby, J. F., *The Selfhood of the Human Person* (Washington, D.C.: Catholic University of America Press, 1996).

Daft, R. L., *Leadership. Theory and Practice* (Fort Worth, TX: Dryden Press, 1999).

Dalla Costa, J., *The Ethical Imperative: Why Moral Leadership is Good Business* (Toronto: HarperCollins, 1998).

Davidson, D. K., *Selling Sin: The Marketing of Socially Unacceptable Products* (Westport, CO: Quorum Books, 1996).

Davis, K., 'Can Business Afford to Ignore Corporate Social Responsibilities?', *California Management Review*, 2 (1960): 70–6.

Davis, K., 'Understanding The Social Responsibility Puzzle', *Business Horizons*, 10, 4 (1967): 45–51.

Davis, K., 'Five Propositions for Social Responsibility', *Business Horizons*, 18, 3 (1975): 19–24.

Davis, K. and R. L. Blomstrom, *Business and its Environment* (New York: McGraw-Hill, 1966).

De George, R., *Business Ethics* (New York: Macmillan, 1982).

De George, R., 'Ethical Universals, Justice, and International Business', in F. N. Brady (ed.), *Ethical Universals in International Business* (Berlin: Springer, 1996): 81–96.

De George, R., *Business Ethics*, 5th edn (Upper Saddle River, NJ: Prentice Hall, 1999).

De George, R., 'Ethical Issues in Information Technology', in N. E. Bowie (ed.), *The Blackwell Guide to Business Ethics* (Oxford: Blackwell, 2002): 267–88.

De George, R., 'Intellectual Property and Pharmaceutical Drugs: An Ethical Analysis', *Business Ethics Quarterly*, 15, 4 (2005): 549–75.

De George, R., 'The History of Business Ethics', in M. J. Epstein and K. O. Hanson (eds), *The Accountable Corporation, Volume 2* (Westport: Praeger, 2006): 47–58.

Deal, T. E. and A. A. Kennedy, *Corporate Cultures* (Reading, MA.: Addison-Wesley, 1982).

Deane, P., *The First Industrial Revolution* (Cambridge: Cambridge University Press, 1965).

Delener, N., 'An Ethical and Legal Synthesis of Dumping: Growing Concerns in International Marketing', *Journal of Business Ethics*, 17, 15 (1998): 1747–53.

De Pree, M., *Leadership is an Art* (New York: Dell Books, 1990).

DesJardins, J., 'Virtues and Business Ethics', in W. M. Hoffman, J. M. Moore and D. A. Fredo (eds), *Corporate Governance and Institutionalizing Ethics* (Lexington, MA: Lexington, 1984).

DiMaggio, P. J. and W. W. Powell, 'The Iron Cage Revisited: Institutional Isomorphism and Collective Rationality In Organizational Fields', *American Sociological Review*, 48, 2 (1983): 147–60.

Donaldson, T. and T. W. Dunfee, 'Towards a Unified Conception of Business Ethics: Integrative Social Contracts Theory', *Academy of Management Review*, 19 (1994): 252–84.

Donaldson, T. and T. W. Dunfee, *Ties That Bind: A Social Contracts Approach to Business Ethics* (Boston, MA: Harvard Business School Press, 1999).

Donaldson, T. and L. E. Preston, 'The Stakeholder Theory of the Corporation: Concepts, Evidence, and Implications', *Academy of Management Review*, 20, 1 (1995): 65–91.

Doris, J., *Lack of Character: Personality and Moral Behavior* (New York: Cambridge University Press, 2002).

D'Orts, A., *Derecho Romano Privado,* 9th edn (Pamplona: Eunsa, 1997).

Douglas, P. C., R. A. Davidson and B. N. Schwartz, 'The Effect of Organizational Culture and Ethical Orientation on Accountants' Ethical Judgments', *Journal of Business Ethics,* 34, 2 (2001): 101–21.

Drennan, L. T., 'Ethics, Governance and Risk Management: Lessons From Mirror Group Newspapers and Barings Bank', *Journal of Business Ethics,* 52, 3 (2004): 257–66.

Drucker, P., *Managers: Tasks, Responsibilities, Practices* (New York: Harper & Row, 1974).

Drucker, P., 'The New Meaning of Corporate Social Responsibility', *California Management Review,* 26 (1984): 53–63.

Drucker, P., *The New Realities* (London: Mandarin, 1989).

Drucker, P., *The Practice of Management* (Oxford: Elsevier, 2005).

Duska, R. F. and J. A. Ragatz, 'Purpose of Business', in R. W. Kolb (ed.), *Encyclopedia of Business Ethics and Society* (Los Angeles: Sage, 2008): 210–16.

Dutton, J. E., P. J. Frost, M. C. Worline, J. M. Lilius and J. M. Kanov, 'Leading in Times of Trauma', *Harvard Business Review,* 80, 1 (2002): 54–61.

Edwards, M., *Civil Society* (Cambridge, UK: Polity Press, 2004).

Eglise Orthodoxe Russe, *Les Fondements de la Doctrine Sociale. Introduction par le Métropolite Cyrille de Smolensk et de Kaliningrad* (Paris: Cerf, 2007).

Ehrlich, P. R. and D. Brower, *The Population Bomb* (New York: Ballantine Books, 1968).

Eisenhardt, K. M., 'Agency Theory: An Assessment and Review', *Academy of Management Review,* 14, 1 (1989): 57–74.

Elegido, J. M., 'Intrinsic Limitations of Property Rights', *Journal of Business Ethics,* 14 (1995): 411–16.

Elegido, J., 'The Just Price: Three Insights from the Salamanca School', *Journal of Business Ethics,* forthcoming (2009).

Elkington, J., 'Towards the Sustainable Corporation: Win–Win–Win Business Strategies for Sustainable Development', *California Management Review,* 36, 2 (1994): 90–100.

Elkington, J., *Cannibals with Forks: The Triple Bottom Line of 21st Century Business* (Oxford, UK: Capstone, 1998).

Ellsworth, R. R., *Leading with Purpose. The New Corporate Realities* (Stanford University Press: Stanford Business Books, 2002).

Engelen, P.-J. and L. Liedekerke, 'The Ethics of Insider Trading Revisited', *Journal of Business Ethics,* 74, 4 (2007): 497–507.

Eriksen, E. and J. Weigård, 'The End of Citizenship?', in C. McKinnon and I. Hampsher-Monk (eds), *The Demands of Citizenship* (London: Continuum, 2000): 13–24.

Ethics Resource Center, *Creating a Workable Company Code of Ethics* (Washington, D.C: Ethics Resource Center, 1990).

Evans, W. M. and R. E. Freeman, 'A Stakeholder Theory of the Modern Corporation: Kantian Capitalism', in T. Beauchamp and N. Bowie (eds), *Ethical Theory and Business* (Englewood Cliffs: Prentice Hall, 1988): 75–93.

Fam, K. S. and D. Waller, 'Advertising Controversial Products in the Asia Pacific: What Makes Them Offensive?', *Journal of Business Ethics,* 48, 3 (2003): 237–50.

Feinberg, J., 'The Right of Animals and Unborn Generations', in W. Blackstone (ed.), *Philosophy and the Environment Crisis* (Athens: University of Georgia Press, 1974): 43–68.

Felcher, E. M., 'Socially Responsible Lobbying' (with a response from D. Vogel), *Harvard Business Review,* 86 (2008): 135.

Ferraro, F., J. Pfeffer and R. I. Sutton, 'Economic Language and Assumptions: How Theories Can Become Self-Fulfilling', *Academy of Management Review,* 30, 1 (2005): 8–24.

Finnis, J., *Fundamentals of Ethics* (Oxford: Clarendon Press, 1983).

Finnis, J., *Natural Law and Natural Rights* (Oxford: Clarendon Press, 1986).

Fishman, M. J. and K. M. Hagerty, 'Insider Trading and the Efficiency of Stock Prices', *Rand Journal of Economics*, 23, 1 (1992): 106–22.

Follett, M. P., *Dynamic Administration. The Colleted Papers of Mary Parker Follett*, edited by H. C. Metcalf and L. Urwick (New York, London: Harper & Brothers, 1940).

Fontrodona, J. and A. J. G. Sison, 'The Nature of the Firm, Agency Theory and Shareholder Theory: A Critique from Philosophical Anthropology', *Journal of Business Ethics*, 66, 1 (2006): 33–42.

Frankel, P. E., J. Fred D. Miller and J. Paul, *Human Flourishing* (New York: Cambridge University Press, 1999).

Frederick, R. E., 'An Outline of Ethical Relativism and Ethical Absolutism', in R. E. Frederick (ed.), *A Companion to Business Ethics* (Oxford: Blackwell, 2002): 65–80.

Frederick, R. E., *Corporation, Be Good! The Story of Corporate Social Responsibility* (Indianapolis, IN: Dog Ear Publishing, 2006).

Freeman, R. E., *Strategic Management: A Stakeholder Approach* (Boston, MA: Pitman, 1984).

Freeman, R. E., 'The Politics of Stakeholder Theory: Some Future Directions', *Business Ethics Quarterly*, 4, 4 (1994): 409–29.

Freeman, R. E., 'A Stakeholder Theory of the Modern Corporation', in T. L. Beauchamp and N. E. Bowie (eds), *Ethical Theory and Business*, 5th edn (Englewood Cliffs, NJ: Prentice Hall, 1997): 66–76.

Freeman, R. E., 'Divergent Stakeholder Theory', *Academy of Management Review*, 24, 2 (1999): 233–6.

Freeman, R. E., 'Business Ethics at the Millennium', *Business Ethics Quarterly*, 10, 1 (2000): 169–80.

Freeman, R. E. and R. Velamuri, 'A New Approach to CSR: Company Stakeholder Responsibility', in A. Kakabadse and M. Morsing (eds), *Corporate Social Responsibility (CSR): Reconciling Aspirations with Application* (Hampshire: Palgrave Macmillan, 2006): 9–23.

French, P., 'The Corporation as a Moral Person', *American Philosophical Quarterly*, 16 (1979): 207–15.

French, P. A., *Collective and corporate responsibility* (New York: Columbia University Press, 1984).

Frey, R. G., *Interests and Rights: The Case against Animals* (Oxford: Clarendon Press, 1980).

Friedman, H. H., 'The Impact of Jewish Values on Marketing and Business Practices', *Journal of Macromarketing*, 21, 1 (2001): 74–80.

Friedman, M. and R. D. Friedman, *Capitalism and Freedom* (Chicago: Chicago University Press, 1962).

Friedman, M., 'The Social Responsibility of Business is to Increase its Profits', *New York Times Magazine*, September 13 (1970): 32–3, 122, 126.

Friedman, T. L., *The World is Flat. A Brief History of the Twenty-First Century*, 2nd revised and expanded edn (New York: Farrar, Straus & Giroux, 2007).

Fritz, N. K., 'Claim Recall and Irritation in Television Commercials: An Advertising Effectiveness Study', *Journal of the Academy of Marketing Science*, 7, 1 (1979): 1–12.

Frost, P., *Toxic Emotions at Work: How Compassionate Managers Handle Pain and Conflict* (Cambridge, MA: Harvard Business School Press, 2003).

Frydman, C. and R. E. Sacks, 'Executive Compensation: A New View from a Long-Term Perspective, 1936–2005' (6 July 2007). *FEDS Working Paper No. 2007–35; AFA 2008 New Orleans Meetings Paper*. Available at SSRN: http://www.ssrn.com/abstract=972399

Gaa, J. and P. Dunmore, 'The Ethics of Earnings Management', *Chartered Accountants Journal*, 86, 8 (2007): 60–2.

Gable, C. and B. Shireman, 'Computer and Electronics Product Stewardship: Are We Ready for the Challenge?', *Environmental Quality Management*, 11, 1 (2001): 35–45.

Gangemi, J., 'What the Nobel Means for Microcredit', *Business Week Online*. 16 October 2006. Available at: http://www.businessweek.com/smallbiz/content/oct2006/sb20061016_705623.htm

García López, J., *Los Derechos Humanos en Santo Tomás de Aquino* (Pamplona: Ediciones Universidad de Navarra, 1979).

Garrett, J. E., 'Unredistributable Corporate Moral Responsibility', *Journal of Business Ethics*, 8, 7 (1989): 535–45.

Garrett, T. and B. Klonoski, *Business Ethics* (Englewood Cliff, NJ: Prentice Hall, 1987).

Garriga, E. and D. Melé, 'Corporate Social Responsibility Theories: Mapping the Territory', *Journal of Business Ethics*, 53, 1–2, August (2004): 51–71.

Geach, P. T., *The Virtues* (Cambridge: Cambridge University Press, 1977).

George, W. W., *Authentic Leadership: Rediscovering the Secrets to Creating Lasting Value* (San Francisco: Jossey-Bass, 2003).

George, W. W., *True North. Discover your Authentic Leadership* (San Francisco: Jossey-Bass, 2007).

Gilligan, C., *In a Different Voice: Psychological Theory and Woman Development* (Cambridge, MA: Harvard University Press, 1982).

Gioia, D. A., 'Response: Practicability, Paradigms, and Problems in Stakeholder Theorizing', 24, 2 (1999): 228–32.

Goffee, R. and G. Jones, 'What Holds the Modern Company Together?', *Harvard Business Review*, 74, 6 (1996): 133–48.

Goodpaster, K. E. and J. B. Matthews Jr, 'Can a Corporation have a Conscience?', *Harvard Business Review*, 60, Jan/Feb (1982): 132–41.

Goodwin, D. K., 'Emotional Strength', *Leadership Excellence*, 23, 10 (2006): 13.

Green, D. and M. Griffith, 'Globalization and its Discontents', *International Affairs*, 78, 1 (2002): 49–68.

Green, R. M., 'Guiding Principles of Jewish Business Ethics', *Business Ethics Quarterly*, 7 (1997): 21–30.

Greenleaf, R. K., *Servant Leadership. A Journey into the Nature of Legitimate Power and Greatness* (New York: Paulist Press, 2002).

Greenwood, M., 'Stakeholder Engagement: Beyond the Myth of Corporate Responsibility', *Journal of Business Ethics*, 74, 4 (2007): 315–27.

Guha, R., 'Radical American Environmentalism and Wilderness Preservation. A Third World Critique', *Environmental Ethics*, 11 (1989): 71–84.

Habermas, J., *Moral Consciousness and Communicative Action* (Boston, MA: MIT Press, 1990 [1983]).

Habermas, J., *Justification and Application: Remarks on Discourse Ethics* (Boston, MA: MIT Press, 1993).

Habish, A., J. Jonker, M. Wagner and R. Schmidpeter (eds), *Corporate Social Responsibility Across Europe. Discovering National Perspectives of Corporate Citizenship* (Heidelberg: Springer, 2004).

Haeffner, G., *The Human Situation: A Philosophical Anthropology* (Notre Dame, IN: University of Notre Dame Press, 1989).

Hagen, J. M. and S. Choe, 'Trust in Japanese Interfirm Relations: Institutional Sanctions Matter', *Academy of Management Review*, 23, 3 (1998): 589–600.

Halpern, D., P. Reville and D. Grunewald, 'Management and Legal Issues Regarding Electronic Surveillance of Employees in the Workplace', *Journal of Business Ethics*, 80, 2 (2008): 175–80.

Handy, C., 'The Citizen Corporation', *Harvard Business Review*, 75, 5 (1997): 26–28.

Handy, C., 'The New Language of Business', *Director*, 52, 7 (1999): 50–3.

Handy, C., 'What's a Business For?', *Harvard Business Review*, 80, 12 (2002): 49–55.

Haniffa, R. and M. Hudaib, 'Exploring the Ethical Identity of Islamic Banks via Communication in Annual Reports', *Journal of Business Ethics*, 76 (2007): 97–116.

Harman, G., 'The Non-existence of Character Traits', *Proceeding of the Aristotelian Society*, 100 (1999–2000): 223–6.

Harrington, J., *Organizational Structure and Information Technology* (Englewood Cliffs, NJ: Prentice Hall, 1991).

Hart, S. L. and M. B. Milstein, 'Creating Sustainable Value', *Academy of Management Executive*, 17, 2 (2003): 56–67.

Hart, S. L., *Capitalism at the Crossroads: Aligning Business, Earth, and Humanity*, 2nd edn (Philadelphia: Warthon School Publishing, 2007).

Hartman, E. M., *Organizational Ethics and the Good Life* (New York/Oxford: Oxford University Press, 1996).

Hartman, E. M., 'Can We Teach Character? An Aristotelian Answer', *Academy of Management Learning & Education*, 5, 1 (2006): 68–81.

Harvey S. J. J., 'Reinforcing Ethical Decision Making through Organizational Structure', *Journal of Business Ethics*, 1 (2000): 43–58.

Hausman, D. M. and M. S. McPherson, 'Taking Ethics Seriously: Economics and Contemporary Moral Philosophy', *Journal of Economic Literature*, 31 (1993): 671–731.

Havard, A., *Virtuous Leadership: An Agenda for Personal Excellence* (New York: Scepter, 2007).

Herman, S. W., *Durable Goods: A Covenantal Ethics for Management and Employees* (Notre Dame, IN: Notre Dame University Press, 1998).

Hernández, R., *Derechos Humanos en Francisco de Vitoria* (Salamanca: San Esteban, 1984).

Hofstede, G., *Culture's Consequences: Comparing Values, Behaviors, Institutions and Organizations across Nations* (Thousand Oaks, CA: Sage, 2003).

Hofstede, G. and G. J. Hofstede, *Cultures and Organizations: Software of the Mind* (New York: McGraw-Hill, 2004).

Holliday, C., 'Sustainable Growth, the DuPont Way', *Harvard Business Review*, 79, 8 (2001): 129–32.

Holme, R. and P. Watts, *Corporate Social Responsibility: Making Good Business Sense*, The World Business Council for Sustainable Development. Available at: http://www.wbcsd.org/DocRoot/IunSPdIKvmYH5HjbN4XC/csr2000.pdf 2000)

Hosmer, L. T., 'Trust: The Connecting Link between Organizational Theory and Philosophical Ethics', *Academy of Management Review*, 20, 2 (1995): 373–97.

Hosmer, T., *Moral Leadership in Business* (Boston, MA: Irwin Publishers, 1994).

Hughes, G. J., *Aristotle on Ethics* (London: Routledge, 2001).

Hunter, J. C., *The Servant: A Simple Story About the True Essence of Leadership* (Roseville, CA: Prima Publishing, 1998).

Husted, B. W. and J. De Jesus Salazar, 'Taking Friedman Seriously: Maximizing Profits and Social Performance', *Journal of Management Studies*, 43, 1 (2006): 75–91.

Ip, P. K., 'Is Confucianism Good for Business Ethics in China?', *Journal of Business Ethics*, forthcoming (2009).

ISEA (Institute of Social and Ethical Accountability), *Accountability 1000 (AA1000) framework. Standards, guidelines and professional qualification. Exposure draft* (1999). Available at: http://www.accountability21.net/uploadedFiles/publications/AA1000%20Framework%201999.pdf

Jackall, R., 'Moral Mazes: Bureaucracy and Managerial Work', *Harvard Business Review*, 61, 5 (1983): 118–30.

James Jr., H. S., 'Reinforcing Ethical Decision Making Through Organizational Structure', *Journal of Business Ethics*, 28, 1 (2000): 43–58.

Jansen, E. and M. A. Von Glinow, 'Ethical Ambivalence and Organizational Reward Systems', *Academy of Management Review*, 10, 4 (1985): 814–22.

Jaroszynski, P. and M. Anderson, *Ethics. The Drama of the Moral Life* (New York: St Paul, 2003. Originally published in Polish under the title: Etyka: dramat życia moralnego, in 1992).

Jensen, M. C., 'Value Maximization, Stakeholder Theory, and the Corporate Objective Function', *European Financial Management*, 7, 3 (2001): 297–317.

Jensen, M. C. and W. Meckling, 'Theory of the Firm: Managerial Behavior, Agency Cost, and Owenership Structure', *Journal of Financial Economics*, 3, 4 (1976): 305–60.

Jones, T., 'Instrumental Stakeholder Theory: A Synthesis of Ethics and Economics', *Academy of Management Review*, 20, 2 (1995): 404–38.

Josephson, M., *Ethics in the Workplace: Resource Reading Materials* (Marina del Rey, CA: Josephson Institute of Ethics, 1997).

Kaler, J., 'Understanding Participation', *Journal of Business Ethics*, 21, 2/3 (1999): 125–35.

Kamat, S., 'NGOs and the New Democracy', *Harvard International Review*, 25, 1 (2003): 65–9.

Kanov, J. M., S. Maitlis, M. C. Worline, J. E. Dutton, P. J. Frost and J. M. Lilius, 'Compassion in Organizational Life', *American Behavioral Scientist*, 47, 6 (2004): 808–27.

Kant, I., *Grounding for the Metaphysics of Morals*, 3rd edn (Indianapolis, IN: Hackett, 1993 [1785]).

Kanugo, R. and M. Mendonca, *Ethical Dimension of Leadership* (Thousand Oaks, CA: Sage, 1996).

Kaptein, M., 'Business Codes of Multinational Firms: What Do They Say?', *Journal of Business Ethics*, 50 (2004): 13–31.

Kaptein, M. and M. Schwartz, 'The Effectiveness of Business Codes: A Critical Examination of Existing Studies and the Development of an Integrated Research Model', *Journal of Business Ethics*, 77, 2 (2008): 111–27.

Karnani, A. G., 'The Mirage of Marketing to the Bottom of the Pyramid: How the Private Sector Can Help Alleviate Poverty', *California Management Review*, 49, 4 (2007): 90–111.

Keeley, M., *A Social Contract Theory of Organizations* (Notre Dame: Notre Dame University Press, 1988).

Keeley, M., 'Continuing the Social Contract Tradition', *Business Ethics Quarterly*, 5, 2 (1995): 241–56.

Keffer, J. M. and R. P. Hill, 'An Ethical Approach to Lobbying Activities of Businesses in the United States', *Journal of Business Ethics*, 16, 12/13 (1997): 1371–9.

Kelly, C., P. Courek, N. McGraw and J. Samuelson, *Deriving Value from Corporate Values* (2004). Available at: http://www.aspeninstitute.org/atf/cf/%7BDEB6F227-659B-4EC8-8F84-8DF23CA704F5%7D/VALUE%20SURVEY%20FINAL.PDF

Kerr, S., 'On the Folly of Rewarding A, While Hoping for B', *Academy of Management Journal*, 18, 4 (1975): 769–83.

Kidder, R. M., 'Universal Human Values', *Futurist*, 28, 4 (1994): 8–13.

Kirkpatrick, S. A. and E. A. Locke, 'Leadership: Do Traits Matter?', *Academy of Management Executive*, 5, 2 (1991): 48–60.

Koehn, D., 'A Role for Virtue Ethics in the Analysis of Business Practice', *Business Ethics Quarterly*, 5, 3 (1995): 533–9.

Kohlberg, L., *Essays on Moral Development. The Philosophy of Moral Development: Moral Stages and the Idea of Justice* (San Francisco: Harper & Row, 1981 (Volume 1), 1984 (Volume 2)).

Kolm, S.-C., *Modern Theories of Justice* (Boston, MA: MIT Press, 1996).

Koslowski, P., 'The Ethics of Banking. On the Ethical Economy of the Credit and Capital Market, of Speculation and Insider Trading in the German Experience', in A. Argandoña (ed.), *The Ethical Dimension of Financial Institutions and Markets* (Berlin: Springer-Verlag, 1995): 180–232.

Koslowski, P., 'The Common Good of the Firm as the Fiduciary Duty of the Manager', in G. J. Rossuw and A. J. Sison (eds), *Global Perspectives on the Ethics of Corporate Governance* (New York: Palgrave Macmillan, 2006): 67–76.

Kotter, J., *A Force for Change: How Leadership Differs from Management* (New York: Free Press, 1990).

Kotter, J. and J. Heskett, *Corporate Culture and Performance* (New York: Free Press, 1992).

Kowalczyk, S., *An Outline of the Philosophical Anthropology* (New York: P. Lang, 1991).

Koys, D. J. and T. A. Decotiis, 'Inductive Measures of Psychological Climate', *Human Relations*, 44, 3 (1991): 265–85.

Kracher, B. and C. L. Corritore, 'Is There a Special e-Commerce Ethics?', *Business Ethics Quarterly*, 14, 1 (2004): 71–94.

Krausz, M. (ed.), *Relativism. Interpretation and Confrontation* (Notre Dame, IN: Notre Dame University Press, 1989).

Kreps, D. M., *Microeconomics for Managers* (New York: W. W. Norton, 2003).

Kurzynski, M. J., 'The Virtue of Forgiveness as a Human Resource Management Strategy; *Journal of Business Ethics*, 98, 1 (1998): 77–85.

Laczniak, G. R., 'Ethics of Marketing', in R. W. Kolb (ed.), *Encyclopedia of Business Ethics and Society* (Los Angeles: Sage, 2008): 1336–43.

Langlois, C. C. and B. B. Schlegelmilch, 'Do Corporate Codes of Ethics Reflect National Character? Evidence from Europe and the United States', *Journal of International Business Studies*, 21, 4 (1990): 519–39.

Larmer, R. A., 'Whistleblowing and Employee Loyalty', *Journal of Business Ethics*, 11, 2 (1992): 125–8.

Lazonick, W. and M. O'Sullivan, 'Maximizing Shareholder Value: A New Ideology for Corporate Governance', *Economy and Society*, 29, 1 (2000): 13–35.

Lee, R. W., L. Fabish and N. McGaw, 'The Value of Corporate Values' (Spring 2005). Available at SSRN: http://www.ssrn.com/abstract=956170

Leland, H. E., 'Insider Trading: Should it be Prohibited?', *Journal of Political Economy*, 100, 4 (1992): 859–87.

Lewis, C. S., *The Abolition of Man* (London: Curtis Brown, 1987).

Lilius, J. M., M. C. Worline, S. Maitlis, J. Kanov, J. E. Dutton and P. Frost, 'The Contours and Consequences of Compassion at Work', *Journal of Organizational Behavior*, 29, 2 (2008): 193–218.

Lindsay, R. M., L. M. Lindsay and V. B. Irvine, 'Instilling Ethical Behavior in Organizations: A Survey of Canadian Companies', *Journal of Business Ethics*, 15, 4 (1996): 393–407.

Llano, C., *El Empresario ante la Responsabilidad y la Motivación* (Mexico: McGrawHill-Ipade, 1991).

Llano, C., *La Enseñanza de la Dirección y el Método del Caso* (Mexico: Ipade, 1996).

Llano, C., *Dilemas Éticos de la Empresa Contemporánea* (Mexico: Fondo de Cultura Económica, 1997).

Llano, C., *Humildad y Liderazgo: ¿Necesita el Empresario ser Humilde?* (Neucalpan, Mexico: Ediciones Ruz, 2004).

Locke, J., *The Two Treatises of Civil Government*, Richard Aschcraft (ed.) (London: Routledge, 1989 [1689]).

Logsdon, J. M. and P. Forsythe, 'Maquiladoras', in R. W. Kolb, *Encyclopedia of Business Ethics and Society* (Thousand Oaks: Sage Publications, 2008): 1324–5.

Maak, T., *Responsible Leadership in Business* (New York: Routledge, 2006).

Maak, T., 'Responsible Leadership, Stakeholder Engagement, and the Emergence of Social Capital', *Journal of Business Ethics*, 74, 4 (2007): 329–43.

MacInerny, R. M., *Etica Thomistica: The Moral Philosophy of Thomas Aquinas* (Washington: Catholic University of America Press, 1997).

MacIntyre, A., *After Virtue. A Study in Moral Theory*, 2nd edn (London: Duckworth, 1985).

MacIntyre, A., *Whose Justice? Which Rationality?* (Notre Dame, IN: University of Notre Dame Press, 1988).

MacIntyre, A., 'Plain Persons and Moral Philosophy: Rules, Virtues and Goods', *Convivium*, 2nd series, 5 (1993): 63–80. Reprinted in: Kelvin Knight (ed.), *The MacIntyre Reader* (Cambridge: Polity Press, 1998). pp. 136–52. Quotations are from this reprint.

MacMillan, K., K. Money and S. Downing, 'Successful Business Relationships', *Journal of General Management*, 26, 1 (2000): 69–83.

Maher, T. E. and Y. Y. Wong, 'The Impact of Cultural Differences on the Growing Tensions Between Japan and the United States', *SAM Advanced Management Journal*, Winter (1994): 40–6.

Mangan, J. T., 'An Historical Analysis of the Principle of Double Effect', *Theological Studies*, 10 (1949): 41–61.

Manne, H. G., *Insider Trading and the Stock Market* (New York: Free Press, 1966).

Manne, H. G., 'Insider Trading: Hayek, Virtual Markets, and the Dog that Did Not Bark', *Journal of Corporation Law*, 31, 1 (2005): 167–85.

Manning, D. J., 'Benefits of Environmental Stewardship', *Review of Business*, 25, 2 (2004): 9–14.

Marcoux, A. M., 'A Fiduciary Argument Against Stakeholder Theory', *Business Ethics Quarterly*, 13, 1 (2003): 1–24.

Marcus Aurelius, *The Meditations* (London: Penguin, 2006).

Margolis, J. D. and J. P. Walsh, *People and Profits?: The Search for A Link Between A Company's Social and Financial Performance* (Mahwah, NJ: Lawrence Erlbaum Associates, 2001).

Margolis, J. D. and J. P. Walsh, 'Misery Loves Companies: Rethinking Social Initiatives by Business', *Administrative Science Quarterly*, 48, 2 (2003): 268–305.

Maritain, J., *The Person and the Common Good* (New York: Charles Scribner's Son, 1947).

Maritain, J., *Man and the State* (Chicago, IL: University of Chicago Press, 1951).

Maritain, J., *The Rights of Man and Natural Law* (New York: Gordian Press, 1971[1943]).

Marsden, C., 'In Defence of Corporate Responsibility', in A. Kakabadse and M. Morsing (eds), *Corporate Social Responsibility. Reconciling Aspirations with Application* (New York: Palgrave Macmillan, 2006): 24–39.

Marsnik, S. J., 'Trade Secrets and Corporate Espionage', in R. W. Kolb (ed.), *Encyclopedia of Business and Society* (Los Angeles: Sage, 2008): 2090–3.

Maslow, A. H., 'A Theory of Human Motivation', *Psychological Review*, 50 (1943): 370–96.

Maslow, A. H., *Motivation and Personality* (New York: Harper & Row, 1954).

Maslow, A. H., *Motivation and Personality*, 2nd edn (New York: Harper & Row, 1970).

Matten, D. and A. Crane, 'Corporate Citizenship: Towards an Extended Theoretical Conceptualization', *Academy of Management Review*, 30, 1 (2005): 166–79.

Matten, D. and J. Moon, "Implicit" and "Explicit" CSR: A Conceptual Framework for a Comparative Understanding of Corporate Social Responsibility', *Academy of Management Review*, 33, 2 (2008): 404–24.

Maury, M. D. and D. S. Kleiner, 'E-Commerce, Ethical Commerce?', *Journal of Business Ethics*, 36, 1/2 (2002): 21–31.

Max-Neef, M., *Human Scale Development* (New York: Apex Press, 1991).

McGuire, J. W., *Business and Society* (New York: McGraw-Hill, 1963).

McMahon, T. F., 'Morality and the Invisible Hand', *Philosophy and Public Affairs*, 10, 3 (1981): 247–77.

McWilliams, A. and D. Siegel, 'Corporate Social Responsibility and Financial Performance: Correlation or Misspecification?', *Strategic Management Journal*, 21, 5 (2000): 603–9.

McWilliams, A. and D. Siegel, 'Corporate Social Responsibility: A Theory of the Firm Perspective', *Academy of Management Review*, 26, 1 (2001): 117–27.

Meadows, D. H., D. L. Meadows, J. Randers and W. W. Behrens, *The Limits to Growth* (New York: New American Library, 1972).

Melé, D., *Ética en la Dirección de Empresas* (Barcelona: Folio, 1997).

Melé, D., 'Early Business in Spain: The Salamanca School', *Journal of Business Ethics*, 22 (1999): 175–89.

Melé, D., 'Loyalty in Business: Subversive Doctrine or Real Need?', *Business Ethics Quarterly*, 11, 1 (2001): 11–26.

Melé, D., 'Not only Stakeholder Interests. The Firm Oriented toward the Common Good', in S. A. Cortright and M. Naughton (eds), *Rethinking the Purpose of Business: Interdisciplinary Essays from the Catholic Social Tradition* (Notre Dame: University of Notre Dame Press, 2002).

Melé, D., 'Organizational Humanizing Cultures: Can they Create Social Capital', *Journal of Business Ethics*, 45, 1 (2003): 3–14.

Melé, D., 'Exploring the Principle of Subsidiarity in Organizational Forms', *Journal of Business Ethics*, 60 (2005): 293–305.

Melé, D., 'Religious Foundations of Business Ethics', in M. J. Epstein and K. O. Hanson (eds), *The Accountable Corporation* (London: Praeger Publishers, 2006): 11–43.

Melé, D., 'Religious Discrimination', in R. W. Kolb (ed.), *Encyclopedia of Business Ethics and Society* (Los Angeles: Sage, 2008a): 1811–13.

Melé, D., 'Corporate Social Responsibility Theories', in A. Crane, A. Williams, D. Matten, J. Moon and D. S. Siegel (eds), *The Oxford Handbook of Corporate Social Responsibility* (Oxford/New York: Oxford University Press, 2008b): 47–82.

Merton, R. K., *Social Theory and Social Structure* (New York: Free Press, 1957).

Messner, J., *Social Ethics. Natural Law in the Modern World* (St. Louis, USA: Herder, 1965).

Messner, J., *La Cuestión Social* (Madrid: Rialp, 1976).

Metzger, M., D. R. Dalton and J. W. Hill, 'The Organization of Ethics and the Ethics of Organizations. The Case for Expanded Organizational Ethics Audits', *Business Ethics Quarterly*, 3, 1 (1993): 27–43.

Metzger, M. B. and D. R. Dalton, 'Seeing the Elephant: An Organizational Perspective on Corporate Moral Agency', *American Business Law Journal*, 33 (1996): 489–576.

Miceli, M. P. and J. P. Near, *Blowing the Whistle: The Organizational and Legal implications for Companies and Employees* (New York: Lexington Books, 1992).

Michelin, F., *And Why Not? Morality and Business* (Maryland: Lexington Books, 2003).

Milgram, S., *Obedience to Authority* (New York: Harper & Row, 1974).

Mill, J. S., *Utilitarianism*, George Sher (ed.) (Indianapolis; IN: Hackett Publishing Company, 2001 [1863]).

Milliman, J., J. Ferguson and K. Sylvester, 'Implementation of Michael Porter's Strategic Corporate Social Responsibility Model', *Journal of Global Business Issues*, Spring (2008): 29–33.

Mintzberg, H., *The Nature of Managerial Work* (Englewood Cliffs, NJ: Prentice-Hall, 1973).

Mintzberg, H., 'The Manager's Job: Folklore and Fact', *Harvard Business Review*, 53, 4 (1975): 49–61.

Moberg, D. J., 'Role Models and Moral Exemplars: How Employees Acquire Virtues by Observing Others?', *Business Ethics Quarterly*, 10, 3 (2000): 675–96.

Mommsen, W. J., *The Political and Social Theory of Max Weber: Collected Essays* (Chicago: University of Chicago Press, 1992).

Moon, J., 'The Contribution of Corporate Social Responsibility to Sustainable Development', *Sustainable Development*, 15, 5 (2007): 296–306.

Moon, J., A. Crane and D. Matten, 'Can Corporations Be Citizens? Corporate Citizenship as a Metaphor for Business Participation in Society', *Business Ethics Quarterly*, 15, 3 (2005): 429–53.

Moore, A., 'Employee Monitoring and Computer Technology. Evaluating Surveillance vs Privacy', *Business Ethics Quarterly*, 10, 3 (2000): 697–709.

Moore, G., 'Corporate Moral Agency: Review and Implications', *Journal of Business Ethics*, 21 (1999): 329–43.

Moore, J., 'What is Really Unethical About Insider Trading?', *Journal of Business Ethics*, 9, 3 (1990): 171–82.

Moriarty, J., 'On the Relevance of Political Philosophy to Business Ethics', *Business Ethics Quarterly*, 15, 3 (2005): 455–73.

Moses, J., *Oneness: Great Principles Shared by All Religions* (New York: Ballantine, 2001).

Moss, A. L., *Selling Out America's Democracy: How Lobbyists, Special Interests, and Campaign Financing Undermine the Will of the People* (New York: Praeger, 2008).

Mounier, E., *Personalism* (Notre Dame, IN: University of Notre Dame Press, 2001 [c1952]).

Murphy, P., *Eighty Exemplary Ethics Statements* (Notre Dame, IN.: University of Notre Dame Press, 1998).

Murphy, P., 'Character and Virtue Ethics in International Marketing: An Agenda for Managers, Researchers and Educators', *Journal of Business Ethics*, 18 (1999): 107–24.

Murphy, P. and G. R. Laczniak, *Marketing Ethics: Cases and Readings* (Englewood Cliffs, NJ: Prentice Hall, 2006).

Murphy, P. E. and G. R. Laczniak, 'An Ethical Basis for Relationship Marketing: A Virtue Ethics Perspective', *European Journal of Marketing*, 41, 1/2 (2007): 37–57.

Myers, L. A., 'Consumer Sovereignty', in K. W. Robert (ed.), *Encyclopedia of Business Ethics and Society* (Los Angeles: Sage, 2008): 439–41.

Naess, A., *Ecology, Community, and Lifestyle* (Cambridge: Cambridge University Press, 1989).

Nash, L. L., *Good Intentions Aside. A Manager's Guide to Resolving Ethical Problems* (Boston, MA: Harvard Business School Press, 1990).

Naugthon, S. and T. Naugthon, 'Religion, Ethics and Stock Trading: the Case of an Islamic Equities Market', *Journal of Business Ethics*, 23 (2000): 145–59.

Nelson, R., 'Training on Ethics: Cummins Eng. Co.', *Journal of Management Development*, 11, 4 (1992): 21–33.

Newton, T. J., 'Creating the New Ecological Order? Elias and Actor-Network Theory', *Academy of Management Review*, 27, 4 (2002): 523–40.

Northouse, P. G., *Leadership: Theory and Practice*, 4th edn (Thousand Oaks, CA: Sage, 2007).

Novak, M., *Business as a Calling – Work and the Examined Life* (New York: Free Press, 1996).

Novak, M., 'The Judeo-Christian Foundation of Human Dignity', *Journal of Markets & Morality*, 1, 2 (1998): 107–21.

Oderberg, D. S., *Moral Theory. A Non-Consequentialist Approach* (Oxford: Blackwell, 2000).

OECD (Organization for Economic Cooperation and Development), *OECD Principles of Corporate Governance* (Paris: OECD Publications Services, 2004).

Oliverio, M. E., 'The Implementation of a Code of Ethics: The Early Efforts of One Entrepreneur', *Journal of Business Ethics*, 8, 5 (1989): 367–74.

Orlitzky, M., F. L. Schmidt and S. L. Rynes, 'Corporate Social and Financial Performance: A Meta-analysis', *Organization Studies*, 24, 3 (2003): 403–41.

Ostas, D. T., 'Fraud', in R. W. Kolb (ed.), *Encyclopedia of Business and Society* (Los Angeles: Sage, 2008): 931–5.

Oxford English Dictionary, 2nd edn (Oxford: Oxford University Press, 1989).

Oxford Concise Dictionary of Quotations, 3rd edn, Oxford: Oxford University Press (1993).

Paine, L. S., 'Managing for Organizational Integrity', *Harvard Business Review*, 72, 2 (1994): 106–17.

Paine, L. S., 'Moral Thinking in Management: An Essential Capability', *Business Ethics Quarterly*, 6, 4 (1996): 477–92.

Paine, L. S., 'Does Ethics Pay?', *Business Ethics Quarterly*, 10, 1 (2000a): 319–30.

Paine, L. S., *AES Global Values* (Boston, MA: Case study, Harvard Business School, 2000b).

Paine, L. S., *Value Shift* (New York: McGraw-Hill, 2003).

Paine, L. S. and M. A. Santoro, *Sears Auto Centers (A) (B) and (C)* (Cambridge, MA: Harvard Business School Cases, Harvard Business School Press, 1993).

Paladino, M., P. Debeljuh and P. Delbosco, *Integridad. Un Liderazgo Diferente* (Buenos Aires: Emecé Editores, 2007).

Palmer, I., J. Benveniste and R. Dunford, 'New Organizational Forms: Towards a Generative Dialogue', *Organization Studies*, 28, 12 (2007): 1829–47.

Pascal, B., *Pensées* (Paris: Gallimard, 1954).

Passmore, J., *Man's Responsibility for Nature* (New York: Scribner's, 1974).

Pava, M., *Business Ethics: A Jewish Perspective* (Hoboken, NJ: Ktav Publishing, 1997).

Pava, M., 'The Substance of Jewish Business Ethics', *Journal of Business Ethics*, 17 (1998): 603–17.

Pava, M., 'Corporate Accountability', in K. Kolb (ed.), *Encyclopedia of Business Ethics and Society* (Los Angeles: Sage, 2008): 451–5.

Pérez-López, J. A., *Liderazgo y Ética en la Dirección de Empresas, la Nueva Empresa del Siglo XXI* (Bilbao: Deusto, 1998).

Pérez-López, J. A., *Fundamentos de la Dirección de Empresas*, 5th edn (Madrid: Rialp, 2002).

Peters, T. J., *Thriving on Chaos* (New York: Alfred A. Knopf, 1988).

Peters, T. J. and R. H. Waterman, *In Search of Excellence: Lessons from America's Best Run Companies* (London: Harper & Row, 1982).

Petrick, J. A. and J. F. Quinn, *Management Ethics. Integrity at Work* (New Delhi: Sage, 1997).

Petrick, J. A. and J. F. Quinn, 'The Integrity Capacity Construct and Moral Progress in Business', *Journal of Business Ethics*, 23, 1 (2000): 3–18.

Pettigrew, A. M., 'On Studying Organizational Cultures', *Administrative Science Quarterly*, 24, Dec. (1979): 570–81.

Phillips, M. J., 'Corporate Moral Personhood and Three Conceptions of the Corporation', *Business Ethics Quarterly*, 2, 4 (1992): 435–59.

Phillips, R., R. E. Freeman and A. C. Wicks, 'What Stakeholder Theory Is Not', *Business Ethics Quarterly*, 13, 4 (2003): 479–502.

Pieper, J., *The Four Cardinal Virtues: Prudence, Justice, Fortitude, Temperance* (Notre Dame, IN: University of Notre Dame Press, 1966).

Plato, *Complete Works*, John M. Cooper and D. S. Hutchinson (eds) (Indianapolis, IN: Hackett Publishing Company, 1997).

Polo, L., *Ética: Hacia una Versión Moderna de los Temas Clásicos* (Madrid: Unión Editorial, 1996).

Pontifical Council for Social Communications (PCSC), 'Ethics in Advertising' (1997). Available at http://www.vatican.va/roman_curia/pontifical_councils/pccs/documents/rc_pc_pccs_doc_22021997_ethics-in-ad_en.html

Pontifical Council for Justice and Peace (PCJP), *Compendium of the Social Doctrine of the Church* (Città del Vaticano: Libreria Editrice Vaticana, 2004). Available at http://www.vatican.va/roman_curia/pontifical_councils/justpeace/documents/rc_pc_justpeace_doc_20060526_compendio-dott-soc_en.html

Pope John Paul II, Encyclical-Letter 'Laborem exercens', on the human work (1981). Available at http://www.vatican.va/edocs/ENG0217/_INDEX.HTM

Pope John Paul II, Encyclical-Letter 'Sollicitudo rei Socialis', on human development (1987). Available at http://www.vatican.va/edocs/ENG0223/_INDEX.HTM

Pope John Paul II, Encyclical-Letter 'Centesimus annus', on economic and social issues (1991). Available at http://www.vatican.va/edocs/ENG0214/_INDEX.HTM

Pope Leo XIII, Encyclical-Letter 'Rerum Novarum', on social order (1891). Available at http://www.vatican.va/holy_father/leo_xiii/encyclicals/documents/hf_l-xiii_enc_15051891_rerum-novarum_en.html

Porter, M. E. and M. R. Kramer, 'Strategy & Society: The Link between Competitive Advantage and Corporate Social Responsibility', *Harvard Business Review*, 84, 12 (2006): 78–92.

Prahalad, C. K., 'Strategies for the Bottom of the Economic Pyramid: India as a Source of Innovation', *Reflections: The SOL Journal*, 3, 4 (2003): 6–18.

Prahalad, C. K., *The Fortune of the Pyramid: Eradicating Poverty Through Profits* (Philadelphia: Warthon School Publishing, 2004).

Prentice, W. C. H., 'Understanding Leadership', *Harvard Business Review*, 39, 5 (1961): 143–51.

PriceWaterhouse Change Integration Team, *The Paradox Principles. How High-Performance Companies Manage Chaos, Complexity, and Contradiction to Achieve Superior Results* (Chicago: Irwin, 1996).

Preston, I. L., *The Great American Blow-Up: Puffery in Advertising and Selling*, revised edn (Madison: University of Wisconsin Press, 1997).

Pruzan, P., 'The Question of Organizational Consciousness: Can Organizations Have Values, Virtues and Visions?', *Journal of Business Ethics*, 29, 3 (2001): 271–84.

Puffer, S. M. and D. J. McCarthy, 'Finding the Common Ground in Russian and American Business Ethics', *California Management Review*, 37, 2 (1995): 29–46.

Purser, R. E. and C. Park, 'Limits to Anthropocentrism: Toward an Ecocentric Organization Paradigm?', *Academy of Management Review*, 20, 4 (1995): 1053–89.

Quinn, D. P. and T. M. Jones, 'An Agent Morality View of Business Policy', *Academy of Management Review*, 20, 1 (1995): 22–42.

Rachels, J. and S. Rachels, *The Elements of Moral Philosophy* (New York: McGraw-Hill, 1995).

Ramirez, S., *La Prudencia* (Madrid: Palabra, 1978).

Rawls, J., *A Theory of Justice*, revised edn (Oxford: OUP, 1999 [1971]).

Regan, T., *The Case for Animals Rights* (Berkeley: University of California Press, 1983).

Rice, G., 'Islamic Ethics and the Implications for Business', *Journal of Business Ethics*, 18 (1999): 345–58.

Robins, F., 'The Challenge of TBL: A Responsibility to Whom?', *Business & Society Review*, 111, 1 (2006): 1–14.

Roels, S. J., 'The Business Ethics of Evangelicals', *Business Ethics Quarterly*, 7, 2 (1997): 109–22.

Roman, R., S. Hayibor and B. Agle, 'The Relationship Between Social and Financial Performance', *Business & Society*, 38, 1 (1999): 109–25.

Román, S., 'The Impact of Ethical Sales Behaviour on Customer Satisfaction, Trust and Loyalty to the Company: An Empirical Study in the Financial Services Industry', *Journal of Marketing Management*, 19, 9/10 (2003): 915–39.

Romar, E. J., 'Virtues is Good Business: Confucianism as a Practical Business Ethics', *Journal of Business Ethics*, 38, 1/2 (2002): 119–31.

Romar, E. J., 'Globalization, Ethics, and Opportunism. A Confucian View of Business Relationships', *Business Ethics Quarterly*, 14, 4 (2004): 663–78.

Rosanas, J. M. and M. Velilla, 'Loyalty and Trust as the Ethical Bases of Organizations', *Journal of Business Ethics*, 44, 1 (2003): 49–59.

Saeed, M., Z. U. Ahmed and S.-M. Mukhtar, 'International marketing Ethics from an Islamic Perspective: A Value-Maximization Approach', *Journal of Business Ethics*, 32 (2001): 127–42.

Salanie, B., *Microeconomics of Market Failures* (Cambridge, MA: MIT Press, 2000).

Sartre, J.-P., *Being and Nothingness: An Essay on Phenomenological Ontology* (London: Routledge, 2003).

Schein, E. H., 'Organizational Cultures', *American Psychologist*, 45, 2 (1990): 109–19.

Schein, E. H., *Corporate Culture and Leadership*, 3rd edn (San Francisco: Willey, 2004 [1984]).

Scherer, K. R., *Justice: Interdisciplinary Perspectives* (Cambridge: Cambridge University Press, 1992).

Schlegelmilch, B. B. and D. C. Robertson, 'The Influence of Country and Industry on Ethical Perception of Senior Executives in the U.S. and Europe', *Journal of International Business Studies*, 26, 4 (1995): 859–81.

Schminke, M., 'Considering the Business in Business Ethics: An Exploratory Study of the Influence of Organizational Size and Structure on Individual Ethical Predispositions', *Journal of Business Ethics*, 30, 4 (2001): 375–90.

Scholtens, B. and L. Dam, 'Cultural Values and International Differences in Business Ethics', *Journal of Business Ethics*, 75, 3 (2007): 273–84.

Schumacher, E. F., *Small is Beautiful. Economics as if People Mattered* (New York: Hartley & Marks, 1999).

Schwartz, M. S., 'Universal Moral Values for Corporate Codes of Ethics', *Journal of Business Ethics*, 59/2, 1/2 (2005): 27–44.

Scott, A. M., 'Family Responsibility Discrimination', *Employee Benefit Plan Review*, 62 (2007): 35–7.

Sen, A., 'Human Rights and Asian Values', in T. Machan (ed.), *Business Ethics in the Global Marketplace* (Stanford, CA: Hoover Institution Press, 1999): 37–62.

Senge, P., *The Fifth Discipline: The Art and Practice of the Learning Organization* (New York: Doubleday, 1990).

Sharma, A. K. and B. Talwar, 'Business Excellence Enshrined in Vedic (Hindu) Philosophy', *Singapore Management Review*, 26, 1 (2004): 1–19.

Shaw, W. H., 'Business Ethics Today. A Survey', *Journal of Business Ethics*, 15 (1996): 489–500.

Sethia, N. K. and M. A. Von Glinow, *Gaining Control of the Corporate Culture* (New York: Jossey-Bass, 1985).

Shrivastava, P., 'The Role of Corporations in Achieving Ecological Sustainability', *Academy of Management Review*, 20 (1995): 936–60.

Simmons, A. J., *The Lockean Theory of Rights* (Princeton: Princeton University Press, 1992).

Simon, H. A., *Administrative Behavior: A Study of Decision-Making Processes in Administrative Organizations* (New York: Free Press, 1997 [1959]).

Sims, R. R., 'Linking Groupthink to Unethical Behavior in Organizations', *Journal of Business Ethics*, 11, 9 (1992): 651–62.

Sims, R. R., 'Changing an Organization's Culture Under New Leadership', *Journal of Business Ethics*, 25, 1 (2000): 65–78.

Sims, R. R. and J. Brinkmann, 'Leaders as Moral Role Models: The Case of John Gutfreund at Salomon Brothers', *Journal of Business Ethics*, 35, 4 (2002): 327–39.

Singer, P., *Animal Liberation* (New York: New York Review of Books Press, 1990).

Sison, A. J. G., *The Moral Capital of Leaders. Why Virtue Matters* (Cheltenham, UK/Northampton, MA, USA: Edward Elgar, 2003).

Sison, A. J. G., *Corporate Governance and Ethics. An Aristotelian Perspective* (Cheltenham, UK: Edward Elgar, 2008).

Slote, M. A., *The Ethics of Care and Empathy* (New York: Routledge, 2007).

Smart, J. J. C. and B. Williams, *Utilitarianism: For and Against* (Cambridge: Cambridge University Press, 1973).

Smith, A., *An Inquiry into the Nature and Causes of the Wealth of Nations* [1776] (Chicago: Encyclopædia Britannica, 1955).

Smith, N. C. and J. A. Quelch, *Ethics in Marketing* (Boston, MA: Irwin, 1993).

Snoeyenbos, M. and K. Smith, 'Ma and Sun on Insider Trading Ethics', *Journal of Business Ethics*, 28, 4 (2000): 361–3.

Solomon, C. R., *Ethics and Excellence: Cooperation and Integrity in Business* (New York: Oxford University Press, 1992).

Solomon, C. R., *The New World of Business. Ethics and Free Enterprise in the Global 1990s* (Maryland: Rowman & Littlefield Publishers, 1994).

Solomon, C. R., *A better way to think about business: how personal integrity leads to corporate success* (New York: Oxford University Press, 1999).

Solomon, R. C., 'Victims of Circumstances? A Defense of Virtue Ethics in Business', *Business Ethics Quarterly*, 13, 1 (2003): 43–62.

Solomon, R. C., 'Aristotle, Ethics and Business Organizations', *Organization Studies*, 25, 6 (2004): 1021–43.

Somers, M. J., 'Ethical Codes of Conduct and Organizational Context: A Study of the Relationship between Codes of Conduct, Employee Behaviour and Organizational Values', *Journal of Business Ethics*, 30 (2001): 185–95.

Spaemann, R., *Basic Moral Concepts* (London: Routledge, 1989).

Spaemann, R., *Happiness and Benevolence* (Notre Dame, IN: Notre Dame University Press, 2005).

Spaemann, R., *Persons: The Difference between 'Someone' and 'Something'* (Oxford/New York: Oxford University Press, 2006).

Spears, L. C. (ed), *Reflections on Leadership: How Robert K. Greenleaf's Theory of Servant-Leadership influenced today's Top Management Thinkers* (New York: John Wiley, 1995).

Spears, L. C. (ed), *Insights on Leadership: Service, Stewardship, Spirit, and Servant-Leadership* (New York: Wiley, 1998).

Steinmann, H. and A. Löhr, *Gundlagen der Unternehmensethik*, 2nd edn (Stuttgart: Schäffer-Poeschel, 1994).

Sternberg, E., *Just Business. Business Ethics in Action*, 2nd edn (Oxford: Oxford University Press, 2000).

Stiglitz, J. E., *Globalization and its Discontents* (New York: W.W. Norton, 2003).

Stiglitz, J. E., *Making Globalization Work* (New York: W.W. Norton, 2006).

Stone, C., *Should Trees have Standing? Toward Legal Rights for Nature* (Los Altos, CA: William Kaufmann, 1974).

Stone, C., *Where the Law Ends* (New York: Harper & Row, 1975).

Sundaram, A. K. and A. C. Inkpen, 'The Corporate Objective Revisited', *Organization Science*, 15, 3 (2004): 350–63.

Swift, T., 'Trust, Reputation and Corporate Accountability to Stakeholders', *Business Ethics: A European Review*, 10, 1 (2001): 16–26.

Tamari, M., 'The Challenge of Wealth. Jewish Business Ethics', *Business Ethics Quarterly*, 7, 1 (1997): 45–56.

Taylor, C., 'The Diversity of Goods', in A. Sen and B. Williams (eds), *Utilitarianism and Beyond* (Cambridge: Cambridge University Press, 1982).

Taylor, J. S., 'Subliminal Advertising', in R. W. Kolb (ed.), *Encyclopedia of Business Ethics and Society* (Los Angeles: Sage, 2008): 20–1.

Thomas, R. R., *Redefining Diversity* (New York: American Management Association, 1996).

Toffler, B. L., *Tough Choices: Managers Talk Ethics* (New York: John Wiley, 1986).

Toffler, B. L. (ed.), *Final Accounting: Ambition, Greed, and the Fall of Arthur Andersen* (New York: Broadway Books, 2003).

Torraco, R. J., 'Work Design Theory: A Review and Critique with Implications for Human Resource Development', *Human Resource Development Quarterly*, 16, 1 (2005): 85–109.

Treviño, L. K., 'A Cultural Perspective on Changing and Developing Organizational Ethics', *Research in Organizational Change and Development*, 4 (1990): 195–230.

Treviño, L. K. and K. A. Nelson, *Managing Business Ethics: Straight Talk about How to Do it Right*, 3rd edn (Hoboken, NJ: Wiley, 2004).

Treviño, L. K. and G. R. Weaver, 'Behavioral Ethics in Organizations: A Review', *Journal of Management*, 32, 6 (2006): 951–90.

Treviño, L. K., G. R. Weaver, D. G. Gibson and B. L. Toffler, 'Managing Ethics and Legal Compliance: What Works and What Hurts', *California Management Review*, 41, 2 (1999): 131–51.

UN World Commission on Environment and Development, *Our Common Future* (Oxford: Oxford University Press, 1987).

Vachani, S. and N. C. Smith, 'Socially Responsible Pricing: Lessons from the Pricing of Aids in Developing Countries', *California Management Review*, 47, 1 (2004): 117–44.

Vandekerckhove, W. and M. S. R. Commers, 'Downward Workplace Mobbing: A Sign of the Times?', *Journal of Business Ethics*, 45, 1/2 (2003): 41–50.

Velasquez, M., *Business Ethics: Concepts and Cases* (Englewood Cliffs. N.J.: Prentice-Hall, 1982).

Velasquez, M., 'Why Corporations Are Not Morally Responsible for Anything They Do', *Business & Professional Ethics Journal*, 2, 3 (1983): 1–18.

Velasquez, M., *Business Ethics: Concepts and Cases*, 5th edn (Upper Saddle River, NJ: Prentice Hall, 2001).

Velasquez, M., 'Debunking Moral Responsibility', *Business Ethics Quarterly*, 13, 4 (2003): 531–62.

Velasquez, M., 'Natural Law Ethical Theory', in R. W. Kolb (ed.), *Encyclopedia of Business Ethics and Society* (Thousand Oaks: Sage, 2008): 1485–8.

Velasquez, M. and F. N. Brady, 'Natural Law and Business Ethics', *Business Ethics Quarterly*, 7 (1997): 83–107.

Veroutis, A. D., A. I. Ullman, J. A. Fava, D. C. Steinmetz and E. J. Kerfoot, 'Achieving Competitive Advantage Through Product Stewardship and LCA', *Environmental Quality Management*, 6, 2 (1996): 67–72.

Vietzen, L. A., *Understanding, Creating, and Implementing Contracts* (New York: Aspen, 2008).

Vogel, D. J., *Is There a Market for Virtue?* (Washington, DC: Brooking Institute 2005).

Waddock, S. and N. Smith, 'Relationships: The Real Challenge of Corporate Global Citizenship', *Business & Society Review*, 105, 1 (2000): 47– 61.

Waddock, S. A., *Leading Corporate Citizens. Vision, Values, Value Added* (Boston, MA: McGraw-Hill/Irwin, 2002).

Walsh, A. and T. Lynch, 'The Very Idea of Justice in Pricing', *Business & Professional Ethics Journal*, 21, 3/4 (2002): 5–27.

Walzer, M., *Just and Unjust Wars* (New York: Basic Books, 1977).

Warneka, P., T. Warneka and L. Tzu, *The Way of Leading People: Unlocking Your Integral Leadership Skills with the Tao Te Ching* (Cleveland, OH: Asogomi Publishing International, 2007).

Waters, J. A. and F. Bird, 'The Moral Dimension of Organizational Culture', *Journal of Business Ethics*, 6, 1 (1987): 15–22.

Waters, J. A. and F. Bird, 'Attending to Ethics in Management', *Journal of Business Ethics*, 8, 6 (1989): 493–7.

Watson, A. (ed.) *The Digest of Justinian* (Philadelphia, Pennsylvania: University of Pennsylvania Press, 1998).

Weaver, G. R. and L. K. Treviño, 'Compliance and Values Oriented Programs: Influence on Employees' Attitudes and Behavior', *Business Ethics Quarterly*, 9, 2 (1999): 315–35.

Weaver, G. R., L. K. Treviño and P. L. Cochran, 'Integrated and Decoupled Corporate Social Performance: Management Commitments, External Pressures, and Corporate Ethics Practices', *Academy of Management Journal*, 42, 5 (1999): 539–52.

Weber, J., 'Business Ethics Training: Insights from Learning Theory', *Journal of Business Ethics*, 70, 1 (2007): 61–85.

Werhane, P. H., 'The Ethics of Insider Trading', *Journal of Business Ethics*, 8, 11 (1989): 841–5.

Werhane, P. H., 'The Indefensibility of Insider Trading', *Journal of Business Ethics*, 10, 9 (1991): 729–31.

Werhane, P. H. and M. Gorman, 'Intellectual Property Rights, Moral Imagination, and Access to Life-Enhancing Drugs', *Business Ethics Quarterly*, 15, 4 (2005): 595–613.

Werner, J. M., 'Organizational Citizenship Behavior: Its Nature, Antecedents, and Consequences', *Personnel Psychology*, 59, 2 (2006): 484–7.

Wheeler, D., B. Colbert and R. E. Freeman, 'Focusing on Value: Reconciling Corporate Social Responsibility, Sustainability and a Stakeholder Approach in a Network World', *Journal of General Management*, 28, 3 (2003): 1–28.

Whetstone, J. T., 'Personalism and Moral Leadership: The Servant Leader with a Transforming Vision', *Business Ethics: A European Review*, 11, 4 (2002): 385–92.

Whitcomb, L. L., C. B. Erdener and C. Li, 'Business Ethical Values in China and the US', *Journal of Business Ethics*, 17, 8 (1998): 839–52.

White, L., 'The Historical Roots of Our Ecological Crisis', *Science,* 155 (1967): 1203–07.

Whitney, E., 'Lynn White, Ecotheology, and History', *Environmental Ethics*, 15 (1993): 151–69.

Williams, T. D., *Who is My Neighbor? Personalism and the Foundations of Human Rights* (Washington, D.C.: The Catholic University of America, 2005).

Windson, D., 'Corporate Social Responsibility: Cases For and Against', in M. J. Epstein and K. O. Hanson (eds), *The Accountable Corporation. Corporate Social Responsibility* (Westpoint: Praeger, 2006): 31–50.

Wojtyla, K., *Love and Responsibility,* trans H. T. Willets (San Francisco: HarperCollins, 1981. First published in Polish, *Miłoi Odpowiedzialno. Studium etyczne*, Lublin: KUL, 1960).

Wojtyla, K., *Person and Community. Selected Essays* (New York: Peter Lang, 1993).

Wood, D. J., 'Corporate Social Performance Revisited', *Academy of Management Review*, 16, 4 (1991): 691–718.

Wood, D. J. and J. M. Logsdon, 'Business Citizenship: From Individuals to Organizations', in R. E. Freeman and S. Venkatraman (eds), *Ethics and Entrepreneurship*, 2002. Ruffin Series, 2, Special issue of *Business Ethics Quarterly,* 59–94.

Zadek, S., 'The Path to Corporate Responsibility ', *Harvard Business Review*, 82, 12 (2004): 125–32.

Zaleznik, A., 'Managers and Leaders: Are They Different?', *Harvard Business Review*, 55, 3 (1977): 67–78.

Zikmund, W. G., *Business Research Methods,* 7th edn (Ohio: Thomson, 2003).

Zwolinski, M., 'Sweatshops, Choice, and Exploitation', *Business Ethics Quarterly*, 17, 4 (2007): 689–727.

General Index

Index of Companies and Institutions

Printed and bound by CPI Group (UK) Ltd, Croydon, CR0 4YY